Russian Front: Furthest German penetration, Dec. 1941 — Nov. 1942

0   75   150   225

Scale (m.)

-N-

Iaroslavl

Gorkii

OKA RIVER

Kalinin

Moscow

Riazan

Pensa

VOLGA RIVER

Tula

DESNA RIVER

Kursk

Voronezh

Stalingrad

Kharkov

Astrakhan

CASPIAN SEA

Dnieper River

Rostov

DON RIVER

Groznyi

SEA OF AZOV

Odessa

CRIMEA

Sevastopol

B L A C K   S E A

THE SIEGE OF LENINGRAD

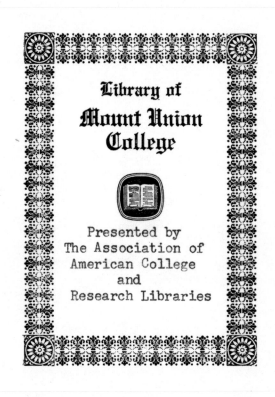

LEON GOURE
The RAND Corporation

THE SIEGE
OF LENINGRAD

STANFORD, CALIFORNIA
STANFORD UNIVERSITY PRESS
LONDON: OXFORD UNIVERSITY PRESS
1962

Frontispiece and
all other photographs, except page 5, top,
by courtesy of Sovfoto.

Stanford University Press
Stanford, California
London: Oxford University Press
© 1962 by The RAND Corporation

Library of Congress Catalog Card Number: 62-8662
Printed in the United States of America

TO MY PARENTS,
who taught me the finer points of my profession

FOREWORD

M<small>R. LEON GOURÉ'S BOOK</small> on the siege of Leningrad is a distinguished achievement. Based on the most careful analysis of sources, both Soviet and German, and making effective use of the memoirs and reminiscences of a host of survivors, it re-creates the conditions of the siege in a memorable fashion. To read this story of the nine hundred days of Leningrad's torment is a traumatic experience, all the more moving because the author spares us rhetoric and lets the facts convey their own horror.

From August 1941 until January 1944, when the Nazis finally retreated, Leningrad was almost completely encircled, thrown back on its own resources, with only a thin trickle of supplies reaching it either by air or through the escape hatch of Lake Ladoga. During this period Leningrad suffered as few cities have been permitted to suffer, with the death toll from starvation, disease, bombardment, and front casualties running into the hundreds of thousands. Yet, somehow, the city held together, enduring the unendurable and hanging on desperately when there was every reason to despair.

The task which Mr. Gouré has set himself in this volume is to explain why Leningrad survived. The tendency among Soviet writers is to cite the magnificent courage and heroism of the Leningraders as proof of the superior virtues of the Soviet system, and particularly of its capacity to tap reservoirs of loyalty and self-sacrifice that no other social or political order can command. Without in any way detracting from the feats of endurance and fortitude that Leningraders performed during the siege, Mr. Gouré suggests that the explanation of their conduct is far more complex than Soviet official versions would concede. It is true that at no point in the siege were there any risings against the Communist authorities nor was there any disposition to surrender en masse to the Nazis. But he also cites evidence to indicate that, in the early period of the siege, at least, there were some who looked forward to a Nazi occupation of the city and that there were also occasional deserters who found their way through the German lines. As Mr. Goure points out, the news of Nazi atrocities helped to harden the will to resist, and the patriotism of the Leningraders, their deep attachment to their beautiful city and their love of country, intensified their desire to hold out.

Mr. Goure places special stress on the strength of the Communist control apparatus in Leningrad, on the fact that it did not collapse in the face of danger, and that it largely maintained its hold on the population throughout the siege. Its efficiency left much to be desired and the population suffered unnecessarily because of its mistakes, but for all its inadequacies it did not lose its nerve, and it kept a firm hand on the throttle. The high proportion of Party members in Leningrad helped to strengthen its power, while the passivity and inertia of the ordinary citizen in the face of authority, qualities that had been instilled and reinforced by more than twenty years of totalitarian rule, eased the problem of control.

Yet, as Mr. Goure also notes, it would be a mistake to conclude that the obedience of the populace was purely a product of terror and effective control. The authorities, to be sure, indulged in a wave of preventive arrests to eliminate the potentially disloyal, and they took stern measures against defeatists, panicmongers, and alleged spies. But as the siege lengthened and suffering intensified, terror lost its force, and Party elite and rank-and-file were driven together in the common desire to survive. With nothing to help them except their own impulse to live, the Leningraders responded with a multitude of ingenious improvisations, doing their best to subsist, to keep industry moving and the front supplied.

Precisely what mixture of motives inspired their sacrifices must remain an ultimate mystery. Hatred of the enemy, love of country, attachment to the cause of Communism, fear of the authorities, and the sheer desire to live were all operative factors. The role that each factor played varied over time, and the reactions of individual Leningraders reflected their place in Soviet society, their past experience, their immediate involvements, and their future hopes. The rich data which Mr. Goure has gathered together and analyzed in this volume illuminate the variety of attitudes that came to the surface during the siege, and even if they cannot be measured with mathematical precision, they nevertheless provide vivid insights into the sources of strain and cohesiveness that characterized Leningrad's behavior under conditions of extreme stress.

Finally, Mr. Goure's study has a broader significance that the alert reader will not miss. The most severe test to which any political system can be subjected is its response to crisis and catastrophe. In so far as the siege of Leningrad can be assumed to have wider meaning, it suggests that the Soviet control apparatus has a toughness and durability capable of sustaining great shocks. No one who reads this volume closely is likely to underestimate the power of Soviet totalitarianism, though he will come away with an appreciation of its weaknesses as well as its strengths. Mr. Goure's balanced appraisal of the implications of the Leningrad experience adds a new dimension to our understanding of the nature of modern totalitarianism, and it deserves to be widely read.

MERLE FAINSOD

PREFACE

THE NINE HUNDRED DAYS' siege of Leningrad appears an anachronism in a war characterized by the mobility of its military operations. Besieging cities and starving them into surrender had ceased to be regarded as a major form of warfare more than a century earlier, when defensive walls lost their power to protect the inhabitants against bombardment. By the second half of the nineteenth century, cities were no longer valued as refuges for military forces too weak to defeat the enemy in the field. In the wars of the twentieth century there have been few prolonged sieges of cities, and those few were usually unplanned. When sieges occurred, it was because the cities had been transformed into military strong points, and in most instances because they were strategic seaports that the defenders tried to deny to the enemy. (Among the port cities that were besieged during World War II were Riga, Tallin, Odessa, Sevastopol, Tobruk, Cherbourg, and the ports of Brittany.) The civilian population played little or no part in the defense, and the issue was settled before the survival of the inhabitants became a major problem.

The siege of Leningrad is unique in modern history both in terms of its duration—it lasted 28 months—and in terms of the hardships and losses suffered by the civilian population. Leningrad, with its more than three million inhabitants, was the largest city to be invested since the siege of Paris in 1870. Unlike most former sieges, in which the population played little part, Leningrad's siege lasted so long, and its industrial facilities were so important, that the population was able to play a vital role both in the defense of the city and in the operation of its war factories. Hence it provides an unusual opportunity for studying the workings of a Soviet urban administrative and political system as well as the attitudes and behavior of a population under extreme stress. The present study attempts to describe the interplay between the population and administrative controls and, at the same time, to give as complete a picture as possible of the appalling conditions in which these controls were maintained.

The documents on the siege of Leningrad are both more numerous and more comprehensive than those dealing with administrative controls and popular reaction to them in other besieged Soviet cities during World War II. Every effort was made to exhaust all Soviet and other printed sources available in this country. Up to 1956, Soviet publications on the siege were largely limited to participants' accounts, a few novels, and the Leningrad newspapers. In 1956 a Soviet historian, A. V. Karasev, pointed out that in the postwar years no significant work on the subject had been published, and that since no effort had been made to exploit the large collections of documentary material available on the siege, people held many erroneous views about it. Between 1958 and 1960 several books and monographs on various aspects of the siege finally appeared. Based on Soviet archives, they provided valuable information for this study. I was fortunate in being able to obtain a microfilm of the *Bulletin of the Leningrad City Soviet of Workers' Deputies* for 1941 and 1944, which was procured by the Library of Congress from the Leningrad Public Library. During a trip to the Soviet Union in 1960, I was also able to visit Leningrad and to see some materials held in the Leningrad Public Library that are not available in the West. Equally valuable and informative were a number of diaries and eyewitness accounts published in the Soviet Union and abroad.

Various Soviet accounts of special problems connected with the siege yielded important data. In the description of military operations, use was made of the unpublished diary of General Franz Halder, former Chief of Staff of the German Army; of most of the available German, Finnish, and Soviet war histories; and of published memoirs of officers who participated in the campaign.

A great deal of information was obtained from a large collection of unpublished German military documents dealing with the siege. Of special interest were German interrogations of Russian defectors and prisoners of war, diaries found on dead or captured Russian soldiers on the Leningrad front, and intercepted letters and radio conversations from Leningrad. To supplement the published and documentary sources seven former Leningraders, who were eyewitnesses to the events described in the study, were interviewed at great length and provided much information not found in printed sources.

I am indebted to many people who gave generously of their time and advice during the preparation and writing of this study.

Special appreciation must be expressed to the seven Russian informants, who at their request must remain unnamed, for their generous contribution of time and information; to Mr. Konstantin Kripton, whose eyewitness report on the siege, specially prepared for me, proved of invaluable assistance; and to Mr. W. Moll, who collected pertinent captured German documents.

For reading the manuscript and for their valuable comments, I wish to express my gratitude to Professor Merle Fainsod, Director, Russian Research Center, Harvard University; Professor Henry L. Roberts, Director, The Russian Institute, Columbia University; and Professors Ulrich Allers, Stefan Possony, and S. Gilbert of Georgetown University. I also wish to thank my colleagues in The RAND Corporation: Bernard Brodie, Herbert S. Dinerstein, W. Phillips Davison, Herbert Goldhamer, and Hans Speier for their suggestions, and Mrs. Elise Kendrick, Mr. Ian C. C. Graham, Mr. Vaughn D. Bornet, Mrs. Ann Greene, Mrs. Eleanor Harris, and Miss Anita Magnus for their editorial assistance.

An earlier version of this study was submitted to Georgetown University in February 1961, in partial fulfillment of the requirements for the degree of Doctor of Philosophy. A shorter account of the siege of Leningrad, with emphasis on administrative controls, was prepared several years ago as part of a continuing program of research undertaken by The RAND Corporation for the United States Air Force.

L. G.

Contents

*M*APS

PART I: *P*REWAR LENINGRAD

Chapter 1

PREWAR LENINGRAD

LENINGRAD is a regal city worthy of having been for two hundred years the glittering capital of the vast Russian Empire. The city was founded in 1703 by Peter the Great in the uninhabited and swampy delta of the Neva River, in order to provide Russia with a "window to Europe." It thus symbolized Russia's break with her oriental past and her adherence to Europe and Western culture. The foreign visitor seldom fails to be impressed by Leningrad's graceful spires, its sprawling palaces and government buildings, its theaters and churches built by Western architects, and he notes that there is none of Moscow's lingering flavor of Byzantium and of the Golden Horde of the Tartars who had ruled Russia for two and a half centuries.[1]

In February 1917 Leningrad acquired a new distinction as the center of the revolution that overthrew the Czarist government, and it was there, too, that in November 1917 the Bolsheviks, led by Lenin and Trotsky, wrested political power from the democratic Provisional Government. In 1918 it ceased to be Russia's capital, when the Bolshevik government, fearing invasion from the West, moved the capital to Moscow. Until 1924 the city's name honored its founder, being first called St. Petersburg, and after 1914, Petrograd. Following Lenin's death in 1924, the city was renamed Leningrad and became enshrined in Communist lore as "the cradle of the Great October Revolution."

Leningrad is the second largest city in the Soviet Union and its most important seaport, as well as a major industrial and cultural center.* According to the 1939 census, its population was 3,191,000; the Leningrad *oblast*, of which Leningrad is the administrative center (each Soviet republic is divided into *oblasts*, or regions), had a population of 6,435,100.[2]

---

[1] Numbered notes will be found at the back of the book, pp. 311–41.
* In 1940 Leningrad's industrial output was valued at 14.1 billion rubles and accounted for 12.3 per cent of the total Soviet production. *BSE*, XXIV (1953), 525.

Because of its size and importance, Leningrad had a high percentage of Communist Party members. At the beginning of World War II there were about 200,000 Party members in the city and 300,000 Komsomols (members of the Young Communist League).[3] Thus about 15 per cent of the city's population was formally affiliated with the Communist Party. The city was also the seat of a substantial Party administration; for it contained both the city and the *oblast* Party committees, and each *raion* (district) of the city and *oblast* had its own Party committee.

In view of Leningrad's importance, the Soviet leaders in 1939 were highly sensitive to the fact that its geographic location made it vulnerable to attack. Indeed, the exposed position of the city had been partly responsible for the transfer of the capital to Moscow in 1918. Leningrad, which is the northernmost city of comparable size in the world, stands at the base of the Karelian Isthmus, where the Neva River flows into the Gulf of Finland. The city was built on both banks of the river and on the many islands formed by its delta. In 1939, the Finnish frontier approached to within 15 miles of the city's northern limits, while Estonia lay some hundred miles to the southwest. Guarding the approaches to Leningrad from the Gulf of Finland was the naval base and fortress of Kronstadt, built by Peter the Great on Kotlin Island, an island lying less than 15 miles from the city. About 20 miles to the east was Lake Ladoga, one of the largest lakes in Europe. Moscow was 450 miles away by rail. Finland and the Baltic states, being small, weak, and politically hostile, could easily become a German springboard for an attack on the Soviet Union, while Kronstadt offered no adequate protection against a landing from the sea to the west of the city.

With Hitler's rise to power, and especially after 1938 when he gave evidence of his intention to expand Germany's borders, the problem of strengthening the security of the Soviet Union in general and of Leningrad in particular became increasingly acute. The earlier nonaggression treaties that the Soviet government had signed with the bordering states were no longer sufficient. Moscow, therefore, sought to move back the frontier in the Karelian Isthmus to a distance of 43 miles from Leningrad, and to establish naval and military bases on several Finnish islands in the Gulf as well as on the Finnish mainland peninsula of Hango. In 1938, using the matter of Leningrad's security to justify its demands, the Soviet government initiated protracted negotiations with Finland.[4] The Finnish government, however, persistently refused to make any territorial concessions.

In the summer of 1939, the Soviet Union began to negotiate simultaneously with the Western democracies and Germany. Moscow asked both sides to agree to the virtual inclusion of Finland, Estonia, and Latvia in the Soviet sphere of influence.[5] Although the Western Allies refused to agree to these demands, Moscow achieved its objectives by the Russo-German nonaggression pact, which was signed in August 1939.[6] In another agreement between Moscow and Berlin, signed on September 28, the Soviet sphere was further expanded to include most of Lithuania.[7] In the same month, Poland was occupied and partitioned between the two totalitarian partners.

With German agreement to Soviet predominance in the Baltic area secured, and with France and England tied down by their war with Germany, the Soviet Union was now able to implement its objectives. By threatening the three Baltic states with invasion, the Soviet government forced these nations in October 1939 to agree to the stationing of Soviet military forces on their territories.[8]

Moscow then turned to Finland. During the negotiations, which began in October, Stalin and Molotov constantly referred to Leningrad's security requirements as one of the principal justifications for Soviet demands.[9] Since Finland refused to accede to these, and since Moscow felt that the Soviet Union had "not only the right, but the duty, to take measures that [would] guarantee the security of the sea and land approaches to Leningrad,"[10] the Red Army attacked Finland on November 30. The war was far more prolonged and costly than Stalin had expected, but after nearly four months of stubborn resistance Finland was forced to yield in March 1940. The Soviet Union received all it had demanded and more, including a 30-year lease on Hango, a number of islands in the Gulf of Finland, the entire Karelian Isthmus with the city of Vyborg, and the northern shores of Lake Ladoga.[11]

After the fall of France, the Soviet Union consolidated its hold on the Baltic states by annexing them outright in July 1940, and thereby restored to a large extent the Russian frontiers of 1914. Leningrad was now at a considerable distance from the frontier, while Soviet bases in the Baltic states and Finland guarded its sea approaches.

Although the Soviet government had succeeded in improving Leningrad's security against attack, the Russo-Finnish War, brief as it was, gave the Leningraders a strong, and sometimes bitter, foretaste of what was to follow. It also revealed how dependent the city was on supplies from other parts of the country and the vulnerability of its supply system to any sort of disruption.

Since the Soviet government had expected weak resistance from the Finns, it had launched the attack with little preparation, relying solely upon forces of the Leningrad military district. Many Leningraders were mobilized, and Leningrad became the main command, production, and transportation center for the Red Army operations in the Karelian Isthmus. The unexpectedly stubborn Finnish resistance soon revealed grave inadequacies in the command and organization of the Red Army, and

eventually forced the Soviet high command to commit nearly half of
its regular divisions to the war. In the end, Soviet numerical and technical superiority succeeded in overwhelming the defenders, but at the
price of some 200,000 casualties, among whom were many Leningraders.[12]

Because of its proximity to the battle lines, various passive defense
measures and other wartime expedients were put into effect in Leningrad. The city was blacked out, the civil defense organization was mobilized and expanded, shelters were prepared, buses and trains were
requisitioned for military use, and public buildings and schools were
converted into hospitals.[13]

More serious, from the standpoint of Leningrad's population, was
the disruption of the food and fuel supply system. The city normally
imported a large part of its food and most of its coal from the Ukraine,
all its oil from the Caucasus, a large part of its lumber and firewood
from the Karelo-Finnish Soviet Republic and elsewhere, all its cotton
from Siberia, and most of its iron and steel from other parts of the Soviet
Union. Local sources provided only some vegetables, peat, bauxite, and
a little lumber.

Past experience with the uncertainties of the Soviet supply system
led the Leningraders, soon after the outbreak of the war, to engage in
panic buying and hoarding of food, thereby creating a food shortage in
the city. The situation was aggravated by the unexpected duration of
the war and the heavy demands made by the military authorities on
the transportation system and local resources. Although there was no
actual hunger, people had to stand in line for many hours without any
assurance of being able to buy what they wanted. All this resulted in
a sharp increase in the prices on the open farm market.

Fuel for heating and cooking, particularly firewood and kerosene,
was also scarce. Since only 7 per cent of Leningrad's homes were
equipped with gas, the remainder of the population and much of the
city's industry depended upon firewood and kerosene, which they
burned in huge quantities.[14] The city required 176 million cubic feet of
firewood annually, which was brought in by rail from places 150 and
200 miles away. Kerosene also had to be imported at the rate of 13,000
tons per month, in addition to 60,000 tons of fuel oil and 2,240 tons of
gasoline.[15] The disruption of the transportation system resulted in a fuel
shortage, and since the winter of 1939–40 was particularly severe, it was
impossible to heat all Leningrad homes all the time. Industry, which
had some stockpiles and was given priority in the matter of supplies,
was less affected by these shortages.

The Russo-Finnish War also had a profound and lasting impact on
the morale of the population and on Party membership. Years of propa-

ganda about the might of the Red Army and the pro-Soviet attitude of workers in other countries had led the people to expect little resistance from the Finns and a quick and easy victory.[16] Since most Russians expected the war to be over in a few days, they were shocked to discover that the Finns were united in their determination to resist and that the Red Army was poorly led and ill-equipped. Consequently, some people believed that they had been misled by the regime, which for years had asked them to make sacrifices in order to build up a strong army, and they began to doubt the Red Army's ability to defend them in the event of a German attack.

It was also evident that not only the rank-and-file members of the Party, but its leaders as well, had believed their own propaganda and were profoundly disturbed to find that their expectations did not correspond with reality. How great an impact the discovery of the true situation made on the leadership may be judged from a statement made to an emergency meeting of the Comintern by Manuilsky, Secretary of its Executive Committee, shortly after the beginning of the war:

> The war with Finland is the expression of the failure of 25 years of effort on the part of the Communist parties, of the Communist International. . . . For a long time we have worked to make fighting against the Soviet Union, the first socialist country, impossible. Until now we believed that the people would refuse to fight against us.
> But it is not so. In Finland even women have taken part in the battle. . . . We shall have to correct many errors, comrades. Events prove that we have not worked well, that our hopes are without foundation. We cannot continue like this.[17]

There was little the Soviet leadership could do to increase quickly the influence of the Comintern abroad, but, with the end of the Finnish war, it had the opportunity to correct some of the shortcomings of the Red Army and improve the country's general preparedness for war. The most important changes took place in the armed forces, whose command system and organization were overhauled. An effort was made to re-equip them with better weapons.[18] At the same time, the fortifications along the old border were dismantled or abandoned, and the army moved forward to defend the new frontiers in Finland, Poland, and Lithuania.

Efforts were made to improve the country's civil defense. Already in March 1939, Marshal Voroshilov, who was then the People's Commissar (Minister) of Defense, had publicly complained about the country's being ill-prepared, which he blamed on the apathy of local officials.[19] Civil defense training of the population was somewhat expanded and accelerated. This training was based on a nationwide 20-hour instruction course initiated in 1935 for members of the *Osoavi-*

akhim* and some other groups of Soviet citizens, many of whom were recruited on what some Leningraders called a "voluntary-compulsory" basis.[20] It was estimated that by 1941 about 38 million people had completed this course.[21] In April 1941 the Central Committee of the Party and the government issued a special joint directive for the improvement of Leningrad's civil defense.[22] It provided for the construction of shelters and the strengthening of the civil defense organization. The war broke out before this directive could be fully implemented, leaving Leningrad inadequately prepared to deal with the expected German air attacks.

The growing international crisis led the authorities to issue various decrees designed to tighten control over labor and increase production. In 1940 a decree was issued increasing the daily work time to eight hours and the work week to six days, prohibiting workers from quitting their jobs without permission, and providing severe penalties for absenteeism.[23] Another decree gave the government the right to order the compulsory transfer of engineering and technical personnel from one place of work to another anywhere in the country.[24] On January 18, 1941, penalties were introduced for tardiness.[25] A provision of the Labor Code of the RSFSR† permitted the mobilization for work in times of emergency of all fit men between the ages of 17 and 45, and women between the ages of 17 and 40.[26]

Little was done, however, to improve the supply system or to increase the stocks of food and fuel in the cities. According to Soviet archives, on June 21, 1941, Leningrad had sufficient food reserves for little over one month.[27] In addition, there were some naval food stores and a certain amount in stock for the use of the armed forces stationed along the Finnish border.

On the eve of the German attack, the city's stockpile of coal and other fuels was sufficient only for normal peacetime needs. The authorities saw no reason to stockpile fuel for the use of Leningrad's industry or electric power plants. This was to have disastrous consequences during the siege.

The authorities also failed to prepare the population for the coming war. Official propaganda stressed the friendly relations between Germany and the Soviet Union and branded every rumor of friction as a Western plot designed to sow discord between two friendly states.

Nevertheless, there were signs that all was not well and that a war

* A society to assist the development of Soviet defense, aviation, and chemical industries. *Osoaviakhim* existed from 1927 to 1948 and was a voluntary civilian organization charged with training the population in military skills and civil defense.

† Russian Soviet Federated Socialist Republic, which includes the Leningrad *oblast* and city.

with Germany might break out at some time. The fall of France had come as a distinct shock to the Soviet leadership, which apparently had counted on a long war of attrition between the Axis and the democracies. It led to a partial mobilization of Russian armed forces and their concentration on the frontiers. These measures, along with official demands for greater industrial output and military preparedness, were not reassuring to the public. Consequently, there was talk of an eventual war with Germany, although people continued to hope that Stalin would somehow manage to keep the country out of it or fight it at a time and place of his choosing. The German victories in the West made a great impression on the population, which began to think of the German army as the most powerful in the world. At the same time, Hess's flight to England had raised the specter of a possible Anglo-German agreement against the Soviet Union. A TASS communiqué of June 13, 1941, denied rumors of an imminent outbreak of war and declared: "The recent transfer of German troops . . . to the eastern and northeastern regions of Germany is, it must be assumed, connected with other reasons which have no bearing on Soviet-German relations."[28] Although this statement reassured most people in the Soviet Union, some of the more sophisticated readers saw in it a clear warning of the storm to come. But neither the city nor the majority of the population was prepared, and for this lack of foresight on the part of the authorities Leningrad was to pay a high price.

PART II: *T*HE GERMAN ATTACK

Chapter 2

THE GERMAN ADVANCE ON LENINGRAD

FROM THE GERMAN point of view, the Russo-German alliance began to lose its *raison d'être* with the fall of France in the summer of 1940. Until then Hitler had worried about the possibility of having to fight a war on two fronts. But once Paris was occupied by the Germans, the Führer again became very conscious of his avowed anti-Communist mission in the world and, even more, of the potential threat of the military strength and political ambitions of the Soviet Union. When England rejected the German peace offer of July 19, 1940, Hitler began to argue that this was due to London's hope of eventual Soviet support.

On July 21, Hitler and his top military leaders held a conference at which the possibility of an immediate successful crossing of the English Channel was recognized as being remote. At the same time the Führer declared: "Stalin is flirting with Britain to keep her in the war and to tie us down with a view to gaining time and taking what he wants, since he knows he cannot get it once peace comes. He has an interest in not letting Germany become too strong, but there are no indications of any Russian aggressiveness against us."[1] Despite his apparent confidence in Stalin's peaceful intentions, Hitler decided to prepare for an attack on the Soviet Union with the aim of capturing most of European Russia. Secret planning for the campaign began immediately.

By December 5 the German army chiefs were ready to submit their plan to Hitler for his approval. This plan called for an advance into the Soviet Union by three army groups, the northern one being aimed at Leningrad, the central one at Smolensk and Moscow, and the southern one at Kiev. Every effort was to be made to destroy the Soviet military forces near the border and to envelop those stationed in the Baltic states. Hitler made it clear during the discussion of the plan that he was far more concerned with the advance in the north and south than with the capture of Moscow. He was particularly bent on the destruction of Leningrad and Stalingrad, which he called the "breeding places of Bolshevism."[2]

In the final plan issued on December 18, the Führer made some basic changes in the missions of Army Groups North and Center by giving first priority to the capture of Leningrad and Kronstadt and the destruction of the Russian forces in the Baltic states. There was to be no advance on Moscow until these objectives had been achieved. The operation was given the code name "Barbarossa."

According to German plans, Finland was to join in the attack on the Soviet Union and assist Army Group North in the capture of Leningrad.[3] As a reward for their help, Hitler thought of giving Leningrad to the Finns after victory had been achieved.[4] Although the German plan assigned Finland an important role in the campaign, nothing had been done to secure Finnish agreement to participate in it. Informal discussions were at last initiated in January 1941, and the Germans met with Mannerheim's refusal to "discuss an eventual German-Finnish military collaboration."[5] Formal negotiations did not begin until May 20 and continued until early June. Although Finland received assurances that Germany would come to her aid if she were attacked, the Finnish Government steadfastly rejected all German proposals for military collaboration in an attack on the Soviet Union. Helsinki insisted on neutrality and refused to make any advance commitments. The only agreement reached, prior to the German attack, was a verbal one providing for Finnish-German military cooperation in northern Finland in the event of a Soviet attack.[6]

In the meantime the German Army was massing along the Soviet frontier and preparing for attack. Army Group North, under the command of Field Marshal von Leeb, assembled in East Prussia and received the following orders:

Army Group North has the task of destroying the enemy forces fighting in the Baltic area, and through the occupation of the Baltic ports and subsequently through the elimination of Leningrad and Kronstadt of depriving the Soviet fleet of its bases. In line with this assignment Army Group North will break through the enemy front with its main weight in the direction of Dünaburg [Dvinsk] and will push its strong right wing of motorized troops across the Düna [Dvina] as rapidly as possible into the area northeast of Opochka, with the aim of preventing the withdrawal of enemy forces eastward from the Baltic area and creating the prerequisite for a further rapid advance in the direction of Leningrad.[7]

To achieve its objectives, Army Group North had at its disposal 30 divisions, of which three were armored and three motorized, and was supported by the First Air Fleet with 430 planes.[8] According to German intelligence, facing the German forces in the Baltic area were 25

Soviet infantry divisions and two Soviet armored divisions.* At the beginning of June these forces began to pull back from the frontier zone and thereby spoiled the German plans to encircle them at the earliest opportunity.[9]

At 3:00 A.M. on June 22, 1941, without any warning, the guns of the invading German armies opened fire, and the troops began their advance. The Russian forces were caught by surprise along the entire front and were at first unable to offer any coordinated resistance. The Luftwaffe caught the Soviet air force on the ground and destroyed a major part of it. The Fourth Panzer Group of Army Group North raced ahead, followed by the infantry of the Eighteenth and Sixteenth Armies.[10]

Although the Red Army was slow to react to the German attack, which Stalin had refused to anticipate, it was quickly active on the Finnish border. The mobilization of the Finnish army on June 17, Hitler's statement on June 22 about German-Finnish military cooperation in the defense of Finland, and a German air attack on Hango caused the Soviet government to discredit the possibility of Finnish neutrality in the Russo-German war. Three hours after the beginning of the German offensive, therefore, Soviet planes attacked Finnish warships and Red Army artillery opened fire along the border.

The Finnish government protested these attacks and hastened to proclaim its neutrality, but to no avail. Further Soviet military operations and air attacks on ten Finnish cities, including the capital, forced the Helsinki government to declare war on June 25.

Meanwhile Army Group North, along with the rest of the German forces, was rapidly advancing. Although the Red Army, after recovering from the initial surprise, tried to counterattack and fought "stubbornly and doggedly,"[11] it was unable to check the onslaught. By June 26, the Germans had reached the Dvina River at Dvinsk and captured Kovno. Riga, Yelgava, and the port of Liepaya fell three days later, and twelve to fifteen Red Army divisions were destroyed. On Hitler's order, Army Group North then halted to regroup.

While the Red Army took advantage of this breathing spell to bring up fresh forces, Hitler met with his military leaders to discuss the future direction of the German advance. The majority of the generals were in favor of concentrating on a drive toward Moscow, but Hitler was more interested in the capture of Leningrad and the Ukraine. It was

---

* Soviet spokesmen and propagandists later asserted incorrectly that the combined German-Finnish forces advancing on Leningrad had over 600,000 men, over 1,000 tanks, 6,000 guns, and nearly 1,000 planes (*BSE*, XXX [1954], 358). Actually the difference in strength between the two forces was greater than was indicated by the number of divisions because a German infantry division had 6,000 more men than a corresponding Red Army division, and 3,500 more men in an armored division (Garthoff, pp. 300–308).

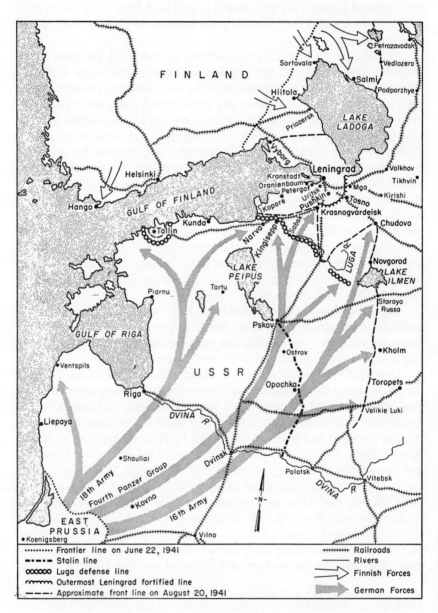

·········· Frontier line on June 22, 1941	+++++++ Railroads
·—·—· Stalin line	——— Rivers
∞∞∞∞ Luga defense line	⟶ Finnish Forces
⌢⌢⌢⌢ Outermost Leningrad fortified line	⟹ German Forces
–––– Approximate front line on August 20, 1941	

THE GERMAN ADVANCE, JUNE 22–AUGUST 20, 1941

finally decided not to divert any forces from Army Group North and to allow it to continue its advance on Leningrad.

On July 2, Army Group North renewed its offensive in the face of stubborn Red Army resistance. The Soviet leadership hoped to stop the Germans on the Pskov defense line, which formed a part of the old fortified Stalin line,[12] but by July 8 the Germans had broken through these defenses with the capture of Pskov and Opochka. At the same time they had penetrated deeply into Estonia. Thus, in the first sixteen days of their offensive, the German armies reached a position from which they could launch an attack on Leningrad.

The German advance on Leningrad was resumed on July 10. The Soviet command hoped to form a new defense line in the Luga area, whither it had rushed thousands of mobilized Leningraders to build fortifications. Fierce Russian resistance, mine fields, and bad roads slowed the advance of the German armor to a crawl. On the flanks, the Eighteenth and Sixteenth Armies made some gains in the direction of Tallin and Lake Ilmen. Although, according to their own estimates, the Germans had achieved definite numerical superiority over the Soviet forces opposing Army Group North, the advance became a series of bloody frontal assaults against a stubborn enemy.

Fearing that this delay would give the Soviet forces time to build more fortifications and raise new divisions, the German command tried to bypass the main Luga defenses by sending an armored corps 47 miles to the west to cross the Luga River at Poreche and Sabsk. By catching the Russian forces off balance, the Germans were able to cross the river in full strength on July 15. They were now in a position to make a quick thrust at Leningrad before the defenders could regroup their forces and fortify the approaches to the city; but the German High Command, despite the pleas of the tank officers, chose instead to halt the advance of the tank corps and to devote the next three weeks to the improvement of roads and the regrouping of forces.

In the meantime Hitler had reached certain conclusions regarding the fate of Leningrad. Halder noted in his diary on July 8:

> It is the Führer's firm decision to level Moscow and Leningrad and make them uninhabitable, so as to relieve us of the necessity of feeding the population during the winter. The city will be razed by the Air Force. Tanks must not be used for the purpose. [It will be] a national catastrophe that will deprive not only Bolshevism but also Muscovite nationalism of their centers.[13]

Hitler also toyed with the idea of diverting substantial forces from Army Group Center to Army Group North to help in the capture of Leningrad. But the forces in the center were engaged in heavy fighting, and it would have been extremely difficult to redeploy large numbers of men and their equipment under the prevailing conditions. According to Halder, "this idea did not come from Hitler's military line of thought but from his political fanaticism, which sought the destruction of Leningrad."[14] Despite the opposition of the army chiefs, Hitler returned again and again to the idea of diverting at least the Third Panzer Group, one of Army Group Center's two panzer groups, to the Leningrad front. Yet he was also afraid of risking his forces in a direct assault on the city.

On July 15, Halder told Army Group North that its immediate mission was not to capture Leningrad but to encircle it. Directive 33 on the future of the Russian campaign, which was issued on July 19, provided for an advance on Moscow by Army Group Center and the diversion of the Third Panzer Group to guard the flank of Army Group North. This, however, did not settle the matter, for the military leaders continued to press the need to reinforce the divisions engaged in the drive on Moscow. Despite numerous conferences with his leaders, Hitler insisted on his initial order of priorities: first Leningrad and the Ukraine, and then Moscow. Finally, on August 12, he relented somewhat and issued a new directive according to which no forces except the Eighth Air Corps were to be diverted from Army Group Center, while Army Group North was to encircle Leningrad and link up with the Finns.

While Hitler was trying to decide what to do about Leningrad, Army Group North with great difficulty beat back numerous Soviet counterattacks and was even forced to make some local withdrawals. Nevertheless, the Eighteenth and Sixteenth Armies made progress by capturing Gdov on July 17 and Tartu on July 27. On August 8, the Germans took Kunda on the Estonian shore of the Gulf of Finland and thereby cut off the Soviet forces defending Tallin. On the same day the advance along the Luga River in the direction of Leningrad was resumed. According to German estimates, the 26 divisions that then formed Army Group North were opposed by some 15 Red Army divisions. Although the latter were reinforced by the hastily organized units of a "people's army" (*narodnoe opolchenie*) from Leningrad, they were unable to check the Germans. The Military Council of the Northern Front, which was directing the Soviet defense, had to report to the General Staff in Moscow on August 13 that "the expectation of holding the enemy with hastily formed and badly organized units of the *opolchenie*, and with reorganized units taken from the Northwest Front after their withdrawal from Lithuania and Latvia, remains completely unrealized."[15]

During the next week, the Eighteenth Army took Kingisepp and Narva, while the Sixteenth Army seized Novgorod and Chudovo. In the center, German armor advanced on Krasnogvardeisk, 21 miles from Leningrad, which formed a part of a hastily built triple ring of fortifications guarding the city. The Soviet forces defending the Luga area were also slowly pushed back.

Meanwhile a second threat to Leningrad had developed on the Karelian Isthmus. When the war broke out, the Finns had been prepared to take defensive action only. Since they faced strong Soviet forces and the Germans were still far away, Marshal Mannerheim decided to proceed with caution.

> The Finnish people probably expected the Army first to recapture Viipuri [Vyborg] and the Karelian Isthmus, not to mention those circles who wanted to go further—to Leningrad! It was my firm opinion that such an undertaking was against the interest of the country, and from the beginning I had informed the President of the Republic and the government that under no circumstances would I lead an offensive against the great city on the Neva. At this early stage, an operation on the Karelian Isthmus might have caused our adversary to think that we aimed at nothing less than Leningrad—without aid from the Germans, who were still a long way from there. It was to be feared that the Russians in such an event might raise sufficiently strong forces to inflict a heavy blow on us.[16]

So it was decided at first to attack north rather than south of Lake Ladoga, and to remain on the defensive on Hango and the Karelian Isthmus. The offensive, initiated on July 10, forged ahead rapidly, and by July 21 the Finns had reached Salmi at the old frontier on the northern shore of Lake Ladoga.

Following these successes, the Finns turned to the recapture of the territory they had lost in the Karelian Isthmus as a result of the Russo-Finnish War. The offensive began on July 31 and made good progress. By August 16 the Finnish forces had encircled Vyborg, captured Hiitola, and advanced some 62 miles along the western shore of Lake Ladoga. While the Red Army sought to evacuate a number of encircled divisions, the Finns continued their advance to the south.

The advance to Krasnogvardeisk had placed the Germans in the rear of the large Red Army forces still defending the Luga area to the southeast. The number of Soviet troops still immediately available was apparently insufficient to ensure the effective defense of the fortified lines. The personnel on hand were either untrained or exhausted from weeks of continuous fighting and retreats.[17] By August 20 the Soviet leaders had decided that Leningrad was in immediate danger of capture.

Chapter 3

LENINGRAD AT WAR

June 22–August 20, 1941

THE WAR BEGAN for Leningrad on a quiet, sunny Sunday morning. At first, few people in Leningrad knew about the war, except the military men on duty; for the leaders in the Kremlin could not immediately decide what to say about it.

In the early morning of June 22 Molotov had listened with horror in the Kremlin while the German ambassador, Count von Schulenburg, read him the German declaration of war.[1] For a short while the Soviet leaders had clung to the futile hope that this was not an irrevocable act, that somehow they could still negotiate and appease the German aggressor. While the Russian troops, reeling under the unexpected German fire, were frantically asking higher headquarters over their radios what they were to do, the Soviet government is reported to have asked Japan "to act as an intermediary on the political and economic relations between Russia and Germany" and to have been "in constant radio contact with the German Foreign Office."[2] When it became obvious that the Germans could not be halted by diplomatic means, then finally, at noon, some nine hours after the start of the attack, Molotov spoke on the radio to inform the people that the Soviet Union was at war. Stalin, even though he was the chairman of the Council of People's Commissars, secretary general of the Central Committee of the Communist Party, and chief of the Politburo, failed to address the nation he headed until July 3.

While waiting for the official word from Moscow, the military and civilian leaders in Leningrad went ahead quietly with their preparations for war. While the population still slept, Red Army guns and planes opened fire against Finland, about ninety miles away. In the city, as a precautionary measure, the civil defense units were alerted and ordered to man their posts by seven o'clock in the morning. Since they were not told the reason for the alert, they assumed that this was just another of the frequent civil defense exercises; they did not learn the truth until Molotov made his statement some five hours later.[3] The authorities also ordered all apartment house janitors to stand guard with their gas masks at the entrances to their buildings.

When the news came, it left all sections of the population stunned. One Communist Party member, who was a civil defense official, is reported to have said: "This news surprised us so much that we did not at first believe our ears."[4] Women in particular took it hard, and many broke into tears. "There were those who sincerely believed that the decisive hour for the clash between two systems had come and that the Soviet Union was ready for it. Many expressed the usual flattery and careerism. . . . There were people who were indignant, at least in the first moment, that an attack had been made on the USSR despite the treaty."[5]

Belief in German military might caused many to fear the outcome of the war. The diary of a Russian officer carried the following entry: "Well, it has come. The war! At first it is difficult to write down the feelings that overcome one, but there is a dominant one: alarm [*volnenie*]. There is no such self-confidence as was the case with Finland, and this is explained by the indubitable strength of the opponent."[6]

But the majority of the population did not anticipate the military disaster that was about to occur. Whatever doubts the war with Finland had created in the minds of many Soviet citizens, most of them felt sure that the Red Army would give a good account of itself. They were not aware that much of the Red Army's equipment was obsolete. In his secret speech on February 25, 1956, at the Twentieth Congress of the Communist Party, Khrushchev said:

Before the war our press and all our political-educational work was characterized by its bragging tone: when an enemy violates the holy Soviet soil, then for every blow of the enemy we will answer with three blows and we will battle the enemy on his soil and we will win without much harm to ourselves. . . .

Soviet science and technology produced excellent models of tanks and artillery pieces before the war. But mass production of all this was not organized, and as a matter of fact we started to modernize our military equipment only on the eve of the war. . . . The situation with antiaircraft artillery was especially bad; we did not organize the production of anti-tank ammunition. Many fortified regions had proven to be indefensible as soon as they were attacked, because the old arms had been withdrawn and the new ones were not yet available there.

This pertained, alas, not only to tanks, artillery, and planes. At the outbreak of the war we did not even have sufficient numbers of rifles to arm the mobilized manpower.[7]

One reaction was common to the overwhelming majority of Leningraders. As every Soviet citizen knew, war, regardless of its outcome, meant shortages and privation, and so the population hastened to the nearest stores and banks to lay in food supplies and to withdraw their savings. People bought indiscriminately whatever was on the shelves of the stores, from cans of caviar to bags of candy.[8]

In the meantime the central government and the local authorities took the first standard war measures. On June 22 the Presidium of the Supreme Soviet issued two decrees, one ordering general mobilization in a number of *oblasts* and republics of the Soviet Union, including Leningrad, the other placing Leningrad as well as other areas under martial law.[9]

There were certain local standing orders in case of war that also went into effect immediately. These included the requisitioning of a considerable number of schools for use as hospitals, the alerting and mobilizing of all civil defense organizations and teams, the placing of *raion* medical-aid stations on round-the-clock duty, and the broadcasting of blackout and civil defense instructions.[10] At the same time a number of security measures were taken. The authorities ordered that all private radios other than the loud-speakers with outlets connected with the local broadcasting station be turned in to the police. The NKVD arrested suspect persons on previously prepared lists as a preventive measure.

The authorities also resorted to the time-honored Soviet practice of calling innumerable mass meetings in all enterprises, offices, institutions, and organizations in order to inspire the proper enthusiasm in the population and demonstrate to the leadership the unity and loyalty of the masses. A special issue of Leningrad's most important newspaper, *Leningradskaia pravda*, which appeared on June 22, 1941, was largely devoted to resolutions passed by various factories, institutions, and organizations, all of which repeated Molotov's words concerning the treacherous and unprovoked character of the German aggression and pledged to work harder, produce more, and destroy the enemy.[11]

Encouraged by the Party, many Leningraders rushed to volunteer for the armed services. Over 100,000 Komsomols expressed their desire to volunteer.[12] There was great confusion at the mobilization centers. In some cases the centers did not know how many mobilization orders they had sent out and how many men had reported, whereas in other instances reservists were called up out of turn and the mobilized men often waited two or three days at the centers before being shipped out to their units. To alleviate this situation the Party rushed thousands of Komsomols and Party members to the mobilization centers, and further helpers were sent in large numbers to the railroad stations to assist in directing traffic and for propaganda work.[13]

There followed several days of relative quiet. Except for a few factories that were ordered to begin conversion to war production and some trenches that were dug for shelter in public parks and in factory yards, there was virtually a return to normal. Restaurants and places of entertainment remained open. Hoarding of food was prohibited, and the initial buying spree tapered off in view of the threatened punishment and the discovery that food was ample. There was an air raid alert in the city on the second day of the war, but it passed without any bombs being dropped.[14] According to several former residents of Leningrad, the first week of the war was a period of business-as-usual, although the excitement among the population and the departure of numerous mobilized citizens, who could not be immediately replaced, curtailed the activities of most agencies and institutions.[15]

But five days after the start of the German offensive the local and central authorities began to recover from the initial shock. Spurred on by the increasingly unfavorable developments at the front, they initiated the first of the flood of new directions and orders, which did not cease until the end of the war.

In view of the deteriorating military situation it was essential to improve the defenses of the city. The Executive Committee of the Leningrad City Soviet* therefore issued an order on June 27 mobilizing the entire city population for defense work.[16] According to this decree, all men between the ages of 16 and 50 and women between 16 and 45 residing in Leningrad or in its suburbs could be called up for work, except workers already employed in defense industries, sick persons, pregnant women, or women caring for young children. Unemployed persons were to work eight hours a day, those already employed or students three hours a day after their regular work or classes. Every seven days of work were to be followed by a four-day rest period. The management in each factory, enterprise, or apartment house was to register all persons subject to this order within twenty-four hours. Failure to perform the work could bring penalties of "loss of freedom by administrative decision for a period of up to six months or . . . a fine of up to 3,000 rubles."[17]

The mobilization was carried out through the *raion* executive committees, which assigned the necessary quotas to the apartment house managers and to the directors of various enterprises, schools, or institutions in the *raion*. Some, if not all, of the directors of plants and institutes made their personnel work overtime even when there was no specific request from the *raion* executive committee, or tried to find

* A city Soviet is a council elected by the inhabitants of a city. It has legislative powers and meets periodically. It elects its own permanent executive committee, whose chairman is equivalent to a mayor in the United States. *Raion* Soviets and executive committees are established in a similar manner.

work for them to do during the prescribed three hours of compulsory labor by lending them at times to other organizations or enterprises.[18] The directors may have been anxious to show their zeal for the cause or may have feared that a failure to act under the compulsory labor decree could be construed as a failure to give full support to the war effort.

Initially the mobilized persons chiefly dug slit trenches and air raid shelters, sandbagged vital installations and valuable statues, or worked in factories as replacements for mobilized workers. During the first weeks many of these activities were poorly organized and coordinated, and there was much confusion.

The picture changed radically with the fall of Pskov on July 8. The leadership realized that the Germans would soon be in a position to assault Leningrad and that the Red Army needed help in halting the enemy's advance. It was therefore decided to use the civilian population in the construction of fortification belts at various distances from Leningrad. Thus began a gigantic effort that was to last for well over three months, gaining increasing momentum as the threat to the city grew.

The fortifications farthest from Leningrad were those built along the Luga River. Others were built closer to the city as dictated by the needs of the retreating Soviet forces. Finally a triple ring of fortifications was built around Leningrad, the outermost line, according to the former commander of the 41st Panzer Corps, extending from Petergof to east of Krasnogvardeisk. (This was the one the Germans reached on August 19.) The second line began on the Neva in the area of Ust-Tosno and then extended via Iam-Izhora to Izhora and the Izhora River. The last line protected Kolpino, Slutsk, Pushkin, the Dudergof heights, and then curved northeast to cover Krasnoe Selo.[19] Beyond this, in the outskirts of Leningrad itself, there were numerous street barricades and fortified houses.

To build these fortifications vast numbers of workers were needed. Since the supply of volunteers was insufficient, the compulsory labor decree was invoked to mobilize the population. This time, of course, it was not a question of three hours of extra work, but of days and weeks of labor away from Leningrad.

The Compulsory Labor Decree of June 27 was clarified and elaborated by two further decrees issued on July 11 and August 9 by the Executive Committee of the Leningrad City Soviet.[20] Control over the mobilization of workers was vested in special commissions formed for this purpose by each *raion* executive committee, which after July 25 were supervised in turn by a general commission composed of five members and headed by A. A. Kuznetsov, one of the secretaries of the

City Party Committee.[21] The decree of August 9 extended the age range of persons liable to compulsory labor from 15 to 55 for men and 16 to 50 for women. As a result of the atmosphere of crisis, the decree also changed the work schedule to seven days of work, followed by one day of rest, for work performed within the city limits, and fourteen days of work and two days of rest for work on the distant fortifications. The duration of the work time could be extended by order of the executive committee. Apparently, some managers of factories and other organizations had been firing workers who were sent away to perform their obligatory service for lengthy periods of time, for the August 9 decree specifically prohibited such practices except when the entire enterprise was being closed down.

The role of the military authorities in the mobilization was restricted to requesting labor from the city authorities, indicating the location of the constructions.

The Party organizations as usual took an active part in the mobilization of the population. The draft orders were frequently issued by the secretary of the Party cell of the institute or enterprise.[22] In schools a mobilization of all physically fit students generally took place at a mass meeting. At a medical school, for example, the secretary of the school's Komsomol organization made the following announcement to the assembled students:

Comrades! Despite firm resistance by our troops, the enemy has succeeded in moving forward. Our city is in imminent danger. Leningrad, the cradle of the Revolution, is threatened. Therefore, after discussing the situation with the military authorities, the Leningrad Soviet and the Party organization in the city have issued the following orders:

1. All studies at institutions of higher learning, with the exception of several technical courses and the last two years of medical school, are suspended.

2. All students, and part of the faculty, will be sent to dig trenches.

3. Upper-class students of high schools will be sent to dig trenches.

4. It is suggested that factory directors allot part of their workers and administrative personnel to dig trenches.

In accordance with this order, Comrades, all first, second, and third year students will report to the institute at eight tomorrow morning with the following equipment: a blanket, change of underwear, personal belongings, a plate, a spoon, and a cup, as well as a two-day supply of food. I warn you now that anyone not appearing at the designated time will be expelled from the institute. The only valid excuse will be a certificate from the institute clinic. No student having outside work will be exempted from digging trenches.[23]

In practice, of course, not everyone liable to mobilization was sent to dig trenches. Administrators, personnel in important public services, workers in defense plants, and many other essential persons were generally not called up. It is also probable that administrators were anxious to retain their best workers in order to keep things going. As a result, since the administrators were often primarily concerned with filling their quotas, little attention was paid to the health or strength of those mobilized. Then, too, the army and the *opolchenie* absorbed a substantial part of the able-bodied population. The bulk of those working on defense construction were therefore older men, women, and adolescents.

There are no precise figures on the number of persons who were mobilized for defense construction, but according to Soviet sources it was somewhere between half a million and a million in all.[24] A report released by the central committee of the Leningrad Komsomol organization stated that by mid-August there were "in Leningrad and *oblast* over one million persons working in the construction zone on the defensive fortifications of the city of Leningrad. The trade schools alone have sent about 60,000 persons to work on the fortifications."[25] In addition, the Leningrad *oblast* authorities mobilized the populations of the villages and towns of the *oblast* for the same purpose. The workers received their normal average pay for the duration of their labor at the construction sites, or a standard pay of six to eight rubles per day for those who had been unemployed.

The mobilized laborers assembled at assigned places in the city in groups, each group under the leadership of someone representing the *raion* authorities, usually a Party member. Each labor column, frequently numbering several thousand persons, was then transported or marched to the construction site. The *raion* executive committees were responsible for transportation and tools. When they arrived at the construction site, often after a long march on foot, the workers were organized into labor brigades and given their assignments. The assignment, which in most instances consisted of building tank traps, trench systems, or fortified positions, had to be completed within a prescribed time. The military authorities established the specifications for each construction and approved it upon completion.

For Leningrad's leadership, the construction of fortifications obviously had top priority. Since the Germans had to be stopped at any cost, it approached this task with single-minded determination and ruthlessness. Inevitably, the population suffered considerable hardships. The people who had to do the work were frequently unaccustomed to such labor. They often had to work for twelve to fifteen hours at a stretch, sleep in barns or lean-tos, and occasionally were subjected to enemy fire. Sometimes they were even overrun by a sudden enemy advance. In other cases they completed one assignment only to start an immediate forced march of six to twelve miles to another construction site. Most of the time they had only the simplest hand tools. Frequently women had to manhandle the heavy concrete obstacles that were constructed against tanks. Many of the people lacked proper working clothes and shoes. Girls and women often came in light summer dresses and shoes, which could not, of course, withstand the wear and tear of the work, the marching, and the outdoor living. It was only after some time had elapsed that the city authorities and employers began to provide the people with more adequate clothing and shoes.

A Soviet publication described the work of one labor column as follows:

> They were obliged to work 12 hours on the first day, and were looking forward to some rest after the strain of the long stretch of heavy digging. But the job was still a long way from completion, and even those who were most exhausted went out on the second shift in order to get it done.
>
> There was no let-up all through the long night, . . . as early as six o'clock in the morning, two hours in advance of schedule, the whole contingent could report that their assignment had been completed.
>
> It was then necessary to switch over at once to a new line 18 miles away.[26]

A 57-year-old woman wrote in a Soviet newspaper: "We have worked for 18 days without a break, 12 hours a day. The soil was hard and one had to work a lot with a pick. This soil could not be worked with a shovel. The dry clay is hard as rock."[27]

These were not the only difficulties. Apparently, the workers, students, and housewives who were mobilized for the job were told before they left that they would be digging from two to five days and were instructed to bring enough food for that period. But in practice, as one Soviet publication confessed, people "remained a long time."[28] Housewives who had left their families at short notice naturally became worried when made to remain longer than expected. One eyewitness reports that after five days of work, when the workers were informed that they would have to remain to dig more fortifications, no one dared to protest except the housewives, who "moaned and carried on."[29]

Food was also a problem. The poorer families had only small reserves of food that they could take along. Then, in mid-July, food rationing was introduced. There was some disagreement as to who was supposed to feed the workers, the civilian authorities or the army, and, as a result, the workers sometimes went hungry. Eventually, however, the feeding of the workers was taken over by the city authorities.

The general hardiness of the population and its adaptability to the harsh requirements and dangers of the digging operations were quite remarkable. Fortunately for the people and the leadership, it was summer, so that life in the open was possible. The soil, moreover, was manageable—the construction operations would not have been feasible in winter. In each group apparently a number of people always turned up who knew how to build shelters and lean-tos, how to make camp-

fires and cook on them, and the like; with their help, the city-bred
workers managed to eat and sleep outdoors.

Workers toiled to the point of exhaustion and some became ill from
drinking bad water, or were hurt during the work. It is reported that
many hospitals were filled with people sick with dysentery.[30] First-aid
groups, and sometimes even complete medical teams, were attached to
the workers' columns.

It was inevitable that there would be criticism and grumbling, but
initially, at least, many believed in the usefulness of the undertaking
and worked with considerable zeal. Members of the elite* also participated in the construction effort. Some Komsomol and Party members certainly took their role as leaders seriously enough not to want
to avoid unpleasant tasks. One eyewitness records in his memoirs that
when a woman technical secretary of the faculty of an institute, who
had been working uninterruptedly on the construction of fortifications,
was offered a chance to be relieved, she refused, saying: "I, as a Komsomol, must set an example. These days we cannot take a rest."[31] But
a large number of Party people, nearly 10,000 of them, functioned as
political officers or propagandists and apparently did little digging
themselves.[32]

When the Germans overran the defense lines built by the workers
or when the Red Army withdrew without using them, the construction
workers began to question the value of their task and sometimes slowed
down their efforts. One informant called the digging "nonsensical" and
asserted that many people believed that the "fortifications were dug in
the wrong places, with pitifully poor equipment, and for very little
purpose."[33] Another informant told his co-workers: "This is like the
sea building a sand bank—there are thousands and thousands of people
putting in a tremendous effort to produce very little."[34] According to a
Soviet source, there were also instances when the lack of news about
the military situation gave rise to various rumors that caused the workers
to panic.[35]

The unexpected duration of the assignments, the bombings or rumors
of bombings and strafings of workers by German planes, and other hardships also produced some resentment and indignation. At least a few
people felt that it was due entirely to mismanagement by the authorities
that construction brigades were exposed to enemy fire. Others were
indignant that physically unfit persons and adolescents were made to
work so hard or were endangered by enemy guns. A few accused the

---

* The term "elite" is used here and throughout the text to include all persons
in positions of authority in all fields, and all members of the Party and of the Komsomol, except for the highest city and Party leaders, who are described by the term
"leadership."

authorities of instituting the mass mobilization in order to prevent popular unrest or rebellion. There was a noticeable tendency to blame difficulties on the callousness and blind zeal of the elite and on the lack of foresight of the top leadership, and there was evidence of some glee when members of the elite were called on to work.[36] The authorities in turn attempted to bolster the workers' morale by sending thousands of Party propagandists to the construction sites.

In most instances even those who complained or had little faith in the value of the fortifications worked very hard. Many were motivated by genuine patriotism and a desire to help the army. Another reason for this zeal, of course, was that the workers knew they would not be released until their task was completed and until the site they were digging had been accepted by the army. For this same reason some volunteered to work longer hours to hasten the completion of the task, so that they could go home sooner. There is no indication that people failed to report for duty once they were notified by the authorities; nobody wished to suffer the penalties that such an act would incur. The speed with which the extensive fortification belts were thrown up around Leningrad by a population working with primitive hand tools and sometimes under fire testifies to the industry of the workers.

The results of the operation were truly impressive, although the manpower cost was undoubtedly high. According to one Soviet source, "over 14 million man-days were used on the construction of fortified lines."[37] Another Soviet source speaks of 20 million man-days.[38] In terms of actual work performed there is no precise agreement among the various sources. One Soviet source gives the total length of earth walls as over 620 miles. Other sources speak of 370 to 435 miles of antitank ditches; 185 miles of abatis in wood; 5,000 earth, timber, and concrete pillboxes; and over 370 miles of barbed wire entanglements.[39] In contrast to the skepticism of some workers, the Germans seem to have felt that the fortifications materially contributed to the defense of Leningrad and to the slowing down of the German advance.

When it became obvious that the Germans were capable of overrunning most of the Soviet Union, Moscow in despair decided not only to mobilize all citizens for defense work, but also to create a "people's army," the *opolchenie*. Because of its voluntary aspect, this typically Soviet undertaking had psychological advantages that a compulsory mobilization of all persons capable of bearing arms would have lacked. The call to the population at large to join in the defense of the fatherland had an obvious psychological appeal, and its successful implementation gave at least the image of mass patriotism.

Already on June 24, the city and *oblast* Party committees had decided to organize Destruction Battalions to fight possible German parachutists. By July 5, 79 battalions were recruited with a total of over 17,000 men, including a large proportion of Party, Komsomol, and NKVD personnel.[40]

On June 27 Leningrad's highest military and Party organs decided to organize an *opolchenie* army of 200,000 men, with one division for each of the city's *raions*. On June 29–30, a Military Council of the *opolchenie* army was formed and a staff. To organize and supply the *opolchenie*, commissions were set up in each *raion*. These commissions were composed of the secretaries of the *raion* Party committees, the heads of the *raion* military commissions, the heads of the *raion* NKVD offices, and the secretaries of the *raion* committees of the Komsomol. Recruiting commissions were organized in every factory and large economic or municipal institution, as well as in large offices. Each commission was composed of the secretaries of the Party organizations, the secretaries of the Komsomol organizations, and representatives of the *raion* Party committee, the *raion* military commission, and the trade union. Usually the director of the enterprise also sat on the commission.[41] The executive committees of the *raion* Soviets requisitioned schools and other buildings to house the volunteers, provided facilities for feeding them, and arranged with the military boards for instructors and supervisory personnel. But the actual recruiting drive was primarily the responsibility of the Party organizations, "with the active participation of Komsomol and trade union organizations."[42] According to a postwar Soviet article, the "Party organizations of enterprises and offices spent twenty-four hours a day checking the declarations of the volunteers. In those days the *raion* Party committees organized themselves as recruiting teams for the formation of *opolchenie* regiments and divisions."[43]

The recruiting drive began on June 30 and went into high gear after July 3 with a concentrated propaganda barrage conducted by the press and Party propagandists. At innumerable public meetings in factories, plants, institutes, unions, and places of public gathering, Party agitators and secretaries of Party committees appealed for volunteers. The official propaganda line copied Stalin's statement of July 3 to the effect that "the Red Army, Red Fleet, and all citizens of the Soviet Union must be ready to defend each foot of Soviet soil, fight to the last drop of blood for our cities and villages, and demonstrate the courage, initiative, and enterprise characteristic of our people."[44] The workers in the factories passed resolutions asserting their readiness to respond to Stalin's appeal by volunteering en masse for the *opolchenie*.[45]

The response to the Party appeal was gratifying. This was due not only to genuine patriotism, which undoubtedly existed, but in many instances to a desire to demonstrate loyalty to the regime. The way in which the recruiting was frequently done made this almost inevitable. The recruiting commissions called on individual employees to appear before them and asked them to volunteer, putting the question in such a way that refusal became a sign of disloyalty. One informant was told, "You are a Soviet man; you cannot refuse to volunteer. I advise you not to refuse."[46] Another informant was assured that the state of his health "is of no significance, what is important is the very fact of volunteering and thereby displaying one's political attitude."[47] He asserts that some of his colleagues who had volunteered petitioned the *raikom* (the Party committee of the *raion*) to mobilize forcibly all those who had refused to volunteer. As a result, these people were once more made to appear before the Party secretary and again asked to volunteer. Certainly in most cases when a prospective volunteer was asked by the secretary of the Party committee of his place of work "Do you want to help our Fatherland?" he did not dare refuse.[48] The recruiting drive was thus turned into a deliberate demonstration of personal loyalty and patriotism. The health or usefulness of the volunteer thereby became of relatively less consequence. This attitude is even described in one Soviet war novel: the secretary of a *raikom* is said to have instructed the directors of enterprises to recruit people "without considering too closely their age or their health."[49] Even cripples volunteered and sometimes successfully pushed their cases by threatening the military authorities with complaining to the Party if they were refused.[50]

To volunteer and thus to "display one's political attitude" was all the easier because few people had any clear idea of what they were volunteering for. Some thought that they would serve in guard units within the city, whereas others believed that they would be called upon to fight only if the Germans actually entered Leningrad.[51] Probably the vast majority of volunteers, knowing their own lack of military training and experience, expected to go through a lengthy period of training before being exposed to enemy fire.

In any event, the propaganda and pressure that the Party brought to bear made the recruiting drive a great success. Entire families volunteered. In many factories, schools, and institutes nearly all employees, technicians, and managerial personnel rushed to register. It is reported that 80 writers, 40 per cent of the Union of Leningrad painters, and 2,500 university students volunteered. Some schools and institutes lost up to 90 per cent of their male students.[52] In the forefront of the volunteers marched the "vanguard of the proletariat"—the Party and the Komsomol. Within a few days of the start of the drive, a substantial portion of the Party bureaucracy had exchanged their desks for *opolchenie* barracks. According to the proud boast of the secretary of one *raikom*,

Many leading Communist Party members of the *raion* joined the *opolchenie*. Among them were 25 members of the *raion* committee, 62 directors of enterprises and secretaries of Party organizations, and 23 members of the *raion* committee staff [*apparat*].

Some primary organizations were thus reduced to half of their number. The Party groups in the Zhdanov factory sent two-thirds of their Communists to the front; the secretaries and deputy secretaries of shop Party organizations alone amounted to 58 people.[53]

According to the *Bolshaia sovetskaia entsiklopediia,* 57 per cent of the Communist Party organization and 75 per cent of the Komsomol organization of Leningrad volunteered for the *opolchenie,* so that the Party and Komsomol people composed from 20 to 45 per cent of the *opolchenie* units.[54] Other Soviet sources report that 20,000-30,000 Party members and 18,000 Komsomols served in the *opolchenie* and other militarized units.[55] Most of the more important Party officials were made officers or political officers. The recruiting drives moved rapidly ahead, and by July 6 over 100,000 persons had been selected.[56] In all, according to Soviet claims, some 160,000 Leningraders, 32,000 of them women, volunteered in July and August of 1941; the total of registrants, after a renewed draft of volunteers was carried out in August and September, rose to 300,000. It was Leningrad's proud boast that it had over twice as many people in the *opolchenie* as Moscow.[57]

In fact, in view of the character of the recruiting drive, the number would have risen even higher had it not threatened to bring the entire Party and administrative machinery, industry, and public services to a complete standstill. Since few able-bodied Leningraders wished to run the risk of having their loyalty questioned by refusing to volunteer, it became necessary for the management and Party organizations in important factories and institutions to reverse their position and prevent their key men from marching off. In the Kirov Works, according to the director, "everybody without exception volunteered. We could have sent 25,000 people if we had wanted to; we let only 9,000 or 10,000 go."[58] Similarly, when the Elektrosila Works decided to form an *opolchenie* regiment, "everybody able to bear arms signed up," so that a selection had to be made if the factory was not to cease operation.[59] Consequently, those who were sent off were often people who could be spared and who were of least value to the enterprise. Less vital institutions had actually to stop the majority of their activities for a time. In fact, it soon became evident that Leningrad, thanks to the energy of its Party and administrative organizations, had in the best Soviet tradition overfulfilled the plan.[60]

It now became apparent that it would not be possible to withdraw so many men from production and organize them into units within so short a time. Some volunteers had been marched directly to temporary barracks, whereas others had been sent home to await a call. The situation in the barracks, where desperate efforts were being made to sort out the volunteers and organize them into units, was chaotic. In view of these difficulties and the worsening military situation, it was decided on July 4 to abandon the plan to form fifteen divisions and to proceed instead to the immediate formation of three *opolchenie* divisions, which were desperately needed at the front. The 1st Division was organized by July 10, the 2nd Division by July 12, and the 3rd Division by July 15. Each division was built around large groups of workers from major factories. Thus the 1st Division was primarily recruited from the Kirov Works and became known as the Kirov Division.[61]

Each division had about 10,000 men organized into three infantry regiments, an artillery regiment, and a tank battalion. These units were largely untrained and very short on armament and equipment. In all three divisions nearly half of the men had no previous military training. Less than 5 per cent of the officers had infantry training, the others being political appointees or reservists with technical specialization.[62]

The process by which those who had volunteered were selected to serve in these three *opolchenie* divisions was quite haphazard. Those who were selected were by no means always better fitted to be soldiers than those who remained behind. Since the selection was largely based on employment in a number of major factories, people with weak hearts, arthritis, asthma, and other diseases, who had volunteered in a gesture of patriotism and loyalty, found themselves shouldering rifles and being sent off to battle.

The manner in which the *opolchenie* divisions were prepared for combat was indicative of the Soviet leaders' pessimistic estimate of the military situation. Although, according to Khrushchev's speech at the Twentieth Congress of the Communist Party of the Soviet Union, Stalin sent all available reserve rifles to Leningrad, and although many Leningrad factories were ordered to produce weapons and equipment for the *opolchenie*,[63] there was a marked shortage of equipment in the *opolchenie* divisions. There were not enough rifles, uniforms, or entrenching tools for all the men. Each division had a few light artillery pieces and one or more machine-gun battalions. The bulk of the infantry regiments were issued rifles, and when there were not enough of them, the soldiers were armed with hand grenades or Molotov cocktails.[64]

Although the *opolchenie* divisions were untrained, the emergency was too great to allow sufficient time to prepare them for combat. As soon as they were formed, they were sent into battle. Thus the 1st *Opolchenie* Division was formed on July 10 and arrived at the front on July 14; the 2nd Division was formed on July 12 and departed for the front on July 13; and the 3rd Division moved out to the fortifications defending Leningrad the day of its formation on July 15.[65] All three divisions soon were engaged in heavy fighting.

The Leningrad leaders and propagandists did not hide the fact that the *opolchenie* was ill-prepared to fight the Germans. But the Leningrad press published numerous reports on how the volunteers were learning soldiering in actual battles and how successful they were.[66] The leaders consoled the population, if not themselves, with the idea that "although it lacked the necessary training and military experience," an *opolchenie* division made up for this with its "strong spirit."[67]

As far as the elite was concerned, it had been easy to volunteer into the *opolchenie* as long as this was essentially only a demonstration of personal loyalty to the regime. But it was quite another matter when some of the volunteers realized that the *opolchenie* would fight. Some then tried either to avoid being selected for combat or to pull strings to get released from the *opolchenie*. But although a few displayed panic, others showed real patriotic zeal and dedication to the cause (probably the younger and therefore more highly indoctrinated members of the elite in particular). A Party member and civil defense official, for example, who could easily have remained at his post, volunteered to serve in the *opolchenie* and later in a partisan unit. When he was not sent to the front with his *opolchenie* unit, this man wrote in his diary: "I was very hurt, for it is against my character to remain sitting around in the civil defense staff, to receive and pass on orders. . . . I yearn with my whole being to participate actively in the destruction of the monster that has thrown itself on our Union." When he was accepted by a partisan unit and ready to leave for the front, he wrote apropos of his farewells to his wife: "How she feared this separation! I pity her greatly, her and the boy, for we three love each other very much. But duty to the fatherland comes before personal feelings and interests."[68]

The population's attitude toward the *opolchenie* varied in proportion to the danger and discomfort involved. Some resented the manner in which the Party leaders forced them to join, although, of course, there were many willing volunteers. Some saw in the *opolchenie* a sign of Soviet military weakness, a useless and desperate gesture that would have no effect on the outcome, whereas others accepted the official view and believed that the *opolchenie* would prove its worth.[69] The relatives and friends of the volunteers were understandably upset when they discovered that the *opolchenie* units were made to fight with little training and few weapons, and some people saw in this another instance of the Soviet regime's callousness and lack of regard for the suffering of the population.[70]

The further deterioration of the military situation led in mid-July to a new recruiting drive. By decision of the Military Council of the *Opolchenie,* it was decided to assemble some of the remaining smaller *opolchenie* units in Leningrad into the 4th *Opolchenie* Division. Shortly after its organization on July 19, this division, too, was sent to the front.[71]

This was followed by a decision to recruit four additional divisions. Marshal Voroshilov proposed to call them "Guard" divisions. The organization of three divisions began after July 24 and was completed by August 8. Most of the men were recruited from the 34,000 *opolchenie* volunteers still remaining in the city. As in the previous case, the divisions were long on Party members and short on training. Nevertheless, all divisions were sent into combat a few days after they were formed. The 4th Guard Division was organized on August 13 to provide replacements for the others.[72] At the end of August this division was renumbered as the 5th Guard Division and was sent into combat in the second week of September.[73]

In addition to these divisions, it was decided on July 4 to form independent artillery and machine-gun battalions, each made up of 800 to 1,200 men. In all, fifteen battalions were formed. On July 12 four were sent to the front, while ten others engaged in the construction of fortifications. All of them were short of weapons and trained men.[74]

Apart from the ninety destruction battalions that were organized by August, Voroshilov and Zhdanov on July 12 ordered the formation of partisan units. Each *opolchenie* division trained some units, and others were recruited in the major factories. The Kirov Works, for example, formed ten partisan units. These units had a very large proportion of Party members, Komsomols, and NKVD personnel. In all, some 15,000 partisans were sent from Leningrad to operate behind the German lines. In the summer of 1941 the local partisan movement in the German occupied area around Leningrad was quite small. There were only 639 activists, organized into 125 units, who were reinforced by 68 Party organizers sent from Leningrad. Thus the overwhelming majority of the partisans who operated behind the German lines were recruited in Leningrad.[75]

It is difficult to assess the role played by the *opolchenie* in defending Leningrad. There is no doubt that some *opolchenie* divisions were actually used in combat. German records repeatedly mention encounters with them.[76] Soviet sources claim that they fought at Kingisepp, Luga, and the immediate approaches to Leningrad.[77] In these engagements the divisions paid the price of their inexperience. According to Soviet statements made to foreign correspondents, four divisions were virtually wiped out, whereas others had about 50 per cent casualties.[78]

Specifically, the director of the Kirov Works stated in 1943, apropos of the elite Kirov Division, that it was "no secret that a large portion of the workers' division never came back. Their losses were very heavy."[79]

Soviet propagandists have, of course, insisted that the *opolchenie* played a vital role in halting or slowing down the German advance.[80] A number of former Leningraders, on the other hand, maintain that the military value of these divisions was small or nil, because they proved themselves unable to withstand any serious enemy pressure.[81] According to a postwar Soviet source, "The battleworthiness of the *opolchenie* divisions, which were formed within a few days and which were poorly trained and insufficiently prepared for battle operations, was particularly low, although they did possess high morale."[82] The Germans themselves tended to minimize the *opolchenie's* military worth, but did on occasion pay respect to its spirit.[83] In general, it would seem that the Soviet leadership considered the situation desperate enough to warrant throwing away lives to slow down the German advance, and although this technique was very wasteful of manpower, it did accomplish its purpose, at least to some extent. But actually neither the Red Army nor the political leaders had a very high opinion of the military worth of the *opolchenie,* and in September the remaining units were transferred to the regular forces or dispersed among them in the guise of reinforcements.[84] Other survivors were demobilized.

During this same period, the Party organizations also conducted a recruiting campaign for the Red Army, encouraging people to volunteer for service in the regular armed forces. These volunteers were persons who were not liable for mobilization until later, as well as many who were not liable for it at all. Among the volunteers were also large numbers of Party members and Komsomols. According to Soviet sources, 146,000 Komsomols volunteered, among them many women.[85] In all, the Party sent to the armed forces about 70,000 Party members and 185,000 Komsomols, most of them during the first three months of the war.[86]

In some cases the volunteers were motivated by other considerations than those of patriotism or display of loyalty. Prominent among these were the expectation that everybody would be mobilized sooner or later and the realization that the families of volunteers received higher allowances from the government than ordinary draftees. From this came the saying "The wolves [the leadership] are satisfied, and the sheep, if not satisfied, get something out of it."[87]

Although a large proportion of those who had volunteered for the *opolchenie* were sent to the front, the authorities sought to train larger numbers of Leningraders in order to provide replacements for the armed forces and for the purpose of defending the city if the German advance were to reach it. On July 20 the staff of the *opolchenie* army ordered compulsory military training for most able-bodied male residents still in Leningrad. In each city *raion*, instructor groups were organized, made up of three to five reserve officers, to supervise the training. Training units were also formed in the large factories, schools, and institutions. A sixteen-hour general training program was drawn up, and the population was required to take the training after regular work hours. In addition, special training in artillery, machine guns, mortars, tanks, and communication was given to select persons. Typically, the authorities overlooked, when instituting this program, the conflicting demands made on the population. The administration and the Party sought in each case to fulfill each demand, and sometimes did so on paper, but this was not possible in reality. Thus it happened that although Soviet propaganda claimed that 102,000 persons received training out of the 151,294 persons who were liable for it, in actuality only 72,379 attended the training course and only 50,377 finished it.[88] The trainees were then organized into seventy-nine battalions. Most of those who failed to attend the training were engaged at that time in building fortifications outside of Leningrad.

Since the training involved a large number of workers, it was decided to organize armed worker detachments in the factories. It was initially planned to form 150 detachments composed of 600 men each. When possible, the directors of the enterprises were put in command of the detachments. These detachments were reinforced by weapons platoons and artillery batteries recruited from among those who received special training. In addition to the basic sixteen-hour training course, those who completed it were given a further thirty hours of training. The training was conducted for three to four hours after work. This meant that after June 27, when an eleven-hour workday was instituted, the workers remained in the factories a total of fourteen to fifteen hours each day.[89]

While these attempts were being made to halt the German advance on the ground, other measures were being taken to prepare Leningrad for the expected air attacks. The fact that these attacks were slow in materializing was apparently a development unhoped for by the Leningrad leadership. Like all other measures taken by the authorities that involved mobilizing the efforts of a large number of people, these measures were carried out as campaigns, with a great deal of noisy propaganda and much inefficient use of manpower. But in the end things did get done, more or less satisfactorily.

At the moment of the German attack on the Soviet Union, Leningrad's civil defense preparations were far from complete. The city was organized as follows: It was divided into nineteen civil defense districts, and each district was divided into two sectors. Operational civil defense commands and groups were organized in each sector and were under the command of the chief of police of each sector. On June 22 the Leningrad civil defense had only 14,000 members, many of whom had to be given additional training. Additional thousands of civil defense workers had to be recruited and trained.[90]

On June 23 the city's Executive Committee and the Bureau of the Party Committee issued a joint order providing for the formation of nearly 10,000 fire-fighting teams in the factories and apartment houses.[91] Although air raids were expected from the moment of the German attack, it was not until June 27 that Order No. 1 of the Civil Defense Organization of Leningrad was issued. It ordered a twenty-four-hour watch on all buildings, described the alert and all-clear signals, provided for a complete blackout of the city, and directed local groups to be responsible for the initial fire fighting and salvage work. It also provided for the removal of inflammable materials from the vicinity of buildings and attics, for the covering of attic floors with a ten-centimeter layer of sand, and for the storage of additional barrels of water and boxes of sand to fight incendiary bombs and fires. Finally, the order authorized the administrators of enterprises, offices, and houses to recruit a sufficient number of people not only to fulfill the specified tasks, but also to be available for other civil defense work in each building.[92] Additional detailed instructions on fire-prevention measures in homes, factories, and public buildings were issued by the Executive Committee of the City Soviet on June 30.[93]

Although the trained civil defense commands in the city had manned their posts from the first day of the war, it was obvious from the start that wide popular participation in civil defense would be necessary if the work were to be effective. The difficulty was compounded by the fact that the supply of trained civil defense cadres and reserves continued to disappear because of mobilization for military service, construction of fortifications, evacuation, or volunteering for the *opolchenie*. All of these campaigns appear to have taken precedence over civil defense needs; for example, even a fully trained staff member of a civil defense command post could volunteer for and be accepted by the *opolchenie*.[94]

The answer was another mass mobilization. On July 2 the Council of People's Commissars of the USSR decreed "universal compulsory training in air and chemical defense for the entire adult population within the ages of 16 to 60." The trained persons were to be organized into "self-defense" groups. Children between the ages of 8 and 16 were also to be trained in "individual measures of defense against air raid attacks."[95] Exempt from participation in these "self-defense" groups were invalids, pregnant women, and women with children under 8 years of age. The trainees were to receive 28 hours of instruction, which were to be given at schools or at places of employment or residence. In schools and houses it was to be the responsibility of the *Osoaviakhim*, while the city executive committee had to supply the necessary equipment. In enterprises and institutions the directors were responsible for the training, while the equipment was to be supplied by the appropriate People's Commissariat (Ministry) or by City Departments.

On the same day, the Council of People's Commissars of the RSFSR decreed that the leadership and organization of the "self-defense" groups would be the responsibility of the local Soviets and specified that the Leningrad "self-defense" groups had to be organized and trained within one month.[96] The decrees also ordered the organization of civil defense "self-defense" groups in all apartment houses, factories, office buildings, and institutions within five days. A further order of the chief of the local civil defense, issued on July 22, directed that all wooden structures and fences near houses be torn down to lessen the fire hazard and that around-the-clock fire watch be maintained on the roofs and in the attics of all buildings. Furthermore, the "self-defense" groups were made completely responsible for putting out all fires in their own buildings or on the street and also were to come to the assistance of neighboring groups.[97]

On July 27 the Executive Committee of the Leningrad City Soviet decided to simplify the situation by dumping the whole problem in the laps of the individual administrators of houses and buildings. The apartment house administrators and the "commanders" of public buildings were made personally responsible for "organizing civil defense and fire-fighting precautions in their buildings, for forming self-defense groups and fire-fighter squads, for training and equipping these squads, and for seeing to the prompt and unhesitating execution of all orders from the chief of local civil defense of the city of Leningrad."[98] In order to fulfill these instructions, the administrators and commanders were authorized to draft "in a compulsory fashion" all persons residing in the building in their care who were not employed in industry, and to assign tasks to resident workers and employees during their free time. These tasks included guard duty on roofs, in attics, on stairways, and in the entrance halls of buildings, and work with fire-fighting squads or with "self-defense" groups. The order made it clear that anybody refusing to serve in a "self-defense" group or to stand guard duty would be liable to punishment under wartime laws. Supervision and control over the proper implementation of this order were assigned to the chief of the militia, the chief of the fire department, and the chief of the Leningrad housing administration.

Thus in the usual "voluntary-obligatory" fashion many persons who had somehow escaped the *opolchenie*, military service, or factory work became part-time civil defense workers. According to informants, people sometimes volunteered for civil defense in the hope of avoiding fortification work. The main weight fell, of course, on the women and young people. In one *raion* alone there were said to be 16,000 women doing civil defense work.[99] There were also older men who served in their free time. There were people who did double duty, working for civil defense at their place of employment and also at home. The physical burden on working people was undoubtedly great, since they had to stand watch on roofs or do other guard duty after eight to eleven hours of regular labor. Despite difficulties the authorities, to no one's great surprise, managed to recruit, at least on paper, the proper number of civil defense personnel within the prescribed period of time. Thus by August 28 the civil defense organization claimed to have about 107,000 persons registered as members of "self-defense" groups.[100]

To improve the training program the Party decided to set up Party organizers in the larger buildings to help prepare the population for civil defense, which meant that the Party organization closely supervised the whole program.[101]

Finally, each large office or public building, apartment house, and factory was provided with a permanent civil defense group drafted from among the employees. Schools had civil defense groups composed of teachers and students, and the philharmonic orchestra organized a group of musicians to stand watch and fight fires. Larger housing units had their own medical or first-aid units. Around-the-clock watch was maintained on each building, with the understanding that each civil defense team was immediately responsible for fire fighting, rescue work, and the like, while the fire department and the *raion* civil defense organization would move in only if the local units were unable to cope with the situation.[102]

To deal with possible large-scale damage from heavy air raids, the Executive Committee of the City Soviet decided on July 17 to form two repair and rescue regiments and three independent civil defense battalions. The first regiment was drawn from the personnel of the Administration for Housing Construction, and the second from the Administration for Construction of Cultural and Public Buildings. One battalion was formed to deal with road and bridge repairs, another with repairs to the water system, and the third for housing repairs. Each regiment had 2,051 men and each battalion 600 men.[103] Furthermore, in order to deal with large fires in the more vulnerable areas of the city, such as the harbor and large warehouse and storage areas, the Leningrad City Committee of the Komsomol decided, in the first half of

August, to organize a Komsomol fire-fighting regiment of 1,614 men from among students.[104] The organization of this regiment was completed by September 1. At the same time the Komsomol also organized another militarized regiment for the purpose of assisting the police in maintaining public order. By September this regiment had 2,160 members, including many women.[105] The personnel of these regiments wore uniforms, and their work was not restricted merely to civil defense tasks. At various times they were used for the construction of fortifications, the laying of mine fields, communication, battlefield reconnaissance, and other nonpassive defense tasks.

By September the civil defense organization had officially a total of 196,198 members as against the 14,000 it had in June.[106] In fact, all this figure shows is the usual administrative success in filling quotas on paper, since the actual number of persons who were active in civil defense was far smaller. According to the Chief of Staff of Leningrad's civil defense, his organization had in September a total of 63,000 members, including nearly 3,000 "self-defense" groups.[107]

The city's civil defense organization was operated by a staff that after July 23 was headed by Chief of Antiaircraft Defense of the Northern Front Command. The Komsomol regiments were under the control of the NKVD. In addition, on August 6 an Extraordinary Commission was formed for the purpose of combating slackness in the civil defense preparations and to help direct the organization. This commission was composed of a deputy chairman of the City Soviet, the chief of the city's civil defense organization, a secretary of the city's Party committee, and the chief of Leningrad's police administration.[108]

The actual training of the civil defense workers appears to have been hurried and superficial. In addition, the newspapers published a few articles on such subjects as how to put out incendiary bombs, and the radio broadcast a number of lectures on civil defense methods. The equipment of the civil defense groups varied, but was always of the simplest kind. Each group usually was equipped with helmets, axes, crowbars, shovels, buckets, extinguishers or hand water-sprayers, hoses, and sand, and the authorities sometimes supplemented this with one or two impregnated suits for work in gas-contaminated areas. Since the amount of equipment apparently depended in part on the size and importance of the building for which the group was responsible, and in part on the initiative, persistence, and connections of the house administrator or building commander, it followed that some buildings were very poorly equipped.

Steps were also taken to improve the existing air raid shelters and medical first-aid posts, and to increase the number of such facilities. Large-scale work on shelters, mainly in the form of reinforcing basement ceilings, began in July. In addition, numerous slit trenches were dug in parks, gardens, and around factories, and in some cases large dugouts were also built. By August 20 Leningrad had sufficient air raid shelters for 918,000 persons and slit trenches for 672,000.[109] This fell far short of the needs of Leningrad's population, especially since the slit trenches, owing to the swampy soil, were not very deep and deteriorated rapidly with the onset of fall rains and cold.

The Red Cross and the public health authorities established nearly 5,000 medical first-aid posts to deal with air-raid casualties. A large number of hotels, schools, and public buildings were requisitioned to serve as hospitals, and a total of 18,000 blood donors was registered.[110]

In July the Soviet armed forces captured some gas shells from Army Group North. This fact and subsequent reports indicating that the Germans were considering the use of poison gases against Leningrad led to a decision to provide the city's population with gas masks.[111] The authorities warned the population that "the Hitlerite bandits are prepared to use vile means—poison gases."[112] Although few gas-proof shelters were available, Leningrad's chemical industry provided gas masks for the majority of the city's population.[113]

A few general measures were carried out to reduce the vulnerability of the city to air attacks. Public buildings and monuments were protected by sandbags, and a few, such as the Smolny Institute, were extensively camouflaged with netting. Factories were apparently not camouflaged. Windows were covered with strips of adhesive paper to reduce the danger from broken glass.

Air defense was provided by fighter planes, antiaircraft guns, and barrage balloons. The fighter planes available for Leningrad's defense were generally obsolete and were constantly being reduced in number as airfields were swallowed up by the enemy advance. The antiaircraft artillery, on the other hand, was more effective. The many parks and city squares, as well as the wide streets and the hundred or so islands in the Neva, allowed for extensive deployment of antiaircraft weapons. Light guns were sometimes mounted on the roofs of large buildings. In the harbor and on the Neva River, antiaircraft fire was supplemented by the fire from guns of warships stationed there.

Numerous alerts were sounded in the city, but except for a bomb dropped by a German plane on July 18 there were no actual attacks.[114] Eyewitnesses mention in their recollections and diaries that there were sometimes as many as four alerts a day and that on one particular day twelve alerts were sounded.[115] Although Soviet sources claim that in the period of June 22 to September 6, 128 German raids on Leningrad were beaten off before they could reach the city, there is no evidence that the Germans had actually attempted such attacks.

Nevertheless, during this period 76 alerts were sounded in Leningrad.[116] The alerts were announced over the radio loud-speakers, which, by orders of the Executive Committee of the City Soviet, were to be kept turned on all the time, and by the sounding of all available sirens and factory whistles. Between the sounding of the alert and the all clear, the radio broadcast the ticking of a metronome, presumably to inform the population that the alert was still on.[117]

The civil defense regulations were strictly enforced, especially after August 6, when a check by the authorities showed that some regulations were not always properly obeyed.[118] During alerts everybody not on duty was ordered by the militia and the air raid wardens into shelters. At nighttime, of course, many people, in the absence of real bombing, were reluctant to use the shelters, particularly if these were not located in the building in which they lived. Where possible, people preferred to take shelter in multistoried houses, since they quite reasonably assumed that they had more cover overhead in such buildings. Failure to maintain discipline during alerts or blackouts was punishable by fines.[119] In fact, failure to obey any civil defense regulation could lead to an accusation of sabotage or refusal to maintain discipline in wartime, which in turn could lead to a court-martial.

According to informants, the population in general felt that the civil defense preparations were extensive and probably adequate, although they recognized that there were undoubtedly cases of unpreparedness on the part of some house managements and that many of the civil defense personnel had little training. Most Leningraders were inclined to regard civil defense measures favorably because they served to protect the individual and his property. Most people seem to have worked conscientiously not only to safeguard their own houses, but also to sandbag public buildings. The physical hardship connected with this labor appears to have been accepted with a considerable degree of willingness and good humor, particularly by young people, who sometimes participated enthusiastically in civil defense units.

Some older people were less enthusiastic and questioned the wisdom of entrusting civil defense to "a bunch of women and girls."[120] Nor were people unaware of the absurdities or risks connected with some of the official civil defense instructions. When a civil defense instructor told one girl, "You are standing on the roof. Here is the sand. If an incendiary bomb drops through the roof, you . . . ," the girl sarcastically replied, "And if it is an explosive bomb?"[121]

There were also instances of negligence and of theft of fire-fighting equipment. Thus a report of the Local Civil Defense Administration, issued in July, stated that a check on the maintenance of fire extinguishers in factories, offices, and houses had revealed that the administrators had often recruited "casual persons" to care for such equipment and that there had occurred "instances of mass misuse on the part of persons doing this work."[122] In some instances these persons had even removed the chemicals from the extinguishers and had sold them, replacing them with valueless substitutes.

Defense of the city was only one of the problems with which the central and local authorities had to deal. A very complex and difficult task was that of reorganizing industry and converting it to war production. The German advance continually added to the problem by forcing industrial installations to evacuate and by eliminating source after source of raw materials and electric power.

There is ample evidence that adequate plans for mobilizing Soviet industry in the event of war had not been made. At the outbreak of the war the Soviet economy was still striving for the most part to fulfill the peacetime goals of the Third Five Year Plan. A "mobilization plan" had been adopted for the second half of 1941 and for 1942, establishing a program of ammunition production and preparing for the conversion of industry, especially machine building, in the event of a war. This plan also ordered that Soviet enterprise "stockpile the materials and semi-manufactures essential for war production in the mobilization reserves of enterprises."[123]

It was not possible to implement the program fully in the short time prior to the German attack, and the limited scope of the program made it of little use after June 22. Consequently, a week later the Soviet government adopted a plan for the third quarter of 1941 that made the first attempt at converting the country's economy to a wartime basis; output of war material was to be increased by 26 per cent. However, because of the unexpected German advance into the Soviet Union, which threatened to capture many of the industrial regions, the government was unable to put this plan into action. Instead, on August 16, it had to adopt another plan that provided for the removal of many key enterprises from western Russia to Siberia and the construction there of new industrial war production centers.[124]

The problem of converting industry to war production within the shortest possible time was no simple matter, and changing the basic plans only contributed to the confusion. According to Voznesensky, then chief of the highest Soviet economic planning body, the State Planning Commission, "war industry was reinforced by transferring to it enterprises from other branches of the economy," and raw materials and supplies were reallocated from nonessential plants to the war industry. Furthermore, the "allocation and rationing of metals, fuels, electric energy, and other types of raw materials and supplies were strictly centralized."[125]

Leningradskaia pravda described the task faced by industry as follows:

What does it mean to convert a factory to wartime conditions? It means to learn quickly, without losing an hour, to change over to producing those goods that are most needed today and to make the output two, three, or even ten times greater than before. It means to plan, to build, and to acquire skill with new machines and apparatus much faster than before. It means that the administrators, directors, shop chiefs, and foremen must learn to fulfill the plan with fewer workers, engineers, and office workers, and must make the entire factory organization more maneuverable and flexible.[126]

It also meant economizing on power, fuel, and raw materials, and converting the small enterprises and shops that had been producing consumer goods to the production of war goods, for which the same machinery often had to be used.

In this program several new methods were used. One was the expansion of the "principle of cooperation." Whereas previously cooperation had been practiced only within ministries (People's Commissariats), it was now to operate between the different industries as well as between the ministries. What exactly was meant by "cooperation" was not explained. Another method was to make wider use of industrial reserves of machinery and material. It is reported, for example, that when a new type of production in Leningrad required some 450 machines, they were requisitioned from Leningrad's industries and made available for the new production line.[127]

The administrative arrangements for these measures were complex. Since the city's heavy industry was under the direct control of ministries, all of which were located in Moscow, the local managers often could not act without instructions from their superiors in the capital. The extreme centralization of administrative controls and the fear of criticism tended to paralyze the initiative of Leningrad's industrial managers, who found it safer to execute orders, no matter how unrealistic, than to take independent action. The degree of this centralization of decisions is illustrated, for example, by the fact that when in August the Leningrad authorities sought to expand the production of bottles for Molotov cocktails, it required a decision from the State Defense Committee, the highest executive organ in the USSR at that time, to allow one of the Leningrad bottling plants to convert to this type of production.[128]

At the same time the local Party leadership on the city and *raion* level also had a hand in supervising and directing industrial operations. The secretaries of the *raikoms* were said to have given "daily assistance to the plants, works, and organizations, and headed up the work of placing industry on a war basis."[129] Local control over industry increased, of course, as the Germans cut off the city more and more completely; but contact with and direction from Moscow never ceased and, despite the siege, never lost importance.

The actual mobilization and conversion of industry took time and effort, despite and sometimes because of the speed with which they were put in hand. Soviet propaganda naturally boasted about its success. Thus one factory was said to have taken less than four weeks to begin mass producing a new type of equipment that had never been made in Leningrad before.[130] But it is probable that effective and uninterrupted mass production of new items actually took considerable time. The individual plant director and his engineers were hard put to it. It was easy to issue new directions, but difficult to implement them.

The attempt to convert Leningrad's industry to war production met serious difficulties in connection with raw material and labor supply. Despite standing instructions requiring Leningrad's factories to stockpile raw materials, there was a severe shortage from the very beginning of the war in a number of critical materials. Thus in June Leningrad's entire stock of TNT was only 284 metric tons. There was also a shortage of steel, nonferrous metals, and other essential materials. Yet, according to the new production plans, Leningrad's industry was required to produce all types of military equipment, ranging from armored trains and artillery to mess kits.[131]

Some of these shortages were partly overcome by the use of substitutes. Leningrad's scientists developed a new explosive and devised methods by which cast iron and a mixture of iron and fiber were substituted for steel in the manufacturing of shell casings.[132]

The other chief difficulty was that while the Party and administration appealed to industry to "work harder, better, more productively," the available trained labor force had been sharply reduced as a result of the various mobilizations.[133] As mentioned earlier, the Kirov Works, for example, which produced ammunition, tanks, guns, and heavy equipment, released nearly one-third of its employees for service with the *opolchenie*. The Stalin Metallurgical Factory lost 1,300 workers to the *opolchenie* alone, and more were drafted into the army.[134] The Elektrosila Works, the largest electric motor plant in the USSR, suffered a similar loss.[135] Although the shipyards were required to make urgent repairs on naval vessels, 25,000 yard workers were mobilized for military service.[136] One source estimates that as a result of mobilization and volunteering, "from 60 to 70 per cent of the factory workers were newcomers and inexperienced."[137]

Initially, the military departments of the *raion* Party committees helped to find replacements for the departed workers. Retired workers and the wives of soldiers and workers were recruited as replacements.

Additional help was drafted under the compulsory labor decree. A large portion of the clerical and administrative personnel in factories was transferred to the production lines. Students from the factory schools were sent to work in the factories.[138]

But the new workers could not, of course, compensate for the loss of skilled labor. In the Stalin Factory, for example, "all the welders of the plant could fulfill only 50 per cent of the program."[139] Engineers were forced to work at machines to keep up production norms and many factories failed to fulfill the prescribed output plans. Because of the lack of replacements, skilled workers sometimes worked on rush orders for twenty-four to thirty-six hours at a stretch.[140] Later some factories managed to bring back some of the skilled workers who had left with the *opolchenie,* but many others had already been killed in battle.

Of course, some workers did increase production and overfulfilled their individual norms. Some increase in output was also obtained as a result of the obligatory overtime work that everybody was forced to do, but this was probably offset by the difficulties described above. The level of production may be indicated by the emphasis that Soviet propagandists gave to the necessity for wide application of Stakhanovite working methods. On July 12 the city's Komsomol committee began organizing production competition among young factory workers for the purpose of encouraging them to fulfill production norms by 150–200 per cent.[141] As usual the Party cells and committees in each factory as well as the *raikoms* did their utmost to help. One of their roles was to organize the training of the new workers.

To achieve the objectives set for industry the Soviet leadership needed to tighten its control over labor. Several new labor laws were issued. On June 26 the Presidium of the Supreme Soviet of the USSR authorized the directors and managers in industry, institutions, transportation, agriculture, and trade to institute up to three hours of overtime for their employees. Adolescents under 16 years of age could be required to work up to two hours overtime, for which they were to be paid at the rate of time and a half. In addition, the decree canceled all leaves to which the workers were entitled.[142] Management was given the authority to prevent resignation from work for most causes other than service in the armed forces.

To improve the state's control over the dwindling labor supply, the Committee for the Registration and Distribution of the Labor Force was formed on June 30 in Moscow. This committee, composed of representatives from the Council of People's Commissars of the USSR, the State Planning Commission, and the NKVD, could mobilize and redistribute labor after reviewing requests for workers from factories and new construction sites. To increase flexibility of labor, the

Council of People's Commissars of the republics and *krais* (territories—
a larger subdivision than *oblasts*) and the *oblast* executive committees
were authorized on July 23 to transfer at will workers and employees
from one factory or work place to another.[143] This decree in effect
voided completely the labor contract that each worker normally had
with his employer. Workers were now in the same position as soldiers
in the Red Army, having hardly any rights and being under the complete control of management and the state authorities.

In August a system called "barrack conditions" (*kazarmnoe polo-
zhenie*) was introduced. It restrained a part of the labor force from
leaving factory premises at night. There were several reasons for this
measure. Probably the most important one initially was the desire to
provide each industrial installation with a trained worker defense unit,
always on the premises and ready at a moment's notice to defend the
factory if the Germans were to enter the city. A further reason was
probably to keep a labor force on hand for emergency work assignments and to reduce the loss of time that the return of the workers to
their homes after work entailed. The workers restricted under this
measure were permitted to go home once a week to visit their families.[144]

There were other measures, direct and indirect, that were also highly
effective in reinforcing the authority of management over the workers.
Management could exempt workers in defense industries from military
service. But this exemption was valid only as long as management was
willing to retain a worker in such an industry. In general, any worker
who was fired from his job, unless he managed to find another employer
immediately, was liable to be drafted under the compulsory labor decree and sent to dig fortifications at the front for minimal pay. To be
fired from a job had two other possible consequences. One was the loss
of the privilege of belonging to the highest food ration category. The
other was the danger of being denounced to the NKVD and turned over
to a military tribunal for failing to support the war effort.

The Party organizations continually exerted pressure on labor to
push productivity. Party propaganda held up the better workers as
an example to others. The press praised the Stakhanovites and urged
all factories to adopt the "correct" method of having each worker operate several machines at once. Workers were given the following warning: "If yesterday the Party strove for the maintenance of the strictest
labor discipline, the complete liquidation of absenteeism, then today
laxity and dallying are the more inadmissible."[145]

In the factories a more personal form of pressure was brought to
bear as well. Factory newspapers and bulletin boards in the shops
stimulated production by censuring the laggards and praising the Stakhanovites. One factory newspaper wrote, "Drillers, you are preventing

the delivery of war supplies," and urged them to increase their output.[146] In another factory signs proclaimed: "Comrade winders! Work like Lutskaia—this is the duty of each Soviet patriot."[147] In some cases, signs were posted at each machine bearing the slogan "What have you done for the defense of Leningrad?" and showing each worker's output for that shift.[148] Elsewhere, daily report sheets and wall graphs showed the performance of each worker, to the shame of the less productive. Shock workers were honored by having little red flags placed at their machines, sometimes with the inscription "Master of Labor Productivity."[149] Other means of increasing output were meetings called to discuss the reasons for the lag in one shop or another, or mock trials held by other workers. There is reason to believe that these methods of shaming workers were fairly effective.[150]

The population seems to have accepted most of the labor measures as necessary or inevitable. What some people resented was the excessive zeal of some of the administrators, who found occasions to display their own loyalty at the expense of their employees. When people were sent to do work for which they were not suited or kept at work when there was little for them to do, they were quick to recognize this mismanagement or misuse of authority and to resent it. There was apparently, as in peacetime, impatience with the frequent and time-consuming mass meetings called by Party propagandists. However, in the opinion of some informants, the order requiring part of the labor force to live in the factory was not unpopular, since the workers benefited from the additional rest and the food at the canteens.[151]

There were few attempts to disobey the labor regulations. Those who wished to avoid unpleasant tasks tried to do so legally by obtaining medical exemptions or by seeking transfer to duties that would free them from those they disliked. Joining civil defense organizations was one way to do this.

The efforts to increase the productivity of Leningrad's industry were further disrupted by the industrial evacuation that began in July 1941. As the Germans came closer to Leningrad, an increasing number of factories were ordered by Moscow to pack up and leave for new locations in Siberia. To move large quantities of machinery chiefly by rail was a difficult operation, and the evacuation was only partly successful.

After the fall of Pskov, and particularly after the breaching of the Luga line, the fate of Leningrad was very much in doubt. Consequently, the removal of industrial equipment had to be carried out at great speed. The nearer the enemy approached, the hastier became the evacuation. First ordered to leave were some optical instrument plants and some aircraft plants, both essential industries.[152] They were followed by factories producing tanks and other war goods, particularly

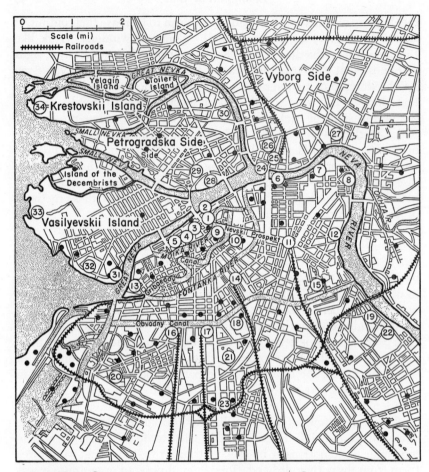

THE CITY OF LENINGRAD

those that were urgently needed in the new war production centers in Siberia. Usually a factory shop was evacuated as a unit, taking along its best and newest machinery. The equipment evacuated from Leningrad, like that from other Soviet cities, suffered considerable damage in transit. According to eyewitnesses, the "dismantling and crating was carried out with such carelessness that part of the equipment was broken."[153] More equipment was destroyed during the trip by German air attacks.

The evacuation was disrupted by transportation difficulties. By July the Germans and Finns had cut all major lines leading from Leningrad except the one going to Moscow. This one line rapidly became overloaded with military traffic. By mid-August this last rail link was cut by the German advance on Mga.

Because of the disorganization of the railway system, the speed of the German advance, and possibly the lateness of the evacuation orders, much machinery that had been packed or loaded on freight cars failed to leave before the city came under siege. According to Soviet sources, over 2,000 freight carloads of machinery remained trapped in the railway freight yards of Leningrad.[154] The equipment left in open cars soon began to rust and deteriorate. A large part of this machinery remained on the freight cars during the entire winter of 1941–42. The chief engineers of the Elektrosila Works said that "the trains with Elektrosila's heavy equipment were left standing in the Leningrad railway yards. They remained there until March 1943 [*sic*]."[155] Much of the stranded equipment was later moved to the east in the winter and summer of 1942. Because of administrative confusion, the evacuation orders issued to factories were often not rescinded even when their machinery failed to get away. Nor did the city's leadership or the plant management apparently have the authority or the initiative to return this equipment to the plant.

The exodus of Leningrad's industry, which took about a year to complete, was fairly extensive. How many factories succeeded in leaving before the beginning of the siege is not clear. According to a Soviet official, 92 of the largest enterprises were evacuated.[156] Another source reports that 86 factories were completely or partly removed.[157] Despite Leningrad's desperate need for arms and munitions, and the Party's exhortations to the workers to produce more for the front, the productive capacity of industry belonging to the People's Commissariat for Arms Production was reduced by 48 per cent and that of the People's Commissariat for Munitions Production by 50.6 per cent, resulting in an over-all reduction by 48.7 per cent[158] in the productive capacity of Leningrad's defense industry.

Some shops from each factory nearly always remained behind and were eventually converted to war production. Some of these, such as foundries, were too bulky to be evacuated; much of their equipment could not be moved at all. Others were auxiliary shops, not essential to the operation of the evacuated plant. Then some shops were engaged in or were suitable for carrying out repairs of naval or army equipment, or had machinery which, though too old to be worth moving, was useful to Leningrad's defense. In some cases the factory buildings emptied by evacuation were used to house the equipment of other plants whose old locations were endangered by the German advance or by bombardment.[159]

Along with the factories, a large number of managers, technicians, engineers, and skilled workers were also evacuated. The evacuation plan obviously called for the presence of at least part of the original labor force if the evacuated plants were to be satisfactorily reconstructed and operated in the east. As far as can be determined, only skilled and semiskilled labor was ordered to leave. The evacuees were authorized to take their families along, unless the latter were not free to leave because of their work, and to take a certain amount of luggage. The workers traveled in fourth-class passenger cars or in freight cars, while leading administrative and technical personnel were often evacuated by air. Each factory management drew up a list of the workers to be evacuated; the families had to obtain their authorization for departure and their travel papers from evacuation bureaus formed under the *raion* executive committees. In all, 164,320 workers and employees are reported to have been evacuated prior to August 27.[160]

In addition to industries, 92 institutions of various kinds, such as academies, hospitals, research institutions, and some theaters, were evacuated.[161] There appears to be no evidence that any governmental or Party organizations were evacuated at this time. Some effort was made to remove art and cultural treasures from the city; parts of the contents of the Leningrad Public Library and of some museums were evacuated or their contents stored in safe places in anticipation of enemy air attacks. But many works of art and historical treasures near Leningrad were left to fall into the hands of the Germans; and other art treasures in the city were destroyed during the bombardment.[162]

The authorities made some effort to evacuate the civilian population. This evacuation was partly obligatory and partly voluntary. At the start of the war some families sent their children and women out of town in anticipation of air raids; other women and children who were away on vacation delayed their return.

At the end of June the Leningrad Soviet decided to evacuate from the city 392,000 children and to send them to rural districts in the Leningrad, Kalinin, and Yaroslavl *oblasts*. The children were to be sent off with whatever school, orphanage, or children's home they belonged to. On June 29, the first ten trains, carrying 15,192 children, left Leningrad for the countryside. Some of the children were sent in the direction of the advancing Germans, for example to Pskov and Novgorod. Soon afterward the German advance and enemy raids on the rail lines, which killed some children, forced the authorities to bring many of the evacuated children back to Leningrad, but according to a Soviet historian, the authorities charged with the evacuation continued to issue the same instructions, out of sheer inertia, and some of the children were sent off as before in the wrong direction. After a while the children were reassembled and this time evacuated farther east, to the Kirov and Sverdlovsk *oblasts* or beyond. At this time some of Leningrad's food stocks were also being evacuated, and part of these supplies were used to feed the children.[163]

According to an order of the Executive Committee of the Leningrad Soviet of July 19, 1941, parents had to pay for their evacuated children on the basis of a scale fixed according to the average monthly income of one member of the family.[164] If, for example, such a family member earned over 281 rubles, he paid 210 rubles. The children were accompanied by their teachers and sometimes by parents.

According to an official Soviet report, 216,691 children were evacuated in the period between June 29 and August 27.[165] Some who had been sent to the country by their parents on an individual basis later returned. For a variety of reasons many children remained in the city.

In addition to children, unemployed people, women, and old people were authorized to leave on a voluntary basis, as were those who managed to obtain a release from their jobs or a transfer to other jobs elsewhere in the country. A number of wives of officials apparently left the city. As the situation worsened, some army officers tried to arrange for the evacuation of their families. By August 10, a total of 467,648 persons had been evacuated. On that date it was decided to evacuate from the city an additional 400,000 women and children up to the age of 14. Less than a week later the growing danger to Leningrad forced the Council on Evacuation in Moscow and the Leningrad Soviet to raise this number to 700,000, to be evacuated at the rate of 30,000 daily. The German advance prevented this evacuation from being completed. By August 29, a total of 636,203 persons had been evacuated, including 147,500 refugees from the Baltic states and 9,500 persons accompanying evacuated equipment or livestock.[166]

The execution of this evacuation was far from smooth and became increasingly chaotic as the danger to Leningrad intensified. Authorization for evacuation had to be obtained from commissions headed by the secretaries of the *raion* Party committees that were attached to each *raion* executive committee.[167] The commissions checked whether the applicant had been properly released from all labor obligations or employment. If he had been, he was given a travel order showing his destination, which was frequently prescribed by the authorities regardless of his wishes. The papers sometimes also showed the date of departure, the car number, and the compartment number. Whether the amount of baggage that an evacuee could take with him was limited or not is unclear. In any case, except for the upper members of Leningrad society, most people could take only what they could carry. While the street cars still ran, it was possible to obtain transportation to the railroad station, but when they stopped, the evacuee generally had to rely on his own physical strength to get himself and his possessions there.

There was much confusion, because in many cases the heads of the families were evacuated separately from their wives and children, and sometimes the children were separated from their parents. Consequently, it happened that the parents were evacuated while the children remained behind. Some of the children who had been evacuated earlier and subsequently sent back to Leningrad found their parents gone. On August 21, for example, a group of scientists of the Leningrad branch of the Academy of Sciences of the USSR sent the following letter to the Leningrad Executive Committee:

> In connection with the decision about the compulsory evacuation of mothers and children from Leningrad, the *raion* Soviet issued at that time to the members and wives of members of Leningrad's departments of the Academy of Sciences notices about their obligatory departure with their children from Leningrad before August 18. Up to the present time not only has this train not left, but its date of departure has not been fixed. Now the Leningrad departments of the Academy of Sciences will be evacuated on August 23, which means that a situation arises in which the members of the Academy of Sciences will leave before their families are evacuated from Leningrad.[168]

Sometimes the evacuees had to wait for days at the Leningrad railroad stations or in the marshaling yards before their train left. At other times they were left stranded en route, either because their train was requisitioned for other use, or because the line was blocked by military traffic or damaged by German air attacks. Food and water for the evacuees often became a serious problem because of the delays and the slowness of travel. It was fortunate that it was summer time, since the majority of the evacuees traveled in unheated freight cars.

The popular attitude toward evacuation was complex. Evacuation orders greatly upset the population, not only because they indicated how extensive the threat to Leningrad was, but even more because they increased people's uncertainties about their future. The majority of the population was torn between fear of staying and fear of leaving. At one extreme, disaffected elements did not want to leave because they hoped to be liberated by the Germans. At the other extreme, those who were afraid of the Germans or of being caught in the fighting for Leningrad were anxious to go.

But above all people feared the hardships that would be their lot if they became refugees. The sight of the refugees who had fled to Leningrad affected many people's views. One woman gave this description of her feelings: "Evacuation . . . we are to be refugees. Refugees—that is something terrible. I have seen refugees. And on top of that to be refugees under the Bolsheviks. . . . During the other war [World War I] everybody helped them. But now? Even if they wanted to—nobody has anything."[169] Other women inquired of the evacuation commissions: "But what awaits us there? We may have to live with little children under the open sky. . . . Will they give us work there?"[170] Letters from those already evacuated or stories told by returnees from earlier evacuations all spoke of the hardships involved.[171] Also frightening were the rumors and accounts of German bombings and strafings of evacuation trains.[172] Moreover, people hated the thought of abandoning their possessions, acquired with so much difficulty and so hard to replace under Soviet living conditions. The spread of what a Soviet source calls "hostile and provocative rumors" at evacuation centers was difficult to suppress.[173]

Another important factor in the reluctance of many Leningraders to leave was the fear of breaking up their families and of being separated for a long period. Many felt that come what might, it was better for the family to be together. The earlier evacuation of the children had understandably upset the population. Rumors that convoys of children had been bombed or that they had been sent in the direction of the German advance created near panic among their parents.[174]

Finally, some were reluctant to leave because, so they said, they did not want to abandon their beloved city and its people in time of danger. While in some cases this may have been merely an excuse behind which lay other motives, it is probable that there were people who actually felt ashamed to leave. Love of their city undoubtedly exercised considerable influence on the attitude and behavior of many Leningraders. An evacuated teacher is said to have written, "I am ashamed that I left Leningrad."[175] Some people felt that to leave was cowardly, and those who remained sometimes referred contemptuously to the evacuees as "rats."[176]

So while many were eager to leave, many others hesitated. The Germans were an unknown and to some extent frightening quantity. Some people argued that "Bolshevism is a known evil, but it is said

that a known evil is better than an unknown one." The whole question
of evacuation was obscured in people's minds by uncertainty. "Is it
really necessary?" some asked. "The ship may not actually be sinking,"
said others.[177] In one captured letter was the statement: "I do not know
whether I should leave, too. I do not want to leave."[178] The Jews in
Leningrad were also uncertain whether to leave or to remain. Many
of them discounted the reports of German anti-Semitism and atrocities,
believing them to be mere Soviet propaganda.[179]

Finally, since the public was not always clear as to what the evacuation policy was, all sorts of rumors circulated and discouraged departure. There were reports that children would be evacuated, but that
mothers had to stay because they were needed. There were numerous
rumors that "nobody was permitted to leave."[180] The authorities were
also confused. One informant tells the following story. A Jewish family
had hesitated for a long time before deciding to leave, but finally made
up their minds when they became frightened by reports of German
atrocities in the occupied areas. When they requested the authorities
to release them from work and to give them travel permits on the
ground that their lives would be endangered if they remained, they were
arrested. The reason: "spreading defeatist rumors by saying that the
city would be captured by the Germans."[181]

Some of the mismanagement of the evacuation inevitably led to
indignation and criticism. Reports that valuable space had been wasted
for the evacuation of the props of some second-rate theaters produced
widespread resentment and criticism. Some bitterness was also caused
by better evacuation conditions being given to the elite and the upper
strata of the intelligentsia, who were frequently flown out and allowed
special baggage and food privileges.[182] Yet, judging from available
sources, it would appear that such inequality of treatment was accepted
by most and that the safeguarding of valuable people was even regarded
as essential. One Party member is reported to have said: "The wrong
people are being evacuated. Why, one cannot leave the academicians.
First of all, there is nothing for them to do near the front, but most
important—how can one let the Germans have such people?"[183]

Evacuation was one of the few areas in which many people had a
limited choice of action. It is clear that some people failed to avail
themselves of the right and opportunity to leave Leningrad, whereas
others who should have remained managed to obtain permission to
leave. Many sources report cases in which people, from academicians
to simple workers, did everything they could to avoid compulsory
evacuation, sometimes even faking illness.[184] The wife of one informant
could have left, but decided to stay because her husband could not
obtain a release from his job. In another case, parents sent their boy

temporarily to a nearby farm to avoid any compulsory evacuation of children, but brought him home a little later.[185] There are reports of workers arguing and pleading with their factory managers not to be included in the compulsory evacuation, because they did not want to leave their native city, their factory, and their friends.[186]

But it is also clear that those who actively tried to avoid compulsory evacuation were in a minority. Furthermore, they did not try to do so illegally, which was not possible in view of the authorities' tight control over residence permits and ration cards. The overwhelming majority clearly obeyed the compulsory evacuation orders, no matter how they felt about them. With few exceptions the only people who exercised a choice were legally entitled to do so; that is, they were among the voluntary evacuees.

There was little if any illegal evacuation. The control exercised by the authorities over rail and highway travel made unauthorized departures very difficult. A person leaving his job without permission was liable to severe penalties. All former Leningraders who were interviewed agree that in Leningrad there was no panicky unauthorized evacuation of the kind that occurred in Moscow in October 1941.[187] Some people did leave in a quasi-legal manner by managing to register as relatives of members of bona fide evacuation groups from factories, theaters, hospitals, or institutes, or by arranging to be sent on assignments to safer areas.[188] The latter course, naturally, was possible only for persons in responsible positions. In general it is clear that the leadership did not wish to retain in the city nonproductive elements of the population and had no objection to their leaving the city. But it maintained strict control over the movements of the "useful" elements, which included all who directly or indirectly contributed to the defense of Leningrad and of the Soviet Union.

When the Germans came closer to Leningrad, some members of the elite became very frightened. Since illegal evacuation was virtually impossible, they sought ways to obtain the necessary permission to leave. The existence of the cowardly official and Party member who manages to find a legal excuse to be evacuated is described in Soviet novels. In one such novel a member of a *raion* executive committee refuses to join a partisan group or to remain in Leningrad because he is convinced that the city will be taken by the Germans. To save himself he pretends that he has to accompany an evacuated factory to the Urals, where, he claims, new strength will be forged for a Soviet counterblow. The author stresses that this man is a weakling and a coward who is treated with contempt by his wife, the heroine of the novel, who chooses to remain in Leningrad.[189]

But most of the elite were trapped by circumstances into doing their

duty regardless of their feelings, since there was no escape from Leningrad. Short of legal evacuation there was nowhere for the elite to hide.
Consequently, its members generally put up a bold front vis-à-vis the
population and the leadership and, lest they be suspected of improper
attitudes, faithfully carried out orders from above.

Many members of the elite, however, did avail themselves of their
privileged status to arrange for the evacuation of their families. To
some extent this was indicative of their pessimism concerning the fate
of Leningrad and of the fact that most of them had no illusions about
what life under German occupation would be like. One Party member
from Pontonnaia, near Leningrad, who volunteered to fight in a partisan unit, made the following entry in his diary for August 20. The note
refers to his wife: "Galia also wants to leave with Anna for her birth-
place in the Saratov *oblast*. I was in complete agreement with her
decision and advised her not to wait too long, but to leave if she had
decided to do so. How could I have discouraged her from leaving,
when, in the event that the Germans take Pontonnaia, she would hardly
escape with her life, being the wife of a partisan."[190] Apparently the
top leadership did not regard the evacuation of the families of the elite
as indicative of insufficient confidence in the regime and in the final
victory.

Although by the end of August the official estimate of how many
Leningraders remained in the city was 2,489,400, the actual number of
civilians in Leningrad was considerably larger owing to the influx of
great numbers of refugees who were fleeing before the German advance.[191] Refugees were reaching Leningrad from several directions
at once. From the north came those who had been settled in the areas
conquered from the Finns in 1939 and, later, those who lived in the
Karelian Isthmus. By sea came evacuees from Riga and Tallin, mostly
the families of Soviet soldiers and Soviet officials. From the south and
west came others who either had to, or wanted to, flee from the German
advance. When the Germans and Finns came closer, a large proportion
of the 176,000 inhabitants of the towns near Leningrad also sought
refuge in the city.[192] Consequently, despite the evacuation and mobilization, there was no marked reduction in the number of civilians in
Leningrad.

On July 8 a special Evacuation Commission was organized by the
Leningrad *oblast* Soviet to deal with the refugees. In each of the city's
raions an evacuation committee was formed, and special evacuation
assembly points were organized at each railroad station. The committees requisitioned schools or empty barracks near the railroad stations
to house the refugees. In all, some forty-two communal centers were
hurriedly established, where the refugees stayed until they could be

sent farther east.[193] With the exception of a minority who had the necessary connections in the city to allow them to find temporary quarters with friends and relatives, the refugees remained in the care of the city authorities. Most of them were used as laborers at minimal pay and received the lowest category of food rations. The authorities did their best to get rid of the refugees by evacuating them as quickly as possible. They were not only concerned over the problem of taking care of large numbers of destitute persons, but also afraid that enemy agents might enter Leningrad in the guise of refugees. Furthermore, the refugees undermined the morale of the Leningraders by spreading defeatist stories. Only those refugees who had the right connections in Leningrad, or who were needed there, were allowed to stay. But when the Germans cut off the land access to the city, it was no longer possible to remove the refugees, so that many remained.

The administrative structure responsible for taking these measures (and many more) to improve the defenses of Leningrad and place the city and its facilities on a war footing was a complex one. Its organization remained unchanged for the first two months of the war. In effect, authority resided in the city and *oblast* Party committee, which was headed by Zhdanov, and in the Leningrad City Soviet Executive Committee, which was headed by Popkov. Leningrad had been put under martial law on June 22, and this, according to Soviet law, placed all powers in the fields of defense, preservation of public order, and state security in the hands of the highest local military commander, in this case Lieutenant General Popov, the commander of the Leningrad garrison.[194]

Although the Presidium of the Supreme Soviet of the USSR had reacted automatically and immediately when the Germans attacked, by issuing the martial law decree, the implementation of this decree and of a number of other measures was delayed. The reasons for this delay are by no means clear. It is possible that the leadership in Moscow was too shocked and confused by the events to be able to act swiftly. It is also possible that it may have been deemed undesirable to resort to measures that implied a certain pessimism on the part of the authorities. But we do know that the Leningrad leaders looked to Moscow for cues and cleared their decisions with the Kremlin.

It was not until June 27 that General Popov issued his Order No. 1, which was a verbatim copy of one issued by the Moscow city garrison commander on June 25.[195] It is difficult to avoid the impression that the Leningrad garrison commander actually copied his order from *Pravda* after it arrived in Leningrad on June 26. Work in offices was to begin at 8:30 for those of local and *oblast* importance and 9:00 for those of union and republic importance. Places of entertainment, restaurants, and places of public gathering were ordered to close by 10:45 P.M. The order established a curfew from midnight to 4:00 A.M. and closed the city to all persons who were not either specifically authorized to reside in Leningrad or equipped with special passes issued by their place of employment. The order was to go into effect on June 29.[196]

From this time on the population was subjected to increasingly tighter controls by the administration. Regulations were issued in Moscow for the entire Soviet Union, and by the local authorities in response to specific local needs and developments. The executive organs of the city and *raion* Soviets retained official control over the population and had the power to mobilize it as requested by the military leadership. In practice, the city and *oblast* Party organizations ran, or at least supervised, all activities.

This formal arrangement was not changed by the creation of a State Defense Committee under Stalin's chairmanship on June 30, 1941. The members of this committee were Stalin, Molotov, Voroshilov, Malenkov, and Beria. The committee concentrated "all power of state authority" in its hands, and its decisions were completely binding on "all citizens and all Party, Soviet, Komsomol, and military organs."[197] It had power to organize the armed forces and defense; to control the distribution of supplies to the army and the civilian population; and to control transportation, agriculture, stockpiling of all types of fuel and heating material, new construction, labor reserves, and allocation of labor and materiel.[198] The committee as a rule issued its orders directly to the responsible administrative organs and acted through its local representatives.* The State Defense Committee maintained close control over the administration of Leningrad; it determined policies that specific administrative organs or the Leningrad Party committee had to implement. Leningrad's general reliance on Moscow's initiative and instructions was a normal feature of the Soviet hierarchy of authority.

The formal arrangement, as in prewar days, had little to do with the real structure of authority. The actual decisions or transmittal of decisions and supervision over the execution of orders and directives were made by the Party organs, in particular by Zhdanov and the other secretaries of the *raion*, city, and *oblast* Party committees. This applied to most major as well as minor decisions, except in those cases when the Moscow organs issued direct instructions to their subordinates in Leningrad. Party representatives, as seen above, participated in, and in effect directed, all committees and commissions, such as those dealing with

---

* It is reported that in August Molotov and Malenkov visited Leningrad at the request of the State Defense Committee to ascertain the situation on the spot (Saparov, p. 17).

the recruiting and formation of the *opolchenie*, civil defense, mobilization for the armed forces or for defense construction, conversion of industry to war production, and so forth. They also issued direct orders to the population or the industry. For example, on July 10 it was the city Party committee that issued orders for the production of Molotov cocktails, and it was the city committee of the Komsomol that organized competitions among workers and formed civil defense and guard regiments.[199]

The awkwardness of this administrative process is obvious. The overlapping of authority and the making of decisions in Moscow, by people unfamiliar with and far removed from local conditions, were often detrimental to Leningrad's defense. No improvement in the arrangement was made until Leningrad was actually cut off, when the Military Council of the Leningrad Front was created; but even then final authority for all major decisions continued to rest in Moscow.

In view of the gravity of Leningrad's military situation, the city's leadership considered it particularly important to set up adequate safeguards against enemy agents, saboteurs, and parachutists, and ways of keeping the population in check. Street patrolling by the militia (the Soviet regular police force) and by the armed forces was therefore instituted, and guards were posted at all factories and important buildings.[200] The militia, with the assistance of Komsomol guard units, also spot-checked the identity cards of passers-by. It maintained check points at the entrances to the city to verify the documents of people entering or leaving Leningrad, and of those coming from or going to the front-line zone (which was under the control of the military). Persons leaving for or returning from fortification construction work were checked at the railroad station. The militia also maintained order and enforced strict observance of curfew and civil defense regulations. Furthermore, it was responsible for issuing residence permits and for seeing that no unauthorized person remained in the city.[201] The Komsomol guard units were later credited with the arrest of 12,653 "violators of revolutionary order and public safety" during the first ten months of the war, most of them during the first four months.[202]

It is not clear to what extent these activities were supplemented by the forces of the state security police (NKGB). There were several security police and border guard regiments in the city and near the front, since Leningrad was the headquarters for the Finnish border guard forces; some of these units were incorporated into the destruction battalions and partisan regiments. Others saw action at the front. Informants agree that the NKGB troops were not much in evidence in the city and that the ordinary control and security measures were carried out by the militia and the Komsomol.

Maintaining control over the movement of the population within the city was not too difficult. Even under peacetime conditions no person could reside within any Soviet city without registering with the militia and obtaining from it a residence permit. Illegal residence was punishable by up to two years of imprisonment.[203] The house managements were responsible for seeing that no unauthorized person resided in their buildings. The twenty-four-hour guard that had been placed on buildings was intended in part to provide a check on all who entered and left the buildings.

On July 30 the city's executive committee decided, in view of the state of martial law and "on the basis of instruction by the military authorities," to tighten registration requirements. House managers and private owners were ordered to ensure that new residents completed registration with the police within twenty-four hours. Factory and office managers were warned against employing persons not in possession of a residence permit. The delinquent managers were threatened with fines and imprisonment.[204] These control measures were obviously intended not only to prevent infiltration by German agents, but also to keep army deserters from finding refuge with friends or relatives in the city.

The Soviet authorities had always been nervous about enemy agents, and their propaganda had constantly warned the population to be on the lookout for spies. With the outbreak of the war, a sort of mass hysteria or spy mania swept the population and lasted well into the fall of 1941. This hysteria affected most persons, regardless of their attitude toward the Germans. The general conviction that numerous German agents, saboteurs, and parachutists were present in Leningrad was probably fostered in great measure by the press, which daily warned against them and reported numerous enemy parachute drops all over Russia.[205] Even Soviet literature gives spies considerable space. In one Soviet play dealing with the operations of an elite sailor brigade on the Leningrad front, the following agents appear: a German agent of long standing who is posing as a clerk, a former monarchist who had helped him, and a traitor who when captured by the Germans agrees to work for them.[206] There are nearly as many traitors in the play as heroes.

People became suspicious of everyone. Guards were posted everywhere. Streetcar conductors stopped calling out street names "in order to make it more difficult for spies to orient themselves." And the population went spy-catching.[207] As might be expected, the most enthusiastic at the game were the young people, although many adults also took part. Suspicious dress (that is, too Western in style), an accent, or any suspicious behavior, such as appearing to be taking notes or asking questions, was enough for the population. Documents were not

accepted as proof of innocence because the enemy agent was expected
to have a complete set of such papers on him. Captured suspects were
often beaten before they were turned over to the militia. Among the
victims were many intellectuals who affected such Western items of
clothing as hats, ties, or vests, as well as members of the minority na-
tionalities who spoke with accents. There were also instances of excessive zeal, possibly as a result of rumors, when people seized and even
beat militiamen on the suspicion that they were disguised Germans.
There were of course numerous denunciations to the militia and the
NKVD. But in fact there is no evidence to show that any bona fide
German agents were actually caught.

The NKVD did not limit its interest to actual enemy agents. In any
case, in the customary Soviet view the terms "enemy agent" or "fifth
columnist" encompassed a very broad category of persons. According
to the Soviet writer Vishnevskii, "many fifth columnists had come in
together with the refugees; some conscious [fifth columnists], others
unconscious—that is, stupid old peasants who were filling everybody
up with rumors and enemy propaganda."[208] Moreover, to the NKVD,
potential agents or collaborators were equally dangerous. In this category fell people with anti-Soviet or deviationist records, those of foreign
origin or with foreign names, families of people in concentration camps,
and those who either had themselves served in the imperial Russian
government before the revolution or were related to people who had.
The connection between treason and class origins was illustrated in an
article by a state security police officer:

A favorite method of the German fascist occupiers is to frighten the population and produce confusion and panic in the rear. This method is widely
used against us. It was particularly used in the first months of the war when
the enemy entered upon the territory of the Leningrad *oblast* and began the
offensive on Leningrad.

In that period German intelligence, recruiting the remnants of hostile
classes, sought to spread through them fascist and defeatist propaganda.

Through its agents—former kulaks, merchants, nepmen, and other trash—
the German fascists tried to convince the population that the Soviet Union
would be defeated. . . .

A counterrevolutionary group of former officers of the Czarist army was
conducting defeatist propaganda.[209]

The security police, of course, did not wait for these "class enemies" to
become active. Among the preventive arrests and deportations mentioned earlier were those of a number of intellectuals of the older generation who either happened to have been born in Germany or had anti-
Soviet records; some of these people were even executed. According
to one report, a secret directive from Moscow on July 12 ordered that
all arrested persons of German, Baltic, or Finnish origin were not to

be released even on completion of their prison terms.[210] Many of the Soviet citizens of German, Baltic, or Finnish origin who made up about 12 per cent of Leningrad's population were either arrested or ordered to leave the city.[211] In all probability the inmates of concentration camps located in and around Leningrad were also removed to the interior of the country.

This process of preventive arrest and forced evacuation of "unreliable" elements was probably not completed until the spring of 1942. No figures exist on the number of arrests; but the Germans frequently received reports from Russian prisoners of war and deserters that Leningrad was under "NKVD terror,"[212] a story that the prisoners may have told to ingratiate themselves with their captors.

It is impossible to assess the extent to which these security and police measures contributed to the continued effective control exercised by Leningrad's leadership. They were in no way unusual and were taken in most other large cities or in areas threatened by the German advance. The ruthlessness and lack of discrimination with which this action was carried out was typical of the operation of the NKVD. The Stalinist concept of "the enemy is in our midst," which gained such prominence during the 1930's, provided ample justification for these precautionary measures and their method of implementation. Since the enemy within could be as dangerous as the enemy without, the probability that the police action would strike at a large number of innocent persons was of little consequence. While it is not possible to guess how many residents of Leningrad were politically unreliable or disaffected, it is likely that their number was substantial. The purges of the 1930's had hit Leningrad's population and Party members very hard, and there were probably many families who had some cause to dislike the Communist regime. In addition, there were still many older people in the city who had seen better days before the revolution and intellectuals who dreamt of the freedom of the West. Whether the bulk of those arrested or deported were actually more disaffected than many of those who remained in Leningrad is not ascertainable; but there is no doubt that these arrests and deportations had a restraining effect on people's behavior in both Leningrad and other large cities.

Another aspect of the leadership's policy was the use of propaganda as a means of maintaining public morale and loyalty. It was pointed out earlier that among the very first security measures was the confiscation of all privately owned radio receivers, a step taken to deny the population news from outside and access to enemy propaganda. To avoid this confiscation was very difficult, if not impossible. The owner of a private radio had to register his name upon purchase of the instrument and pay a nominal tax each year. Consequently, the militia knew the names of the owners and could check on their compliance with the order. Instead, the population was permitted to use cheap, small loud-speakers, which were connected by wire to the local public-address system, and people were thus able to listen to official news and propaganda. Since the loud-speaker system was also used to announce air raid warnings, there was a tendency to keep the loud-speakers switched on all the time.[213]

When the Germans approached the city, all private telephones were disconnected. The purpose of this measure is not clear. It is possible that part of the telephone network was requisitioned for military use, or that it was a measure to conserve electric power. But whatever the reason, the result was that it was more difficult for people to keep in touch with each other.

Deprived of outside news, the population was exposed to the full blast of Soviet propaganda. This was the special realm of the Party, which always believed that no activity could be carried out successfully without political indoctrination. According to the secretary of the Leningrad City Party Committee:

> The network of agitators was significantly expanded. Lecturers spoke in enterprises, offices, army units, induction centers, movie theaters; they taught the factory agitators.
> The characteristic feature of agitation in this period was its mass character. In the large enterprises of the city—in the Bolshevik, Stalin, Kirov, and Elektrosila works, as well as in other factories—the lectures and meetings were attended by 2,000–3,000 workers. Discussions in the factory shops were attended by 200–300 persons. In a relatively short time tens of thousands of lectures and discussions had been conducted.[214]

Mobilization, however, had depleted the ranks of the Party propagandists and "agitators," while the need for them was even greater than before. To replace the losses and expand propaganda activity the Party drafted many Party members who had no previous experience in this work. In many *raions* and factories the newcomers formed the majority of the agitator groups. In addition, the city Party committee formed a group of 150 lecturers for special duties, and groups of 40 to 50 lecturers were organized in each *raion*. The number of agitators was quite large. For example, during the construction of the fortifications, 8,000 agitators were sent to work among the workers.[215]

Lectures were not the only form of propaganda organized by the Party. In the first three months of the war the Party claimed to have printed many millions of copies of various pamphlets, posters, proclamations, and leaflets. Bulletin boards on which newspapers were posted (the so-called "Tass windows") were set up everywhere—in the factories, on the streets, and in shops and offices—to report the official war news, as well as city and factory news, and to publicize outstanding examples of individual behavior. Finally, there were the Party political instructor-organizers, mentioned before, who worked among the residents of individual apartment houses.[216]

In all cases in which mass public participation was called for, like the *opolchenie* or defense construction, the Party published special newspapers for the participants. The *opolchenie* newspaper was called *Na zashchitu Leningrada* ("For the Defense of Leningrad"), and the one for the fortifications construction workers was called *Leningradskaia pravda na oboronnoi stroike* ("*Leningradskaia pravda* for the Defense Construction Sites"). The partisans had a paper called *Narodnii mstitel* ("The People's Avenger").

Up to June 22, the Soviet propaganda machine had treated Hitler as a partner and the Western powers as warmongers. One of the principal objectives of Soviet propaganda after the outbreak of war was to reverse this line and persuade the people that the friend of yesterday was in reality a monster. Hitler's aim, it was now said, was to become master of the world. It was pointed out that he had already deprived many nations of their independence.

In time, the description of German war aims became quite specific. Stalin in his speech on July 3 said:

The enemy is cruel and implacable. He is out to seize our lands, which have been watered by the sweat of our brow; to seize our grain and oil, which have been obtained by the labor of our hands. He is out to restore the rule of the landlords, to restore Czarism, to destroy the national culture and the national statehood of the Russians, Ukrainians, Byelorussians . . . and the other free peoples of the Soviet Union, to Germanize them, to convert them into the slaves of German princes and barons. Thus, the issue is one of life and death for the Soviet State, of life and death for the peoples of the USSR; of whether the peoples of the Soviet Union shall be free or fall into slavery.[217]

While this catalogue of German objectives lacked consistency, it was supposed to leave the Soviet citizen in no doubt about how dire the consequences of a German victory would be. Stalin's analysis was, of course, repeated dutifully *ad nauseam* by Soviet propaganda and faithfully incorporated into all the declarations, resolutions, and editorials passed by mass meeting or published in the press.

To strengthen the image of a bloody and inhuman enemy, the daily war communiqués issued by the Soviet Information Bureau began in July to publish reports and descriptions of German atrocities. The bulletins particularly emphasized that in the territories occupied by the Germans the defenseless population was shot, tortured, and maimed by the enemy soldiers.[218] At the same time the press reported that the enemy stripped the population of all food and other possessions and left it to starve. The communiqués were supplemented by feature articles and purported prisoner-of-war interrogations.

In addition to this effort to spread fear and hatred of the enemy among the people, Soviet propaganda appealed to the patriotism and particularly to the local and individual pride of each Soviet citizen. In the case of Leningrad, the city's history and traditions were particularly emphasized, since the people of Leningrad never ceased to regard themselves and their city as something unique, something superior.

This feeling was compounded of many factors. Most Leningraders felt tremendous pride in their city, a feeling that was often enthusiastically shared by newcomers. For the intelligentsia, cultural life in Leningrad had always been a little more in touch with Western thought than that in Moscow. In the words of one wartime visitor:

> From numerous remarks that were made during the evening I felt how deeply Leningrad still felt its closeness to Europe, how very much alive the "Western" traditions of the city still were—traditions of Peter the Great and Pushkin—and what a large place was held in these people's outlook by the sea. More even than in Moscow, perhaps much more than in Moscow, one was conscious, in talking to those Leningrad writers, of a real thirst for close future contacts with the West; they thought in terms of harbours and ships— ships that carried passengers to and fro, and goods, and books and music, and paintings and gramophone records.[219]

To many Leningraders, Moscow was a rival that had to some extent unfairly deprived their city of its glory and importance, but was itself only a crude, administrative town devoid of real sophistication and refinement.[220] Soviet propaganda therefore set about reminding the population of Leningrad that the city had never been conquered by an enemy, that it was the cradle of the revolution, and that its workers had always set an example for the rest of the Soviet Union.[221]

Individual pride was appealed to by constant descriptions of the heroism of others. Part of the daily news communiqués was devoted to the heroic deeds of individual soldiers or small groups of soldiers at the front, or civilians on the production line. The daily press published articles praising such actions. In all fields of endeavor the press pointed out by name specific persons who were particularly devoted to their tasks as an example to others. Thus, during the formation of the *opolchenie, Leningradskaia pravda* wrote:

> The best people of our city take their place in these ranks.
> "My son voluntarily joined the Red Fleet five years ago. I cannot remain at home now when things are like this. I cannot remain sitting when there is fighting with the base fascist band." Thus speaks an old Putilovets [worker in the Putilov or Kirov Works], Petr Alekseevich Solovev, a participant of the heroic defense of Petrograd in 1919, decorated with the military order of the Red Flag. . . . "I am joining the *opolchenie* to assist the Red Army," declares a young locksmith of the Stalin Factory, comrade Dmitriev. "I will not spare my life when the happiness of the fatherland is involved."[222]

Similarly, a 57-year-old woman, who was digging trenches, appealed to the "young mothers, dear sisters" in Leningrad to join her.[223] As to those who failed to do their duty, they were declared in advance to be traitors and cowards, despised by their fellow citizens.

Soviet propaganda also attempted to create the impression that the masses gave enthusiastic support to the regime and the war effort by publishing the resolutions of factory or office workers and of units of the *opolchenie* and the armed forces. This expression of public support also pictured the laggards, defeatists, or cowards as isolated and as going against the views of the overwhelming majority of their fellow citizens. For example, the resolution of the collective of the Bolshevik Works read: "In these times of danger through which our fatherland is passing, we, the workers, engineers, technicians, and employees of the Bolshevik Works, reply to the perfidious enemy attack by joining, as a body, the people's *opolchenie*."[224]

The workers of the Kirov Works wrote: "The Kirovites, who are ardent patriots of their socialist fatherland, will do everything necessary for the speediest defeat of the enemy. Our splendid Red Army will receive in ever increasing quantities the war goods so necessary for the complete destruction of the brown fascist plague."[225]

If the propaganda was unrestrained in its appeals to popular pride and patriotism, it was much more reticent about the true situation at the front. Only the Soviet Information Bureau was authorized to issue daily news communiqués. Even when Leningrad was besieged, the local Leningrad Defense Council did not publish any special reports on the local military situation. The official communiqués, which were issued twice daily in Moscow, were extremely vague about the extent of the German advance. In general the fighting was described as taking place "in the direction of" a certain city, while the loss of that city was either not announced at all or reported only after great delay. This also applied to those enemy operations that were of particular concern to Leningrad.

For example, fighting "in the direction of Pskov" was not reported until July 12, although the city had actually been taken by the Germans on July 8. At the same time, nothing was said of the German advance on Riga, Tallin, and Gdov, or of the crossing of the Luga at Poreche. Pskov continued to be reported as a battleground until July 24, when communiqués simply ceased to refer to it. Fighting around Porkhov continued to be reported until August 2, although that city had actually been lost on July 12. The advance of the Eighteenth Army was merely described as taking place "in the Estonian sector of the front." On August 23, without any previous mention, a communiqué reported the loss of Kingisepp and told of fighting in the Novgorod area. By August

20 the communiqués had still reported nothing specific concerning the fighting in Estonia, nor was anything said about the battle around Krasnogvardeisk or Luga.[226]

By playing down the defeats and retreats of the Red Army, Soviet propaganda undoubtedly hoped to preserve the optimism of the population. Yet it thereby ran the grave risk of far greater popular disappointment when it finally revealed the magnitude of the disasters.

In July and early August there was little in the official news that would have indicated to the people of Leningrad that their city was seriously threatened by the Germans. The possibility of a disaster was never mentioned without denying that it would occur.[227] For example, the resolution made by an *opolchenie* unit on July 22 said: "We, the defenders of the city of Lenin, declare with firm conviction: The enemy will not break through. The fascist cannibals will not walk the streets of Leningrad, they will not drink the water of the Neva, they will not breathe Soviet air."[228]

Toward the end of July and particularly in August, there were increasing references to the defense of Leningrad, but without any indication of its urgency. Instead, all statements breathed the firm conviction that the Germans would fail to reach the city.

This optimism about the outcome of the war was, of course, one of the main themes of Soviet propaganda. Although it was admitted that victory would not come easily, the final outcome was never held to be in doubt. In his speech of July 3 Stalin had publicly confessed that the enemy had a temporary advantage in manpower, weapons, and know-how, as well as the advantage of surprise.[229] Similarly the press did not minimize the difficulties facing the nation:

The struggle with the fascist horde, armed to the teeth, entails serious difficulties; it requires mobilization of all resources, maximum effort, and readiness to make any sacrifice in the name of the fatherland.

Whatever these difficulties might be they should not and cannot frighten the people, who have been tempered in overcoming them, who have achieved freedom and happiness in a stubborn struggle with numerous enemies of the toilers.

Our times are heroic times.[230]

But the final outcome was said to be certain because of the past record of victories of the USSR, because the forces of the Soviet Union were "countless" and "inexhaustible," because the entire free world was fighting against Hitler, and finally because the enemy was morally weak and his soldiers afraid of a real fight.[231] Soviet propaganda never failed to create the image of a leadership firmly resolved to fight at any cost and to win regardless of difficulties.

Thus the Soviet citizen was appealed to on every possible ground to work harder and to fight harder and to be loyal to the leadership. If his information about the situation at the front was sketchy, he was aware that he faced a long and bloody struggle and that the regime wanted him to make every sacrifice in the name of the final, inevitable victory of the fatherland.

The population, however, did not have to rely entirely on official propaganda for war news. Inevitably it acquired a good deal of information (as well as misinformation) from people in the *opolchenie* and those doing fortification work. Not only did both undertakings indicate how grave the situation was, but also the participants were often able to judge the extent of the German advance and the state of the Red Army. Additional information was brought to Leningrad by refugees and visiting army men.

The terse communiqués of the Informburo could not completely hide the true situation from the population, although few people knew the exact extent of the military disasters. One former Leningrader wrote in his diary: "From the veiled communiqués of the Soviet Informburo it is nevertheless absolutely clear that the Red Army is unable to stop the German offensive on any one of the defense lines."[232] Consequently, the population tended to interpret the official news pessimistically and often assumed the worst. People were also irritated by the section of the daily communiqué that was devoted to the description of super-human deeds by individual soldiers or small units of Red Army men. This, it is reported, led to the sarcastic saying: "We are winning, but the Germans are advancing."[233]

It was natural under these circumstances that all kinds of rumors circulated among the population. The greater the efforts of the authorities to hide the truth, the more widespread became the popular reliance on word-of-mouth information. Many rumors dealt with the military situation. To explain why the Germans had not bombed Leningrad as had been expected, some claimed that the city was defended by up to 20,000 Soviet planes, while others asserted that Hitler had decided to capture Leningrad intact.[234] In the nearby towns it was rumored that Leningrad was bombed nearly daily.[235]

In this situation, far from tolerating increased freedom of speech, the authorities took steps to restrict it and suppress undesirable rumors and information. All rumors favorable to the enemy, as well as reports casting doubt on the survival of Leningrad or on the inevitable victory of the Soviet Union, came under the heading of "enemy propaganda," and persons responsible for circulating them became *ipso facto* German agents in the eyes of the police. To assist the NKVD, the "Party organized a campaign to wipe out loose talkers, panicmongers, and *provocateurs*."[236] On July 22 the *Gorkom* ordered all *raion* Party committee secretaries to assign political organizers in every apartment house for the purpose of mobilizing all resident Party and Komsomol members and patriots to indoctrinate the population and to guard it against enemy agents, panicmongers, and rumormongers. This order was to be carried out within three days.[237]

For the majority of the population "a word to the wise" was enough. This word was given by the press and over the radio. On June 28 *Leningradskaia pravda* warned the population against enemy agents and went on to declare emphatically that "loose talk [was] a crime against the fatherland."[238] Examples such as that made of one woman who was held responsible for spreading false rumors and who was accordingly found to be a "fierce enemy of the Soviet people and a daughter of a [Czarist] police colonel"[239] led most people to take the warning to heart and exercise great caution in conversation, particularly with strangers or in public. On July 6 the Supreme Soviet passed a law that made persons responsible for spreading "false rumors that provoke unrest among the population" liable to trial by military tribunals and subject to two to five years' imprisonment, if these acts did not merit even harsher punishment under the law.[240] Consequently, most people tended to hide their true feelings, at least when dealing with strangers. Furthermore, the population had learned the need for discretion during the prewar purges. The fact that rumors and remarks circulated despite these threats and restrictions indicates the nervousness of the population and the inability of the Soviet authorities ever to achieve complete control over the conversation of a whole nation. But as long as the controlling agencies were in evidence, public expression of doubt or of antiregime sentiments was unusual, although it was on the increase as the fall of Leningrad appeared to be more imminent.

There were a few subjects that Soviet propaganda avoided entirely. Prominent among these was the anti-Semitism of the Germans. Nothing was said about the German massacre of the Jews or about the fact that the Jews were a special target for German terrorism. This had some serious consequences for the Jewish population of the Soviet Union, which often failed to realize the danger it was in when it had to choose between fleeing or being captured by the enemy.

Another theme that Soviet propaganda failed to emphasize was the anti-Communist character of the German invasion. The issue was pictured not as Fascism vs. Communism, but as Germany vs. Russia. In line with this, the war became the "Second Fatherland War" or the "Great Fatherland War of the Soviet Union."*

---

* The "First Fatherland War" was the Napoleonic invasion of Russia in 1812.

It was, of course, made clear that only the Party and Stalin were able to mobilize the country and knew how to lead it to victory:

In these times of the Great Fatherland War the Bolsheviks are setting an example of unprecedented heroism on the battlefields, in the factory shops, and on the *kolkhozes* [collective farms]. They have the masses behind them for the defense of the beloved fatherland. . . . By setting a personal example they foster in each soldier of the Red Army selfless heroism, contempt for death, bravery, Bolshevik organizing ability, and iron discipline. By setting examples of selfless labor they draw after them the collectives of the enterprises and assure that the orders for the front will be fulfilled ahead of time.[241]

Consequently, the Party (or, more broadly speaking, the elite) was expected to put into effect the measures decided upon by the leadership and to set an example for the rest of the population. In effect the Party retained and even expanded its traditional role as the goad of Soviet society and the Soviet system. The goading took the habitual form: a combination of cajoling and threats, carried out in the usual Soviet spirit of being sure to "fulfill and overfulfill the plan" even at the price of gross inefficiency and even when it involved the dislocation of the very measure the Party was trying to enforce. Everybody, of course, clearly understood that behind the Party stood the NKVD and the military tribunals.

The Party paid a price for its claim to leadership: a large number of Leningrad Party members, especially rank-and-file members, and Komsomols paid with their lives for their leadership role, since many of them volunteered or were drafted by the Party for combat duty.

Inevitably the war brought about some changes in the composition of the Party. Since it represented the executive arm of the leadership and was essential to the preservation of the leadership's control over the population, the numerical losses that the Party had suffered as a result of the mobilization and volunteering of many of its members for the army and the *opolchenie,* and the evacuation or transfer of others to the interior, had to be made up. This replacement took two forms. One was an intensive recruiting drive for new Party members. The other was the widespread practice of promoting persons from within the Party ranks to responsible positions.

For the first two months of the war, in view of the dislocation of *raion* Party administration, the direction of each *raion* Party committee was placed under the control of committees of three, each headed by the first secretary of the *raion* Party committee. On August 9 the Bureau of the City Party Committee abolished this system on the ground that it "lowered the organizational and political Party work."[242]

The recruiting drive had both practical and psychological value. On the practical side it meant that the leadership was able to replace some of the thousands of Party members and Komsomols who had left the city or had been killed in battle. On the psychological side it committed more people to the support of the regime. Furthermore, the leadership could reasonably expect that at least some new Party members would be more energtic in their work than some of the older elements.

The recruiting drive was aimed primarily at those segments of the population that were closely identified with the Party and the regime: the so-called non-Communist *aktiv* and the Komsomol. There were two basic themes: the assertion that every "true patriot" must identify himself with the Party, and the hint that acceptance of membership in time of danger was a true measure of loyalty to the regime. "To sincere Soviet patriots the interests of the Party are infinitely dear and near. They are eager to formalize their blood ties with the Party, and by joining its ranks they become outstanding fighters on the labor front and on the battlefront against the enemies of their fatherland."[243] Young volunteers for the army or the *opolchenie* were asked to join under the slogan "to die with the Party card in hand."[244]

Often among those recruited were people whose military or labor records made them outstanding examples to others. When they joined, the Party could hope to identify itself with their glory or successes. An editorial in the *Leningradskaia pravda* of August 10, 1941, listed the following among those who asked or were asked to join: a fighter pilot who had shot down a German plane, Stakhanovites in factories, engineers and technicians who were successfully overcoming production difficulties, and well-known intellectuals.[245] Heroic deeds on the battlefield were often rewarded by membership in the Party. Consequently, the majority of the new members belonged to the younger element of the population.

The scope of the recruiting drive was extensive, if it can be judged by the total increases in Party membership during the war: namely, a rise from 3,876,885 members at the beginning of the war to 5,760,369 in January 1945.[246] Although there are no month-by-month figures available, Soviet sources claim that during the first year and a half the Leningrad Party organization inducted into its ranks 21,627 new members, of which 15,170 became candidates and 6,457 full members, and over 45,000 Leningraders joined the Party while serving in the armed forces.[247] By November 1943 the number of new members in Leningrad was reported to have grown by 35,000.[248]

The success of this membership drive reflects a high level of morale among at least one segment of the population. While the battlefield was still far from Leningrad, many people may have joined the Party for career reasons. But careerism alone cannot explain the subsequent growth of membership when the survival of Leningrad and even of the Soviet regime as a whole was much in doubt. To join at such a time took courage and true loyalty. Those who joined while serving in the *opolchenie* or in the armed forces knew that they had much to fear if captured by the Germans; furthermore, they were supposed to set an example to others of bravery and readiness for self-sacrifice. With understandable satisfaction the secretary of the Leningrad City Party Committee wrote in 1943: "The best indication of the growth of the prestige of the Communists, of the great authoritativeness of Party organization, is the steadfast aspiration of the workers and employees to join the ranks of the Bolshevik Party. Never before has the attraction of the Party been so great as in the days of the war and the blockade of the city."[249]

The promotion of personnel from the lower ranks to responsible posts that had been vacated because of mobilization, fighting, evacuation, and later starvation changed the character of the elite to some extent. This process, which began with the outbreak of the war, was to continue during most of the rest of the siege. Writing in 1942, the secretary of the Kirov *raikom* noted that in a "short while several tens of thousands" of Party members had left the city; he continued: "The situation that arose in Leningrad, and particularly in our *raion,* helped us to find a large number of splendid people who often would have remained unnoticed in normal, peacetime conditions."[250]

In industry the evacuation of the old managerial personnnel often led to the promotion of younger men. In the cases of the Kirov Works and the Kanonerskaia Factory, for example, which were only partly evacuated and had retained some shops, foremen were promoted to the directorships of the factories. In other cases, assistant directors or assistant chief engineers were promoted.[251]

The loss of trained and experienced personnel undoubtedly had many drawbacks. But the energy and devotion that the new men generally brought to their positions were valuable assets to the top leadership. In turn the newly appointed leaders knew that they had been offered an opportunity to show their mettle and make their careers quickly, and that a failure to live up to their new responsibilities would weigh heavily against their records. The exact extent of this promotion policy is not known, but it was certainly of some magnitude. According to one source, by February 1942 a full 90 per cent of the personnel of some *raikoms* were new people.[252]

Although some Party members were revealed to be cowards in the crisis, others modeled their behavior on what they felt their role as leaders demanded and did not try to avoid difficult or unpleasant duties. There were undoubtedly truly dedicated Communists and patriots among them.

Indicative of the attitudes that many Party members held are some of the letters written by Leningraders to soldiers, letters that later fell into German hands. One such letter ran: "I know that you have been engaged in the defense of the glorious city of Lenin against the fascist barbarians. I am sure that you will fight courageously and boldly against these bloodthirsty barbarians, as a Communist should, for our beloved city of Lenin, the cradle of the proletarian revolution. I wish you a speedy victory."[253]

Another letter gave the admonishment "Do not fall into the hands of these reptiles and don't shame your family." A mother wrote her son: "Dear boy! If you love your mother, fulfill her prayer and be a good soldier. . . . All who are dear to you have gone forth to defend the fatherland."[254] Although allowances must be made for the fact that the writers of these letters may have expected the mail to be censored, their content cannot be entirely disregarded, since the record of captured letters shows that many other people wrote mainly to complain about conditions.

It was inevitable that the military defeats and the administrative blunders would affect the morale of the elite. Like ordinary citizens, many Party members, Komsomols, and other members of the elite had firmly believed in the correctness and foresight of Stalin's foreign policy and in the might of the Red Army. To them the success of the German invasion came as a great shock, which was aggravated by the apologetic and plaintive tone of Stalin's speech of July 3. While performing their various duties, many members of the elite had ample opportunity to discover how ill-prepared the country was for war. They could see for themselves the great difference between reality and past propaganda. They also saw how some of their superiors failed to live up to their positions and responsibilities. The resulting disappointment undoubtedly led some to become cynical and disgusted. It may also have led them to engage in some *sotto voce* criticism of the top leaders, but only rarely did this result in a complete rejection of the Soviet regime or in actual disaffection. The elite had no real choice, since it stood to lose most from a German victory.

Since the elite had to enforce the many demands made by the leadership on the population and since controls were greatly tightened, there was no real improvement in the relationship between the elite and the population. The elite, under orders from above, could not relax its controls. Under the prevailing conditions, there was no possibility of bringing about any appreciable change in the normal relationship that existed between the ruling elite and the subordinate population. The elite could not save itself except by mobilizing the population and leading it in the defense of the city regardless of cost. One eyewitness said that "although on one hand the Soviets organized the defense of Lenin-

grad very well, on the other they forsook the concern for the person,
for the 'living man,' as Stalin used to say."[255]

The burden that the situation placed upon the ordinary Leningrader
was great indeed. In addition to the numerous tasks set him by the
leadership, he was plagued by problems of daily living. Because his
standard of living was already low, these problems became acute as
the war progressed.

The chief problem was that of obtaining food and consumer goods.
Thanks to its privileged position in matters of income and sources of
supplies, the elite was less affected than the population. In the period
from June 22 to August 20 the food situation was as yet far from serious.
The authorities had forbidden the hoarding of food and other supplies
at the outbreak of the war, and the stores continued to have their
normal supply of goods for sale. Possibly some items such as fats were
sold in limited quantities, but such restrictions were not unusual even
in peacetime.

On July 18 the rationing of food and consumer goods was introduced
throughout the country.[256] Ration cards were issued to the population
by the city administration through the *raion* executive committees,
through the heads of enterprises, offices, and schools, and through the
apartment house managers, all of whom were responsible for keeping
exact records in their own areas of jurisdiction. To facilitate registration of the *raion* population, special commissions were established under
each *raion* executive committee. All working persons received their
cards at their place of employment, and those who were unemployed
received them at their place of residence. Each ration card was good for
one month. The ration system divided the population into four categories based on each person's importance and contribution to the war
effort. The first and highest category included managers of defense
enterprises, technical and engineering personnel, defense workers, key
personnel in utilities and services, the armed forces, troops of the NKVD,
and other persons in similar jobs. The next category included office
workers in nonessential jobs, including education. The lowest category
comprised all unemployed persons. In addition there was a category
for children under 12 years of age. No special mention was made of
Party officials and full-time Party workers, but they were presumably
included in the first category.[257]

The ration of bread, the basic food of the population, was set at a
fairly high level. According to official Soviet sources, people in the
first category received 800 grams* of bread per day; those in the second,

* Eight hundred grams are equivalent to 28.2 ounces, 600 grams to 21.2
ounces, and 400 grams to 14.1 ounces. An average loaf of rye bread in the United
States weighs 15 ounces, but Soviet bread is wetter and thus heavier.

600 grams; unemployed persons, 400 grams; and children under 12 years of age, 400 grams.[258] According to Leningrad Party records, workers received in addition to bread 800 grams of butter, 2,000 grams of cereal, and 2,200 grams of meat per month. For other sections of the population, the rations in these items were again lower: office workers received 1,500 grams of cereal and 1,200 grams of meat; dependents, 1,000 grams of cereal and 600 grams of meat; and children under 12 years old, 1,200 grams of cereal and 600 grams of meat.[259]

The rations were generally regarded as generous, although the population did not always receive all items listed on the ration cards. According to one source, "the quotas under the rationing were larger than the amount we ever used before it was introduced."[260] The availability of food in Leningrad was also commented upon by a Party man from a nearby town, who made the following notation in his diary on August 17: "The food served here is not very good, but it is nice that one can buy here all sorts of things: butter, sugar, candy, sausages. I bought some things and sent them home because at home we cannot get anything."[261] On the next day he again noted in his diary further food purchases for his family. Restaurants were still open. Workers and employees could get meals in their factories or office canteens. In addition to the ration, food could be purchased on the open market but at high prices.[262]

With the approach of the Germans, many food items other than bread began to disappear from the stores; consequently, it became of paramount importance to belong to a high ration category and to remain in it as long as possible. This in turn gave the authorities a very powerful lever for the control of the population. The families of servicemen and of officials working away from Leningrad were in a particularly difficult position. The low living allowance and small rations granted them by the authorities made them particularly vulnerable to rising prices on the open market and declining supplies in the official stores. Although the frantic purchasing of food that had occurred at the outbreak of war declined, the population was not optimistic. It had little faith in the official assurances that supplies were plentiful; consequently, hoarding of food continued, although more cautiously. The more energetic and enterprising citizens went out into the countryside after the start of rationing to buy additional food supplies. This practice appears to have been fairly widespread. Sometimes people digging fortifications took vegetables from abandoned fields. More frequently they bought produce or bartered for it with farmers near Leningrad. The population resorted to individual initiative, on the basic assumption that under the Soviet system a man's only way of survival was to look after himself.

The people's attitude toward the war and the Germans was far from uniform. There were patriots and defeatists, loyalists and anti-Communists, brave men and cowards. One informant said:

> People waited for the Germans and were afraid of the fighting; they hoped for the arrival of the Germans and they hated them and were ashamed of the defeats of the Red Army; they were patriotic and yet they hated the Soviet regime; they wanted to stay for the liberation and then sought to leave; they supported the regime but did not believe that Leningrad would hold out; they expected a complete defeat and yet made every sacrifice to save the city from the enemy.[263]

The general attitude was one of excitement and nervousness, which increased as the danger to Leningrad became more evident. Popular attitudes naturally varied continually, as people changed their minds from day to day under the impact of a multitude of impressions and information. It is probably correct to say that although most people were to some degree critical of the regime, they remained basically patriotic or at least politically passive.

There were varying attitudes toward the war and its probable outcome. Some people were genuinely shocked and angered by the German surprise attack on the Soviet Union; some welcomed it as promising liberation from Communist rule. One woman wrote in her diary: "Is our liberation truly approaching? No matter what the Germans are like—it cannot be worse. And what do we care about the Germans. We shall live without them. Everybody has the feeling that at last the thing for which we have all been waiting for a long time, and for which we did not even dare to hope, has come about."[264]

Yet even those who were disaffected, like the woman quoted above, were not devoid of patriotic feelings. Thus the same woman, after expressing her hope for a German victory, wrote: "There is no doubt that the Germans will win. Forgive me, God! I am no enemy of my people, of my motherland. I am no monster." And later: "According to rumors our army is shamefully retreating."[265]

Some of the older generation of Leningrad workers and intellectuals were opposed to the Communist regime and did not expect the Soviets to win, but were nevertheless loath to see Leningrad or Russia conquered by foreigners. One family with anti-Soviet sentiments is reported to have decided to leave because the wife was Jewish. They felt they could not be sure of what the Germans would do; according to this account, if the invaders had been anybody but the Germans, they would have stayed.[266]

Because the speed of the German advance made the eventual capture of Leningrad seem inevitable, more and more people began to console themselves with the hope of better treatment under German rule. Some are said to have argued that the Germans were "cultured people" who would bring "order" into the Soviet chaos. Others recalled favorably the German occupation of Russian territory during the First World War.[267] According to all informants, the official reports of German atrocities were widely disbelieved. In 1943 Alexander Werth, a British correspondent, was told by a Soviet staff officer: "At first . . . our people didn't much believe in German atrocities, until they saw them with their own eyes."[268]

The favorable view of the Germans held by some Leningraders was reinforced by rumors or wishful thinking to the effect that in the occupied territories the Germans were treating the population particularly well. In the popular mind the signs of good treatment seem to have been an ample supply of food and to a lesser extent freedom of religion. There were rumors that German planes had dropped white bread, a very scarce item, to workers digging trenches and that they had put bread and other foods on sale in the occupied areas as in peacetime.[269] Some old women are said to have argued: "What about Hitler? He can't be worse than what we have now, but at least they will permit us to have churches and pray to God."[270] An indication of how some of these people felt was inadvertently revealed during the Nuremberg War Crimes Trials by the rector of the Prince Vladimir Church, who was then appearing as a witness for the Soviet prosecutor. He described how his church was hit by a bomb on Easter Sunday, 1942, killing thirty worshipers. The remaining members of the congregation rushed up to the rector and asked, "Little father, how can we understand this? How can we believe what was said about the Germans—that they believe in God, that they love Christ, that they will not harm those who believe in God?"[271]

But there were many other Leningraders who were less optimistic. Their feelings are probably best described by this statement from a captured letter: "We live like a pea leaf—we tremble."[272] Relatives advised some families by letter to leave because the "fascist dogs" would have no mercy on women and children.[273]

The popular attitude toward the leadership and the elite was not uniform. According to all informants, who were mainly anti-Communist, Zhdanov and Marshal Voroshilov (who was then commanding the Soviet forces defending Leningrad) were neither loved nor respected. The former was sometimes called a "coward" and a "pig," and the latter was spoken of with contempt.[274] Stalin's conciliatory and plaintive speech of July 3 shocked the population. Some were expecting him to announce his resignation, and many blamed him for his lack of foresight and for the unpreparedness of the Soviet Union. The elite was unpopular among many people partly because of its privileges and partly because of its role as the agent and whip of the leadership. Consequently, there was some glee when the elite was called upon to work or fight with the masses. The popular dislike of the elite found expression in such rumors as that officials and their families were seeking to leave Leningrad, or that the Party people and NKVD men accompanying work columns hid in cellars during German air attacks.[275] The most disaffected elements looked forward to the settling of accounts with their Communist overlords. The wife of a Party member was warned by some old woman: "When the Germans come, we will denounce you."[276] One worker is reported to have said, "Well, we'll be going through the apartments soon to take care of people who need it."[277]

The majority of the population, however, apparently did not question either the right of the leadership to institute whatever measures it deemed necessary or the need to defend the Soviet Union, and they looked to the elite for guidance. Despite criticism of the usefulness of some of the measures (and even more of the ways in which they were executed), most people knew that they had to rely on the energy and wisdom of their leaders to save Leningrad.

We might expect to find these confused and contradictory attitudes reflected in the behavior of the Leningraders. Nothing was further from the truth. In nearly all phases of activity the population did exactly what the authorities wished it to do, although not always for the "right" reason. There was a clear distinction between the morale or attitude of the population and its behavior. One reason for this was that the population felt helpless to resist the controls imposed upon it. It was seldom given the opportunity to make a choice. Belief in the all-powerful and all-knowing state and fear of its police apparatus left most Soviet citizens feeling insignificant and helpless, unable either to oppose the authorities or to manage without them. Even those who were most disaffected feared to awaken the suspicions of the police and thus be arrested, and possibly evacuated, before the liberation they hoped for. One former Leningrader described the situation as follows:

The *apparat* of the NKVD with its special police and troops was always on the alert. Wartime laws were in effect. In a place where everybody knew one, one had always to be above reproach—at work, at home. . . .

The least suspicion or accusation of unwillingness to carry out one's obligations to the "motherland" could put a person into a still worse situation. . . . That is why everybody worked hard. The more one wished for the coming of the Germans, the harder one worked. Since one knew that all duties in the home—from standing watch to spreading sand in the attic—were called forth by events foreshadowing something new and better, these things were done not without some pleasure and joy. Finally, it was also nice to show one's zeal to the regime, even while there was some hope of breaking away from it.[278]

Some people hoped to ensure the success of their careers simply by enthusiastically carrying out orders. As a matter of fact, in spite of the grumbling, pessimism, and criticism in private, all directives of the leadership were obeyed except for the brief panicky buying of food. According to all informants, the population was too disciplined and too well aware of the penalties for disobedience not to do what was demanded of it. Furthermore, patriotism played a major role. One source reports that it was not fear, but conscience, that inspired the people's obedience in carrying out the many tasks assigned to them.[279] This was particularly true in the case of measures providing for the safety of the population.

Thus, despite the nervousness of the population and despite the critical or even hostile sentiments of some of its elements toward the Soviet regime, the Leningrad leadership preserved complete control over the situation and had no real difficulty in securing popular obedience in the execution of its orders. Since the firm hand of the authorities was felt by everyone in every aspect of life, the Leningraders outwardly behaved like loyal and patriotic citizens, no matter what their private views might have been.

Chapter 4

THE GERMAN ASSAULT ON LENINGRAD
August 20–September 25, 1941

HAVING REACHED THE AREA of Krasnogvardeisk, some seventeen miles south of Leningrad, on August 19, the Germans stopped their direct advance on the city. The Eighth Panzer Division, which had spearheaded this advance, turned south to attack from the rear the large Soviet forces that had been bypassed earlier and that were still defending the Luga River line. The rest of August was spent on the encirclement and destruction of these forces, ending with the German capture of 21,000 prisoners and great numbers of tanks and guns.[1]

While the bulk of the Fourth Panzer Group was engaged in this operation, the other two armies on both flanks of Army Group North continued to attack. On the left the Eighteenth Army took Tallin on August 28 after very heavy fighting. The defending Red Army elements were evacuated by sea to Leningrad in an operation that cost the Soviet navy numerous warships and transports.* Other elements of the Eighteenth Army Group made slow progress north of Kingisepp toward Kotly and Kopore. On the right flank the 56th Panzer Corps successfully fought and destroyed large Soviet forces south of Lake Ilmen, while farther south German troops advanced to Toropets and engaged in hard fighting east of Kholm. To the north of Lake Ilmen, the Germans attacked from Chudovo along the railroad and highway in the direction of Leningrad, while another unit advanced north toward the vital railroad station Mga on the Leningrad–Moscow railroad line, Leningrad's

---

* Two hundred ships participated in the evacuation. Of the 29 large transports that escaped from Tallin, 25 were sunk, 3 had to be beached on Hogland Island, and only one reached Kronstadt. In addition, 10 warships were sunk (Grechaniuk, p. 247).

last link with the Soviet capital. On August 27 the Germans reached Tosno after passing through extensive Soviet mine fields, and pushed on to Krasnyi-Bor and Iam-Izhora southeast of Leningrad. They succeeded in crossing the Izhora River by the end of the month, but encountered the fortified belt that had been built by the Leningraders between Ust-Tosno and the Izhora River and were unable to expand this bridgehead. To the northeast the Germans cut the Leningrad–Ovinichi rail line, and, by August 30, they had advanced to the area of Mga as well as the Neva River at Ivanovskoe. Thus the fortification belt guarding Leningrad from the Gulf of Finland to the Neva River east of Kolpino was reached along a considerable part of its length, while the last rail line connecting Leningrad with the outside was cut at Mga.

During this time the Finns had been developing their offensive in the Karelian Isthmus. The attack on Vyborg began on August 22 with a Finnish attempt to encircle the city. The Soviet forces there counterattacked strongly, but on August 25 the Finns cut the Vyborg–Leningrad railroad line. Part of the Russian forces thus trapped managed to escape to Björkö, where they held out for another two months, while the other pocket of resistance was mopped up by September 1. On August 29 the Finnish forces entered Vyborg, and two days later they reached the 1939 Russo-Finnish frontier at Mainila. On September 2 they took Koivisto, and a few days later the Soviet forces in the eastern part of the isthmus also withdrew to the pre-1939 frontier.

The stage was thus set for the final assault on the city. But at that time it was by no means certain that such an assault would be made, because Hitler was unable to decide what to do with Leningrad once it was captured. Furthermore, some German army chiefs were pushing him to authorize a German drive on Moscow and to let Army Group North be satisfied with encircling Leningrad. On August 21 Hitler issued an order that rejected Moscow as the immediate German objective and instead gave top priority to the seizure of the Ukraine and the Crimea and to the encirclement of Leningrad by combined German-Finnish forces.[2] Army Group North was instructed, as it had been on August 12, not to attempt a direct assault on the city, but to carry out a speedy encirclement of it.

There appear to be several reasons why Hitler sought to avoid a direct attack on Leningrad. One of these was his dislike of street fighting, which, on the basis of the experience in the battles of Warsaw, Minsk, Smolensk, Kiev, and Tallin, had revealed itself to be very costly. Hitler also was impressed by Soviet propaganda statements promising a house-to-house defense of Leningrad.[3] According to Ciano, the Führer made these views clear to Mussolini in a conversation that took place on August 25:

The Führer declared that he does not intend to fall in with the Russian attempt to prolong the struggle in the cities by street fighting, for which the Russians are specially prepared. He does not intend to destroy the great urban agglomerations but wishes to make them fall after having won the battle which will annihilate the Soviet military forces around them. This is what he intends to do in the case of Leningrad, whose urban area contains some four million inhabitants and whose fall will take place shortly after the complete destruction of the Soviet troops surrounding the city. By avoiding street fighting, which does not lead to any useful result, one, above all, saves important forces.[4]

Another reason for Hitler's attitude was his inability to reach any decision on what to do with several million Leningraders who "could be neither eliminated nor fed."[5] By the end of August Hitler thought he had found a solution to this problem. In a letter dated August 30, Field Marshal Keitel informed the army chiefs that since the Germans would be unable to feed the people of Leningrad, the Führer felt that they should be forced out of the city and permitted to escape eastward into Soviet-controlled territory. Field Marshal Brauchitsch and General Halder considered this proposal to be impracticable and therefore pointless. They also felt that the question of a direct assault on Leningrad was still open.[6]

The successful encirclement of Leningrad required close cooperation with the Finns and a considerable Finnish advance below the old frontier on the Karelian Isthmus. The Germans therefore renewed their efforts to obtain Finnish agreement on military operations. While fighting on the isthmus was at its height, Mannerheim received a letter from Keitel requesting the cooperation of the Finnish army in an attack on Leningrad.[7] Keitel also asked that the offensive east of Lake Ladoga be pushed across the Svir River in order to make contact with the Germans advancing on Tikhvin. Mannerheim rejected the request on August 28, but the Germans once more strongly urged that the Finns join in the attack on Leningrad. On August 31 this request was once again rejected. Mannerheim intended to move his forces only a short distance beyond the frontier to the narrowest part of the Karelian Isthmus, where he planned to establish a defense line. On September 4 Keitel arrived in Finland to ask again for a Finnish attack on Leningrad; he received the same negative reply. Thus at the moment when the Germans were preparing for the encirclement and capture of Leningrad they still could not obtain Finnish agreement to collaborate in this vital undertaking. As a result a substantial gap was to remain between the two armies, which left Leningrad with free access to Lake Ladoga.

On September 1 the German forces were poised south, southwest, and southeast of Leningrad at a distance of twelve to twenty-two miles

from the city's outskirts. But despite this proximity to their final objective, the Germans found serious obstacles in the way of any further
advance. The defending Red Army forces had been regrouped and
reinforced by *opolchenie* units and by sailors of the Baltic fleet organized into marine brigades and were supported by the heavy naval
guns of the warships stationed in Leningrad and Kronstadt. Furthermore, the Germans had to break through the triple line of extensive
fortifications to which the civilian population of Leningrad was constantly adding.

But Hitler, disregarding these difficulties, had no doubt that the
operation would be successful. On September 5 he changed his mind
and agreed to an offensive aimed at Moscow, with a reinforced Army
Group Center.[8] Since he believed that the encirclement of Leningrad
was about to be achieved, the Leningrad area was to become a "sub-
sidiary theater of operations." Army Group North was to capture
Schlusselburg on the shore of Lake Ladoga and to encircle Leningrad
along a siege line which could be held by a mere six to seven divisions.
Contact with the Finns was to be made on the Svir River, although the
Finns had made no agreement to cooperate. The next day, Directive
No. 35 was issued, stating in part:

On the northeast front it is essential, in cooperation with the Finnish
Corps attacking on the Karelian Isthmus, to encircle the enemy forces fighting in the Leningrad region (after Schlusselburg has been captured as well),
so that by September 15 at the latest a substantial part of the mechanized
troops and of Air Fleet 1, particularly the 8th Air Corps, be freed for employment with Army Group Center. Before this, the close encirclement of
Leningrad, at least in the east, is to be achieved, and, if the weather permits,
a major air attack by the Luftwaffe on Leningrad is to be carried out. It is
particularly important to destroy the waterworks.[9]

The directive also ordered a crossing of the Neva River east of Leningrad and an advance to the Svir after the encirclement of Leningrad
had been completed. Although the plan did not envisage actual assault on the city, it did include breaching its fortification lines and
joining the Finns on the Karelian Isthmus as well as along the Svir River.

In the meantime Army Group North had not altogether given up
hope of capturing Leningrad. During the first week of September the
Sixteenth and Eighteenth Armies had made slow but steady progress
against strong Soviet resistance. On September 8 the Germans had
taken Schlusselburg, thus eliminating Leningrad's last communication
by land with the rest of the country. On September 7 the Finns reached
the Svir east of Lake Ladoga and stopped to turn their attention to the
capture of Petrozavodsk on the shore of Lake Onega. For their part the
Germans, still hoping to link up with the Finns south of the Svir River,

began to advance slowly in the direction of Volkhov. During the first ten days of September Leningrad was also subjected to its first artillery and air bombardments. But it was south of the city, where the Germans were closest to it, that the prospects of capture seemed most likely.

Early in September Army Group North drafted a plan for an attack in the direction of Leningrad that was to be spearheaded by the 41st Panzer Corps advancing from the area of Krasnogvardeisk. The attack, which was initially planned for September 5, was not executed until September 9. The offensive was launched despite strong Soviet attacks in the area between Lake Ladoga and Lake Ilmen, attacks by which the Red Army attempted to relieve the pressure on Leningrad. The 41st Panzer Corps made slow progress in the face of strong enemy fire and also because of the numerous fortifications, but nevertheless by the end of the first day succeeded in breaching the first fortified line. On the next day, while still able to advance against the Dudergof heights, one of its divisions had to go to the assistance of the German forces, which were in difficulty at Krasnogvardeisk. An indication of the fierceness of the fighting is the fact that on September 10 the 6th Panzer Division lost four divisional commanders in one day. By nightfall on September 10, after suffering heavy losses despite extensive air support, the Germans took the Dudergof heights. On the next day the 1st Panzer Division took Hill 167, the highest elevation in the Dudergof area and a key position of the last Soviet fortification line. "In front of the victorious troops stood the city of Leningrad in the sunlight, only twelve kilometers away, with its golden cupolas and towers and its port with warships that tried with their heaviest guns to deny us possession of the heights."[10]

To the west the Germans penetrated into Krasnoe Selo and captured Krasnogvardeisk, which had been bypassed by the 41st Panzer Corps. Elsewhere, two army corps attacked toward Slutsk, Pushkin, and Izhora with the objective of reaching Kuzmino. They became involved in heavy fighting and made very slow progress despite massive air support. On the left flank the Eighteenth Army, bypassing Soviet forces along the coast of the Gulf of Finland, struck toward Uritsk, which was only four miles from Leningrad.

Despite the slow progress, the attacking troops felt certain that they would soon be in Leningrad and were therefore shocked to be informed on September 12 that the city was not to be taken but merely encircled and that the attack was to be pushed only as far as the Petergof–Pushkin road.[11] But the severity of the fighting forced Hitler to modify his earlier schedule. A new directive was issued on September 13, which stated: "In order not to weaken the attack on Leningrad, the armored and Luftwaffe forces must not be withdrawn before a close envelopment (within artillery range) is achieved. Therefore the date set by Directive 35 . . . for the withdrawal of a part of the mechanized forces and a part of Air Fleet 1 can be moved back by a few days."[12]

Although the Red Army was making desperate attacks along the Volkhov River to save Leningrad and fighting tenaciously for every foot of ground around the city, the Germans continued to battle their way through the fortifications. On September 14 the 41st Panzer Corps reached the Pulkovo heights, beating back all Russian counterattacks. Having crossed most of the fortified belt, the German tank forces were poised for the last dash into the city, which was now only about seven miles away. But at that moment, according to plan, they were ordered to halt and establish defensive positions in preparation for their withdrawal three days later to serve with Army Group Center. Thus the fruits of the victory were denied to them at the very instant when they seemed within their grasp.

On the next day the Eighteenth Army completed its advance to Uritsk, thereby cutting off the Soviet forces along the Gulf of Finland between Kopore and Oranienbaum and approaching to within four miles of the outskirts of Leningrad. Two days later it completed the encirclement of Soviet forces around Oranienbaum. This pocket was to survive until January 1944. On the right Pushkin was taken, and heavy fighting developed for Slutsk and Kolpino. On September 17 Alexandrovka, the terminal of a Leningrad trolley car line, fell into German hands, but on that same day the armored and motorized divisions began their transfer to Army Group Center. The Germans did reach Slutsk and the vicinity of Kuzmino, but their attack on Kolpino failed.

The defending Soviet forces had managed to prevent a close encirclement of Leningrad (that is, within medium artillery range), partly because they were able to use troops from the static Finnish front and partly because the Germans, already suffering from very heavy losses, weakened their attack by the withdrawal of the armored divisions. On September 18 Halder noted in his diary:

> The ring around Leningrad has not yet been drawn as tightly as might be desired, and further progress after the departure of the 1st Armored Division and the 36th Motorized Division from that front is doubtful. Considering the drain on our forces on the Leningrad front, where the enemy has concentrated large forces and great quantities of materiel, the situation will remain critical until such time as hunger takes effect as our ally.[13]

Fighting continued until September 25, marked by minor German advances and numerous fierce Soviet counterattacks aimed primarily at breaking the encirclement. The Germans took Detskoe Selo and Petergof and reached Volkhovstroi east of Leningrad, not, however, without encountering fierce resistance everywhere. In view of the exhaustion

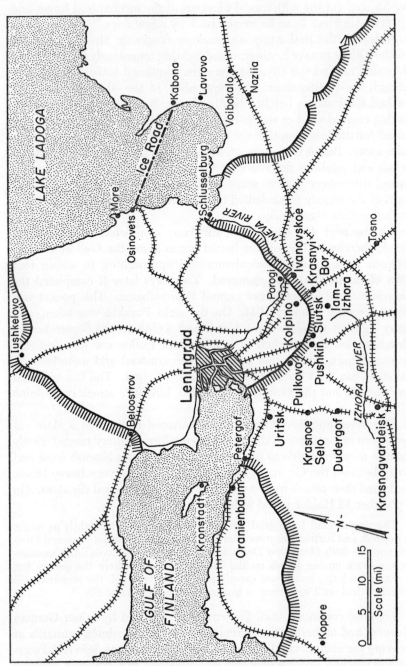

THE FRONT LINE ON SEPTEMBER 25, 1941

of the Germans, the crossing of the Neva River and a junction with the Finns was out of the question. Nor, as had been hoped, was it possible to approach the city to within range of light artillery. By September 24 Army Group North, hard pressed to beat off strong Soviet counterattacks, had to acknowledge that it lacked the forces to continue its advance on Leningrad with any hope of success. It consequently had no choice but to break off its attacks and pass to the defensive along the Leningrad front. The troops began to dig in; but although anticipating a long siege, they were confident that starvation would eventually force the defenders of Leningrad to surrender.

In retrospect it would seem that it is one of the ironies of the Second World War that Hitler, who had so stubbornly insisted on making Leningrad one of the major objectives of the German campaign in Russia and who had persisted in this view against the advice of his army chiefs, was also responsible for saving the city from capture. By withdrawing the armored divisions just at the moment when the capture of the city seemed certain, Hitler had saved Leningrad. According to a German staff officer, he had done so because "He thereby wanted to avoid the losses of human life and materiel to be expected from fighting in the streets and squares of this Soviet metropolis against an outraged population and hoped to gain the same end by cutting off the city from all lines of supply."[14] The German Führer apparently had a healthy respect for the fighting spirit of the Russian "Untermensch." Yet, as Halder noted, Hitler had decided not to take Leningrad when his chances of success were greatest, "only to seek later, time and again, to possess it."[15]

Chapter 5

THE BATTLE OF LENINGRAD
August 20–September 25, 1941

Bᵧ AUGUST 20 the outlook for Leningrad ap-
peared very grim. The German advance to the area around Krasnogvardeisk, which had bypassed the Luga River defense line, constituted a grave threat to the city, since only a few disorganized Red
Army units stood between it and the enemy. It was obvious to the
leadership that the best Soviet efforts to stop the German forces were
proving fruitless. Recalling the situation a few months later, the commander of the Leningrad front, Lt. Gen. M. Khozin, wrote: "During
this time the command of the Red Army tried every means to bar the
road to Chudovo, Krasnogvardeisk, and Krasnoe Selo to the enemy. But
our few troops, tired from the continuous fighting and always numerically inferior, could hold the enemy drive only for a short time. While
this fighting was in progress, withdrawals were prepared to lines of
resistance created beforehand."[1]

In this grave, if not desperate, situation an appeal to the troops of
the northwest front was issued on August 20, signed by the principal
members of the Military Council of the Northwest Front, Voroshilov
and Zhdanov: "A threat hangs over Leningrad. The insolent fascist
army pushes toward our glorious city—the cradle of the proletarian revolution. . . . Our holy duty is to bar the road to the enemy at the gates
of Leningrad with our breasts."[2]

On the next day an appeal, signed by Voroshilov, Zhdanov, and
Popkov, was addressed to the population of Leningrad:

Comrade Leningraders! Dear friends! Our dearly beloved city is in
imminent danger of attack by the German fascist troops. The enemy is striving to penetrate into Leningrad. . . . The Red Army is valiantly defending
the approaches to the city: our navy and air force are striking at the enemy
and repelling his attacks. But the enemy has not yet been crushed, his resources are not yet exhausted, and he has not yet abandoned his despicable,
predatory plan to capture Leningrad.[3]

When during the following week the situation further deteriorated, the city's leadership was forced to accept the prospect of the enemy's reaching and possibly even penetrating Leningrad. On September 2 the press sounded the alarm in the following words:

The enemy is at the gates of Leningrad! Grave danger hangs over the city. The forces of the Red Army are fighting in the immediate vicinity of Leningrad, holding in check and overcoming the assault of the insolent enemy, who with his last strength tries to break through to the city. The success of the Red Army depends on the heroic, valiant, and firm stand of each soldier, commander, and political worker, and also on how active and energetic the assistance given to the Red Army by us Leningraders is.[4]

On September 9 the Germans, who had now advanced to within heavy artillery range of the city, renewed their assault. The leadership was understandably pessimistic. According to some reports, Stalin is said to have ordered the destruction of all vital installations and facilities in Leningrad if their capture appeared inevitable.[5] Important papers and archives were apparently ordered destroyed to prevent their falling into enemy hands.[6]

The climax of the crisis was reached when the German tanks broke through the last fortified line less than ten miles from the city. The defenders could not count on any help from outside, since the fall of Schlusselburg on September 8 had cut the city's land communications with the rest of the country. A German penetration into Leningrad seemed unavoidable, and the leadership issued an order on the night of September 16 directing all worker defense units in the southern part of the city to man their posts: "On the Moscow highway, at the gates of Elektrosila [Works] one could expect at any moment to see the forward elements of the enemy appear."[7] Later a Soviet official told a foreign correspondent: "The loss of the southern half of Leningrad was not entirely out of the question. It is horrible to think of it, but at that time one had to consider the possibility of seeing the Germans in the Winter Palace, and of shelling them from the fortress on the other side of the Neva."[8]

At this point Leningrad's leadership was seriously concerned over the morale and loyalty of the armed forces, from whom it was demanding desperate efforts to save the city. In view of the defeats, heavy losses, poorly trained replacements, and shortage of certain types of weapons and ammunition, it was reasonable to expect that morale would not be good. But since the Soviet leadership tended to equate poor morale or even grumbling with potential political disaffection, it reacted violently when it encountered either. The leadership's ideas of what constituted treasonable or defeatist behavior on the part of the Red Army troops covered many actions that by Western standards would not merit such a definition.

On August 16 Stalin and other members of the Army High Command had issued an order declaring that all those who surrendered to the enemy, regardless of circumstances, would be treated as deserters and directing the immediate execution of any soldier who spoke of deserting or tried to surrender.[9] A few days later a special order was issued to the troops defending Leningrad. It said in part:

Individual soldiers, commanders, and political workers are forgetting . . . their pledge and are revealing in battle a criminal absent-mindedness, faint-heartedness, and cowardice. Not only are there commanders and political leaders who do not set an example of courage and audacity and do not carry along their soldiers by their example, but there are also loathsome self-seekers who hide in foxholes and do not lead the fight. Such disgraceful individuals cannot be tolerated in the Red Army. Those who fail to perform their duties have no place in our ranks.[10]

On September 9 the Military Council of the 55th Army, which was defending Pushkin, reported that some divisional commanders had withdrawn without orders, that others were drunk, and that discipline was deteriorating among the troops.[11] A few days later Zhdanov and General Zhukov (who was then in command of the Leningrad front) complained about the comportment of the 8th Army, which was defending the Oranienbaum area. They declared that it was not only endangering the defending forces by its actions, but it was betraying them; that its soldiers were running away at the first shot; and that all who failed in their duty were to be executed.[12]

The incident that seemed to have produced the greatest anguish among the Soviet leadership occurred on or about September 20. Some German officers, dressed in Russian uniforms, entered the position of a Red Army battalion and tried to persuade the soldiers to desert. A few did desert, and the Germans were permitted to leave unmolested.[13] Apparently some version of this or of a similar incident reached Stalin, who, on September 22, issued the following personal order to the troops and administration of the Leningrad front:

According to rumors, the Germans who are advancing on Leningrad are sending old men, women, and children from the occupied territories as representatives to the Bolsheviks with the request that they surrender Leningrad and make peace.

It is said that there are among Leningrad's Bolsheviks people who consider it inadvisable to use weapons against such representatives.

If there are really such people among the Bolsheviks, then in my opinion they should be the first to be extirpated, for they are even more dangerous than the fascists. I advise you not to be sentimental, but to attack the enemy and his helpers whether they are voluntary or not. . . .

No mercy for the Germans . . . no shielding of their representatives, whoever they may be.[14]

Following this, the Military Council of the Leningrad Front warned the troops:

All traitors to the fatherland who try to commit treasonable acts, hold conversation with the enemy, or desert to the other side are to be fired upon without warning and destroyed by any available means.

The commanders and commissars of the units in which treasonable "fraternization" and treason to the fatherland occur are to be arrested and turned over to the military tribunals.

The Special Section of the NKVD of the Leningrad front is to take immediate steps to arrest and commit to trial the family members of traitors to the fatherland in accordance with paragraph 6 of Article 68-1 of the Criminal Code. . . .

All soldiers of this front are to be informed that everyone who fails to take action against traitors and criminals, lets them escape, or reveals cowardice and disorder in such cases is to be mercilessly destroyed as a helper of the fascist master.[15]

After this a number of arrests and executions of officers, commissars, and soldiers for treasonable actions or for unauthorized withdrawals were announced, and in some cases whole units were disbanded.[16]

These harsh measures were undoubtedly justified in some cases. Army morale was poor, and some soldiers sought to desert either to the Germans or to Leningrad, whose fall they believed to be imminent. For instance, 310 deserters were intercepted in the area of one German army corps during the period of September 20 to 26, and an even larger number deserted during the following week.[17]

But the real measure of the Soviet leadership's distrust of the army lay in its attempt to suppress the normal grumbling peculiar to all soldiers the world over and regarded as natural in Western armies. The NKVD and the political officers of the Red Army appeared to expect their troops not to complain at all. An example of grumbling that political officers considered "hostile" was the following exclamation of a tired soldier during a position change: "Oh, Comrade Stalin, why do you torment us so?"[18] The political officer of the battalion reported this man to his regimental superior.

The leadership resorted to other control measures than the threat of execution or arrest. To bolster morale and keep closer watch on the soldiers, the number of reliable Party men, Komsomols, and political workers in the front lines was greatly increased, so that each company had 15 to 30 Party members.[19] Various orders were also issued at the highest level to maintain a strict surveillance of potentially disaffected troops, particularly of those in the best positions to desert to the enemy. Constant checks were made of Estonian, Polish, Finnish, and other soldiers of "foreign origin."[20]

There is reason to believe that the morale of the Red Army was not actually so poor as the Soviet leadership feared. The Germans at least were of this opinion. In September a German report stated: "The Red Army men who fall into our hands are mostly the worst soldiers, who report under the fresh impression of a first combat experience. In contradistinction to their statements, it is clear that many troop units, whether from conviction or under pressure of the commissars, fight very well and resist up to their total annihilation."[21] The continuing fierce Soviet defense of the approaches to Leningrad seemed to bear out this German estimate.

Nevertheless, by mid-September it must have appeared to the Soviet leadership that only a miracle could save Leningrad. Hitler made this miracle possible when he ordered the armored advance stopped just when it was about to enter the city. This came as a great surprise to the city's leaders, who had hardly expected the enemy to throw his victory away. Whether they realized that this was due to a German decision rather than to successful Soviet resistance, as claimed by their propaganda then and later, is not known. It would appear that at some time during this period the Soviet High Command was informed by its espionage network in Germany, the so-called *Rote Kapelle*, of the "decision of the high command to encircle Leningrad rather than to occupy it."[22] Whether and when Leningrad's leadership was apprised of this intelligence cannot be ascertained, but it should be noted that in all subsequent statements by the leaders the possibility of a renewed assault on the city was always mentioned.

The possibility of declaring Leningrad an "open city," or surrendering it in order to spare it battle damage and street fighting, was apparently never seriously entertained by Moscow. Soviet military tactics clearly showed that Stalin was determined to defend every foot of Soviet soil and that, whenever possible, every city was to be defended to the last. No Soviet city was to be spared battle damage or civilian casualties as long as such resistance helped to slow down the German advance and inflicted losses upon the enemy.

Knowing this, the Leningrad leadership took various additional defense measures. Foremost among them was the mobilization of further thousands of Leningraders as reinforcements for the hard-pressed Red Army and for units intended to fight in the streets of the city.

On August 21 the Military Council of the Northwest Front, the Leningrad City Party Committee, and the Executive Committee of the City Soviet published a joint appeal to the population:

Let us assist the fighting Red Army in Leningrad by forming new *opolchenie* units. Let us arise all together to the defense of our city, our homes, our families, our honor and freedom. Let us carry out our sacred duty as Soviet patriots! We will be indomitable in the struggle against cowards, panicmongers, and deserters; we will maintain the strictest revolutionary order in our city.

Armed with iron discipline and Bolshevik-style organization, we will courageously meet the enemy and inflict on him a devastating defeat.[23]

On the next day the *Leningradskaia pravda* echoed their appeal in its editorial: "All who are able to bear arms, who value the honor and freedom of our fatherland, consider it their duty to be fighting in the ranks of the people's *opolchenie,* to help the Red Army beat back the enemy and to defend our beloved city, our homes, our wives and children."[24] New *opolchenie* units were hurriedly formed. They were recruited as before, except that even less attention was paid to the physical condition of the volunteers and even more pressure was brought to bear to procure volunteers.[25]

The authorities appealed in particular to the youth of the city, boys and girls of 16 to 18, to volunteer. On September 7 the Komsomol published an appeal, stating that in moments of danger the heroic youth of the city had always stood in the front ranks of the defenders.[26] A meeting of students was called by the Komsomol on September 14, at which direct appeals were made for all to volunteer. Describing this meeting, a Soviet official told a foreign correspondent:

That day [September 14] our various high school students held an enormous meeting with the Komsomol, as a result of which every single young man still in town volunteered for immediate service. Hundreds of thousands of young people volunteered that day and in the next day or two.

Only one thousand did not volunteer. We said, "We want no cowards here." And we—said good-bye to them.[27]

The reporter added that the last phrase was spoken "in a very ominous tone."

Since it was necessary to throw into battle every available soldier, new sources of manpower had to be found. The leadership therefore mobilized for military service workers from enterprises that had to close, had been evacuated, or had to curtail production.[28] Another possibility was to release and mobilize persons serving jail sentences. Apparently those condemned to less than five years in concentration camps were sent into the army, while those condemned to five years or more were evacuated.[29]

The principal effort was directed to the organization of workers' battalions. By August 28 there were officially 36,658 persons serving in these units. On August 20 the authorities decided to assign all such battalions to "barrack" status, with a daily obligatory three-hour training period for their members.[30] Because of the seriousness of the military situation, it was decided also to arm them, but there was actually little equipment available for them. In addition to some rifles and machine guns, the workers were mainly armed with Molotov cocktails and hand grenades; they also had some 10,000 shotguns, and about 12,000 small caliber and training rifles "donated" by the city's population.[31]

The purpose of these units was to defend each *raion* and factory if the Germans succeeded in penetrating into the city. In the case of the Kirov Works, for example, which was located not far from the battle line, one of its workers said: "We decided on a circular defense. We fortified the whole area so that if necessary we could defend ourselves. In addition to the *opolchenie* we formed other volunteer units. The others could do as they pleased, but we, the Kirov workers, were not going to give up our plant."[32]

On September 1 three additional *opolchenie* divisions were organized from among the workers' battalions and sent to the front. Following this, and after some additional recruiting, there remained in the city a number of workers' units of varying sizes, totaling some 15,000 men who were eventually organized into four rifle brigades.[33] Some of them saw action in November, when Leningrad was required, despite its weakness, to exercise pressure on the Germans in order to help divert enemy forces then attacking Moscow.[34]

Although the combat value of these last-ditch forces was obviously low, they were the best the leadership could produce under the circumstances. There are even reports that housewives and children were asked to throw stones or boiling water on the Germans if they entered the city.[35]

Although the population was not surprised by these defense preparations, it had a very low opinion of its ability to contribute to them. Many persons felt that fighting was for soldiers and that the leadership had no business asking civilians to sacrifice themselves. The idea that, as a last resort, civilians should fight the enemy with boiling water, hand grenades, and bottles filled with gasoline struck many Leningraders as a useless undertaking, since if the army were unable to stop the Germans, civilians were hardly likely to do so.[36]

Some soldiers and members of the *opolchenie*, believing the battle to be lost, sought to desert and hide in the city, or feigned illness. How frequently this occurred is not known, but on September 17 the population was reminded by the authorities of the law subjecting anyone who harbored a deserter to trial by military tribunal, and house administrators were instructed to be on the lookout for such persons.[37]

Although fortifications continued to be built outside Leningrad, the main effort to fortify the city was not actually made until September, or in the words of the director of the Kirov Works, "during the worst days, when we thought the Germans might break through to Leningrad."[38] Not until after September 15 were the Elektrosila Works fortified with barricades and strong points built out of metal parts and pieces of machinery.[39] This tardiness is another indication that the leadership had been caught unawares by the swiftness and force of the German attack and that it had not expected the enemy to reach the city, but had clung to the hope of halting him on one of the outer defense lines. It is also possible, of course, that the leadership did not receive its orders to hold and defend the city to the last until the height of the crisis. If so, it is a significant comment on the lack of initiative of Zhdanov and his collaborators that they failed to take steps on their own.

The defense lines being prepared in the city utilized as far as possible the natural obstacles to an enemy advance provided by the canals that bisected the entire southern part of Leningrad. The main defense lines were in the suburbs from Uritsk to Verkhnee and on the Obvodnoi and Fontanka canals, although the city was fortified throughout.[40] It is also reported that a defense line was built south of the canals, along the railroad line connecting the port with the Neva, which would have included the industrial complexes of the Kirov and Electrosila Works.[41]

For the street-by-street defense of the city, antitank ditches and a large number of stone and timber barricades were built across streets. These barricades were several feet high and several feet thick and were equipped with firing slits. In some places streetcars, sometimes filled with sand, were used as barricades. A number of wooden, earthen, and concrete pillboxes were built. In the zone where the Germans were most likely to appear, cellars, stores, and sometimes upper windows of buildings were sandbagged, boarded, or bricked up, and provided with firing slits for machine guns and riflemen. For the most part, these emplacements were not manned or equipped with weapons, but were apparently intended to be used as strong points only if the Germans penetrated into the city. Areas along the sea front, including Krestovskii Island, were fortified to guard against a possible enemy attack across the ice after the sea had frozen.[42]

This construction program took several months to complete. Quantitatively, it was quite impressive. About 16 to 19 miles of barricades and antitank ditches, over 4,000 pillboxes, and 17,000 firing positions in buildings are said to have been built.[43] But they were generally of such poor quality and so badly planned that, in the spring and summer of 1942, a complete new program of fortification construction had to be carried out.

In September the construction of a fortified belt in the immediate outskirts of the city was begun, but could not be completed and made effective until the front was stabilized.[44]

It is thus apparent that when the German armored units broke through the triple fortification belt in mid-September, Leningrad itself was not sufficiently fortified to offer any serious obstacles to a further German advance.

To strengthen the defenses, extensive use was made of naval artillery, part of which was taken off the ships and mounted into fixed positions or placed on railroad cars.[45] The situation was obviously so desperate that even the antique guns of the cruiser "Aurora," which had been made into a national monument for its role in the Bolshevik revolution in 1917, were sent to the front.[46]

As before, the population provided the bulk of the labor force for the construction of the fortifications within the city and on the outskirts. On August 29, the Leningrad authorities issued another order "on the drafting of the population for work on the defense of Leningrad on the basis of obligatory labor." According to the order, the actual mobilization and the planning of the assignments of the labor force were "the responsibility of the executive committees of the city of Leningrad and of the *raion* Soviets."[47] Only 50 per cent of any civil defense group could be drafted at one time, and they could be put to work only in the city or its immediate vicinity, in order to be available when the bombings began. Since a large proportion (eventually in fact the majority) of the draftees were women, the *raion* executive authorities were directed to organize children's homes and special rooms in the apartment houses where children could be left while their parents performed their assignments.

On September 3 the Military Council of the Leningrad Front ordered the mobilization of 80,000 persons for the construction of fortifications. The workers received an extra daily bread ration above their regular ration and one cooked dish. In view of the short rations, this constituted a certain inducement to work for some people. In addition some 10,000 soldiers also worked on the fortifications.[48] Because of their proximity to the front lines, the workers were often exposed to enemy fire, and in many instances they remained on the construction sites for long periods of time, so that their families did not know what had become of them.[49]

In view of the justified pessimism of the leadership during the September crisis, some measures were also taken to deny to the enemy use of the city in case of its capture. These included the mining and laying of demolition charges under factories, buildings, bridges, port and railroad installations, and other vital structures. The hundreds of bridges across the canals, as well as across the Neva and its tributaries, were mined at this time.[50] Various buildings including factories were mined, so that they could be collapsed across important streets in order to form barriers to the German advance.[51] This preparation for demolition was apparently a matter that required a decision at the highest level. Intercepted radio messages make it clear that the order did in fact come from Moscow and that the Leningrad authorities made several reports to the capital on the progress of their preparations.[52] How complete the preparations for demolishing the city were is not known.

The demolition preparations were strongly resented by some elements of the population. The Leningraders appeared to draw a distinction between damage caused by the Germans, over whom they had no control and who were expected to do their worst to the city, and destruction initiated by Soviet authorities; they apparently felt that the latter were supposed to prevent damage, not cause it. Then, too, Leningraders had strong proprietary feelings about their factories and their city's landmarks. They feared that the destruction of the factories would deprive them of their livelihood. One eyewitness reports the following conversation with a worker: "And what are we supposed to do after the factories have been blown up? We can't be without factories. Even if the Germans come—we have to work in order to eat. We will not blow them up."[53] Despite these sentiments,* there are no indications that anyone tried to prevent the army engineers from laying the demolition charges.

Leningrad's preparations for repelling a German ground attack were seriously hampered by the beginning of the artillery and air bombardments of the city. By early September the Germans had advanced sufficiently close to Leningrad to bring the city under long-range artillery fire. On September 4 the first artillery shell exploded in the streets of Leningrad; on September 6 the first German bombs fell on the center of the city.[54] This bombardment was to continue with varying degrees of intensity until January 1944.

Actually, the German ability to bombard Leningrad was quite limited. In the area of Army Group North, the Germans had only 886 planes, 604 of which were bombers and dive bombers. Opposing them, according to German estimates, were some 115 Soviet fighters, numerous antiaircraft guns, barrage balloons, and searchlights. But most of the German planes were required for support of the German army. When the German Eighth Air Corps was withdrawn and sent elsewhere, on September 29, the attacking forces lost most of their dive bombers and were left with fewer than 300 planes of all types.[55]

The total amount of German artillery with sufficient range to reach Leningrad was also quite small. At that time there were only "a few

---

* Similar sentiments were expressed by Moscow workers when it was rumored in October 1941 that their factories would be destroyed (Dinerstein and Goure, p. 214).

heavy artillery regiments," primarily equipped with 150mm and 210mm guns, stationed seven to ten miles southwest of the city.[56]

Nevertheless, the bombardment was quite intense during the months of September through November. While the volume of artillery fire tended to increase in time, that of the air bombardment declined after October as a result of the shortage of planes and adverse weather conditions. In the period of September 4 to November 30, the city suffered 272 artillery bombardments lasting a total of 430 hours. During September Leningrad was struck by 5,364 shells, during October by 7,590 shells, and in November by 11,230 shells.[57] In all, the Germans fired some 30,154 artillery shells against Leningrad during 1941, which was about 20 per cent of the total shells fired against the city in the war.[58]

The first large air raid occurred on September 8 and did considerable damage. Following this the German air attacks increased in intensity. In September there were 23 raids, 12 of them at night, during which 987 high-explosive and 15,100 incendiary bombs were dropped. In October there were 38 raids, during which the Germans dropped a total of 812 high-explosive and 43,290 incendiary bombs, and in November another 38 raids with 1,256 high-explosive and 6,540 incendiary bombs.[59] In all, during 1941, the Germans made 108 air raids and dropped on Leningrad over 3,000 high-explosive and 66,000 incendiary bombs, which represented 71 per cent of all high-explosive bombs and 96 per cent of all incendiary bombs dropped on the city during the entire war.[60]

The actual tonnage of explosives dropped is not given in the available material, but was probably not very great, since a large portion of the German bomber force was made up of dive bombers that carried relatively small bombs. But although the raids or shellings were not heavy individually, they were frequent. The Germans deliberately spaced out their attacks in order to interfere as much as possible with the activities of the population. For example, the artillery bombardment on September 15 lasted, in all, over eighteen hours.[61] Sources mention nine alerts on September 9, twelve alerts on September 11, eleven alerts on September 13, six alerts on September 19, eleven alerts on September 23 lasting a total of seven and one-half hours, and ten alerts on October 4 lasting over nine hours.[62] During the period of September through November, 251 air raid alerts were sounded.[63]

The largest attacks occurred on September 19 and 27. On September 19, Leningrad was subjected to six air attacks by 264 planes, which dropped 528 high explosives and about 2,000 incendiary bombs; in addition, the city was struck by 242 heavy artillery shells. On September 27, the city was attacked by 197 planes.[64]

The bombardment caused considerable damage and many casualties. The Germans concentrated their fire against factories, food storage areas, electric power stations, water-pumping and water-purification plants, military installations, and naval vessels; but they also struck numerous residential buildings. It would appear that they made little effort to destroy the administrative and political centers of Leningrad. Although, officially, the main Party administration and military organs remained throughout the siege in the historic Smolny Institute, this building, as far as can be determined, never suffered a single hit, although the area around it was severely damaged. Other military, city, and police authorities were housed in buildings concentrated in a small area around the Admiralty in the heart of the city; yet they appear to have suffered little significant damage. The only administrative target that the Germans tried to destroy, probably for political and ideological reasons, was the headquarters of the secret police, located in a block of buildings near the Liteinyi bridge. According to all sources, this area suffered severe damage, but the police headquarters emerged almost unscathed.

Considerable damage was inflicted on industrial installations, utilities, and food warehouses. For example, the air raid of September 8 caused 144 fires (including 46 large ones), 62 of which occurred in factories and 52 in residential and office buildings. In all, during September the raids caused a total of 11,528 fires and damaged or destroyed 26 factories.[65] Those that suffered most were the factories located in the southern portion of the city, since they were within easy range of the German artillery—in some cases, close enough to the front lines to be observable by the enemy through field glasses.

Damage to utilities appears to have been far less extensive. The Germans succeeded in destroying only one of the minor electric power plants in the city and the gas works.[66] This had relatively little effect on the city, since, as was noted earlier, only a small percentage of the population used gas. The water works were subjected to intensive enemy fire. According to Popkov, the main water works, located on the Neva in the heart of the city, was hit during the siege by 62 bombs, 272 incendiary bombs, and 155 shells, but continued to operate. More serious was the damage to water mains, which were cut in 5,609 places throughout the city, so that, despite repairs, leakage was still causing a loss of 20 per cent of the water supply in 1943.[67]

The Germans also inflicted serious damage on ammunition and weapon depots and on food plants and warehouses. On September 8, for example, the bombardment caused 78 large fires that destroyed, among other things, the large Badaev food warehouses and the Red Star butter plant.[68] Other warehouses, flour mills, and refrigeration plants were also damaged or destroyed during this period, including some belonging to the army.[69]

Each air raid and artillery bombardment killed and wounded a number of civilians, especially factory workers. During the fall, 681 persons were killed and 2,269 wounded by artillery fire alone.[70] According to another Soviet source, 15,529 persons were wounded and 4,481 killed during 1941 by the air and artillery bombardments.[71] In all, 16,747 civilians were killed and over 33,000 wounded by enemy fire in Leningrad during the war.[72]

Although the bombardment of Leningrad never achieved the magnitude of that suffered by London or Berlin during the war, it nevertheless severely tested its civil defense organization. It was fortunate for Leningrad that the leadership had had two months in which to prepare the city for bombardment. Despite the primitiveness of its equipment, the civil defense organization proved generally effective, thanks largely to the sturdy construction of the houses, the relatively small volume of the bombardment, and the lavish use of manpower.

Although most of the civil defense groups were composed of poorly trained women and teen-agers, they showed remarkable efficiency, most of them working with great energy and determination. Officially, the "self-defense" groups are credited with extinguishing over 5,700 fires during the course of the war. Eventually 32,270 members of the "self-defense" groups were decorated.[73]

Even though Leningrad had expected air attack since the beginning of the war, there were many instances when the authorities showed lack of foresight. For example, only after the bombing of two hospitals was an order issued on September 23 to have stretchers placed near the beds of severely ill or severely wounded patients, so as to be ready to move them in case of need, and to have rope ladders placed in hospital wards to permit patients to escape from the building.[74] Some of the hastily erected street barricades had been stretched across streets from wall to wall, so that they sometimes not only interfered with traffic but prevented fire engines and ambulances from reaching disaster areas. The authorities also committed the astonishing blunder of concentrating much of Leningrad's food reserves in a few warehouse areas. The Lenin and Kirov flour-milling *kombinats,* along with the Badaev warehouses, held nearly the entire flour reserve for feeding the civilian population. On September 4, Popkov, as chairman of the Executive Committee of the City Soviet, had been instructed to check on measures for protecting the food and fuel reserves from enemy bombardment; but no action was taken to disperse them until after September 8, when a considerable portion of the supplies was destroyed.[75]

The bombardment initially caused some panic among the population. Even though the air attacks had been expected, they caused bitterness against the Germans as well as against the Soviet leadership. Some people expressed surprise that the enemy found it necessary to bomb what they believed was already his.[76] The destruction of historic landmarks, according to several informants, caused more sadness than anger, although it is likely that some people took this as proof that the Germans were engaging in indiscriminate bombing. Although, of course, the destruction of homes, hospitals, schools, and utilities was resented, it was nevertheless generally accepted as being inevitable under the circumstances.[77] Some people, particularly women, tended to blame the leadership for its inability to protect the population from enemy fire.[78] The population was disappointed in the effectiveness of the large concentration of antiaircraft artillery, barrage balloons, and other air defense weapons. Although prior to September it had been rumored that Leningrad's air defense was too strong for the Germans, by mid-September the inhabitants believed that the Germans flew at will over the city.[79] Although the Leningraders were able to witness numerous air battles,* they thought that Leningrad's fighter defense was poor on the ground that it did not prevent the Germans from bombing the city. Popular disappointment led to criticism of the leadership, which had for years assured the population that the Soviet air force was invincible.

The Leningrad authorities made no effort to hide from the population the damage caused by the bombardment. The attacks were, in any case, too frequent for this to be possible. All that was done was to clear the streets of rubble and pull down walls that were in danger of collapsing.[80] Damage to factories and military installations was to some extent kept secret from the population, since only those employed in such places could see what had happened. But this did not preclude the workers from discussing the damage with their families and friends. The grapevine was very effective in disseminating this kind of information among the population. The burning of the Badaev food warehouses, for example, became known throughout the city immediately after the raid. Four informants report that although they had not known the whereabouts of the food stocks, they were told of the destruction of these warehouses as soon as they emerged from the shelters after the air raid.

Since the population generally tended to view factories, government buildings, warehouses, and military installations as legitimate targets for enemy fire, they measured the risks to themselves and to their homes in terms of their distance from such targets. Lacking confidence in the

---

* The Soviet authorities claimed to have shot down 132 enemy planes during September (Karasev, *Leningradtsy v gody blokady,* p. 150).

antiaircraft defenses and believing that antiaircraft emplacements were likely targets for enemy attacks, they resented the authorities' decision to mount light antiaircraft weapons on the roofs of some large buildings or in the backyards and playgrounds of some apartment buildings.[81]

Following the initial shock and anxiety caused by the bombardment, the population quickly adjusted itself to the new situation and came to accept the danger and discomfort with a good deal of fatalism. There is no indication that these attacks were able to paralyze any of the major defense or municipal activities, although they created much hardship and interfered with work and sleep. The effects of the bombardment on everyday life are described in the diary of one eyewitness in an entry dated September 12:

> For three days things have been thus: starting in the morning—alerts, firing of antiaircraft guns, air battles overhead. Barely have people formed a queue to buy bread—they must scatter; on the ride to work—one has to get off the trolley car three or four times to take cover in trenches, hallways, or shelters. In the evening and at night—bombings. In the morning it is frightening to see familiar buildings destroyed or smoking . . .
>
> Kind, dear Leningraders! We waited, we prepared—but did anyone think that it would be like *this*?[82]

Many rumors circulated among the population about the number of casualties and the extent of the damage caused by the bombing. Some of these rumors reflected a wish to make the attacks appear less frightening. For example, it was said that a large unexploded bomb that had fallen near a hospital was "loaded with sugar" and that many duds contained notes saying "we help the best we can," presumably put there by pro-Communist workers in Germany.[83]

People took what precautions they could to protect their personal belongings. Some took their prize possessions with them into the shelters. Most carried all their vital personal papers and documents in their pockets to prevent them from being destroyed at home. For the same reason some Leningraders wore their best clothes, while others dispersed their clothing and most valuable possessions among friends and relatives throughout the city to reduce the chance of their being wiped out by a single hit.[84]

The shelters were uncomfortable, since they were generally not equipped for sleeping and were at first not heated; consequently, the Leningraders found it hard to spend a large part of their days and nights there. During alerts people usually tried either to reach "reliable" shelters in multistoried buildings or to stand away from windows and near strong walls on the lower floors of buildings. During the first weeks of the bombardment most people slept in the shelters or ran for cover every time they heard a German plane. But after a while many people became used to the situation and took cover only when bombs or shells were falling nearby.[85]

The population participated with energy and willingness in civil defense work. Incendiaries were smothered with sand or thrown off the roofs by the watchers. Everybody helped to put out fires. If there were not enough people, additional help was drafted on the spot from among passers-by and neighboring houses. If the building could not be saved, everybody joined in to save the possessions of the residents. Many children were also active in civil defense, serving not only as messengers but as roof-watchers and fire fighters. Sometimes children formed themselves into well organized, unofficial civil defense groups that proved successful in putting out numerous incendiary bombs.[86] All of this allowed the regular civil defense and fire-fighting units to take care of the public and industrial buildings, in whose preservation the population was less interested.

Since the southern districts nearest to the German lines were the most exposed to enemy artillery fire and in the greatest danger in case of a German breakthrough, the Leningrad leadership decided to relocate a part of this area's industry and population to safer districts. This relocation began in September and continued for some time. In all, according to Soviet archives, 28 factories, including several from the suburbs, were partly or completely moved.[87] Usually the factory shops that were moved were those working on military production, whereas those engaged in less vital production, or those whose equipment was too heavy to move, remained behind and continued to operate under fire. For example, only the lamp and the marine-engine shops of the great Elektrosila Works remained in their old location.[88] The relocated shops were generally dispersed among various factories located on the northern bank of the Neva River, or were given the space left by evacuated factories.

It was also decided to move the inhabitants of the exposed districts to safer parts of the city. About 54,000 persons were moved (some going by streetcar, others by foot), and these were quartered in empty schools and offices, or else in apartments and rooms whose occupants had been evacuated or were away in the army or on missions.[89] Some were moved in with residents who had excess living space. The evacuees had to leave most of their furniture and other belongings behind, to be retrieved later when the immediate emergency had passed.

The defense of Leningrad required a continuous supply of war materiel for the troops. Up to the end of August the city's industry had been in the process of reorganizing and expanding its war production. But this effort, as was noted earlier, was repeatedly disrupted by labor and supply shortages, enemy bombardment, industrial evacuation, and other defense measures. In addition, there was much administrative confusion, since the major part of Leningrad's industry depended on Moscow for its finances, its production and evacuation orders, the supplying of raw materials or semifinished goods, and even for orders to close down production. At the same time, in view of the emergency, the Military Council of the Leningrad Front and the city's Party leadership were acquiring extensive powers to cut across the usual administrative structure in order to satisfy local requirements. The council had the authority to order changes in production, to pool labor, raw materials, fuel, and machinery, and to transfer these from one plant to another without regard to their ministerial affiliations and without compensation to the ministry or industry so affected.[90] This resulted in a great deal of confusion, because the administration in Moscow was often poorly informed about conditions in Leningrad, and because the Moscow and Leningrad authorities did not always coordinate their decisions, particularly in matters of evacuation, over which Moscow had primary authority regardless of the production needs of Leningrad.[91] The uncertainty of Leningrad's leadership about what turn the fighting would take compounded the confusion.

The result was that factory managers either received orders that under the circumstances were unrealistic or impossible to fulfill, or else received no orders at all and did not know what to do. In the absence of new directives from Moscow, factories that had been ordered to prepare for evacuation continued to dismantle their machinery even though it could no longer be shipped out and was badly needed for the defense of the city.[92] Moscow, apparently failing to appreciate the situation, kept issuing further evacuation orders that the factory managers had no choice but to obey.[93]

Of course the leadership and the armed forces, while mobilizing large segments of the labor force for a last-ditch defense, were at the same time appealing to the factory workers to increase the production of war goods. An editorial in *Leningradskaia pravda* from this period stated:

The success of the courageous and daring defenders of Leningrad—who are standing, weapons in hand, face to face with the enemy; who are defending our city, life, and freedom with their breasts—depends directly on the extent to which the workers and toilers of Leningrad, who have remained at their machines in the plants and factories, continuously supply the army with new weapons and war materiel.[94]

As in the preceding months, industry continued to recruit women, retired workers, students in factory training schools, and workers from factories that were either closed down or nonessential in order to replace the departed workers. The authorities often frustrated these attempts by drafting into military service workers from closed or nonessential factories instead of transferring them to other factories.[95] In most instances the number of recruited workers fell far short of the number of those who had left, so that most factories continued to suffer from a severe labor shortage. The lack of skill of the new labor force made it difficult to maintain a high production level and forced a simplification of the production processes.[96]

To maintain production, workers in the factories and on the railroads were required to work even during air raids, since otherwise the frequency of the alerts and their long duration would have seriously impaired the operations of industry and transportation. Workers were allowed to leave their machines only when bombs or shells were actually dropping nearby.[97] Work was constantly being disrupted by the bombardment, especially in the factories located near the front lines. A Leningrad woman reports in her diary that in one factory on September 17, the workers spent seven hours, with only brief interruptions, taking cover under railway cars.[98]

The artillery bombardment in particular, since it could not be preceded by any warning, caused heavy casualties among the workers and naturally affected morale. One factory director, describing this situation to a foreign correspondent in 1943, said:

You also ask how they take it? Well, I don't know whether you've ever been for any length of time under shell fire. But if anybody tells you it isn't frightening, don't you believe it. He's a liar. There is no soldier and no civilian who is not frightened. I am the director here and I am frightened. But the real thing is not to show it. And I don't. And everybody else here knows how to act and how to behave in a bombardment. But this frequent shelling nevertheless has an effect on people's psychology. In our experience a direct hit has a very bad effect for twenty-four or forty-eight hours. In a workshop that's had a direct hit, production slumps heavily for twenty-four or forty-eight hours, or stops almost completely, especially if many people have been killed or injured. It's a horrible sight, all the blood, and makes even some of our hardened workers quite ill for a day or two. But, in the long run, it doesn't matter. Two days later, they are fully back at work again, and do their best to make up for the time lost by what's called "the accident."[99]

Another informant made a similar comment: "I must say it was difficult at first to get used to the bombing, and if anyone says it doesn't frighten him, don't you believe it."[100]

The workers, of course, had no choice but to work despite these conditions. The control measures discussed earlier—the freezing of labor at its place of employment, the punishments for tardiness and absenteeism, the forced transfers to other factories in or outside the city, trial under wartime laws for anything that the authorities cared to label "sabotage"—all had their effect in preventing unauthorized movements. The food-rationing system also served to discourage workers from leaving the plants, since workers were entitled to the largest rations. Then there were also many patriotic workers who felt it their duty not to let down the soldiers, among whom, of course, they had relatives and friends. In fact, some workers, apparently inspired by propaganda and patriotism, reportedly worked many hours overtime to complete their assignments. Thus, for example, the *Leningradskaia pravda* of October 2 reported that "Having remained in the boiler room without relief for 30 hours and then having received only a few hours of rest, Comrade Vinnikov again resumed his post. In three days, Comrade Vinnikov worked five 12-hour shifts at a hot furnace."[101]

In most instances, Leningraders who had to work in exposed and dangerous locations did not try to avoid doing so, although some of them, as is reported in one diary, said farewell each morning to their families in case they did not come back.[102]

The operations of industry were increasingly hampered by fuel shortage. On September 1, Leningrad had sufficient petroleum products for 18 to 20 days, and industry had enough coal for 50 days. By the end of the month industry had exhausted its liquid fuel supply and in most cases its coal supply as well.[103] Furthermore, on September 1, the military authorities had sufficient aviation gasoline for only ten days and gasoline for vehicles for seven days.[104]

Electric power was also in very short supply. Before the war Leningrad obtained its electric power from six large hydroelectric power plants located at some distance from the city and from a number of thermoelectric plants (some large and some small) located in the city. The latter produced less than half of the total amount of electricity needed by Leningrad, and most of them operated on coal imported from other parts of the country.[105] By September the hydroelectric power stations had been either captured or cut off by the Germans.[106] This put the entire burden on thermoelectric plants in the city, which had sufficient fuel for only 80 to 100 days. Furthermore, some were damaged by the German bombardment. Consequently, the available monthly electric power output dropped from a prewar level of 10.8 million kilowatt-hours to 3.9 million kilowatt-hours in October.[107] It therefore became necessary to ration electric power for industrial use, and this in turn led to a decline in Leningrad's industrial output.

The continuing German advance forced the authorities to review their program for evacuating the population of Leningrad. On August 14 the Council of Evacuation of the Council of People's Commissars of the USSR had decided to evacuate an additional 700,000 persons from the city. After the Germans had severed all railroad lines to Leningrad on August 29, the Military Council of the Leningrad Front ordered the continuation of the evacuation and raised the number of persons to be evacuated to 1,200,000.[108] In actuality this was a meaningless decision, since large-scale evacuation was no longer possible.

Following the capture of Mga by the Germans, the only means of supplying Leningrad or evacuating its population was by air or water across Lake Ladoga. The airlift was organized only very slowly and did not begin to operate effectively until October. Even then, of the 64 twin-engine transports of the DC-3 type assigned to the operation by the State Defense Committee, only 20 to 22 were operational at any one time.[109]

On August 30, the State Defense Committee ordered a supply line for Leningrad to be established across Lake Ladoga.[110] Since in peacetime there had been little traffic on the lake, there were neither sufficient boats nor sufficient harbor facilities to transport large numbers of persons and supplies.[111] On September 9 the Military Council of the Leningrad Front decided to develop a small port at Osinovets on the Leningrad shore of the lake. The port was to handle five barges daily by September 18 and twelve barges daily by September 25. Actually, as a result of a severe drop in the water level of the lake, bad weather, and a shortage of ships, this program was not fulfilled.[112] Twenty barges were assigned to transport food and other supplies from Lodeinoe Pole and Volkhovstroi to Osinovets, but actually only sixteen barges were put into operation and several were wrecked by storms and enemy bombing.[113] Thousands of Leningraders and farmers were mobilized to deepen the Osinovets harbor and build piers and jetties.[114]

The authorities were slow to appreciate the transport difficulties and kept ordering people to leave the city. This led to chaos. People waited for days at the railroad stations, or in trains in the marshaling yards, or at the boat landings in Osinovets. A Soviet official who was a witness to these events noted in his diary:

With catastrophic tardiness we are trying to clear the city of women and children; they are assembled, loaded into railway cars, and sent ten to twelve kilometers to Sortirovachnaia or Rybatskaia, or somewhere else, where they remain standing on the track, eight to ten trains at once. They stand three days, five, a week, waiting to be sent on at any moment; the people cannot get in touch with their relatives, who imagine that they have departed long since. The majority are without money, there is hardly any food; the food [they had put aside], which was barely sufficient for the trip, had to be eaten on the spot.[115]

Between August 11 and August 29, about 168,500 persons were evacuated by rail.[116] After that the evacuation was reduced to a trickle.

Instead of evacuating over one million persons as planned, only about 40,000 managed to leave the city during September.[117]

Despite the growing danger to Leningrad, the bombardment and the deteriorating living conditions, many of the persons who could have been evacuated still refused to go. One Leningrader noted in her diary on September 7 that although she did not wish to leave her home and her city, she thought that people with children should leave. "But they are obstinate. Recently they nearly created an uproar at the Smolnyi: 'Our husbands are here, and they want to send us off someplace else.' "[118] The Party leaders and organizers were supposed to persuade and encourage people to leave, but some of the local Party leaders actually helped to sabotage the evacuation. In their eagerness to demonstrate the patriotism and loyalty of the people in their care, they had encouraged them to refuse evacuation. According to a representative in Leningrad of the State Defense Committee: "Some members of the local organs of power even made a show of pride [that people were refusing to leave], regarding the refusal of citizens to evacuate as an expression of patriotic sentiments, and thereby in effect encouraged people to remain. One could often hear them say: 'Our population is ready to work in forward battle positions, but does not want to leave Leningrad.' "[119]

During this period the population was asked by the leadership to contribute to the war effort in other ways than by working. The battle for Leningrad was taking place just at the time when the Red Army was re-equipping its forces with winter clothes and shoes. Apparently the supplies of these that were stored in the city were insufficient, and the trains carrying additional supplies were prevented by the German advance from reaching Leningrad. Various shoe and clothing factories began to make boots and uniforms, but could not produce enough. Consequently, with true Soviet "spontaneity" the workers of one factory publicly appealed for donations of winter clothes for the army, and their appeal, as could be expected, was echoed by all other factories and institutions.[120] The Komsomols and school children went from apartment to apartment collecting clothes and shoes, as well as money to buy wool and flannel. At the same time, housewives and girls formed sewing and knitting circles to make winter clothes for the soldiers.[121]

When on September 6 the government instituted a collection of money and valuables for a national defense fund, the Party in Leningrad and its satellite organizations made a considerable effort to fulfill their collection quotas, since they felt that this would demonstrate their zeal and efficiency. In the factories the workers contributed at least one and sometimes two or more days' wages. By September 22 the Leningraders had collected 587,500,000 rubles in cash or valuables.[122]

The population was accustomed to campaigns to collect funds for special purposes, and it was understood by all that a refusal to contribute could, and probably would, be interpreted as an expression of defeatism and disloyalty. Few dared risk this. Of course, there were probably many people who were eager to contribute out of patriotism or loyalty to the regime; but others were less happy to do so, either because they had little money to spare or because they disliked the pressure that the Party brought to bear.

The threat to Leningrad forced the authorities to tighten and reorganize some of the administrative systems of the city and to create new organizations. On July 13 Zhdanov had been appointed member of the Military Council of the Northwest Front, which was under the command of Marshal Voroshilov. Military councils were institutions dating back to prerevolutionary days, but had become especially important since 1917. In 1938 the Main Military Council of the Red Army was organized, of which Stalin was a member, Zhdanov becoming a member of the Main Military Council of the Naval Forces. Following the German attack on the Soviet Union, military councils were organized for each front and army under the chairmanship of the officers commanding these forces. The military councils dealt with all military and administrative problems, other than strategic and tactical ones, in the zone of operation of their forces.[123] Voroshilov, who, it will be remembered, was the chairman of the Military Council of the Northwest Front, was also a member of the all-powerful State Defense Committee, which was headed by Stalin and which directed the entire war effort of the country. The addition of important and trusted Party members to the military councils ensured that the fronts and armies would have the support and assistance of the local administrative and Party institutions, while at the same time it permitted the Party to keep a close check on the military commanders. Zhdanov subsequently listed himself in his addresses and orders to the troops as a member of the military council as well as a secretary of the Central Committee of the Communist Party, while in his addresses to the population he appeared as a secretary of the Leningrad City Party Committee.[124]

After mid-August it was no longer possible to maintain northern and northwest front commands. On August 23 the northern front was divided into the Karelian and the Leningrad fronts, and the northwest front was put under the direct control of the High Command of the Soviet Armed Forces.[125] After the Germans had cut the northwest forces in half, the command of the northwest front was merged with that of the Leningrad front. On August 24 the Military Council of the Leningrad Front was organized. The composition of this council reflected the role of the city as the main battleground and main objective of the enemy. Voroshilov was its first chairman, since he was also commander of the front; but the council included such civilian political and administrative leaders as Zhdanov, Kuznetsov, and Kapustin, all of them secretaries of the city Party committee; Shtykov, secretary of the *oblast* Party committee; and Solovev, chairman of the *oblast* executive committee.[126] Voroshilov's chief of staff and the commander of the Baltic fleet were also on the council. In addition, two secretaries of the *oblast* Party committee were appointed members of the military councils of the armies of the Leningrad Front, and a secretary of the city's Party committee was assigned to the Military Council of the Baltic Fleet.[127] The Military Council of the Leningrad Front, as the highest authority in the area (since it had been expressly formed to "organize the defense of the city"), was able to command the "unhesitating obedience of all Party, Soviet, and economic organizations as well as of all citizens."[128]

The various members of the council held unequal rank. In general, orders to the armed forces were signed by the front commander, the chief of staff, and Zhdanov, and only occasionally also by Kuznetsov and others. Eventually both Zhdanov and Kuznetsov were given the rank of general. Orders to the population were sometimes signed by the entire membership of the council, whereas at other times the names of junior members did not appear. In view of Zhdanov's high rank in the Party, he either had over-all control of the council or shared the top position with the military commander, while the other members were responsible for specific sectors.

Despite their high ranks, Voroshilov and Zhdanov were by no means free to reorganize the administrative system in their area without Stalin's approval. Their attempt to do so aroused Stalin's anger. On August 20 they had decided, in view of the gravity of the military situation, to create the Military Council for the Defense of Leningrad, which was charged with the supervision of fortification construction, the military training of the population, the production of armaments, and the employment of workers' battalions.[129] The membership of this council was made up of two secretaries of the city's Party committee, Kuznetsov and Kapustin; the chairman of the Executive Committee of the Leningrad City Soviet, Popkov; the commander of the Leningrad *opolchenie*, General Subbotin; and a member of the military council of the *opolchenie*, Antiufeev.[130] According to a former representative of the State Defense Committee in Leningrad, Stalin telephoned Voroshilov and Zhdanov the next day, expressed his displeasure "that a council for the defense of the city had been organized without his permission," and stated that he "thought it wrong that neither Voroshilov nor Zhdanov participated in that organ once it was created."[131] Voroshilov and Zhdanov argued that this military council was established merely to assist the Military Council of the Northwest Front, which was already overburdened with duties, and that both men wanted to have more time "to direct the military operations on whose outcome the fate of Leningrad depended"; but Stalin refused to listen.[132] At his insistence, the composition of the council was changed to include Voroshilov and Zhdanov in addition to the existing members Kuznetsov, Subbotin, and Popkov. This decision was obviously an expression of Stalin's displeasure. Instead of having their task made easier, Voroshilov and Zhdanov were obliged to head two councils. This arrangement could not continue for any length of time, and as soon as it was practicable, or safe, the Military Council for the Defense of Leningrad was eliminated. It functioned only for six days and a little later, on August 30, it was formally abolished by the State Defense Committee, and its functions were transferred to the Military Council of the Leningrad Front.[133]

There was nothing extraordinary in the organization of a council for the defense of Leningrad. Similar councils, composed of representatives of the Party, military, and security organs, were formed in Sevastopol, Stalingrad, Tula, Rostov, and Murmansk. These councils were established under the authority of the State Defense Committee, to which they remained responsible for all actions; their powers, however, were extensive, and they were not operationally under the direct control of the State Defense Committee. They were able to institute a state of siege, resettle the population from one part of the city to another, give local industry special production orders, organize the *opolchenie* and other defense units, mobilize the population and the transportation facilities for defense work, and control food distribution and the maintenance of food reserves.[134]

The Military Council of the Leningrad Front was unique in that, unlike the councils of the other cities mentioned above, it remained under the direct control of the State Defense Committee.[135] Zhdanov, although not a member, frequently acted as a representative of the State Defense Committee, particularly after Voroshilov's removal in September. It is not clear from the published material how much freedom of action the council had under this arrangement. As far as can be ascertained, it had a free hand in the mobilization of the population and in certain other defense and control measures, but was less independent in matters pertaining to food control, industrial operations, evacuation of factories and civilians, and the like. That the council had unusually great authority is demonstrated by its ability to remove and punish members of the special section of the NKVD in the Red Army.[136] It is also probable that because of its importance the city's leadership could often secure better cooperation and help from Moscow than other military councils of Soviet cities.

It is indicative of the close control maintained over the Military Council of the Leningrad Front by the State Defense Committee that, despite the presence of Voroshilov and Zhdanov in the city, two members of the State Defense Committee, Molotov and Malenkov, were sent to Leningrad in August or September of 1941 "to organize its defense."[137] Their purpose in coming seems to have been either to determine the defensibility of Leningrad or to resolve a dispute on this question between Voroshilov and Zhdanov. According to rumors, Voroshilov favored the surrender of the city.[138] At any rate, he was relieved of his command and replaced on September 13 by General Zhukov, who a month later was recalled to Moscow to direct the battle there.

Although the Military Council of the Leningrad Front had over-all control, the local authorities had to be prepared "for possible fighting within the city, in the streets of Leningrad."[139] For this purpose they organized the Internal Defense Staff of Leningrad, which was headed by Colonel Antonov. The staff prepared plans for the street-by-street defense of the city and had command over the 36,000 men in the *opolchenie* and the workers' battalions.[140] "The Internal Defense Staff worked under the guidance of the city committee of the VKP(b) [the Party] and the Executive Committee of the Leningrad City Soviet of Workers' Deputies, and in operational matters was subordinate to the Military Council of the Leningrad Front."[141]

Each city *raion* in turn formed defense staffs. Each staff was made up of the *raion* Party secretary, the chairman of the *raion* executive committee, the chief of the *raion* section of the NKVD, and the chief of the *raion* military reserve training commission. To assist these staffs, each large industrial plant or major office organized a *troika* (committee of three), composed of the director, the secretary of the Party organization, and the chairman of the trade union committee.[142] This arrangement was put into operation on September 16, when a secretary of the Moscow *raion* Party committee ordered the workers' units of the Elektrosila Works to take up their defense posts and prepare to fight the advancing enemy.[143]

Centralization and coordination of the administrative bodies were certainly necessary. However, the actual efficiency of the system appears to have been impaired by overlapping and hazy areas of responsibility, by the subordination of Leningrad to the direct orders of Moscow, and by the necessity for deciding many minor administrative matters at a fairly high level. Control did not always run according to the formal organization described above. The Party leadership retained a leading role throughout by dominating all of the organizations. Particularly at lower levels, authority was firmly in the hands of the *raion* or unit Party secretary. One NKVD colonel stated: "Not all the forces that have been set up for the defense of Leningrad are under a single leadership. Everybody is concerned with defense—the civil authorities, the Party committees, the military leaders, as well as single plants and enterprises—but they are not united under one command."[144]

Yet in spite of everything, there was a good deal of respect for legal formalities. The Executive Committee of the City Soviet dealt with such matters as issuing orders to the population, operating the utilities, and dispensing food and fuel, and Popkov signed the decrees, although the Military Council of the Leningrad Front actually determined what would be done.

On the whole, the efficiency of this command system depended less on its organization than on the energy and ability of those who headed it. At the top, Zhdanov, Popkov, Kuznetsov, and others seem usually to have acted with the necessary vigor. At lower levels the caliber of the administrators varied, and a certain number of failures came to light, which led to some officials being replaced.[145] The initiative shown by the *raion* officials was uneven. In general, the city's leadership had considerable will and determination, although at times it showed a lack of foresight and imagination.

The immediate threat to Leningrad forced the authorities to tighten their security and control measures over the population even further. To prevent the infiltration of Leningrad by enemy agents and at the same time to prevent Russian soldiers from deserting either to the enemy or to the rear, the military authorities forbade all unauthorized movements by soldiers or civilians in the front-line areas or through the forward barbed-wire obstacles and instituted strict controls to the rear of these areas by establishing military and police checkpoints that could be crossed only with special passes.[146] These measures had an additional advantage in that they kept the population in ignorance of the morale and state of the army and prevented the army from being infected by possible civilian defeatism. The checkpoints also had orders to prevent refugees from the battle area from entering the city. Instead they were assembled in special facilities and, while it was still possible, were shipped into the interior of the country. The militia and the house managers were again instructed on September 17 to be on the lookout for persons who did not have proper papers or had failed to register with the militia; anyone harboring them was threatened with severe punishment.[147]

On August 24 the executive committees of the city and *oblast* Soviets issued new curfew regulations "in order to strengthen revolutionary order in Leningrad and its suburbs." The curfew now extended from 10:00 P.M. to 5:00 A.M., and the sale of alcoholic beverages was prohibited after 8:00 P.M.[148] Curfew orders were legally the responsibility of the garrison commander. The fact that the executive committees issued them rather than the garrison commander is an example of how administrative responsibilities overlapped. In 1942 such orders were again issued by the garrison commander.

It was widely believed, as has been noted earlier, that the city was full of resident German agents whom the Germans had either placed there before the war or parachuted in later, and that "remnants of destroyed classes" were being recruited by these agents.[149] The bombardment served to strengthen this belief. Most sources described the work of these agents as consisting of undermining the morale of the population and signaling to enemy planes with rockets and lights, from which they received the name "rocket men" (*raketchiki*).

To deal with enemy parachutists and rocket men, the authorities organized in each *raion*, in addition to the Komsomol and militia patrols, special destruction detachments made up of members of the Komsomol and of the NKVD, each 150 to 200 strong.[150] On September 15 the Leningrad City Committee of the Komsomol decided to organize in each *raion* special security units made up of five to ten persons; their duties were to catch spies and rocket men and to form guard units to protect the railroad and railroad stations against sabotage.[151] On September 25 a Komsomol regiment of over 2,000 members was placed on active duty for the purpose of helping to preserve public order and security. At the same time, the Germans estimated that there were some 250 militiamen in each of the city's *raions*, most of them armed only with pistols.[152] At the height of the battle for the city a part of the militia was sent to the front to fight. To make up for these losses the authorities recruited mostly women.[153]

According to all informants, the NKGB troops were not much in evidence in the city. Most or all of their regiments were in fact at the front, either fighting or performing security work in the rear of the army.[154] But the state police organization in the city was still making some preventive arrests and was on the lookout for enemy agents.

There were few Red Army units in the city, since the leadership was trying to stem the German advance by throwing in all available reserves. The majority of those that had remained in Leningrad were made up of workers' battalions, *opolchenie* troops, and special guard units, all of which had been recruited from among the population. It would thus seem that the leadership did not possess many reliable security forces in Leningrad capable of dealing with large-scale popular unrest or rebellion. The control system was also weakened by the reduction in the number of Party members present in the city and by the fact that some of them became afraid of the people; this was particularly true of the lowest level of Party members.

Widespread rumors about the so-called rocket men caused a great deal of popular excitement. All informants recall that the population firmly believed in their existence. It was also widely believed that thousands of ethnic Germans who resided in Leningrad were disloyal. Rumors spread the story that the subversive operations were being directed by the "50 Abteilung Gestapo."[155] Regardless of individual attitudes toward the Germans, the population was uniformly hostile to these agents and actively participated in apprehending them. Leningraders apparently drew a distinction between the invading German army, which some people, at least, were prepared to welcome as liberators, and the advance guard of enemy agents. One reason for this was the belief that the rocket men signaled the location of targets to the German bombers; but a more important reason appears to have been a popular revulsion against any secret or subversive enemy activity, even on the part of those who were perfectly ready to accept outright conquest and occupation.

Actually, there is no evidence from German or Soviet official sources that the rocket men really existed. Many suspected persons were guilty of nothing more than carelessness in violating the blackout. It is significant, for instance, that an NKVD officer writing an article citing several subversive cases makes no mention of any rocket men.[156] But the belief in the existence of rocket men persists even in current Soviet literature on the siege of Leningrad.[157] There is, however, no indication that there was any organized or extensive contact between the Germans and any of the disaffected elements of the population in Leningrad, and there are no reported instances of genuine sabotage or other subversive acts instigated by the Germans. Most bona fide German agents were sent into Leningrad at a later date, from outside, and were used for the purpose of collecting intelligence.

As for the elements within the population that the authorities classified as enemy agents—that is, deserters, defeatists, speculators, rumormongers, and the like—the technique used to combat them was to mobilize the population to act as the eyes and ears of the authorities.[158] "Let us be vigilant and ruthless in dealing with cowards, panic-mongers, and deserters. Let us establish the strictest revolutionary order in our city," were the words of an appeal made on August 21.[159] On September 2 *Leningradskaia pravda* wrote: "No mercy to those who violate revolutionary order and public safety, to marauders, speculators, and hooligans who might try in these dangerous times to interfere with the workers of Leningrad in defending their city and fulfilling their sacred duty as patriots."[160]

The inhabitants were thus at the mercy of every busybody and juvenile spy-catcher. Large numbers of school children were particularly active in assisting the security operations of the militia and Komsomol. The average citizen, although willing to denounce people for what he believed to be spying or subversive activities, was less inclined to do so in the case of grumbling, rumormongering, and other expressions of discontent and anxiety. To combat these undesirable forms of behavior, the authorities had to rely on the regular security forces and Party activists.

There was actually very little activity that could be classified as anti-Soviet. Most disaffected citizens did not dare to oppose the authorities openly. The only instances of "organized" resistance that were reported were insignificant in their limited scope and intentions. A secret police officer reported that in September the imminent fall of Leningrad led "former Czarist officers, merchants, and the former Petersburg autocracy" to prepare for their liberation at the hands of the Germans:

> These animals showed their true faces. Assuming that the Germans would occupy the city at any moment, they, upon instructions from their fascist masters, began to draw up lists of Communists, of the Soviet *aktiv*. . . . The former officers and civil servants, headed by the White officer Vasiliev and the former member of the Petersburg Circuit Court Merkulov, began to organize in the city so-called "house committees." These committees were charged with collecting information on the Communists living in each house, on Komsomols, and on employees of the Soviets.[161]

One "agent," the son of a former Czarist officer, was said to have drawn up plans for the economic reconstruction of Leningrad under German occupation. Another "agent" and "German spy" formed a "series of counterrevolutionary groups" and organized a clandestine fascist "government." The police officer's article listed a number of "mentally retarded" teen-agers and "morally depraved women," children of parents who had been punished by the Soviet regime, and other spies and saboteurs, all of whom, of course, were caught in time: "In October a counterrevolutionary gang of fascist teen-agers, whose parents had been at one time condemned for anti-Soviet activities, was arrested. The aim of this gang was to give the Germans armed assistance in capturing the city. Their plan was to carry out armed raids on stores and food warehouses at the moment when the Germans reached the suburbs."[162]

It is clear that if these counterrevolutionary groups really existed, they involved very few people and in fact took no action, since they prepared to act only if the Germans took the city. It is also obvious that the last group described was not a group of counterrevolutionaries at all, but a gang of thieves seeking to profit from the disorder expected during the street fighting.

Since the leadership was trying to mobilize all available reserves, it now wanted to instill in people a sense of urgency and a readiness for self-sacrifice. Consequently, the leadership no longer made any attempt to hide the gravity of the crisis, although it still failed to give the Leningraders a clear picture of the military situation. There was in any case little possibility of hiding the danger, since everyone was aware that the Germans were within artillery range of the city. The newspapers and radio broadcasts were largely devoted to exhortations and appeals. Factual news, as before, was limited to the official bulletins of the Information Bureau released by Moscow, or to special feature reports on local matters. No maps of the Leningrad front were published in the city's newspapers. Yet it was inevitable that under siege conditions the Leningrad press devoted increasing space to local rather than national matters.

From August 22 to September 2 the warning given by Voroshilov, Zhdanov, and Popkov on September 21 that the enemy was trying to enter Leningrad was repeated nearly every day, either by the press or in published resolutions of factory workers.[163] While there were assurances that the Red Army would be victorious, propaganda did not go so far as to guarantee victory. Victory was made conditional on the people's energetic participation in the defense of the city and their readiness for self-sacrifice. This was particularly true of the propaganda after September 2. On that day the enemy was alleged to be "at the gates of Leningrad"; it would be impossible to stop him, the people were told, without "the most strenuous fight demanding sacrifice and privations"; preparations for street fighting were said to be necessary.[164] On September 16, at the height of the crisis, *Leningradskaia pravda* ran the headline "The Enemy Is at the Gates." It warned that a German penetration into the city was possible at any moment.[165] After that the propaganda was very cautious in admitting that the danger had declined.

In view of the proximity of the fighting, the inhabitants had in fact a fairly accurate idea of the general situation around Leningrad. No one doubted that the city was in immediate danger. The sound of guns at the front was audible throughout most of the city, and people knew of the evacuation of the southern districts. The stabilization of the front after September became known both because Soviet propaganda claimed that it had occurred and because the Germans had failed to enter the city when expected. The general location of the front line inevitably became common knowledge, since it was so close.

As before, the Informburo was not very helpful in presenting a true picture of the situation. It made no mention of the proximity of the enemy. Nor did the communiqués report the fall of Schlusselburg and Mga. Of course, these omissions did not remain a secret for long in Leningrad. The fact that the Germans had cut the last railroad line at Mga soon came to be known because those scheduled to be evacuated were forced to return and all further evacuation proceeded by air and water.[166] After a while even the official publications spoke of the blockade of Leningrad, but no mention was made of the exact extent of the German encirclement.

The control measures instituted by the authorities and the fact that the leadership gave no evidence of serious weakening had their effect on popular behavior. Even though the fall of Leningrad appeared imminent and even though (according to all informants) it was generally believed that the city contained large numbers of disaffected persons who eagerly awaited the coming of the Germans, or at least wanted an end to the fighting under any conditions, public expressions of anti-Soviet sentiments then and later remained largely restricted to private conversations between family members or friends. There were no public demonstrations, speeches, or appeals. Except for standing in line, waiting for food or transport, people had little occasion to exchange views in public; and all informants report that the Leningraders were generally afraid to talk too freely while waiting in line because they believed the authorities were watching. Consequently, only when darkness provided anonymity for the speaker or when a particularly exasperating situation occurred, such as a long wait in line for food, were there any public expressions of discontent.

Soviet propaganda, of course, continued its efforts to instill in the population hatred and fear of the Germans and to preserve a high level of morale. To this end it emphasized the same themes as earlier: the cruelty of the enemy, local and national patriotism, the examples set by loyal citizens, and the inevitability of a Soviet victory. Because popular participation in the defense of the city was essential, because the outcome of the struggle was so uncertain, and because life under these conditions was so difficult, it was particularly desirable to show that surrender was a horrible alternative to continued resistance. In the appeal of August 21 to the population of Leningrad, the leadership described the objectives of the enemy as follows:

He is out to wreck our homes, seize our factories and mills, plunder our public property, drench the streets and public squares with the blood of innocent victims, torment the civilian population, and enslave the free sons of our country. . . .

In his ferocious hatred of our country and our people, this vile and malicious foe does not shrink from bombing peaceful cities or from shooting women and children. [167]

The description of German atrocities soon became more specific. For example, an appeal addressed to the women of Leningrad used these words:

Do you know what the fascists have done at the approaches to Warsaw? They executed 5,000 people—mostly women and children. They buried them in a ditch and built a road over the spot.

The dishonored girls of Belorussia are still moaning. The maddened mothers of Chernigov are still crying. Ragged and naked orphaned children are roaming the streets of Kiev.

Remember this; defend your children, whose lives are now threatened.[168]

To appeal to local patriotism, propaganda referred as before to Leningrad's glorious history, its cultural and artistic heritage, its role as the cradle of the Russian revolution, and the fact that it had never yet been captured.[169] Propaganda also called upon the collective and individual pride of the citizens: it appealed to collective pride by contrasting the individual coward or defeatist with the collective body of inhabitants eager to resist, and it appealed to the individual by placing upon him the responsibility for the fate of the city:

If the insolent enemy tries to break through to our city, he will find his grave here. We Leningraders, men and women, all the patriots of the city, acting as one—from the smallest to the biggest—will throw ourselves into the deadly fight with the fascist robbers. We will fearlessly and unselfishly defend each street, each house, each stone of our great city.[170]

Or again: "The enemy is at the gates! Let each Leningrader clearly realize that the fate of our city depends now in large measure upon himself, on his conduct, his work, his willingness to make every sacrifice, his courage."[171]

The resolutions of the factory workers all spoke of their united decision to fight on to death and not give up the city, and warned the soldiers that the people would not tolerate cowards or deserters in the ranks of the army:

With great pain and bitterness we hear that among you [soldiers] there are sometimes cowards and deserters. . . . The coward and deserter thinks that he will succeed in hiding from the people's censure and anger. He is mistaken. He will be cursed by his own mother, his wife will turn from him, his name will be spoken with loathing by his own children. With hatred and contempt—that is how his friends and comrades will greet him. A bullet in the head—that is what such a scoundrel and self-seeker will get. For a dog —a dog's death![172]

In their appeals to women, young people, workers, and other groups, the leadership tried to show that all were united in their will to resist the enemy. They also continued to hold up for example individual acts of heroism, whether in the factory or at the front, and special instances of devotion to duty. Among the techniques used on the armed forces was a letter campaign, which consisted of school children asking the soldiers to kill the enemy and drive him back. One such letter read:

Darling Father: I am studying very hard here at home, as I promised you I would. You at the front must strike harder at the enemy who had the gall to attack our great cities and villages. Defend my home, the city of Leningrad, where I was born and where I have grown up.

Give all your comrades my Pioneer [Communist children] salutations, so that, together with you, they will destroy the enemy as soon as possible.[173]

Workers and other civilians also sent letters and delegations to the front asking the soldiers to fight harder and promising to send them more weapons. Conversely, military delegations were sent to the factories and other organizations asking the civilians to do their utmost to help the army.

Another propaganda theme aimed at overcoming the feeling of being forgotten by the rest of the country, a feeling that the besieged population was apt to get. After the appeal of August 21, messages of encouragement and support (principally from groups of factory workers) began to arrive from all over Russia. Stalin did not send a message, but there was one from Kalinin, chairman of the Presidium of the Supreme Soviet, who wrote in August: "Comrade Leningrader! The entire Soviet Union is with you—everybody, little or big, is watching with great attention and excitement your selfless struggle with the enemy. Thousands upon thousands would have liked to be in the forward positions with you."[174]

Much was made of a poem by the Kazakh poet Dzhambul called "Leningrad, My Children," which was reprinted by the Leningrad press, distributed in leaflet form, and posted on billboards all over the city.[175] Of course, Leningrad reciprocated when Moscow, Odessa, or other cities were in danger.

Editorials in the local press also reminded the inhabitants, particularly during the critical period of the battle, that the eyes of the whole country were upon them. On September 11 the editorial in *Leningradskaia pravda* was headed "Leningraders, the whole country is with you"; it continued:

In this hard, grim struggle we are not alone. Millions of workers of the Soviet Union and of the whole world are watching our defense effort with excitement. All Soviet citizens are ready to fight with us to the last drop of blood to preserve the city that has given so much for the good of mankind.

The entire Soviet land is with us, heroic Leningraders! With us are the workers of Moscow and the Urals, of Donbass and Baku, of Kiev and Kharkov, the collective farmers of the Kuban and the Ukraine, of the Volga and Siberia. With us are the mountaineers of the Caucasus and the hunters of the Polar region, the cotton growers of Azerbaidzhan and Uzbekistan. The defense of Leningrad is a national undertaking.

The whole country is with us! The whole of progressive mankind is with us! We shall win![176]

The population of Leningrad was also exposed, although to a far lesser degree, to German propaganda, which aimed at undermining the city's morale and speeding its surrender. Since the population had had to turn in its radios to the authorities, the German effort consisted mainly in dropping leaflets over Leningrad and the surrounding countryside. Because the Germans believed that they would be able to capture Leningrad in September, their leaflet campaign was limited in scope.

In an effort to prevent the leaflets from having any effect, the Leningrad authorities forbade the reading or circulating of them and dispatched special squads to the drop areas to collect and destroy them.[177] Inevitably some leaflets were read despite the risks attached to such action. The majority of the population, however, never saw any of them. None of the persons interviewed by the author recalled having seen any leaflets. Yet their contents were widely disseminated by word of mouth.[178]

On the whole the leaflets were too crude and uninspiring to be effective. In August and September they asked that Leningrad be declared an open city to avoid unnecessary destruction and suffering for its inhabitants, denounced the "Jewish-Bolshevik leaders," and ridiculed the city's defense efforts.[179] At no time did they give the population a clear idea of what to expect in case of surrender, except for pointing out that Soviet police terror would end, as would the bombardment.

Many Leningraders felt repelled or insulted by the leaflets.[180] One ardent anti-Bolshevik who had eagerly awaited the arrival of the Germans noted in her diary after reading a German leaflet: "Everybody is in a funereal mood. Have we made a mistake here, too, and are the Germans just the way Soviet propaganda said?"[181] According to another source, people said: "What do they write in the leaflets?—'Little ladies, do not dig your little holes [construction of fortifications].' That is stupid, silly to read. Or that they hold Stalin's son captive. What do we care about Stalin's son? They should tell us what it will be like on their side, what we should expect."[182] Leaflets appealing to the population's national and local patriotism and denouncing the anti-Russian policies of the Communist regime appear to have been more favorably received.[183] However, many Leningraders for obvious reasons were anxious to know more about the Germans and to be reassured about them, and since German propaganda failed to answer their questions, it also failed to weaken their morale; on the contrary, because of its insulting tone, it even tended to strengthen local and national patriotism.

One of the claims that Soviet propaganda reiterated incessantly was that the Party represented the best elements of the Russian people. Purely ideological themes were largely absent from Soviet propaganda: it seldom mentioned that the survival of the Soviet system as such was at stake, or that Bolshevik rule should be defended by the inhabitants, although it did use much Soviet terminology, such as maintaining "Bolshevik discipline" or using "Bolshevik organizing ability." But in the press appeals to the population, whether to join the *opolchenie*, to build fortifications, or to increase industrial production, it was always proudly pointed out that Party and Komsomol members marched in the forefront of the volunteers and worked harder and with more determination than anybody else.[184] On September 7 the city's Komsomol committee appealed to the youth of Leningrad in these words:

In the front lines the Leningrad Komsomols, the youth of Leningrad is fighting bravely. . . . Worthy sons and daughters of our All-Union Communist Party of Bolsheviks.
Be worthy, children of our great fatherland.
Be worthy, citizens of the great city of Lenin. . . . On to feats of arms, youth, for the beloved city, for honor and freedom![185]

Assertions such as the following that the people were rallying around the Party and trusting it to lead them to victory were common:

In the grave days of the Fatherland War the toilers of our country are rallying even more closely around the Communist Party. Constantly new groups of non-Party Bolsheviks seek to formalize their ties with the beloved Party. Soldiers who have shown heroism and bravery at the front, commanders of the Red Army, heroes of Stakhanovite labor, scientific workers, and Komsomols are joining the Party.[186]

Thus the Party's claims to leadership were not made in the name of socialism, but on the basis of the Party's energy, performance, and readiness to set an example for others. In reality, of course, the Leningrad elite did not always measure up to the Soviet ideal. Not all members of the elite were iron-willed, self-disciplined, infinitely devoted, and ready to die at any time for the good of the Party and the country. The elite was after all only human and keenly aware that its own survival was at stake and in doubt. Its morale could not fail to be low. The demoralization and passivity of some of its members presented the leadership with a problem that might have become serious if the population had decided to riot or had revolted.

Since the elite had more access to information than the average citizen, it was more sensitive to bad news from the front. Indications of how frightened and depressed members of the elite were in this period can be found in the radio conversations between Leningrad and Moscow. Thus one functionary told his colleague in Moscow on September 6: "Unfortunately one cannot repeat the news, but there is uneasiness at the top and at the bottom. Things are in a bad way. The word 'bad' is not strong enough. The situation is below zero."[187]

During the next days doubts about Leningrad's survival increased.

One prominent Soviet writer noted in her diary that she was obsessed by the question "Will Leningrad hold out?" and that whereas she did not fear death, she hoped that she would escape torture at the hands of the Germans.[188] On September 24 the Party press admitted that some Party members were not displaying the proper attitude: "In these ominous days when life tests the steadfastness of the Bolshevik ranks, there are some Party members and candidates who show insufficient courage, show faintheartedness. The Party of Lenin and Stalin will not tolerate them for a single day in its ranks."[189]

Of course there was also criticism of the leadership for having been unable to prevent the situation from becoming so desperate. According to one source, some Party members and functionaries made such remarks as "It was wrong to have let it come to a war with Germany, whose army is invincible" and "Everything is badly organized"; others felt that the leadership had shown "complete lack of foresight." One woman said during an air raid: "It is before the war that we should have prepared and worked on serious business and not wasted time on all sorts of nonsense."[190]

As the gravity of the situation became increasingly apparent, some members of the elite, particularly in the lower echelons, began to worry about their own salvation. Since there was no possibility of escaping from the city, their only hope in the event of German occupation would be to go into hiding. But for this they needed the good will of the population if they were not to be denounced to the enemy or killed by anti-Communists. And this was essentially a forlorn hope, since most of the elite believed that there were many enemies of the regime among the population.

As the Germans approached, it would also have been logical for most of the elite to destroy their Party cards and other proofs of Party affiliation before going into hiding. But everyone knew that without official permission this was a treasonable act and that to commit it prematurely, while the leadership and its police organs were still in control, could result in harsh punishment. Consequently, there is no indication that any significant number of people actually did so.[191] Whatever destruction of Party cards there was probably occurred more often at the front than in the city, since the chances of being captured were greatest there. It is probable that a substantial number of the elite made preparations to destroy their Party cards, incriminating literature, and portraits of the leaders, and that some may have looked for a place to hide if the Germans entered the city; but few carried out these plans. One informant, for example, reports that he packed all his incriminating books, newspapers, and pictures in a suitcase so that he could drop it in a vacant lot or in the river if the Germans came any closer.[192] According to one source, some uniformed Party members stopped wearing their uniforms for a while in September.[193] But the overwhelming majority did not dare to show any lack of faith in the outcome of the battle. The burning of various official records may have been in part intended to protect certain elements of the elite, and it is possible that the NKVD took some additional steps, either individually or collectively, to safeguard its members or to go underground.

While the fate of Leningrad was still undecided and as long as the leadership was still in control, the majority of the elite, despite their fears and despair, had no choice but to remain at their posts and hope for the best. Since a German victory was the worst possible fate for most of them, it was in their own interest to continue to work and thus possibly delay or even avoid the disaster. The elite also appears to have had many dedicated members who refused to leave the city even when offered the chance, who joined the Party at this most critical time, and who fought and died for the city and the Communist cause. Outwardly, at least, the elite as a whole did not collapse. Consequently, the administrative structure and control system remained intact, giving the population the impression of a determined and active leadership still capable of imposing its will on them.

In return for its support the elite received certain rewards and privileges from the leadership. Its members had a better chance, for instance, of being evacuated from Leningrad than the rest of the population; they could try to manipulate their contacts in the city and in Moscow to arrange for evacuation orders. Of course, those in the higher echelons found this easier than those in the lower. Equally, if not more, important were privileges with respect to housing and, particularly, food. As the siege progressed, these advantages became of decisive importance.

The fact that the Soviet leadership had failed to the very last to anticipate the possibility of a prolonged siege is nowhere more clearly evident than in its failure to stock sufficient food in the city. On August 21 the city had sufficient food for only one month.[194] These reserves were augmented by supplies that were brought in from the Baltic region and from nearby districts endangered by the German advance and by some shipments of food from the Iaroslavskaia and Kalinin *oblasts*. Thus Leningrad received 21,900 tons of cereal and 1,400 tons of flour from the Baltic states, and 45,000 tons of grain, 14,000 tons of flour, and 3,000 tons of cereal from the Iaroslavskaia and Kalinin *oblasts*. In addition, 12,112 tons of meat (including horsemeat) were obtained by slaughtering herds of cattle that had been brought into the city.[195] Despite these additions, the available reserves were very small. During July and August the authorities shipped some of the food out for the use of the children who had been evacuated from Leningrad. On August 2 the Leningrad City Soviet authorized two food and two goods stores to sell special food for gifts to the soldiers. The stores sold 200 tons of special foods, such as chocolate, cocoa, and candy, and one million rubles' worth of the higher-quality cigarettes, before the leadership realized that it had to hoard the available supplies.[196]

The food situation was aggravated by the large number of people who remained in the city when its communications with the outside were cut off by the German advance. The exact number is not known. According to a Soviet historian, on September 6 ration cards for 2,489,-000 people were issued in Leningrad.[197] A former representative of the State Defense Committee, in discussing the food situation, placed the number of civilians in the city at 2,544,000. In addition, he reports that there were 343,000 residents of the surburban towns.[198] These figures did not include children who were living in children's homes, or resident students of trade schools and special schools, or the refugees who had not been given permanent resident permits, none of whom received ration cards. That the number of refugees in the city was very large is indicated by the fact that despite the evacuation, the monthly consumption of flour in August was 4,800 tons greater than during July.[199] It is therefore likely that the actual population of Leningrad was between 3,250,000 and 3,800,000,* of which 400,000 to 800,000 were refugees. Estimates on the total population made by informants and other Leningraders who were interrogated by the Germans varied between three and five million.[200] All who were questioned were greatly impressed by the number of refugees in the city.

A large number of those receiving ration cards were women and children. Out of the 2,443,400 ration cards issued in October, 831,400 were workers' cards, 407,300 were office workers' cards, 745,500 were cards for adult dependents, and 459,200 were children's cards; this gives us a total of 1,204,700 unemployed and dependent persons not counting those who were not entitled to receive ration cards.[201] These figures in-

---

* The population figure varies according to the method of calculation. According to Karasev, 147,500 refugees were evacuated from Leningrad by August 27 and possibly as many as 133,800 were evacuated during the period of September 1941 to April 15, 1942. Actually, a large number of refugees died during that time. Again according to Karasev, the average daily output of bread in Leningrad in August was 2,305 tons, which, at an average daily bread ration of 600 grams, would mean that there were 3,841,660 persons in the city. Karasev states that the daily bread output in August was 193 tons greater than that in July as a result of the influx of refugees; if each refugee received the minimal ration of 400 grams of bread a day this represented sufficient bread for 482,500 persons. But 636,203 persons were evacuated from Leningrad prior to August 27, who at the prevailing rations had consumed 250 tons of bread daily, so that the actual increase in bread consumption was 443 tons. At the rate of 400 grams of bread a day, this would represent a total of 1,107,500 persons. To this number must be added the refugees who reached the city after September (Karasev, *Leningradtsy v gody blokady*, p. 128).

dicate the degree to which Leningrad's authorities failed to complete the evacuation of the nonessential elements of the population from the city.

In the last days of August the city's Party and executive committees made a survey of all remaining food supplies. They found that there was enough flour for 14 days, cereal for 23 days, and meat and meat products for 19 days, which totaled only enough food to last until the end of September. The food reserves of the armed forces were equally low. On September 10 the armed forces had sufficient flour for 7 days, cereal for 14 days, fish for 10 days, fats for 8 days, vegetables for half a day, and horse feed for 10 to 11 days. In other words, on the basis of the prevailing rations they had supplies for only 7 to 14 days.[202]

In view of the scarcity of food reserves and the size of the population, it was clear that if the city faced a prolonged siege, starvation would be inevitable. On September 2, therefore, the bread ration was reduced. Workers and white-collar employees received 600 and 400 grams a day respectively, or 200 grams less than before, while dependents, non-workers, and children received 300 grams, or 100 grams less than before.[203]

In order to stretch the available supplies, it was decided on September 6 to add to the bread all sorts of admixtures, such as malt, corn flour, barley oat flour, soya flour, and other products.* By September 20 these admixtures constituted 40 per cent of the bread.[204]

This first reduction in the food ration appears to have been primarily a precautionary measure on the part of the local authorities. Since it was clear that the available supplies would stretch only for a short time, we may assume that the leadership did not believe in the likelihood of a prolonged siege. It is also possible that the leadership was awaiting a decision from Moscow on whether to surrender the city or whether to defend it.

On September 8 the Badaev food warehouses and several other storage areas were totally destroyed during a German air raid. According to eyewitnesses, "that night the streets ran with melted chocolate and the air was rich and sticky with the smell of burning sugar and wheat."[205] A Soviet writer then in Leningrad noted in her diary that the Badaev warehouses were "the central stores in Leningrad, the heart of the food supply system."[206] Popkov admitted in 1943 that "one of the reasons why we were short of food in the winter of 1941 was that some of our most important food stores were destroyed in an air raid."[207]

---

* There were 17,920 tons of various admixtures in Leningrad. On September 15, for example, the bread was made up of 52 per cent rye flour, 30 per cent oat flour, 8 per cent barley flour, 5 per cent soya flour, and 5 per cent malt.

The actual loss, while considerable, may not have been as great as some people believed. According to a former Soviet official, 3,000 tons of flour and 2,500 tons of sugar were destroyed in the Badaev warehouses.[208] Nevertheless, under the circumstances this was a severe loss, although it was possible to salvage some of the food.[209]

How the leadership came to commit so grave an error of judgment as to concentrate a large part of Leningrad's food reserves in one area, and in wooden buildings at that, despite its expectation of early air attacks on the city is difficult to understand. One possible reason is the administrative confusion that prevailed in the area of food control. According to a Soviet official, the food supply was "under the control of a dozen different economic organizations," none of which could make a move without instructions from Moscow.[210] Furthermore, the leadership had not anticipated a siege and thus had not been especially concerned with safeguarding the food reserves.

The administrative chaos in the area of food control had also led the various responsible agencies, in the absence of instructions from Moscow, to dispense the produce under their jurisdiction at the usual rate.[211] Finally, on September 10, the Council of People's Commissars of the USSR issued an order "on the norms of food supply to the troops and population of Leningrad" according to which the food rations were further reduced.[212] The daily bread ration of workers and office workers was reduced by 100 grams and that of adult dependents by 50 grams. At the same time, the monthly cereal ration was reduced by about a pound, and sugar and meats by 300 to 400 grams.* The fact that this decision was made by the Council of People's Commissars indicates the degree of centralization of decision then prevailing in the USSR; it also suggests that Moscow had reached a decision at that time to attempt to hold Leningrad at all costs.

The local authorities were given control over the food reserves and their distribution. The remaining civilian and military food reserves were pooled and placed under the authority of the Military Council of the Leningrad Front; they were administered by a committee, headed by Kuznetsov, that was known as the Food Supply Committee of the Leningrad Supply Committee of the Party.[213] To conserve food, the sale of supplies in the free market at higher prices was prohibited.[214] Because of shortages in specific types of food, various substitutions were

* Workers received 1,500 grams of meat, 1,500 grams of cereal, 2,000 grams of sugar, and 950 grams of fats; office workers received 800 grams of meat, 1,000 grams of cereal, 1,700 grams of sugar, and 500 grams of fats; adult dependents received 400 grams of meat, 600 grams of cereal, 1,500 grams of sugar, and 300 grams of fats; children under 12 years received 400 grams of meat, 1,200 grams of cereal, 1,700 grams of sugar, and 500 grams of fats (Pavlov, pp. 46–47).

made. Instead of meat, the population was issued "sausages of third quality"; cereal was replaced by potato starch, flour by vegetables, and sugar often by hard candy. In fact the population increasingly failed to receive all the rations to which it was entitled. The official rations of twenty pounds of potatoes and four to five pounds of cabbage were not issued in September.[215] By seizing the entire potato crop of the farms still under the control of the Leningrad authorities and by harvesting, sometimes under fire, the potatoes in the battle area, the city had a total reserve of 9,652 tons of potatoes or less than eight pounds per person.[216] Consequently, vegetables were issued first to hospitals, factory canteens, and the front-line troops, and only occasionally to the civilian population.

Pooling all reserves and counting all types of food substitutes, it was found on September 12 that the city had sufficient bread grains and flour for 35 days, cereals for 30 days, meat and meat products for 33 days, fats of all types for 45 days, and sugar and candy for 60 days. At the same time the daily consumption of flour, as a result of rationing and the use of admixtures, declined from 2,100 tons in the period September 1–11 to 1,300 tons after September 12, while the daily meat consumption amounted to 246 tons.[217] Thus even with lowered ration rates the city had sufficient food only until the end of October.

The movement of supplies across Lake Ladoga was not enough to maintain even the lowered ratio for any length of time. The State Defense Committee had given priority to the rail shipment of supplies to the lake, and Mikoyan had been given the task of organizing and directing the flow of supplies to Leningrad.[218] The airlift, for example, brought into the city only 40 to 45 tons of all types of supplies daily, although, according to directives issued by the State Defense Committee on September 20, it was supposed to deliver 100 to 150 tons a day.[219] The amount of food brought in by the 16 barges operating on Lake Ladoga also fell short of the transport plans. In 36 days only 9,800 tons of supplies were delivered to the port of Osinovets, which at the prevailing rate of rationing was sufficient food for only eight days.[220] According to another Soviet source, during September only 172 tons of food were brought daily to Leningrad as against an average of 2,000 tons consumed daily by the population.[221]

The rationing system, as before, gave preferential treatment to the essential or valuable elements of the population. Because of this discrimination and the reduction in rations, a certain amount of abuse, including the black-market sale of ration cards, soon developed. Cards were issued to employed persons by their employers, who sometimes issued two ration cards to one worker, or gave out unauthorized workers' ration cards instead of lower-category cards.[222] The Germans tried to disrupt the rationing system by dropping false ration cards by air, an operation that had little effect because new cards were issued soon after.[223] The attempt was not repeated.

The worsening food situation caused considerable excitement and anxiety among the population. The food shortage was not unexpected, since past experience had taught the people that such shortages always occurred in times of crisis; but the lowered rations made it obvious that many people would have to go hungry if the military situation remained unchanged for any length of time. The population was given no information about the actual state of the food reserves, except to be told that the reductions in rations were largely due to the destruction of the Badaev warehouses.

This many people apparently found hard to believe. Some Leningraders could not conceive that their leadership had been so careless as to fail to disperse the food supplies. Apparently some people preferred to think that the food reserves were larger than admitted by the authorities because they did not wish to face the prospect of starvation, or perhaps because they did not want to believe that their leadership, on which they were so dependent, could have been so grossly incompetent. Others, possibly more embittered or more imbued with anti-Soviet sentiments, chose to think that the authorities had stored the food in the suburbs and had been forced to destroy it because of the German advance, or that the food had been deliberately evacuated from the city to prevent it from falling into the hands of the Germans.[224] The informants also suggested that some people believed that the food shortage was artificially created by the authorities in order to keep the population dependent on the leadership and thus prevent a rebellion. It is interesting to note that in nearly all instances those who criticized the leadership preferred to believe that it was acting in a rational and calculated manner, no matter how Machiavellian its objectives were. Moreover, the full significance of the food situation was not yet grasped by most Leningraders in September; they expected the battle to result in a German victory or end with the re-establishment of communications with the outside. This tended to lessen popular anxiety about the future availability of food.

Nevertheless, many Leningraders, despite official prohibitions, attempted to lay in food stocks and find new sources of supply. Although the sale of food in the open markets in Leningrad was prohibited, there was no absolute control over or prohibition against the sale of private supplies by farmers to city dwellers, if the latter came to them to buy. Consequently, some Leningraders still sought to visit nearby villages to obtain food from the peasants, usually on a barter basis. The prohibition against hoarding meant that people returning to the city were liable to search by the militia, but this did not deter many Leningraders from trying, often successfully, to bring food into the city. In this respect the population apparently was sufficiently motivated to disregard the leadership's orders.

At this time the population also began to buy up those food items that were still unrationed, such as mustard, pepper, bone meal, starch, and laurel leaves. Only coffee and chicory were in ample supply.[225] Somewhat later cough drops and castor oil, which was to be one of the last remaining sources of fat, became popular.[226] Of course, supplies of these items were soon exhausted.

Considerable hardship was imposed upon the population by the poor organization of the sale of food. The authorities reduced the number of food stores in Leningrad, rather than expanding them as had been done in Moscow. By an order of the Executive Committee of the Leningrad City Soviet, issued on August 24, only 59 food stores and 54 bread stores were to remain open to the population.[227] Under the rationing system, bread had to be purchased daily, which forced the Leningraders to spend many hours standing in line.[228] It was also necessary to stand in line to buy other goods. One woman noted in her diary that she waited five hours to buy two kilograms of sugar beets.[229] People also spent hours going from one store to another in the hope that one of them would have for sale some of the rationed items that were issued only at irregular intervals. All this caused criticism of the authorities.

It was inevitable that a certain amount of criticism would be voiced over the inequalities of the rationing system. While the Leningraders, as before, took for granted the necessity of issuing larger rations to soldiers and workers, they dreaded having their wives and children go hungry and resented the privileged position of some elements of the elite, at least those they considered to be parasitic or opportunistic.[230] This privileged position was in a sense flaunted before the workers by the fact that the canteens and restaurants of the institutions and factories continued, as before the war, to serve different menus to the workers and the managers, the latter being in turn separated into the middle and upper elite. "The principle on which food was issued in enterprises was," as one informant put it, "based on rank."[231] But jealous though many Leningraders may have been of the privileged position of the elite, they did little more than occasionally grumble about it. As yet no one was starving, and such discrimination, though disliked, was not new, since it had been a normal feature of the Soviet system even before the war.

Leningrad's isolation affected the living conditions of the population in other ways. Severe shortages developed almost immediately, particularly in all types of fuel. There was little liquid fuel left for heating and cooking. There was only enough coal for heating for 60 to 65 days and only enough fuel for the bakeries for 60 days.[232] Consequently, the population was not issued its normal firewood supply on which the majority were dependent for heating and cooking. Nor could it lay in reserves for the winter, as was usually done during the summer. However, during August and September the shortage of fuel for domestic use was generally not critical. During September the population was issued a last kerosene ration of 2.5 liters per person.[233] By the end of September the situation became more serious, since most of the available coal had been used up and the remaining firewood would have been barely sufficient for two weeks of normal use in summer.[234]

The situation with regard to electric power was worse. On September 6, for instance, a radio message to Moscow from Leningrad explained a temporary interruption in radio transmission as being due to the power shortage and also reported a shortage of power for industrial use.[235] The bombardment also played its part in disrupting the power supply by breaking cables and destroying one minor power station.

On September 11, therefore, by order of the city's executive committee, electricity was rationed.[236] The use of electricity in homes and offices was sharply curtailed. Citizens were forbidden to use electrical appliances in their homes, whether for heating, cooking, or any other purpose. Control over the proper observance of the limits set for electric lighting was given to the house managers. Violators were to be fined five times the cost of the electricity they used above the authorized limit; anyone caught using electrical appliances was to be deprived of electricity and jailed for six months or fined 3,000 rubles. Office and industrial administrators who committed violations were liable to similar fines and jail sentences. The amount of electricity allotted to each household varied with its location and record of normal use. In general, electricity was available for a few hours each day, but at different times in different parts of the city. The hours were often very inconvenient, too—late at night or early in the afternoon.[237]

As noted earlier, all private telephones had been disconnected. In addition, all local telegraph offices were closed, leaving only the central office open. The lack of electricity prevented people from hearing broadcasts over their wired radio loud-speakers, but the public loud-speakers in the streets continued to function both for propaganda and for civil defense purposes.[238]

The shortage of electric power and fuel also affected public transportation. Bus service stopped entirely owing to lack of gasoline. Streetcars continued to operate, but fewer in number, and the lines were sometimes blocked by debris from the bombardment. It became more and more difficult for the Leningraders to travel to and from their jobs or to visit each other.[239]

The authorities did take some steps to try to maintain existing living conditions, particularly with regard to preparing the houses for winter, a yearly feature of life in Leningrad. On September 17 the Executive Committee of the Leningrad City Soviet issued an order directing the *raion* executive committees, the Leningrad housing administration, and the house managers to repair broken windows, roofs, and doors; to prepare the central heating systems for use; to insulate water, sewage, and central-heating pipes in attics, cellars, and empty apartments; and to take other similar measures.[240] These preparations were to be effected largely by the efforts of the residents of the buildings, with whatever material they could find. The house managers were warned that they would be held responsible for all breakdowns due to their failure to make the buildings in their care ready for winter. Actually there was too much else to be done and too little to do it with for much to be accomplished. Many windows and roofs broken by the bombardment were not repaired at all. In view of the shortage of window glass, many windows were simply boarded over hastily with plywood, and many pipes were not sufficiently insulated to prevent their freezing in unheated houses.[241] These omissions later had serious repercussions on living conditions.

In the midst of all these difficulties, many cultural and scientific facilities and organizations continued to function. The research, literary, and other intellectual and cultural institutions still remaining in the city continued their activities. Since people engaged in intellectual work were following set programs, like everyone else, they could not abandon their projects except when ordered to do so or if their institute was evacuated. Libraries—Leningrad's Central Public Library was the second largest in the Soviet Union—also remained open, as did motion picture houses and some theaters.[242]

It was not possible, of course, to maintain even a semblance of a normal atmosphere in the city. Naturally, many people were very pessimistic about Leningrad's chances of avoiding capture. The Germans had successfully overcome all the forces and fortifications that had barred their way; it seemed inconceivable that they would not advance the few remaining miles to the city. One informant was told by a friend, "The state is dying, everything is falling apart, everything is coming to an end."[243] Yet although the population had lost confidence in the efficacy of the remaining defenses, many people expected that the leadership would attempt to defend Leningrad street by street, as Madrid had been defended in the Spanish Civil War, even if it meant the city's destruction. The Leningraders pictured the German conquest not as a military parade but as a fierce battle that would cost the civilians dearly.[244] There were some who felt that the city should be defended to the last and others who believed any defense to be senseless and far too costly.[245] Others, frightened by the bombing and the expected street fighting, said, "If only there was some sort of end to all this," apparently not caring which side won.[246] Not a single informant appears to have doubted that the Red Army would remain loyal and fight to the end. Regardless of whether they were in favor of defense or surrender, most inhabitants knew there was very little they could do to influence events one way or the other.

The increasing likelihood of a German conquest of Leningrad led greater numbers of people to cling to favorable rumors about the Germans, or to engage in wishful thinking. Some members of the intelligentsia, for example, thought that they could continue their usual activities just as well under enemy occupation.[247] Others who were more hesitant, either because of nationalistic sentiments or because of doubts raised by Soviet propaganda about German intentions, felt that the fall of the city could not be avoided, but hoped that it would come about as painlessly as possible.[248]

The situation also tended to undermine the Leningraders' respect for their leaders. Many people apparently were ready to give credence to various derogatory rumors about them. For example, informants report that during September it was rumored that Zhdanov and Voroshilov either had fled Moscow or were living at an airfield in order to be able to flee at a moment's notice.[249] There was also criticism of Stalin, whom some people held responsible for having ordered the last-ditch defense of Leningrad, regardless of civilian cost, and for being prepared to destroy the city if the Germans entered it.[250]

Nevertheless, on the whole the population continued to be conformist in its behavior. Even though some people thought that only a speedy German occupation could prevent destruction of the city and suffering on the part of its inhabitants, no one was willing to take an active part in bringing about Leningrad's surrender. This was not surprising. After all, if the German victory was inevitable, there was no need to help it along. Even those most disaffected thought it foolish or pointless to run risks in order to bring about a situation that they expected to occur in any event.

The majority of the population, however, being torn between a genuine patriotic desire to help defend Leningrad and fear of the consequences of such a defense, kept hoping for the best. Believing themselves to be the victims of circumstances, they did not contemplate action. Moreover, since they were politically passive, the Leningraders continued to rely on the authorities to tell them what to do, and did not conceive of engaging in independent activities so long as the leadership gave no evidence of being ready to abdicate its controls.

PART III: *T*HE SIEGE

Chapter 6

*T*HE THREAT OF COMPLETE ENCIRCLEMENT
September 25–December 15, 1941

A‌T THE END OF SEPTEMBER the Leningrad front was stabilized after months of hard fighting. The Germans reported that "Voroshilov's armies had lost fearfully in blood and their lines of defense were held among others by companies of women, cadets, and workers."[1] But the German forces, too, had suffered heavy losses. Even though Leningrad was now a secondary theater of operations for the Germans, their final objective remained the capture and destruction of the city.

It became evident immediately that, for the purposes of an airtight encirclement and siege, Hitler had halted the attack at an unfavorable moment. The "close encirclement" of the city prescribed in the Führer's plan was in reality a wide arc, too distant from Leningrad to permit bombardment of the city except by heavy long-range artillery. Furthermore, the ring had little depth on the eastern side, so that continuous Soviet attacks were made in this area in an effort to break through to Leningrad. Finally, although the Germans discounted its value, Leningrad retained a line of communication via Lake Ladoga with the interior of the Soviet Union.

The siege line, as it was established in mid-September and as it remained substantially until January 1943, began on the shore of the Gulf of Finland at Novoikerzon and then curved eastward in a semicircle to Petergof and Uritsk, both cities also being on the coast and within sight of Leningrad. Within this arc, which faced the island fortress and naval base of Kronstadt, was the so-called Oranienbaum encirclement defended by the Soviet Eighth Army. No assault on Kronstadt and the western side of Leningrad was possible until the Oranienbaum forces had been destroyed. These forces were supplied by sea, and later over the ice, and were supported by naval and coast artillery. This beachhead not only tied down a number of German divisions needed elsewhere, but also constantly threatened the flank of the German forces that held Petergof and Uritsk. From Uritsk the front swung in a semicircle through Pushkin, Dudergof, Kolpino, and Izhora to Schlusselburg on the shore of Lake Ladoga. Only the western portion of this arc was within artillery range of a major part of Leningrad. From Schlusselburg the front followed the shore of Lake Ladoga for a few miles, then swung sharply southeastward to the vicinity of Kirishi, and from there followed the Volkhov River south, via Novgorod, to Lake Ilmen. At its narrowest point, near Schlusselburg, the depth of the encirclement was less than ten miles. Below Lake Ilmen the German Sixteenth Army had pushed forward during September into the Valdai Hills beyond Demiansk and was in touch with the Ninth Army of Army Group Center. On the Karelian Isthmus the Finnish advance had come to a halt a few miles beyond the old frontier, some 12 to 15 miles from Leningrad. On the eastern shore of Lake Ladoga the Finns and Germans held the northern bank of the Svir River, but were too weak to push across it. The shore of Lake Ladoga between the front and the Svir River was in Soviet hands. Thus a considerable gap existed between Army Group North and the Finns, and the survival of Leningrad depended in large measure on the ability of the Soviet defenders to prevent the junction of these forces.

The months of fighting had inflicted heavy losses on the Red armies defending Leningrad, but had not destroyed them. According to the testimony of von Leeb:

My battles took place mainly as heavy frontal fighting. As a consequence, the number of prisoners captured by my army group in comparison with the number of prisoners taken by Army Groups South and Center is a rather modest one. The number of prisoners taken by the two armies, the 16th and 18th, until the end of December, amounted to approximately 200,000 to 220,000.[2]

The actual size of the defending Soviet forces is not known precisely. In all probability, it was composed of about 200,000 men, exclusive of the *opolchenie*.[3] This force had little offensive capability, since it could not be resupplied from the outside without the greatest of difficulty and then only to a very limited degree. Consequently, Soviet operations tended to shift to the eastern part of the ring, where there was room for maneuver and where the outside relief forces of the Russians could be brought into play. The subsequent history of the fighting on the Leningrad front consisted primarily of Soviet attempts to break the encirclement by attacking from the east and German efforts to retain their grip on Leningrad.

Although Leningrad had been saved from immediate capture, from the viewpoint of the Soviet command the military situation after September continued to deteriorate: the Germans' decision to starve out and destroy the city, their attempt to advance to the Svir River, and their assault on Moscow gave events a far from encouraging turn. All these developments raise further doubts about the ability of Leningrad to survive for any length of time. Yet the loss of Leningrad meant the destruction of the Baltic fleet, the junction of the German forces with the Finns, and the possibility of a wide German encirclement operation aimed at Moscow from the north. The Soviet command therefore had to do its utmost to preserve Leningrad and to relieve the besieged garrison.

The Germans, and particularly Hitler, did not doubt their ability to keep their ring around Leningrad. They were also optimistic about the outcome of the siege, since they assumed that the city would fall like a ripe apple as soon as the inevitable famine set in. In the meantime Hitler, indulging some wishful thinking, issued orders that were totally out of proportion with German capabilities in the area.

To speed the surrender of Leningrad and to avoid any unnecessary drain on the meager food supplies in the area of Army Group North, the Germans had decided that every effort should be made to prevent the encircled population from escaping through the German lines. The exaggerated reports of the besieging forces, claiming that great numbers of civilians were filtering through German positions around Leningrad, had served to confirm the wisdom of this decision, and on September 18 an order had been issued to prevent such escapes at all costs.[4] To spare the sensitivity of the German soldiers, the order provided that artillery should "prevent any such attempts at the greatest possible distance from [the German] lines by opening fire as early as possible, so that the infantry, if possible, [would be] spared shooting on civilians."[5] This order was repeated two months later, when the German news agency DNB also reported that large numbers of civilians had fled from Leningrad through the German lines.[6]

On September 22 Hitler had decided "to wipe the city of Petersburg [Leningrad] from the face of the earth" and to turn down all requests for capitulation.[7] A letter to the Naval Chief of Staff on September 29 elaborated on this decision as follows:

The Führer has decided to erase from the face of the earth St. Petersburg. The existence of this large city will have no further interest after Soviet Russia is destroyed. Finland has also said that the existence of this city on her new border is not desirable from her point of view. . . .

It is proposed to approach near to the city and to destroy it with the aid of an artillery barrage from all weapons of different caliber and with large air attacks. . . . The problem of the life of the population and the provisioning of them is a problem which cannot and must not be decided by us.

In this war . . . we are not interested in preserving even a part of the population of this large city.[8]

Previously the German Naval Operations Staff had asked that in "bombing, occupying, or attacking Leningrad the dockyards, wharf installations, and all of the special naval installations be spared," so that they could be used later by the Germans. Hitler had turned down this request.[9] Apparently there was some discussion of Hitler's order, for on October 7, 1941, it was announced:

The Führer has again decided that a capitulation of Leningrad or, later, of Moscow is not to be accepted even if it is offered by the enemy . . . therefore no German soldier is to enter the city. By our fire we must force all who try to leave the city through our lines to turn back. The exodus of the population through the smaller unguarded gaps toward the interior of Russia is only to be welcomed. Before the cities are taken they are to be weakened by artillery fire and air attacks, and their population should be caused to flee.[10]

Hitler's failure to capture the city of course embarrassed him. He "wavered between irrational certitude of victory and recurrent fits of pessimism"[11] and took refuge in bombastic declarations. On November 8 Hitler publicly declared: "[Leningrad] is surrounded and no one will free it again and it will fall into our hands."[12] In answer to statements that the Germans were on the defensive before Leningrad, Hitler said:

We were on the offensive before Leningrad as long as it was necessary in order to encircle Leningrad.

Now we are on the defensive and the opponent must break out, for he will starve in Leningrad. I will not sacrifice one more man than necessary. If today there were someone to relieve Leningrad then I would give the command to storm the city and we would take it by storm, for whoever advanced from the East Prussian border to within 10 km. before Leningrad can also march these 10 km. into the city. . . .

I have no interest in any such cities as Leningrad, but only in the destruction of the industrial centers of Leningrad. If it suits the Russians to blow up these cities, they save us, perhaps, much work.[13]

Actually the forces necessary for storming the city were no longer available, but the statement once more indicated that Hitler planned to destroy Leningrad and its population. This German plan appeared to leave Leningrad's population little choice, since a surrender was not likely to improve their situation to any considerable extent.

Hitler's grandiloquent order to wipe out the city completely had little hope of being realized; for, to put it into practice, it would have been necessary for the Germans not only to have at their disposal a very large bomber force, but also to get close enough to Leningrad to bring to bear medium- and small-caliber artillery. Numerically the air force was too small to comply with Hitler's orders, and furthermore it was seriously handicapped by climatic conditions. By December the Germans had only 100 fighters and 150 bombers as against 185 Soviet planes.[14] The cold had a devastating effect on the German planes: motors refused to run, hydraulic systems did not work, guns did not shoot. There was no preheating equipment. Only 10 per cent of the planes in some squadrons were operational.[15] Since throughout this period a large part of the German air force had to be used in ground support and interdiction operations along the entire front of the army group, there were relatively few planes left for raiding Leningrad.

The artillery available to the Germans for this purpose was also inadequate to accomplish the desired result. Although the Germans apparently had a definite local superiority in artillery, the Russians helped to compensate for their inferiority by dismantling the guns from crippled and immobilized warships and installing them around the defense perimeter of the city.[16] Counterfire from Soviet batteries and Soviet air attacks played a role in limiting the effectiveness of the German bombardment.[17] Prisoners of war reported in interrogations that the German artillery had a high proportion of duds.[18] But since artillery fire was unaffected by the weather, the bombardment of Leningrad continued.

Although Hitler professed certainty about the eventual fall of Leningrad, he nevertheless tried to tighten the German stranglehold on the city even while preparing for a direct advance on Moscow. While the commander of Army Group North had been instructed to surround Leningrad rather than to assault it, he was also instructed "to concentrate his efforts on pushing forward in the direction of Tikhvin and the Murmansk railway."[19] It was hoped that the German-Finnish forces poised on the Svir River would also advance toward Tikhvin, thereby closing the ring around Leningrad and preventing any supplies from reaching it via Lake Ladoga. At that time Tikhvin served as a major supply and rail center both for Leningrad and for the Soviet forces attempting to break through the German encirclement from the east.

At the same time Army Group North was given the task of advancing its right flank into the Valdai Hills to cover and support the advance of Army Group Center on Moscow. If the Germans succeeded in attaining these two objectives, the fall of Leningrad was inevitable.

On October 2 the offensive against Moscow, under the code name of *Taifun,* was launched by 69 divisions, of which 14 were armored. Under Field Marshal von Bock, Army Group Center, which included three armies and three panzer groups, began to advance along a 480-mile front from the Valdai Hills to Romny, some 225 miles from Moscow.

The offensive, which caught the Russians by surprise, made rapid strides. On October 3 the Second Panzer Group under General Guderian took Orel, while the Third and Fourth Panzer Groups attempted to encircle the Russian defenses at Viazma. On October 7 Viazma was taken. Two days later Guderian's forces encircled other large Russian groups in the Briansk area, trapping some 660,000 Red Army soldiers. While these encircled forces were being destroyed, other German units reached Kalinin and Rzhev, about 100 and 130 miles northwest of Moscow, respectively, on October 13. By October 15 the Fourth Army and the Fourth Panzer Group broke through the hastily constructed fortifications at Borodino and captured Kaluga and Borovsk, 90 and 55 miles southwest of Moscow. The remnants of the Red Army then withdrew to new positions about 40 miles west of Moscow.[20]

The collapse of the armies guarding Moscow led the Soviet leadership to expect the fall of the capital. On October 15 a hurried evacuation began, which soon took on the qualities of flight. Governmental and Party agencies, as well as entire industrial installations, left the city. Archives and documents were burned. Hundreds of officials and other members of the elite left with or without authorization. On October 20 a state of siege was declared. Although further unauthorized flight was halted and some order restored, the evacuation of the city continued as the Germans drew daily nearer.[21]

Even though the German advance was slowed down by rains and early snows, which transformed the roads into seas of mud, Mozhaisk and Maloiaroslavets fell on October 18. On the Nara River the Germans were held up by hastily erected fortifications and fresh Russian forces, some of which were beginning to reach Moscow from Siberia. Nevertheless, after mopping up the Briansk pocket, Guderian resumed his attempt to encircle Moscow from the south on October 22. Despite fierce Russian resistance he reached Tula on October 29, but was unable to capture it. At this point the German offensive, bogged down in the mud and in the face of strong resistance, came to a temporary halt, while plans were made for a new assault on Moscow.[22]

In the context of the battle of Moscow, that of Leningrad assumed a new importance in the eyes of the Soviet leadership. Each enemy division tied down at Leningrad was one less available for use against Moscow, and the defense of the capital took precedence over all other considerations. Therefore, although Leningrad's interests would probably have been best served if the defending forces had been given time to reorganize and prepare for a major attack in conjunction with relief forces advancing from outside, the defenders were made to expend their strength in attacks designed to divert German forces from the Moscow operation.

The present war demands many sacrifices. In bloody battles the Hitlerite lords have succeeded in seizing a considerable part of our territory. We have lost much. . . . But the supreme sacrifice—Moscow—we shall not make. Never and at no price! We will lay down our lives, but we will not let the enemy pass to the capital. . . .

The best assistance to Moscow is the defeat and destruction of the Hitlerite bands before Leningrad. . . .

In some sectors of the Leningrad front our front-line troops are continuously attacking the Germans, wearing out and annihilating their forces and equipment. . . . The fascists are suffering great losses before Leningrad; in some sectors under the pressure of our troops they are forced to quit their prepared positions and withdraw.[23]

In order to assist the forces defending Moscow, Leningrad was also required to send them by air over one thousand artillery and mortar pieces and large quantities of shells, mines, communication equipment, and other supplies.[24]

On November 29 General Zhukov, who had left Leningrad to take command of the western front defending Moscow, sent a telegram to Zhdanov thanking "the Leningraders for their assistance to the Muscovites in their struggle with the bloodthirsty Hitlerites."[25]

The Soviet High Command was aware that Leningrad was unlikely to survive if the city remained cut off from the rest of the country. It therefore seemed essential to break the encirclement as soon as possible. Consequently, an attack plan was drawn up that provided for an offensive by the 54th Army from Volkhov, with the objective of capturing Mga, coinciding with an attack by the Leningrad forces that would try to establish a junction with the troops advancing from the East. The 54th Army was placed under the control of the Military Council of the Leningrad Front. At the same time, the Leningrad forces sought to cross the Neva River east of Leningrad. During September they succeeded in establishing a small bridgehead, but despite fierce fighting involving heavy losses were unable to expand it further. To the east the 54th Army began its attack on September 26, but made very little headway. Fighting continued through October with little result. In November the objectives of the Soviet attack changed, turning from the relief of Leningrad to the assistance of Moscow. The Leningrad forces, reinforced by a division of NKVD troops, launched repeated attacks, all of which were repulsed by the Germans. The 54th Army was forced by the German advance on Tikhvin and Volkhov to cease its attacks and to devote all its efforts to the defense of Volkhov.[26]

The Germans had launched an attack in the direction of Tikhvin on October 26. They advanced slowly over very difficult terrain and in the face of strong Russian resistance.[27] On November 9 they finally captured Tikhvin. They also advanced to the vicinity of Volkhov and

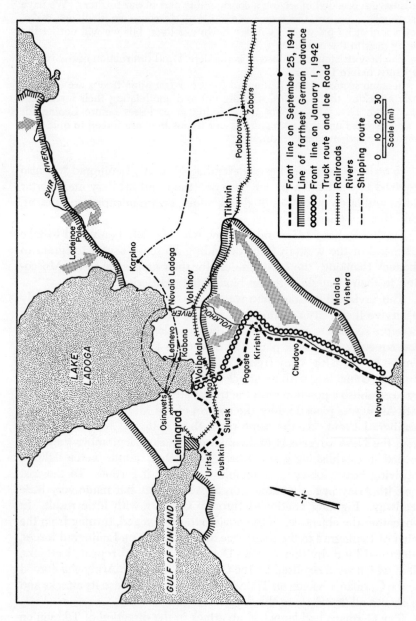

The German Advance to Tikhvin

Voibokalo in the north and Malaia Vishera in the south. There, however, they were halted by the 54th Army without being able to reach the
coast of Lake Ladoga. A contact with the forces advancing south
across the Svir River also failed to materialize. The Finns and Germans
were held up both by Russian attacks and by the need to wait until the
river froze over. In the meantime the forces holding Tikhvin were
having difficulty retaining the ground they had captured and vainly
pleaded for help. Attempts to capture Volkhovstroi and the hydroelectric power plant in Volkhov were beaten off, but the Soviet authorities were forced to dismantle the plant and evacuate it to a safer area.

During the following month both sides engaged in heavy fighting
for Tikhvin and the rail line west of it. The recapture of this city was
essential for the Russians if Leningrad was to survive the winter, even
if the Germans were prevented from joining up with their forces on
the Svir. As long as Tikhvin remained in German hands, it was impossible to supply Leningrad with the food and material necessary to
prevent its fall. If even a minimum flow of supplies into the city was
to be maintained, these would have to be brought by rail near to the
shore of Lake Ladoga, so that the limited number of available barges
and trucks could move them rapidly to the other shore. Thus it was
that Leningrad's fate hinged on that of Tikhvin, and consequently the
Red Army fought desperately to dislodge the Germans from this city.

In the meantime on November 16, with the support of several thousand artillery pieces, the Germans renewed their attack on Moscow.
The cold and the snow, as well as the defending troops, which were
reinforced by large forces from Siberia, slowed the advance to a crawl.
Nevertheless, the Germans continued their attempts to encircle Moscow
from the north and the south and to advance on it from the west. The
Second Panzer Group bypassed Tula and pushed on to Kashira and
Zaraisk. To the north the Germans took Klin, just 50 miles from Moscow,
on November 23, and by December 1 reached Krasnaia Poliana, 14
miles north of the capital. The German forces in the center inched forward against strong Russian counterattacks to a final position 25 miles
from Moscow, but were unable to advance any further. The stage was
set for a general Soviet counteroffensive along the entire front.[28] On
December 6 the Red Army attacked around Moscow and by January 1,
1942, had forced the Germans to retreat along their entire line of advance.

In the Tikhvin area, the Soviet offensive broke through the German
positions on December 4 and forced the Germans to leave the city on
December 8. Retreating from the Tikhvin salient, the Germans suffered heavy losses, many of them caused by the extreme cold. By mid-
December the Russians managed to reopen the railroad supply route

to Lake Ladoga. Two weeks later the Germans had recrossed the Volkhov River and were back in the positions they had held around Leningrad in September, before they launched their abortive offensive on
Tikhvin. Thus at the end of the year the Soviet authorities for the first
time had some grounds for cautious optimism. The *Blitzkrieg* had
failed, and neither Moscow nor Leningrad had fallen to the enemy,
although the fate of the latter was still far from certain.

Chapter 7

LENINGRAD TIGHTENS ITS BELT
September 25–December 15, 1941

THE STABILIZATION of the Leningrad front in September did little to reduce the fears of the city's leadership. It knew only too well the weakness of its military forces and the grave shortages in the city's food, fuel, and military supplies. When the siege began in earnest, the leaders believed that either the German blockade would be speedily broken or the city would eventually be so weakened by hunger and shortages as to make surrender inevitable.

Initially, at least, the possibility of a protracted siege was not seriously considered by Leningrad's leadership, probably because it did not believe that Leningrad could survive a siege for any length of time. One official said later: "We all thought that it would be over in two or three weeks. . . . None of us believed that it would be a protracted affair."[1] Popkov, in an interview, gave this account of the situation: "We were forced to adopt the most drastic measures in the field of food rationing . . . so as to be able to hold out the necessary time until the troops of the Leningrad front could carry out their battle assignments: to break through the ring of the enemy blockade, to defeat and throw back from Leningrad Hitler's robber army."[2]

Yet by October not only had the efforts to break through the German blockade failed, but Moscow itself was in danger of being captured by the Germans. If this were to happen, there was little hope for Leningrad. In mid-October Leningrad's leadership was perfectly aware that Moscow was being hurriedly evacuated and that the Germans might reach it at any time.[3] On October 22 a resolution of Leningrad workers declared: "A deadly peril hangs over our great Moscow."[4] The survival of the Soviet regime and, indeed, of the Soviet Union was in doubt. Matters became even worse less than a month later, when the Germans seized Tikhvin in an attempt to achieve the complete encirclement of Leningrad.

These developments, together with the freezing over of Lake Ladoga, interfered with the shipment of supplies to Leningrad. Rations had to be reduced twice during November and were well below the subsistence level. The leadership was forced to announce that there was no hope of improvement in the immediate future.[5] A Leningrad radio official recalled his feelings of mid-November: "I remember how in the most awful period I laid hands by a miracle on a bottle of vodka. All of us gathered around it. We'd just issued the seventy-seventh news bulletin. I gave a toast: To the hundredth bulletin! This toast seemed just then to be the height of optimism and self-confidence."[6]

But before the hundredth news bulletin could be issued, the German forces around Moscow were driven back and Tikhvin was recaptured. It then became possible to hope that the city might be supplied over the ice of Lake Ladoga, if the Soviet offensives on the Ladoga and Volkhov fronts did not make this unnecessary. By mid-December the leadership, at least, began to feel slightly more optimistic. In the words of a Leningrad staff officer: "The battle of Moscow gave us complete confidence that it would be all right in the end."[7] However, conditions in Leningrad were so bad that during the second half of December the Soviet government made an attempt to resume negotiations with Finland through the Swedish Minister of Foreign Affairs (an overture that was rejected by Helsinki[8]), which may indicate that Soviet confidence was not too great.

Military developments were in any case overshadowed by the even greater threat of starvation. The acute shortage of food made it likely that either the army or the population or both would collapse, or even revolt when driven beyond their endurance by hunger, or that the army would be so weakened and demoralized that the smallest German push would take the city. Particularly in October and November, when the fall of Moscow was expected, and the survival of the Soviet regime appeared in doubt, there seemed to be little point for the Leningraders to continue their suffering. Even if there was no revolt, the food and fuel shortage seemed likely to paralyze the city to such an extent as to render further resistance meaningless.

The leadership was thus forced to realize that unless the supplies reaching Leningrad were considerably increased, there was no hope for the city at all. The emergency effort to bring in supplies by water and air transport had not been sufficient to maintain the ration level established in September.[9] The deliveries fell far short of Leningrad's needs; reserves of food and other supplies were rapidly dwindling. On October 1, for example, the reserves of flour in the city amounted to only

20,052 tons, which had to meet the needs of the armed forces and the population, who, between them, consumed over 1,000 tons of flour per day. One month later there were only 7,928 tons left.[10] Moreover, in early November Lake Ladoga began to freeze over, and shipments by water had to stop altogether. During the operation of the boat lift, the city had received a mere 45,000 tons of food (it had also received some gasoline and some much-needed ammunition).[11]

It became essential to find a way to re-establish communications with the outside over the ice on the lake. The famous ice road, or "life road," to whose existence Leningrad was to owe its survival, thus came into being.

Soviet literature is somewhat contradictory on the question of who should receive the credit for the idea of building the ice road. The contemporary literature gave the credit to Zhdanov and the Military Council of the Leningrad Front, whereas postwar publications, not surprisingly, gave it to Stalin and the State Defense Committee.[12] After the 1956 de-Stalinization, the credit reverted once more to the "city Party committee and the Military Council of the Leningrad Front."[13] In all probability the Military Council of the Leningrad Front initiated the plans for the road, and Moscow then approved them.[14]

In preparing to build the ice road, Zhdanov ordered scientific and technical studies to be made, only to find that little was known about the problem. To complicate the difficulty of planning, the lake did not freeze uniformly: strong winds made the ice pile up, and there were always some crevices that never froze over. The lake was not expected to be solidly frozen until mid-December, but it was impossible to wait that long. On November 18, when the ice was five inches thick, a small reconnaissance party crossed the ice on foot, followed by a man on horseback. At that time the ice was only strong enough to bear horse-drawn sleds with light loads. But four days later a truck column succeeded in crossing (although some of its vehicles fell into the water) and returned on the next day with 33 tons of supplies.[15]

On November 19, the Military Council of the Leningrad Front decided to construct a "military automobile road," which was to cross over the ice of Schlusselburg Bay.[16] The military council and the city Party committee were to organize the road, but since it was a military road, the army was to operate it. A special administration, headed by a major general, was established for this purpose. Civilian personnel, who had been mobilized under the compulsory labor decree for work on the road, or for unloading supplies, were placed under military control. As usual, the Party was an active participant; numerous Party members were mobilized and dispatched to the road to help in its development.[17]

The road had to take account of the German capture of Tikhvin and the threat to the entire road network between that city and Lake Ladoga. Therefore, on November 24, the military council decided to build a road taking in the following points: it was to begin on Cape Osinovets on the western shore and then cross 18.6 miles over the ice to the village of Kabona; from there it was to pass through the trackless swamps and forests around the German salient at Tikhvin; and finally it would end up at the railroad stations of Podborove and Zabore east of Tikhvin—a total distance of about 237 miles.[18] While the road builders on the ice struggled with fissures, thin ice, lost convoys, and arctic blizzards, the road construction units east of the lake had to build an emergency track through the wilderness; they were given only two weeks to complete this operation and consequently paid little attention to road profiles, slopes, or road beds.[19] How desperate the situation was at that moment is illustrated by the fact that whereas at the minimum some fifteen days were needed to complete the ice road, Leningrad had sufficient flour for only seven days.[20] The Military Council of the Leningrad Front requisitioned for service on the road a large proportion of the available army trucks, while the Party and city authorities mobilized whatever vehicles they could find in Leningrad. (On November 26 the chairman of the Leningrad City Soviet mobilized 500 trucks and 100 tank trucks.[21]) Eventually ten trucking battalions were organized, many of the trucks being driven by civilians. These battalions comprised several hundred vehicles, chiefly one- and one-half-ton trucks, although there were also buses and in time three- and five-ton trucks.[22]

The Germans, of course, strafed and bombed the road and, where it was within range, bombarded it with artillery, particularly in the area on the ice track, where a large fissure always caused a pile-up of vehicles. During October, for example, there were 58 air attacks on Osinovets.[23] But enemy action was small hindrance in comparison to the difficulties caused by weather conditions and the primitiveness of the road. Nothing could be done about the blizzards, in which the drivers lost their way, nor about the cold, which killed the drivers and froze the engines, nor about the thinness of the ice. The track between the Ladoga and Zabore was so bad that accidents and losses were frequent. The continued operation of the ice road was an act of desperation, an example of how determined the leadership was to keep going at any cost. In all, 1,004 trucks were smashed or lost while navigating the road, and most trucks required repairs after each trip.[24]

But despite every effort the volume of supplies moved by December fell far short of the 2,000 tons per day that had been planned.[25] The main reason for this failure was the thinness of the ice, which forced the trucks to carry only half loads.[26] Only in January did the lake freeze sufficiently (three feet) to bear the weight of fully loaded heavy trucks.

From November to December the average daily delivery of supplies to Leningrad amounted to 361 tons.[27] Some of the initial shipments consisted almost entirely of gasoline to keep the trucks moving. To prevent the drivers from getting lost the trucks operated in convoys. Round trips often took ten to twenty days because traffic was held up for several days at a time owing to blizzards, breakdowns, poor loading and unloading facilities, improper organization of traffic control, insufficient road marking, lack of watering and fueling points, and other difficulties. Most trucks were in poor condition to begin with, and repairs were hasty or inadequate. Under these conditions control over the drivers was difficult to maintain. There were no norms set; there was no check on those who lagged behind or shirked work.[28]

The real tragedy of the situation lay in the fact that even if it could fulfill the plan, the ice road would be bringing in only the bare minimum of supplies necessary to prevent the complete collapse of the city.

To compensate for the cessation of water transport and the shortcomings of the ice road, an attempt was made to airlift supplies. In mid-October the authorities supplemented the earlier airlift by forming a special group known as the Northern Aviation Group, which flew from bases in Khvoinoe, Chirepovets, Podborove, and Kushever. This group carried mainly food and military supplies for the use of the army. In all, in the period of October 21 to December 31, a total of 3,357 tons of food was flown into Leningrad.[29]

Despite these efforts, by the end of the year Leningrad seldom had more than one or two days of food on hand. Experience soon showed that whereas it was possible for the city to survive and defend itself in the absence of running water, sewerage, fuel, or light, there was no substitute for food. It was this shortage, above all others, that nearly brought Leningrad to its knees.

Once Leningrad was blockaded, it had to live largely from what it had in the cupboard, and the cupboard was nearly bare. The leadership had no choice but to attempt to stretch the available supplies for as long as possible. On October 1 bread rations for all categories were again reduced: workers and technicians were to receive 400 grams a day, and all other categories 200 grams.[30] Actually the new level of rations reduced the daily consumption of flour by a mere 100 tons.[31]

Local food sources in the areas around the city were nearly exhausted, and it was decided to gather together the remaining supplies on the farms outside of Leningrad and ship them to the city. On October 9 the Leningrad *Oblast* Party Committee issued a "strictly secret" order:

1. In view of the exhaustion of local food supply sources and of the stockpiling of the remaining food supplies for the city of Leningrad, the executive

committees of the *raion* Soviets of workers' deputies, the *raion* committees of the VKP(b), and the local organizations are prohibited from issuing to any person food from the stocked supplies (bread, potatoes, vegetables, milk, meat products, as well as cattle), which are reserved for the city's supply.

2. The army quartermasters and chiefs of the special distribution areas must carry out all future special supply measures in connection with the centralized supply "fund" with reference to the needs of other areas. The army quartermasters are authorized to obtain on their own initiative potatoes, vegetables, and other food supplies in the frontal areas from which the population has been evacuated.[32]

Thus it was a whole month after the beginning of the siege before the necessary measures were taken to place the remaining food sources in the *oblast* under centralized control. Whether this delay was due to the uncertainty that prevailed during September about the city's fate, to the lack of proper centralized authority, to the absence of transportation, or even to a simple oversight cannot be ascertained. The order was also an example of the confused lines of administrative jurisdiction and of the predominance of Party agencies in decision-making.

By November 1 only a seven-day supply of flour remained in the city.[33] To stretch this out, the proportion of admixtures in the bread was increased to 68 per cent.[34] The supply of most of the admixtures used previously had been exhausted. A systematic search for stores of food was instituted. When grain was found under the floor of a bakery plant's storage bin, floors of all bins were pulled up, an operation that yielded a total of 389 tons of grain.[35] Perfume factories refined for consumption 1,600 tons of industrial oils.[36] While railroad cars in the Leningrad marshaling yards were being searched for food, 1,000 tons of cottonseed oil cake were found. It was at first feared that this oil cake, which had been originally intended for use as fuel by ships, was poisonous, but experiments showed that it could be eaten. Another admixture that was used consisted of cellulose or sawdust. The bread sold to the population contained at least 10 per cent cellulose and 10 per cent cottonseed oil cake.[37] "It was black like Donets coal, bitter, hard, containing two-thirds admixtures, and this Leningrad blockade bread was of questionable nutritional value."[38] Substitutes also had to be found for other types of foods. The meat industry began to reprocess industrial grease for consumption. Sausages were made from horsemeat, peas, and soya flour; bones were used to prepare soups. In the milk industry natural milk was replaced by soya milk. Even the foam resulting from the preparation of soya milk was reprocessed to produce a type of flour and more milk.[39] In addition, the search parties found 110 tons of malt under the floors of the breweries; 2,000 tons of sheepgut in the port (this was subsequently used to prepare a kind of jelly, which was sold instead of meat); and 500 tons of flour, 100 tons of codfish, and

30 tons of fats in the freight yards.[40] Residues of sugar and cocoa powder were carefully collected in the factories.

When the water transport on Lake Ladoga came to a stop as a result of the freezing of the lake, the authorities had to reduce the rations further. On November 8, the rations of the army were reduced to 2,600 calories a day for front-line troops and 1,600 for those in the rear echelons.[41] On November 12 the Leningrad press and radio warned the people of what was to come: "The Leningraders have suffered much during the months of the siege. But ahead of them are even more severe trials, even greater privations. One must be ready for them. One must look the truth straight and soberly in the face."[42] On the next day rations were reduced to 300 grams of bread for workers and 150 grams for all other categories.[43] This ration was, of course, considerably below the subsistence needs of the population. Most other food items disappeared from the stores. In the canteens and restaurants of factories and offices, the employees received salt water, with one or two cabbage leaves or a few grains of barley in it, in addition to their bread ration. This was their entire meal.[44]

Only seven days after this reduction, the rations were reduced once again. On November 20 they reached their lowest level: 250 grams (about ten slices) of bread for workers and 125 grams for other categories of the population. The authorities further decided to expand the production of the cellulose that was added to flour to 150 tons per day, and the bakeries began to add tree bark and leather scraps to the bread. The official daily ration provided for 1,087 calories for factory workers, 581 calories for white-collar workers, and 466 calories for dependents, as against the 3,005 to 3,555 calories normally considered necessary for adults. In fact, according to Soviet sources, since no staples other than bread were available, or were rarely issued, the actual daily amount of calories consumed by the population was even lower than that provided by the official rations.[45] Thus the majority of the population was forced to subsist on a daily diet of a quarter of a pound of bread, over half of which was made up of admixtures of little nutritional value. This situation persisted until December 25. Although by early December the ice road across Lake Ladoga began to bring in increasing amounts of supplies as a result of the liberation of Tikhvin, the improvement was insufficient to permit an increase in the rations. According to a foreign correspondent, the leadership chose to set aside whatever food reached Leningrad for the use of the army "rather than save a few thousand civilian lives."[46]

The poor organization of the sale of food also continued to add to the difficulties of the population. As conditions deteriorated, the authorities reduced the number of bread stores still further, from 54 in August to 34 in October.[47] This meant that the Leningraders, despite the intense cold, had to spend many hours standing in line. Since the inhabitants were free to buy their bread in any store, the number of purchasers in each store fluctuated from day to day, so that sometimes the supply ran out before everyone could buy his ration.[48] Consequently, housewives would rise at 5 o'clock in the morning to line up in front of the store.[49] Eventually the authorities took steps to remedy this situation. On December 1 everyone was ordered to register with a store of his choice and could receive his rations only from that store.[50] Later, permission was given to workers to obtain their rations at their places of employment.

The failure of the leadership to devise a more efficient method of food distribution, or at the very least to relieve the population of the necessity of having to stand in line in subzero weather for hours at a time, illustrates its lack of imagination and initiative in matters of easing living conditions.

Food became the Leningraders' chief concern. Since survival on the official rations was impossible, the population was forced to seek other means, some of them illegal, to procure additional supplies. Despite the prohibition on hoarding, many people tried to find black-market sources or sought to visit the surrounding villages to barter for food with the peasants, although the militia searched anyone returning from the countryside. In some houses the housing committees or the political organizers searched the apartments of evacuees for food and fuel.[51] In the area of the Badaev warehouses, people scraped the earth to collect some of the sugar and chocolate that had melted during the fire, and some people sold "Badaev sand" or " Badaev earth."[52]

In any event, these limited sources soon dried up, and people turned to less appetizing foodstuffs. First to go into the pot were all the cats, dogs, and other pets. Indeed, in November and December anyone who owned a pet, or could buy one, was considered fortunate. In the black market, dogs and cats sold for the equivalent of an average monthly wage.[53] The authorities did not interfere with these activities, although they frowned on any excessive discussion of the topic, which they regarded as being prejudicial to morale. All other legal sources of food were also used. Children dug for leaves and plants under the snow in the suburbs and gardens. People tried to buy or beg horse and cattle feed. Later they ate bark, leather, carpenter's glue, castor oil, and other unlikely substances.[54]

Inevitably a black market and a barter market appeared. The legality of the barter market was uncertain. In general, people sold or bartered items they had obtained legally or semilegally. For example, a day's bread ration could be exchanged for firewood, lamp oil, or vodka;

expensive articles or furniture could be either sold or exchanged for food. A Soviet writer who visited Leningrad reported: "On the walls of buildings, on fences or garden walls, on wooden boards covering basement windows, hung typed or written announcements. They were offers to exchange a suit or a pair of shoes or articles of gold or silver or pieces of valuable furniture for bread or other foodstuffs."[55] Most transactions in this open or gray market involved very small amounts of food or other goods. One eyewitness recalls having been offered a grand piano for a few slices of bread.[56]

Speculation or illegal black-market operations sometimes involved larger amounts of foodstuffs and dealt in commodities that could only be obtained illegally; these were exchanged or sold for valuable articles. Supplies for such operations were obtained either by theft, or with the connivance of officials or employees of the food distribution and transportation systems. Despits threats of severe punishment, even of death, there was no lack of willing speculators. Apparently, Soviet society always contained an element ready to engage in free enterprise when the returns justified the risks. However, with the progressive tightening of the blockade and the increasing food shortage, most legal and illegal market operations ceased, at least as far as food was concerned, because there remained next to nothing to sell.

The blackout and the black market contributed to a sharp rise in instances of robberies and theft. People were attacked in the street or in their homes and robbed of money, ration cards, and even of their clothes, which could be bartered for food.[57] The militia was not numerically strong enough to control this situation. Sometimes even friends stole food from each other. People looted empty apartments during air raids and bartered the stolen goods for food. In other cases people engaged in elaborate swindles to obtain additional ration cards that they could use for themselves for a short time. Theft of ration cards from persons who had collapsed in the street or had been wounded or killed by enemy fire was also common.[58] Officially, 4,800 ration cards were reported lost in October, 13,000 in November, and 24,000 in December.[59] Lost or stolen ration cards were very difficult to replace. The authorities, afraid of being swindled, insisted on conducting an investigation before making a decision.[60] This tedious and lengthy procedure often meant death for the victims of the theft, since the stage was reached in December when a single morsel of bread could mean the difference between survival or death.

In order to obtain additional food, some people simulated illness in the hope of being admitted into a hospital, where they might receive a little extra food. People dug up valuable flower bulbs from the Botanical Gardens in order to eat them.[61] The diary of a young man, whom the Soviet press would have called a "scoundrel" and "hooligan," gives the following interesting picture of the daily struggle for survival: November 2, 1941:

It is very hard. If only there was enough to eat, at least of what one must have to live on—bread. I would work, even a whole year. . . . The factory offers to let me live in the barracks; they want thus to take care of me. I don't know how I'm going to go on living. It is very hard now. It is very hard to bear this constant hunger even though I have three ration cards for the factory canteen, and I exchanged the bread for alcohol. . . .

November 3:
Today I spent the day in the technical school. I have managed to obtain 1.5 pounds of groats for *kasha* [gruel]. I was also able to buy rubber shoes for Varia.

November 4:
I must soon go again and try to get something to make *kasha*. Today I went three times. . . . I live on only 400 grams of bread [the worker's ration].

November 5:
I have managed to obtain some bread, groats, and a little meat in the canteen.

November 6:
I ate well after drinking 300 grams of port mixed with alcohol. I slept the whole night and my entire free day. For the first time in two months I felt I had had enough to eat.

November 7:
I had guard duty at the factory. I ate five plates of soup and 100 grams of meat. I was very full. In these days one could not have it better. I remained in the factory, in the corridor, overnight. It is warm here. There are no blankets or sheets, but it is still better than to travel to *Lesnoi* or to sleep in the technical school without the knowledge of the director.[62]

People began to hide dead members of the family in order to use the dead person's ration card until its expiration date. Consequently, the authorities were unable to keep an exact count of the deaths occurring in the city.

Only a limited number of people could procure food by these illegal means, so that the majority of Leningraders subsisted largely on their bread rations, hot water, and occasional gruel or other kinds of cereal. People became very concerned about the question of how to eat their daily bread ration:

People are accustomed to think that bread is simply bread and that one gets the same satisfaction from 125 grams [in whatever way one eats it]. That is not true. Bread can be eaten in different ways, and each person must find the most "satisfactory" method for himself. One can eat it by biting off a piece, or by breaking off crumbs. Others cut it: some into thin, transparent slices, some into thick squares. All agree that the crust is the most filling.

The thoughtless ones eat the bread before they have even left the bakery;

the others—they are in the minority—divide the ration into three parts: for breakfast, lunch, and dinner. To know that one can eat one's own piece of bread right away, and to stop oneself from doing it, is an act of heroism.[63]

One Leningrader noted in her diary that she hid her rations so as not to be tempted to eat them all at once.[64]

Surprisingly, despite the extreme hunger, there were no riots or serious disorders. According to the director of the Kirov Works: "People were hungry. But there was not a single serious incident. When the bread vans arrived, there was not a single case of looting. Now and then there were some rows, but never anything serious. Frankly, I find it hard to this day to understand how people resisted the temptation to attack bread vans or looting bakeries. But they didn't."[65] This statement was supported by other Soviet sources and by all informants except one, who reported the looting of a bread van when people became exasperated by a particularly long wait in front of a store.[66] While a few incidents may have occurred, it is evident that there were no instances of serious popular unrest, to the obvious surprise of the leadership.

Survival often depended on the readiness of the family or of small groups to cooperate. On the whole, most people tried to help each other, at least within the immediate family group. One informant, for example, owed his survival to the fact that his sister-in-law, a doctor, gave him part of her larger ration.[67] In other cases people who happened to have some food reserves tried to help friends or orphans.[68] Employed persons often gave part of their own rations to family members, and children sometimes had to be prevented from taking food home from the school canteens for the less fortunate of their families.[69] Often when working members of a family tried to share their rations with less favored members, such as small children or grandparents, they doomed themselves to death from malnutrition without being able to save the others. Of course, there were also instances of families breaking up in bitter fights over a piece of bread or relatives stealing from each other.

The illegal activities of the population were on too small a scale to disrupt or even endanger the rationing system. Although the leadership was unable to put a stop to all black-market activities, it could keep them in check. It was impossible, of course, to prevent the population from seeking ways to obtain additional food, but actually this mattered very little to the authorities as long as these remained unorganized individual efforts. Basically, each Leningrader remained completely dependent on his official ration, and control was maintained by frequently changing the cards.[70] Since no one would have been willing to forego the privileges of a ration card, the leadership was in a position to exercise control over the population through the rationing system. It could recruit labor and direct people to enter voluntarily into various occupations, people were given an incentive to work in the factories and ration categories. Since workers and soldiers received the highest rations, people were given an incentive to work in the factories and volunteered for the armed forces. Similarly, better rations were an inducement to join civil defense and other local defense organizations. Blood donors were given special rations; so people gave blood.[71] Workers in lumber camps and peat bogs received an extra issue of 125 grams of bread daily, and truck drivers on the ice road received 500 grams of bread, as well as other special rations including vodka.[72] Fear of losing their ration status was one of the factors that drove the Leningraders to work and kept them there until they collapsed or died.

According to the available evidence, the population on the whole appears to have accepted the necessity for the discrimination in rations that favored the army and the workers rather than women and children. This did not mean that the people were insensitive to the suffering of their loved ones. The urge to save their families or friends placed an additional emotional and physical burden upon the Leningraders. Everybody was perfectly aware that if the prevailing conditions continued, a high proportion of the population would die. But this awareness, coupled with the belief that the leadership had a right to favor the elements most necessary to the city's defense at the expense of all others, resulted not so much in anger as in resignation, a sort of fatalistic acceptance of the inevitable.[73] The battle for survival was an individual rather than a collective matter. One felt sorry for the others and helped them where possible, but one's own needs and those of one's family came first.

In addition to suffering starvation, people were tortured by cold. Their wasted bodies became acutely sensitive to the abnormally low temperatures of that winter. A student recalls the two basic and "unforgettable" sensations of those months:

First, the feeling of being cold. One gets up with it, one walks with it, one goes to bed with it. It seems to wander around somewhere under the skin; it penetrates the bones and sometimes it seems as if it even enters the brain. One can't escape from it. It penetrates under all shirts, sweaters, and jackets no matter how many one puts on.
The second is the feeling of hunger. This feeling has many shadings—from a dull, painful, sharp, unbearable one, which appears as soon as one has eaten one's ration of 125 grams, to being tortured by phantasies.[74]

Hunger caused weakness, dizziness, swelling of the hands and legs, and painfulness of the joints; moreover, it made people increasingly susceptible to various diseases. In November, when the rations dropped below subsistence level, people began to collapse in great numbers. Memoirs, diaries, and letters speak of people collapsing in the street or at work, too weak to rise, and of others barely able to walk. Those who were not helped often froze to death. One survivor wrote: "I do not know if there is a more unpleasant sensation than the feeling of not having control over one's body. You walk, you wave your arms about, you breathe heavily. But in reality you barely move. Only with the greatest effort can you force yourself to move."[75] Another Leningrader noted in her diary on December 25 how she collapsed in the street:

Recently, I experienced an unpleasant moment: I walked and walked and suddenly I sat down in a snowdrift . . . I sit and I don't understand why I have sat down. And suddenly I understood . . . it was so horrible and—above all—disgusting: to die, but from what? Not from a shell fragment, not from a bomb, but from hunger . . . ! This idea made me so sick, so miserable that I jumped up—I don't know where I got the strength—and even ran a few steps.[76]

But not all could get up by themselves, and an increasing number of people just collapsed and died.[77]

Weakness caused by vitamin deficiency and lack of food became a general phenomenon that few Leningraders escaped. In the popular terminology, this wasting away was called "dystrophy"; there were said to be three stages, the last one being fatal.[78] The number of sufferers from dystrophy rose to 18 per cent of all those receiving medical treatment. Actually the number was far greater, since by no means everybody received treatment; furthermore, even if a person was registered with the authorities as suffering from some other complaint, his illness had often been brought on, either directly or indirectly, by hunger. In November the first cases of death from starvation were officially registered. Soviet records list 11,085 deaths from dystrophy during that month, not counting deaths from other causes.[79]

While there were no epidemics of typhus or other plagues, bad food and water and the extreme cold made dysentery, scurvy, and pneumonia prevalent. People who needed special diets or treatment were among the first to succumb. Recovery from disease was difficult, since living conditions continued to deteriorate and the medical services were unable to do much for the patients. Vitamin deficiencies led to a high death rate among children and old men, while premature births reached nearly 40 per cent as compared with 10 per cent before the war.[80] In December, 85 per cent of all registered patients suffered from dystrophy, and 85 per cent of all patients died.[81] The official records showed 52,881 deaths from dystrophy in December, which equaled the death rate for the entire year of 1940.[82] Actually, as was seen, by no means were all deaths registered or reported by the population. The majority of those who died were men, and in particular men under 25 and over 40 years of age. Women seemed to be less susceptible to dystrophy, at least at first.[83]

The medical facilities were completely unequal to this situation.

Most hospitals were requisitioned for the use of the armed forces; civilians often had to use temporary facilities such as school buildings and hotels. By the end of the year most hospitals were short of rations and medicines and were often without electricity, water, or heat. The number of doctors available in the city was completely inadequate, since 60 per cent of Leningrad's medical personnel were with the army or evacuated.[84] Those who remained were ill themselves and barely able to stand. General practitioners were given two weeks' training and then put to work as surgeons. Home visits were very difficult to arrange; procuring a bed for a sick person in a hospital often involved days of effort and then meant bringing the invalid to the hospital on a sled, since no other transportation was available.[85] Many sick people were left without medical care, and sometimes it was not even possible to hospitalize people with infectious diseases.[86]

One medical student gave the following picture of a hospital in December:

The absence of electricity, heat, and water made work extremely difficult. The temperature in the wards usually stood between 30 and 35 degrees Fahrenheit. The patients lay fully clothed, with coats and blankets, and sometimes even mattresses, piled on top of them. The walls were covered with frost. During the night water froze in pitchers. The hunger had the effect of causing diarrhea among the patients, many of whom from weakness were unable to use the bedpans. Sheets on the beds were filthy—no water for laundering. The only medicine available was sodium bromide, and the doctors prescribed it to the patients under various names.[87]

Another source describes the Evropeiskii Hotel, which had been made over into a hospital and which in December was without light or water:

Small iron stoves were installed in the luxurious rooms of the hotel, and the parquet floors were used as a chopping block for firewood, when wood was obtainable; when it was not obtainable the furniture was chopped up for fuel. All the baths and bedpans were filled with excrement and refuse, all of which froze on the spot. The medical staff could barely stand on their feet through hunger, cold, and hard work.[88]

Doctors worked in overcoats and gloves. Nurses and orderlies sometimes stole the patients' rations. The food deficiencies caused the patients to contract ulcers and gangrene of the fingers. Conditions in the military hospitals were hardly any better.[89]

There was little the leadership could do to preserve the health of the inhabitants, since it was unable to give them enough food; but it made desperate efforts. In an attempt to control scurvy, the Leningrad *oblast* Party committee issued an order on October 31 instructing the Leningrad vegetable and fruit trade organization to extract vitamins from pine needles and to produce daily 30 tons of infusion from them.

The Komsomol played its usual role by leading the collection of the necessary raw material, of which 40 carloads were sent to the city daily for processing. It was made obligatory in all factory and office canteens and restaurants to drink the infusion, and the population as a whole was urged to consume it in large quantities. It appears, however, to have had little effect in decreasing the death rate in the city.[90]

The rising death rate of the population made certain controls, normal to the Soviet system, virtually impossible. Theoretically, each death had to be registered with the Bureau of Vital Statistics, ZAGS, while the militia and the house managers also had to keep records of the persons under their jurisdiction.[91] As more and more people died, this system broke down. Deaths were not always reported to ZAGS or to the militia, either because the families or the house managers were unable to do so, or because relatives deliberately kept the deaths secret in order to make use of the deceased persons' ration cards; at other times the corpses could not be identified, having been stripped in the street of papers and even of clothes.[92] The authorities did not have the personnel or the transportation necessary to determine the identity of such persons. Thus an undetermined number of people simply disappeared without the authorities being able to account for them. A check on the survivors remained in the form of the monthly registration of ration cards.

The collection and burial of corpses now also became a problem. With the rising number of deaths and the lack of vehicles, it was not possible to pick up the bodies at home; instead the population had to bring its dead to the cemeteries or morgues, which were often merely courtyards or dugouts, from which corpses were later removed by truck for mass burial, without coffins.* According to all accounts, corpses were left lying in the streets or yards for long periods of time. People who died alone at home might remain undiscovered for days. There was little the authorities could do to soften the effects on public morale of the ever-growing parade of carts and sleds transporting the dead through the main streets of Leningrad. Under these conditions it was not strange for a worker to approach his factory director with a request such as the following: "Comrade Chief, I have a request to make. I know that today or tomorrow I shall die. My family are in a very poor way—very weak. They won't have the strength to manage the funeral. Will you be a friend and have a coffin made for me, and have it sent to my family, so they don't have the extra worry of trying to get a coffin? You know how difficult it is to get one!"[93]

Many orphaned children had to be taken in by friends or relatives because there was not enough room in the orphanages. Children were

---

* In November the Leningrad undertaker trust buried 9,219 persons and in December 27,463 persons, the rest being buried by friends and relatives (Karasev, *Leningradtsy v gody blokady*, p. 185).

found wandering the streets, or waiting at home for their mothers who had gone out and never returned, or else sitting beside the bodies of their dead parents. Sometimes the rescuers did not know the children's family name and eventually gave them their own.[94]

When there were no relatives, people who were dying sometimes turned to their employers or to the school authorities. A Soviet teacher recalled how a woman came to see her and told her, "My husband is dead. . . . I too will soon die. . . . I am worried about one thing only. What will happen to my son, who is only ten years old?"[95] The teacher promised to see that the boy would be sent to a children's home. Two weeks later the boy came to school with the news of his mother's death.

It was inevitable that the population should become increasingly callous toward the dead and dying. Passers-by often failed to assist people who collapsed in the streets, since they had barely enough strength left themselves to make their way home.[96] A man kept his concern for himself and for those nearest and dearest to him. To help strangers became increasingly a luxury that many could no longer afford.

The same teacher mentioned above, when confronted by one of her students—who with despair in his voice said, "My mother is dying. Is there nothing one can do?"—found that the only help she could offer was to let him take his mother a plate of watery soup from the school's dining room; and even this had to be done in secret.[97]

Usually death came as no surprise. There was so much of it all around that it seemed to have become a part of the daily routine. The struggle for survival was so harsh that there was little time or energy left for violent grief; often even pity called for more emotion than many could summon up. Sometimes death was almost welcome because it meant one less mouth to feed, or one extra ration card. There was often nothing parents could do but watch in silent despair as their children cried from hunger and slowly wasted away.[98]

Shortages of fuel, water, electricity, and transportation were somewhat less disruptive of life and more easily borne than the shortage of food. The most important of these others was the fuel shortage. Most of the supply of firewood available to the population was exhausted by mid-October. After September 25 the Administration of State Reserves began to issue industry with fuels from its emergency stocks according to norms set by the Military Council of the Leningrad Front.[99] These reserves could not, of course, last very long, and it became essential to find additional fuel if industry were to be kept going.

On October 2 the Executive Committee of the City Soviet ordered some of its small reserves of firewood to be distributed among the neediest offices, schools, institutions, and apartment houses.[100] On October 8 the executive committees of the city and *oblast* Soviets decided to organize work groups to collect firewood in the *raion* north of Leningrad.[101] Various groups of workers and students were mobilized and sent to cut trees. Most of them had no experience in this type of work. They lacked the proper clothes and were weakened by hunger. Working with hand tools, they were unable to fulfill the production plan.

On October 20 the executive committee authorized the house administrations to redistribute firewood from empty apartments among the remaining residents of their buildings.[102] This was insufficient to prevent the progressive freezing of the apartments, particularly of those that were empty.

Two weeks later a survey conducted by the Leningrad Soviet and *oblast* executive committees revealed that the production plan of the firewood-cutting crews had been fulfilled by only 1 per cent, and that fewer workers were engaged in the task than had been anticipated. In the Pargolovskii *raion,* for example, there were 216 persons and 27 horses in operation, instead of 800 persons and 300 horses; while in the Vsevolzhskii *raion* there were 136 workers instead of the planned 800.[103] This disastrous situation led Popkov to declare: "We must at all costs have 300,000 cubic meters [10,593,000 cubic feet] of firewood in order to live through December and January; otherwise industry will be paralyzed, and a large number of the buildings with central heating will be frozen."[104] To help out in this situation, the Komsomol organization of the city was mobilized. Two thousand Komsomols, mostly girls, were sent to cut firewood;[105] but at best they could improve matters only slightly.

The shortage of electric power also had serious consequences for the city. As a result of the German advance on Tikhvin, it had become necessary to evacuate the Volkhov hydroelectric power station, the last hydroelectric station still supplying Leningrad.[106] The city produced in October only 3,900,000 kilowatt-hours of electricity, and even this output was increasingly curtailed as a result of the fuel shortage. On November 17 the use of electric lights was limited to the following: the Party headquarters in the Smolny Institute; the army headquarters; the offices of the militia, the *raion* Party and executive committees, and the *raion* military commandants; the civil defense posts; the telegraph and main post offices; the main telephone exchange; factories; and a few other essential offices.[107] There was no electric lighting in apartments and homes. In December many of the less important organizations listed above were also deprived of light, including nearly all hospitals.[108]

On November 17 the use of fuel for heating water in public institutions such as public baths was prohibited, and the heat level in buildings with central heating was set at 53.5° F. in apartment houses, 50° F. in offices, and 46.4° F. in factories.[109] In practice, the central heating in most buildings ceased to function altogether, and most factory workshops remained unheated.

On December 9 the executive committee ordered that excess firewood in the possession of any Leningrader be confiscated, with compensation, and distributed to those in need.[110] The "excess" was all wood above the prescribed norm of 35.31 cubic feet per eight square meters of living space. On the same day, as a result of the further decline in electric power output, 90 streetcars were taken out of service, and eight streetcar lines were abolished.[111] A week later all streetcar traffic ceased. Because of the lack of fuel and the consequent freezing of water pipes, all laundries, barber shops, and public baths closed down. Even the essential bakeries had to interrupt production owing to the water and fuel shortages.

In desperation the authorities tried once more to organize some means of collecting firewood from the surrounding countryside. On December 10 the Leningrad City Party Committee ordered the *raion* executive and Party committees to mobilize within three days 2,850 people to cut firewood. Two days later 1,400 more Komsomols and students were mobilized for the same purpose.[112] Apparently the results of these efforts were not satisfactory since more drastic measures had to be taken later.

About this time the electric power stations began to burn their emergency fuel reserves. On December 15 the director of the First Leningrad City Electric Station reported to Popkov that the station received between 150 and 350 tons of coal a day, whereas it needed 700 to 800 tons to produce the power demanded of it. By mid-December the fuel and power shortage brought the bulk of Leningrad's industry to a halt.[113] According to the director of the Kirov Works, "On December 15 everything came to a standstill. There was no fuel, no electric current, no food, no tramcars, no water—nothing. Production in Leningrad practically ceased. We were to remain in this terrible condition until the first of April."[114]

As fuel disappeared, the freezing led to a progressive breakdown of the water, sewage, and central heating systems in homes. In view of the inability of the authorities to help them, the Leningraders fell back on their own efforts and initiative to find substitutes for the missing services and supplies. Since it was impossible to procure fuel for central heating or for the big stoves that were the normal source of heat in homes, the population sought to obtain or build small temporary stoves. These were known as *burzhuiki* and were made from a variety of materials: tin cans, bricks, metal barrels; they were usually placed on the floor or on a stool underneath the ventilation shafts, which served as chimneys.[115] As a rule, these stoves were used for both heating and cooking. Generally, only one room in an apartment could be heated at all, and then only for short periods of time; everybody lived and slept in this one room.[116] Even then the temperature could be kept barely above freezing. Those who had no reserve firewood stole wood or coals from their place of work, managed to pick some up from damaged houses, burned their furniture or that from abandoned apartments, or even tore up wooden floors for fuel. Food was sometimes bartered for firewood on the open market.[117] According to one Soviet source, five to six logs sold for 1,000 rubles, which represented two and a half months' average wages.[118]

The temporary stoves were often badly built and caused numerous fires, which owing to the water shortage sometimes became quite large. These fires created a serious problem, since there was no gasoline for the fire engines, and consequently the firemen had to go to the scene on foot; moreover, often only about 10 per cent of the firemen were strong enough to perform their duties.[119] On November 30 and again on December 15 the executive committee published prohibitions against the building of stoves and ordered official inspection of those already built; but these restrictions were apparently not obeyed.[120] Nor were the authorities able to prevent the inhabitants from ruining their apartments in an effort to obtain firewood.

When the electric power failed, most Leningraders managed to make various primitive types of lamps, often consisting simply of a tiny wick floating in a little oil or paraffin. Since even oil, kerosene, and paraffin were very scarce, the lamps had to be used sparingly. Much of the fuel for them was obtained in the barter market, where one ran the risk of being sold colored water instead of oil. Candles were in very short supply.[121]

Each household solved the water problem as best it could. Sometimes the water main in the basement still gave some water, while at other times people had to carry it from holes cut in the ice of the river and canals, or from public pumps and a few fire hydrants. In view of the water shortage and the cold, many Leningraders stopped washing and shaving. Washing clothes was a luxury few indulged in. The pollution of some of the drinking water, coupled with the fact that fuel was not available for boiling it, caused much illness among the population.

When the freezing and the bomb damage made the sewage system no longer usable, the population solved this problem in the simplest manner. Garbage and excrement were either thrown into the courtyards and streets, or else dumped in abandoned rooms. Fortunately it was so cold that these practices did not create a serious health problem during the winter.

The streets could not, of course, be kept clear of ice and snow as they usually were. As the accumulated snow and ice made the streets increasingly impassable, the executive committee issued repeated orders mobilizing the population for street-cleaning.[122] On December 12 all workers, employees, and students were directed to spend three hours of obligatory overtime labor to clean the streets; those who were unemployed were to work eight hours: "The duration of uninterrupted work on the part of citizens will be determined by the time necessary to complete the removal of the snow.... The work on snow removal is being performed by the citizens on the basis of obligatory labor and is not to be paid for, and those called upon to perform such work will not be issued free food."[123] But the weakened population lacked the incentive to carry out the order effectively, and most streets were left to accumulate a thick crust of snow and ice, which was not removed until spring.

Faced with this situation within the city, the leadership was forced to accept the prospect of the eventual collapse of Leningrad's defenses, an outcome made particularly likely in view of the battle of Moscow and the loss of Tikhvin. Yet the possibility of voluntary surrender was apparently never seriously contemplated. Moscow's orders were clear: hold on regardless of cost as long as possible, and thereby contribute to the defense of Moscow and the rest of the country. Thus a Soviet colonel wrote: "As a rule, the greatest activities of our forces around Leningrad coincided with the execution of large-scale operations in other sectors of the Soviet-German front and contributed to the successes of those operations."[124]

The decision to continue the defense of Leningrad remained unchanged even when it became clear that it condemned to death hundreds of thousands of Leningraders. In the view of the Soviet leadership, the continued defense of Leningrad served a sufficiently useful purpose to justify any cost in human lives.

Accordingly, the leadership continued to seek ways to strengthen the city's defenses against the possibility of a renewed German assault. The defense forces were certainly not in any condition to inspire great optimism in their leaders. The army was short of weapons and ammunition as well as of clothing and food. It had to hoard artillery shells, issue antiquated rifles, and collect all weapons found abandoned on the battlefield.[125]

Even more serious was the shortage of proper clothing and food. Without these the army was in danger of collapsing, as the following intercepted Red Army report indicates: "One of the men from our battery has frozen feet. He is in a hospital. Both his legs are being amputated. Moreover, there are already 2,000 such cases. . . . We must give each soldier two pairs of socks, or the cold will bring about our defeat."[126] In the end, with the help of the civilian population, enough warm clothing was provided for the troops, who on the whole suffered less from the cold than the Germans. There was, however, no remedy for the food shortage. The army was receiving larger rations than the civilians, but it, too, was starving. In November and December, according to one report, men in the forward positions received daily some 300 to 350 grams of bread, two servings of watery soup, and sometimes 50 to 75 grams of rye hardtack; soldiers in reserve units or rear echelons received only 200 grams of bread and less than 50 grams of hardtack.[127] As a result, many soldiers fell ill or became too exhausted to go on fighting. Discipline declined, and some of the hungry soldiers proclaimed themselves unwilling to risk their lives on empty stomachs, while others went in search of food that might have been overlooked under the snow in the fields. There were said to have been instances of attack and looting of food transports by soldiers.[128]

The inferior quality and character of the replacements also affected army morale. A small number of replacements came from outside the encirclement, usually arriving by boat over Lake Ladoga. They had little training and were equipped with a motley collection of old weapons.[129] Those from within the city were convalescent soldiers, workers out of a job, criminals, and youths of 16 to 17 years of age.[130] The amount of military training received by these men varied, but it was seldom enough for combat requirements. One prisoner reported that he had been shown how to handle a rifle and had fired three shots, after which he was sent into the front lines.[131] Other replacements received as much as two or three weeks of training.

Since many soldiers were native Leningraders, their morale was greatly affected by the fate of their families in the city. The leadership could not entirely hide from the soldiers the conditions prevailing in Leningrad, or the privations that their families were undergoing. This information leaked out through letters, word-of-mouth reports, eyewitness accounts, and reports from newly mobilized men. Although letters were censored, the censorship was not consistently strict, and many Leningraders complained that times were "very hard" or that life was "terrible."[132] Other letters told how impossible it was to obtain food and listed family members and friends who had died or were dying.[133] Delegations of civilians who visited the front also told the soldiers what was going on within the city. The men could not fail to realize that with every passing day the plight of their families was getting worse.

Soldiers whose families lived in other parts of the country, or who had been evacuated from Leningrad, also had reason for concern, since they knew that severe food shortages existed in many areas of the

Soviet Union and that the refugees were usually not welcome in their new homes. Letters like the following inevitably affected the soldiers' morale:

We live very badly. No bread is being issued. Until recently there was still 200 grams. . . .

Oh, my beloved husband, you write me to be energetic! My director chased me out of his office when I asked him for bread. He called after me, "I will hang you on a string!" You know what that means. One cannot get anything for money here. I have tried very hard. . . .

My life is not to be envied, Andrei. It's so hard to live without money. I'm not getting any allowance, and there is no work.[134]

It was not surprising that many Red Army soldiers, with news like this from home and so many battles lost, would doubt the feasibility and desirability of continuing to defend Leningrad. A political commissar of an infantry regiment noted in his report, "One hears individual soldiers speaking of defeat . . . their depression is heightened by doubts about whether the blockade of Leningrad can be broken."[135] In an intercepted letter a soldier wrote on October 30: "Leningrad is encircled by the Germans. It is impossible to get out. Moscow, too, will probably be taken, since that city is also encircled by the Germans. They will not be satisfied until all these cities are taken. As soon as the Germans take these cities, Japan will start a war, and one can only conclude that one will not survive these times.[136]

In another letter a soldier wrote, "Life is hopeless. Probably we will not survive. . . . Probably my life will end here."[137] An NKVD colonel, captured by the Germans, told them: "The troops defending Leningrad are not convinced that they can defend the city."[138]

This situation led to an increase in the desertion rate. After September, when the fall of Leningrad no longer seemed imminent and it was impossible to survive in the city without a ration card and proper permits, desertion into the city was senseless. Desertion to the Germans therefore became more frequent. Even some NKVD troops, who after all were drawn from the same sources as the other Red soldiers and had to live on the same rations, deserted.[139] The problem, in fact, became sufficiently serious throughout the Red Army for the authorities to institute various new control measures. On December 16, for example, the chief of the Political Administration of the Red Army, Mekhlis, ordered that only the most reliable men were to be used for reconnaissance and that they were to operate under the strictest supervision.[140]

Yet despite the deterioration of morale and fighting quality, the defending Red Army forces were by no means ready to revolt or to give up resisting the Germans. On the contrary, the Leningrad units made frequent, if ineffective, attacks upon the Germans and forced the enemy to make the following admission:

The German military leadership is constantly amazed by the toughness and stubbornness of the Russians as well as by their ability to form new troop units . . . . Although the combat value and morale of the "improvised" units is low, the Red Army soldiers and Leningrad workers fight as before with stolid persistence.

Without changing anything in the desperate situation of Leningrad, [the Russians] nevertheless are tying down ten German divisions in the encirclement and preventing their use in other sectors of the front.[141]

The Russians themselves did not have quite this picture of the situation, since they were more aware of how demoralized the army was, despite the relatively good showing that the troops were making in battle. But the front was stabilized, and the battle worthiness of the army was not put to the test to which it might have been subjected if the Germans had renewed their assault on Leningrad. Generally it was more difficult for soldiers to desert to the enemy in a static situation than in a fluid one. Consequently, relatively few chose this course. From the German point of view, a bullet fired by a demoralized soldier was just as painful as one fired by a loyal supporter of the regime. As long as the army leadership remained loyal and the soldiers received enough food to prevent mass starvation, it was unlikely that the army would collapse while the Germans remained on the defensive around Leningrad.

In this same period, after the immediate military threat to the city was over, a more systematic approach to the problem of organizing local defense became possible. The *opolchenie* and workers' battalions could now be trained and used as reinforcements and replacements for the army. Some of the hurriedly mobilized units and some workers' battalions could be sent back to work. Systematic military training for the entire male population, with the objective of providing local defense forces and creating a semitrained replacement pool for the army, could be set up. On September 18 the State Defense Committee in Moscow issued a decree introducing a new system of universal military training (*vsevobuch*) and abolishing the territorial draft system, which the Red Army had used since 1923.[142] A central administration for universal military training was organized in Moscow under the People's Commissariat of War. Some hundred training centers were organized in Leningrad, and instructors were sent to the *raion* military commissions to supervise and direct the training of all able-bodied men between the ages of 16 and 50. The duration of the training course was set at 110 hours, to be taken in the trainees' free time. Some advanced training in truck driving, gunnery, communications, and similar fields was also offered to selected candidates.[143]

The training program started on October 1, but encountered difficulties from the beginning. For one thing, there was some delay in implementing the decree. On November 27 *Leningradskaia pravda* wrote:

Nearly two months have passed since the start of universal military training . . . . In the military training centers of Leningrad the first half of the *Vsevobuch* program is nearing completion. The future Red Army men have successfully completed their training in close-order drill, gunnery, engineering, and tactics, as well as in the technique of bayonet fighting. Defects characteristic of the first days of the training are now largely eliminated. The *Voenkomats* have assembled a staff of instructors of high military qualifications; they have shown care and discernment in handling the selection of commanders at the centers, bringing into these posts men who have had experience in the present war.[144]

The article went on to complain, however, that some of the commanders still came to lectures unprepared and wasted the time of their men.

By the time the training program was able to run its full course, the ranks of the local units were decimated by starvation. According to one Soviet source, during the winter of 1941–42 "many fighters of the *Vsevobuch* could not participate in the training because of illness and hunger. Nearly half of the men of the command staff at the military training points were ill from hunger."[145]

Out of the 26,600 persons who initially participated in the training, over 6,000 were too ill or weak to finish the course, and of these, 800 died of starvation; another 10,000 were given a short course and then sent as replacements to the army; and a further 3,000 dropped out; so that in the end only 7,000 Leningraders completed the training. These figures are in marked contrast to the official claim that between October 1941 and May 1942 about 112,000 persons were given training under the *Vsevobuch* program.[146]

The Military Council of the Leningrad Front believed that, following their attack on Moscow, the Germans would renew their assault on Leningrad. On November 15 the military council organized a special military staff called the Command of the Internal Defense of the City (VOG). In December the VOG was charged with the defense of the ice road against a possible German attack over the ice of Lake Ladoga and was also made responsible for the internal defense of the city, for which purpose it was given command over the NKVD troop, the fire department, the militia, and five workers' brigades.[147]

Work on the fortifications in and outside the city continued for a time; but although it was better organized now, the work was carried out at a declining rate. Fortifications near the front lines and along the canals bisecting the southern part of Leningrad were strengthened, and the defenses surrounding some of the factories were expanded.[148] But by the beginning of winter the shortage of building materials, the intense cold, and the progressive weakening of the population limited the work on fortifications to the tasks that the army designated as most urgent.

When hunger and worsening working conditions began to affect the rate of work, it was decided to establish work norms for the construction workers and to pay them according to their performance. On November 30 the executive committee directed that temporary norms "for the construction of fortifications in winter time" be set for various categories of work.[149] Employed persons were to be paid their total average daily pay if they fulfilled the norms by 100 per cent. Unemployed persons were to be paid 8 rubles a day, and factory and trade school students 70 per cent of the rate set for adults. If the norms were not fulfilled, the pay was to be decreased proportionately. Those who completed their assignment in less than the prescribed fifteen-day work period were to be given two days of rest, while those who did so in less than twelve days were to receive an extra day of rest. Supervisors of the construction sectors were to set norms for other types of work not listed in the order. When no norms were set and the work was less arduous, the pay scale was established at 6 rubles a day (4.20 rubles for trade and factory school students).

In reality, construction work outside the city virtually ceased with the arrival of winter. The frozen earth was too hard to be worked with hand tools, and the workers were too weak or ill to accomplish much. Furthermore, the importance of fortification construction declined as the military situation improved and other tasks became more urgent.

Of course, these labor drafts were unpopular, since the work was hard and had to be performed under very trying conditions. The performance of the draftees was unaffected by the financial penalties incurred when they did not fulfill the prescribed norms. Money was of little value, since there was nothing to buy with it. The controlling factor was what food ration each person could obtain. Construction workers, falling in the category of defense workers, received the largest food ration, and this did provide a certain incentive for working on the fortifications, particularly since many of the draftees were not normally entitled to such rations. But the difficult working conditions and the fact that this hard labor was likely to exhaust the workers' remaining strength acted as deterrents; so that whereas some were eager for the larger ration, others were afraid to perform the work. There was, of course, no way anyone could avoid the draft except for reasons of health. However, as starvation, exhaustion, and other difficulties took their toll, it became increasingly easy to use illness as an excuse.

Meanwhile, the amount of damage and the number of casualties inflicted by the German bombardment continued to increase. As before, the Germans concentrated upon military installations, factories, and utilities; but because of Hitler's orders to destroy the city, an increasing number of bombs and shells were dropped on nonmilitary targets.[150] During the whole of the siege, according to Soviet sources, the Germans destroyed 3,174 buildings and damaged 7,143.[151] In all, over 100,000 shell hits are said to have registered on buildings.[152] How much this represented in terms of total housing space is not clear. In 1943 Soviet authorities claimed that only 8 per cent of the total living space had been destroyed, whereas in 1944 they put the figure at 20 per cent.[153] More recent statements give 40 per cent.[154] The last figure appears to represent the total of all housing destroyed and damaged during the siege, including nearly 10,000 wooden houses torn down for fuel and others damaged by fire or water. In 1944 Popkov asserted that, at the prevailing norm, the buildings destroyed could have housed over half a million people.[155] What proportion of this damage was inflicted in 1941 cannot be determined from the available sources.

Two types of damage to housing were especially serious in the winter of 1941–42. First, as a result of broken roofs, damage to housing caused by the weather was extensive. Second, the breakage of windows during the bombardment, which was more widespread than other forms of damage from enemy fire, imposed particularly great hardships upon the population in view of the severity of the cold, the lack of fuel, and the extreme shortage of window glass. Eighty per cent of all windows are said to have been broken in the end.[156]

The authorities were unable to provide glass or plywood for private dwellings and had very little of it for public buildings. Yet the intense cold, the snow, and the blackout regulations made it imperative to cover up broken windows in some fashion. The population, left largely to its own devices, resorted to putting blankets and carpets over the broken windows, or boarding them up with lumber or plywood when they could get these materials.[157] This meant that many apartments were deprived of daylight. Furthermore, although these makeshifts were better than nothing, they did not, of course, keep out the cold so effectively as glass.

In the long run, for one reason or another, there was hardly a "single building in the city which did not suffer to some extent from the war."[158] In addition, over 9,000 square feet of factory floor space were damaged or destroyed during the siege.[159] This represented 840 industrial establishments destroyed and about 3,000 damaged.[160] A large proportion of this damage was inflicted in 1941, during which period Leningrad suffered the largest number of air attacks and heavy artillery bombardments.[161]

The continuing bombardment and starvation brought about the progressive breakdown of the civil defense organization and also rendered the authorities increasingly less able to cope with the accumulating damage. The intense cold and the physical weakness of the Leningraders put a halt to most of the fire watches on the roofs of buildings. The civil defense teams disintegrated as more and more of their members became ill, died, or were evacuated, and many workers, instead of returning home, slept in their factories and offices.[162]

Bomb damage to water pipes and the shortage of fuel and electricity led to a sharp drop in water pressure. Consequently, fire hydrants often failed to work, and in houses water could not be piped above the ground floors. The low water pressure, coupled with the lack of heat, meant that many of the water pipes in buildings began to freeze, often bursting as a result. Thus there was frequently no water for fire fighting. The Leningraders were often forced to use snow in an attempt to put out fires, and many buildings burned to the ground.

The personnel of the fire brigades and rescue units was weakened by starvation, and sometimes an entire brigade would be too sick to respond to a fire alarm. The following account illustrates this situation. In one apartment the head of the family was found dead by his 15-year-old daughter. The girl, "thin and weak, crushed by her loss, was even unable to cry." Then a neighbor came to tell her that the house was on fire, but the girl was unable to move. The firemen who rescued her and carried out her father cursed their luck. "We don't have enough strength to carry stiffs," they complained.[163] Fortunately the German air bombardment ceased just as the city became most vulnerable to incendiary bombs. Artillery fire did not usually cause fires and required a less elaborate civil defense system.

There was little the authorities could do about the civil defense situation. The air raid warning system was improved to provide a separate alert signal for artillery bombardments. Instead of sounding a general alert, the public address system announced which city district was being shelled so that people in that area could seek shelter. Signs were posted in the main streets indicating which side of the street was safer during an artillery bombardment.[164] These measures at least helped to prevent complete paralysis of the entire city during a bombardment.

Some effort was also made to improve the conditions in the shelters, most of which had not been prepared for prolonged use, particularly not for wintertime. On November 10, the Executive Committee of the City Soviet reported that in a number of city districts public shelters were flooded, were not being properly maintained, or had become refuges for homeless dogs that had somehow avoided being eaten.[165] The executive committee issued instructions, through the *raion* executive committees, that the various factories, offices, organizations, and apartment buildings were to be in charge of the shelters nearest to them, and that by December 15 each shelter was to be equipped with stoves, lights, doors, benches, and other facilities as provided by the civil defense organization's regulations. Since, however, by December 15 neither fuel nor electric power was available, it seems unlikely that anything much was in fact done to improve the shelters.

As before, people continued to do their best to protect their own belongings, but as starvation increased, they showed themselves less inclined or able to rush to the rescue of others. People also began to disregard the civil defense regulations that made it mandatory for all to seek shelter during an alert. The alerts were so frequent that many Leningraders not only lost their fear of them, but preferred to conserve their energy by remaining where they were, at least when no bombs or shells were dropping nearby. At night, particularly, many people chose to stay in bed during alerts. In the streets the militia still tried to enforce the regulations, but their efforts were often openly disobeyed.[166] On November 30 the Executive Committee of the City Soviet noted that a growing number of persons were disregarding the alerts and instructed the militia to enforce the regulations.[167] This proved impossible, however, and until the end of the siege many Leningraders never went into shelters except when they came under direct enemy fire.

In their determination to continue resistance to the Germans, the authorities were also faced with the problem of how to keep the army supplied with weapons and ammunition under blockade conditions. The leadership considered it essential to keep the defense industries going; but this was extremely difficult to do in the face of the severe shortages of raw material, labor, and machinery, the administrative confusion, the bombardment, and the starvation of the workers. In the end, however, it was not so much these difficulties that brought about the virtual cessation of industrial operations as the lack of fuel, water, and in particular, electricity. No industrial or labor control measures instituted by the leadership could overcome the power shortage.

The problem of finding substitutes for various products and raw materials that were no longer available was approached with considerable ingenuity. Among the items in short supply were steel, casting sand, coke, aluminum, textiles, leather, alcohol, various chemicals, explosives and gunpowder, glass, wood rubber, grease, and various fuels.[168] Despite these shortages, the production plan for October required industry to produce 1,465,000 shells and 800,000 mines, as well as tanks, armored trains, and other military equipment.[169]

The leadership gave industry some assistance in finding substitutes, but more often the initiative was left to the factory managers and technicians. When new materials or production methods proved successful, the leadership organized the manufacture of the new materials or introduced the new methods in other plants. The scientists who remained in the city also worked on the problem. A substitute for powder for heavy artillery was discovered and manufactured.[170] The casting shops used

90 per cent burned earth in making molds, instead of the usual 50 per cent, and the foundries used coke with a 50 to 60 per cent admixture of anthracite.[171] To conserve steel and its alloys, some types of artillery shells were made of cast iron, or from a mixture of iron and fibers. In the manufacture of incendiary bombs, kerosene and alcohol were replaced by petroleum and fuel oil mixed with paraffin.[172]

The problem is to produce more tanks, more guns, more rifles, more cartridges, while using less metal, less coal, less copper, less zinc, less energy, and last but not least—less labor power.

The workers say: If a specification demands one hundred pounds of aluminum, make fifty pounds do—even in using fifty pounds you permit yourself an unpardonable luxury. How is this economy to be attained? By renouncing prewar habits, by revising all traditional norms, and constantly rationalizing the processes themselves with the accompanying techniques.[173]

How this affected the quality of the manufactured products is not known, but it certainly did not improve them. In fact, it is probably correct to assume that these measures greatly reduced the durability, reliability of performance, and effectiveness of the weapons and ammunitions so produced. But in view of the situation, this was far better than no production at all.

Of course, not all factories suffered from shortages to the same degree. Some of them had considerable raw material reserves, which, with industrial production curtailed, could have kept them going for a considerable time. But these reserves often had to be distributed among other factories or used in the manufacture of new items not produced before in the city.

Many factories were forced to close down, while others attempted to operate by switching first to gasoline-driven generators and later, when there was no fuel, to hand-manufacturing methods, even resorting to such expedients as using bicycle pedals to keep some lathes going.[174] Symbolic of the situation were the gifts brought by a delegation of Leningrad workers sent to visit soldiers at the front: a few handmade submachine guns.[175] In some cases the production of weapons and ammunition had to be halted in favor of repairing weapons, tanks, and ships, and manufacturing simple military equipment such as mines and bayonets.[176] In the end most factories were closed down, and their workers were employed in cleaning and repairing machines (against the time when production could be resumed), cutting wood, checking the factory's equipment, and trying to keep the water and fuel pipes in working order.

Throughout this period the watchwords of Leningrad's industry had to be initiative and flexibility. The leadership set or approved production schedules, supplied materials when and where it could, and, in gen-

eral, helped out within the limits of its capabilities; but each management of the few factories still operating had to rely largely on its own
resources to find ways of overcoming the difficulties and shortages and
of keeping the plant in production. The leadership kept prodding the
management, but it did not look too closely at the latter's activities, as
long as the defense orders were filled. The formula was very simple:
industry, or what remained of it, had to "provide the front with everything it needed" and fulfill all defense orders in the prescribed time.

Even when there appear to be unsurmountable difficulties in the way,
such as the breakdown of machinery, shortages of raw materials or auxiliary
materials, interruption of electric power supply, weakness or exhaustion of
workers, etc., the chiefs of the enterprises must see to it that the orders are
carried out by the prescribed time. Any excuses, even if they are eventually
confirmed by the events, will not be accepted, for the factory chief has to see
to it that everything needed is on hand. Just as the soldier fulfills his duty at
the post, the worker and office worker must fulfill their duties at their posts
and are to be held responsible, just like soldiers, for their actions.[177]

Zhdanov subsequently gave high praise to industry for its ability to
keep going under the most adverse conditions: "Never before had Leningrad's industry . . . shown such flexibility, such Bolshevik ability,
to get out of the most difficult situations, and to fulfill its task somehow,
as it did in the most difficult months of the winter under the blockade."[178]
While some managers and engineers were eventually overwhelmed
by the difficulties confronting them, others showed remarkable initiative
and ability. In some instances a few managers and technicians, often
working on their own initiative, organized production with what remained of the machinery from an evacuated factory.

These enthusiasts submitted plans for the utilization of the machinery to the authorities and devised new methods of production. They
were not necessarily devoted Party members or even pro-Communists;
they were people who liked to be active and were motivated by the
desire to "do something," by patriotic sentiments, or by an unwillingness
to leave their workers unemployed and possibly starving. Of course,
there was a limit even to the ability of such managers to keep plants going, but the leadership did profit greatly from their enthusiasm and in-
ventiveness.[179]

The managers' difficulties were increased, as usual, by the complexity
of administrative controls and their continuing extensive dependence on
instructions and decisions from Moscow. Thus, according to intercepted
radio conversations between the two cities, Moscow often continued to
decide whether an enterprise was to be shut down or not, what it was
to produce, what financial arrangements were to be made, and what
stocks, equipment, and personnel were to be evacuated.[180]

PAGE 1: *Above:* Supply trucks crossing Lake Ladoga on the ice road. *Below:* Despite the risk of their headlights' attracting German fire, truck convoys travel along the ice road at night.

PAGE 2: Columns of conscripted Leningrad women march off to collect peat and firewood.

PAGE 3: *Above:* With the breakdown of public transportation, people go everywhere by foot; the weak and sick are dragged on sleds. Note the predominance of women. *Below, left:* A starving Leningrader carries his meager daily bread ration from the food store (Winter, 1941–42). *Below, right:* Survivors of the first winter of siege wait for the departure of their evacuation train (Spring, 1942).

PAGE 4: The fuel and electricity shortage forces Leningraders to huddle around improvised stoves in their dark, cold homes (Winter, 1941–42).

PAGE 5: *Above:* People collapsed and died in the streets in the winter of 1941–42. Painting, "By the Fence of the Summer Garden," by N. Kochergin, 1943. *Below:* The inhabitants use children's sleds to transport their dead to the cemetery or morgue (Winter, 1941–42).

PAGE 6: *Above, left:* Children who have survived the first winter of siege seek the warmth of the early spring sun. *Above, right:* The bombardment forces the inmates of children's homes to spend long hours in air-raid shelters. *Below:* Infants in a children's nursery get some fresh air between shellings.

PAGE 7: *Above:* Women work brigades are sent out to improve the fortifications around Leningrad. Here they are seen building antitank defenses on the outskirts of the city. *Below:* Reinforcements trudge to the front along streets choked by snow and ice.

A part of Carcassonne bombardment

There were conflicts over priorities and decisions. Many managers appealed to Moscow to have decisions by local authorities overruled, as the following radio conversation illustrates:

LENINGRAD. I cannot manage here because I can't get the railroad ties sent there.

MOSCOW. Why not? Isn't it possible to get through?

LENINGRAD. That is not the question. I could send the ties by trucks, but I cannot get any trucks.

MOSCOW. I don't understand this: you do have trucks in your city.

LENINGRAD. Of course, but there are no trucks available. Everything is requisitioned, and the Military Council will not release any.* That is why I ask you to send a telegram.

MOSCOW. That is ridiculous. I certainly can ask the People's Commissar to send such a telegram, but he will not understand either how the people there can be so stupid and make difficulties in such a case. What we are doing is for their direct benefit.

LENINGRAD. I have explained all that to them, but nothing can be done with the military and one cannot cope with them. First they requisition everything, and then on top of that they demand that we manage with what we have.

MOSCOW. The hell with it. All right, I will go and send a telegram.[181]

During the battle of Moscow and particularly during the second half of October, the mass evacuation of government ministries, Moscow's major economic administrative authorities, and various important organizations led to temporary breakdowns of the links between Moscow and Leningrad.[182] Many of the Leningrad managers were left at a loose end, without orders, vainly trying to locate their chiefs.

Despite conditions in the city, the Leningrad Party organizations preserved the rituals that always plagued Soviet industry. To have failed to do so might well have cast doubts on the political orthodoxy of Leningrad's leadership. One such ritual was the annual "socialist competition" that took place on the anniversary of the revolution. Thus, on October 5 the Stalin Works publicly appealed to the city's entire industry:

Soon the 24th anniversary of the Great October Socialist Revolution will take place. The Soviet people have a wonderful tradition—to greet the national holiday with new production victories. Our collective warmly praises the Stakhanovites of the Moscow L. M. Kaganovich ball-bearing plant and gladly joins in the pre-October socialist competition. . . . We challenge you, dear comrades, to enter the mass pre-October socialist competition, too.[183]

Since the undertaking obviously had the approval of the highest authorities, the satisfaction expressed by the *Leningradskaia pravda* editorial of October 29 is not surprising: "Upon the appeal of the collective of the

---

* The trucks had been requisitioned for use on the Ladoga ice road, and the railroad ties were needed to extend the tracks so that they would connect with the truck road.

Stalin Works, the workers of the Leningrad industry have entered into the pre-October socialist competition, whose main objective is to intensify the assistance to the front and increase the output of war material. Many works and factories have already made significant achievements in this competition."[184] In view of the weakness of the workers and the lack of fuel and electricity, the socialist competition among the factories remained largely a symbolic gesture rather than a reality.

The Party groups in the factories also organized the traditional "socialist competitions within shifts, among workers, as well as between shifts, in the achievement of the highest daily production norms."[185] In all probability these competitions, which even in prewar days often disrupted industrial operations, were not welcomed by the city's factory managements at a time when they were glad to be operating at all, although the excitement did sometimes stimulate productivity for a short period. The workers, too, could have little interest in these competitions in view of the conditions under which they had to labor and the shortage of food.

Working conditions soon became appalling. The factory shops were unheated. One factory director told a foreign correspondent:

One day in December, in twenty degrees frost, we had all our windows blown out by a bomb, and I thought to myself: "No, we really can't go on. Not till the spring. We can't go on almost without food!" And yet, somehow we didn't stop ... and sure enough within thirty-six hours we were working again—working in altogether hellish conditions, with eight degrees frost in the workshops and fourteen degrees of frost in this office.[186]

Workers in the factories wore their overcoats and kept their gloves on. There was often hardly any light to work by, since electricity was scarce and the windows were often boarded up. The Soviet writer Tikhonov described one factory shop that was still operating at the end of the year:

The sky showed darkly through the shell-holes in the roof, a gleaming layer of ice covered the rafters and walls, carefully shaded, dim electric lamps cast patches of light at intervals, and if you stared intently you would see a good number of people in the various sections of the vast hall.

They were wrapped in all sorts of coverings and threw weird shadows in the feeble light. The sharp lines of their sunken faces would have frightened an outsider.[187]

One factory worker mentions in her diary how some workers were so swollen from hunger that they could not sit down or get up without help, and how others fainted at their machines.[188] During the winter the workers "ate grease from the guns and oil from the machines."[189] Since the remaining skilled and trained workers were mostly older people, they proved particularly susceptible to exhaustion and illness. According to the director of the Kirov Works: "People were terribly cold and terribly hungry. It is no secret that a large number of our people died during those days. And it was chiefly our best people who died—highly skilled workers who had reached a certain age when the body no longer resists such hardships."[190]

Under these conditions, the existing labor control measures were difficult to enforce. In an effort to maintain closer control over the obligatory labor performed by Leningraders, the Executive Committee of the City Soviet instituted on October 20 a system by which the performance and fulfillment of the assigned task of each mobilized person were to be registered in labor books.[191] The book had to be presented by the worker in order to receive payment or compensation for his work. This made it more difficult for the Leningraders to avoid doing the work for which they were drafted.

Industrial workers still could not leave their factories without permission, or be absent from work without proper medical authorization, without running the risk of being prosecuted for violation of labor laws or for sabotage. But in view of the progressive breakdown of public transportation, the absence of telephones, and the physical exhaustion of the administrative staffs, it became increasingly difficult for the factory administrations to check on absenteeism. One factory director said: "But some died at home, and died together with the rest of their families, and in the circumstances it was difficult to find out anything definite. The bodies were taken away, and there was really nobody who could report the man's death to us. And since there was no transportation, we weren't usually able to send people around to inquire. This went on till about the 15th of February."[192]

Control over labor, as mentioned earlier, was exercised primarily by means of the food rationing system. The higher worker ration category not only attracted new labor to industry, but kept most workers at their jobs. The ration card, usually valid for one month, was issued at the place of work or by the *raion* authorities upon the presentation of a certificate from the employer. Bread was often issued at the factory. To be relegated to the lowest ration category, that of the unemployed, meant certain death not only for the worker but also for his family. If a worker was absent, he was listed as sick until the time came for the renewal of ration cards; then he either appeared and proved his illness to be genuine, or was dropped from the factory's rolls.[193] To be dismissed for any cause, or to be left without employment when the factory closed or was destroyed, was, for most people, a great calamity. Such workers had to turn in their ration cards and obtain new ones from the *raion* authorities; but the issuing of a new card, as in cases of theft, took time, so that these people were left without food for days.[194]

Working had other inducements. One of the principal ones was the fact that often workers could eat at the factory canteen, which was sometimes able to provide a little extra food if the management displayed initiative and energy. This hot food usually consisted of a plate or two of watery cabbage soup or very thin gruel, but sometimes there was also a little extra bread.[195] In the diary of an employee at an electric power station there appears the following notation for November 11: "For two days we've been getting cabbage soup made from gray cabbage—a hard wooden-like leaf in salt water, without any trace of fat and with such a smell that it permeates the whole room. One has to eat it without breathing. And when this cabbage is washed and boiled in its sour form, one chokes from the smell."[196] Another worker noted that in December the factory canteen issued for the employees a tub of boiled wheat and a tub of water in which the wheat had been cooked, each worker receiving one tablespoon of the cereal and unlimited amounts of the water.[197]

Little of this food could be taken home, since the management was primarily interested in preserving the strength of the workers. However, it did mean that workers could at least sometimes give part of their bread rations to their families.

Factory managements often tried to develop independent sources of food, either by trading, or by growing vegetables in factory gardens or greenhouses. The factories also organized dormitories for the workers so that they could live at the plant and conserve their strength. Some of the more enterprising ones set up baths and laundry facilities, which were otherwise virtually nonexistent in the city.[198]

Beyond the powerful inducements of extra food or the use of facilities like these, the authorities could only fall back on propaganda in their attempt to inspire the workers to greater effort. There were workers who accepted the repeated statement that it was their duty to keep the defending army supplied. Posters showing a soldier pointing a finger at the reader and asking, "You! How have you helped the front?" were probably effective, at least in implying that unless the workers produced more, soldiers would be killed and the city might fall to the enemy.[199] Shaming laggards in various ways, such as posting their names on the bulletin boards or forcing them to watch how their comrades worked, was also effective in many instances.[200] But the pressure this propaganda could create was minor in comparison with the effect of the ration cards. Later even the leadership spoke in wonder at the workers' will power and refusal to give up altogether, since the extra rations did not compensate the workers for the physical exhaustion entailed in the performance of their tasks.[201] But then it was a wonder that Leningrad held out at all.

In view of the uncertainty of the situation, the authorities in Moscow, particularly those in charge of economic planning, were still anxious to

evacuate the most valuable parts of Leningrad's industry and population. Control over evacuation continued to be vested in Moscow. For
example, in mid-October the decision that the tank shop of the Kirov
Works, together with 11,614 workers and technicians and their families,
should be evacuated by air to Cheliabinsk and Sverdlovsk was made by
the State Defense Committee. The same procedure applied to the evacuation of 6,000 workers of the Izhora Works.[202]

In ignorance of the exact situation, the authorities in Moscow often
issued evacuation orders that could not be carried out. Only one workshop of the Kirov Works could be moved in October, while the rest was
crated and had to wait until the summer of 1942 before it could leave.[203]
In October, too, the huge turbine shop of the Elektrosila Works was
ordered evacuated, although its equipment could not be moved by
plane.[204] A number of other factories had similar experiences. The following radio conversation gives some idea of Moscow's attitude:

MOSCOW. As far as possible you are to send immediately by air the machinery,
material, and labor about which you received instructions some time ago.
LENINGRAD. It cannot be done now.
MOSCOW. Why not? Maybe we should intervene at this end?
LENINGRAD. That is of no use. You won't be able to do anything there either.
It is simply impossible and completely out of the question to send any-
thing now. Do you understand me?
MOSCOW. I understand. How long is this situation going to last?
LENINGRAD. No one knows that.
MOSCOW. You must be able to judge when it will be possible again?
LENINGRAD. It is difficult to judge, maybe at the end of the next month.
Everything is ready to be shipped. But it is not possible to ship now.
MOSCOW [indistinct words].
LENINGRAD. Don't talk so much; you are talking nonsense. I will write you
in detail. When you have read it, you will understand.[205]

Since there were many competing demands for space on the few evacuation planes and boats, it was often up to the higher authorities in Moscow to determine priorities.

The evacuation of a part of Leningrad's skilled workers was motivated not by humanitarian feelings on the part of the leadership, but
rather by necessity. New industries, built around the evacuated factories, were being established in Siberia and in the Urals, and they
lacked trained workers. "Cheliabinsk, for instance, had never made
tanks. It was essential to start this tank production going in the shortest
possible time."[206] The workers from the tank shop of the Kirov Works
and their families were therefore loaded into planes and sent to Cheliabinsk to organize and operate the new tank plant.

At this time, in addition to workers, technicians, scientists, and administrators, who were usually ordered to leave, some people left the

city under less specific instructions; some families of officials and of higher army and navy officers were evacuated, along with certain people who managed to pull the necessary strings to obtain permission to go.[207] An example of this is contained in the following request from the Military Medical Administration of the Northwest Front, addressed to the Council for Evacuation in Moscow: "The wife of the Military First Rank Doctor, Professor Glasunov, is to be authorized to leave the city of Leningrad and to settle wherever she chooses in the unoccupied territory of Russia."[208] By the end of the year a total of 35,114 persons had been evacuated by air from Leningrad. In addition, people were evacuated by boat over Lake Ladoga during October and November, the Leningrad authorities being anxious to rid the city of as many unnecessary persons as possible. This route was especially hazardous because of the storms and German attacks on the ships. Nevertheless, by mid-November, when the boat traffic came to a halt because of the freezing of the lake, 33,479 persons had been evacuated in this fashion.[209]

Some of the workers, technicians, and professional people who left received their orders from the management of their place of work, who in turn had been told by Moscow how many persons of various categories to evacuate. In other instances, individual technicians, Party members, or administrators received their orders direct from Moscow, as is illustrated by the following radio conversation:

LENINGRAD. When must I leave from here?
MOSCOW. You can get ready. A telegram will be dispatched to you in the next few days.[210]

The authorities also sought to evacuate unemployed persons without close family ties in Leningrad, such as retired people, or persons who could obtain release from their places of employment; their departure, however, depended on the availability of transportation.[211]

As before, the popular attitude toward evacuation varied. Despite the horrors and uncertainty of life in Leningrad, evacuation was by no means regarded by all as the most desirable way to escape. Some still wished to share the fate of the city and its inhabitants, or felt ashamed to leave at so critical a time.[212] One Leningrader noted in her diary: "If one has to perish, then let it be here."[213] There were others who would not abandon close friends and relatives. Still others continued to be reluctant because of the known or suspected dangers of the trip; the evacuation boats and planes were often attacked by German aircraft. More than ever, many people were afraid of becoming evacuees in faraway places where they would be among strangers and at the mercy of the local authorities. These fears were reinforced by letters from evacuees complaining bitterly about conditions. Typical of these are the following excerpts from letters intercepted by the Germans:

I fear that this business will take a long time. But we have nothing to live on, and the prices are rising not daily but hourly. . . .

Living here is unbearably expensive. We live together with twenty people in one common room. There is no wood, no beds; we sleep on the floor. If we travel in winter to Siberia in freight cars, we don't know that we will arrive there alive. Probably we will be dead. . . .

How we can travel in this cold and above all in freight cars, I cannot imagine. Maybe we shall not even reach our goal, because we shall die of cold. . . .

You cannot imagine what torment we suffer. Daily we are promised transportation, but up to now there has been no sign of it. . . .[214]

Of course, there were also many Leningraders who saw in evacuation the only alternative to death from starvation or bombardment. These people sought to leave and were jealous of those who managed to do so. But only very few had the opportunity to leave. The vast majority of the population did not expect to escape the privations resulting from the siege.

The deterioration of conditions in Leningrad affected the control agencies as well as those they were supposed to control. While the leadership still sought to exercise total control, it found it increasingly difficult to do so. In the end it was forced to disregard minor violations of rules in the areas of food rationing, or temporarily nonexistent services, and to concentrate instead on preserving the more vital political and security controls. The latter had become particularly important now that it was highly uncertain how long the population would tolerate the conditions imposed upon it. After all, people now doubted that Leningrad or even Moscow would be able to resist the Germans. *Leningradskaia pravda* thus took a typically severe tone on November 12: "Enemy elements are gambling on our food difficulties, trying to sow defeatist sentiments among the people of the city. These fascist agents call for the surrender of the city to the mercy of the enemy. . . . Anyone who tries to make use of our difficulties and privations for hostile agitation cannot be regarded otherwise than as a fascist agent, undermining our rear from within.[215]

The same organizations and agencies as before exercised control, but with lowered efficiency as hunger and cold increased. The ordinary militia became less evident in the streets of the city. Some of its members began to collapse at their posts and die from starvation and exhaustion like the rest of the population. The chief of a militia unit noted in his diary on December 2 that his unit was undermanned by 32 per cent; 26 per cent were so weak as to be unable to rise; 16 per cent could not stand, but could work sitting down; and 26 per cent were available for duty.[216] To assist the militia, it was decided on December 8 to form a Komsomol guard regiment composed of 40–50 Komsomols from each *raion*, most of whom were 16 or 17 years old and all of them very weak from hunger.[217] Other security forces that were still in evidence were the guards posted at all factories, communication centers, and other key points, and the army and shore patrols that guarded military installations. But these forces were small and were not primarily concerned with controlling the behavior of the Leningraders. Supervision of the population by the Party declined because, especially on the lower echelons, Party members, too, were suffering from exhaustion and hunger, and because many members had been evacuated or assigned to assist the army or perform other tasks outside the city.[218] Thus, just when the danger of civil unrest and disobedience was potentially greatest, the leadership's ability to maintain its controls declined.

Tight supervision over all aspects of behavior of individual Leningraders was no longer possible. Increasing numbers of people now began to move without authorization, as death and evacuation left many apartments in the city empty. According to the law, when a person died or was evacuated, leaving his possessions behind, his apartment was to be sealed by the manager after an inventory was made of the contents.[219] The empty apartments were then registered by the manager with the housing department of the respective *raion* executive committee. Legally, no one could obtain or use a new apartment without final confirmation by the committee.[220]

But as the winter progressed, the house managers were less inclined or able to uphold the law. As residents starved to death or moved to better living quarters, whole apartment houses were left nearly or completely empty. Remaining managers increasingly let unauthorized persons have apartments on a temporary, unofficial basis and did not bother to obtain the authorization of the committees or register the fact with the militia. Consequently, there were large numbers of persons occupying living space "on their own initiative."[221] In some cases individual house administrators allowed the residents of upper floors of buildings to move into empty apartments on the lower floor, where they would be safer from artillery fire.[222] The situation was further complicated by the fact that although a number of managers, administrators, and technicians had taken up residence in their offices or factories, they still retained formal possession of their apartments. According to one source, it became very difficult to locate people because no central file existed that could show where they had moved or what had become of them.[223]

Of course, the authorities did not relinquish their claim to any of the controls, but, on the contrary, continued to try to enforce them to the limit of their ability. Violations of rules that did not come under the category of treasonable behavior and that were not major crimes were tried and punished by special administrative commissions. These commissions, however, like the militia and the house administrations that forwarded the accusations to them, were inevitably affected by the conditions prevailing in the city. A survey of the work of these commissions during the months of September and October led the city's executive committee to complain that there were "instances of liberalism in the investigation of individual cases," that the commissions did not use the full legal power granted to them by the wartime laws, and that the militia and house administrations presented their cases in incorrect form and only after much delay.[224] The commissions found their task even more difficult after October.

On the whole, beginning in November if not earlier, control by terror was not feasible and instead the authorities had to rely on control by persuasion and example. It was obviously dangerous to push the hungry and enervated population too far, lest it rebel against the controls altogether. To complicate the problem for the authorities, the earlier techniques of mass propaganda and education could no longer be used.

The major technical difficulty that the propaganda operation encountered was the declining availability of various media. From September to December 1941, it was progressively more difficult to supply copies of the major Leningrad newspapers, and in some cases publication was actually interrupted.[225] It became increasingly necessary to rely on newspapers posted on bulletin boards or in workshops, offices, and streets, or on the reading aloud of newspapers in air raid shelters and at other places of public gathering.[226] The use of radios was also curtailed by the lack of electric power. In time, only some of the public loud-speakers mounted in the streets continued to broadcast. But the shivering and starving population was increasingly disinclined to remain in the open in order to listen. Furthermore, as a result of the shortage of personnel for the radio station, "there were several hours of radio silence during the day."[227]

The propaganda did not try to hide the gravity of Leningrad's situation, although it continued to remain vague on the details of the military picture and never failed to hold out hopes for a relief of the city. On October 21 the fact that the Germans were stopped before the walls of Leningrad was mentioned, but the possibility of a renewed attack was not ruled out.[228] At the same time radio and newspaper propaganda, without being more specific than the official communiqués, made it clear that Moscow was in imminent danger of being taken by the enemy.[229] Here again the propaganda, while hopeful of victory, was unwilling to guarantee that Moscow would be held. The propaganda also did not hesitate to reveal that Leningrad's industry was encountering many production difficulties and held out no hope for a speedy improvement in living conditions. Then, on November 12, the editorial of *Leningradskaia pravda* warned that the enemy planned to starve Leningrad out and that worse was to come: "The Bolshevik Party never hides anything from the people. It always tells the truth no matter how cruel it is. While the siege lasts, one cannot count on an improvement in the supply of food."[230]

Although the ice road began to function in the second half of November, no information about it appears to have been published to improve popular morale. At that time, of course, the success of the ice road was far from assured. The press even indicated that some people were urging the surrender of the city to the enemy.[231]

One of the propaganda objectives, as before, was to instill in the population a fear of the Germans in order to discourage it from thinking of surrender as a possibly attractive alternative. Consequently, the press and radio continued to publicize alleged instances of German atrocities and German plans to kill the city's population. Interrogations of captured Germans and excerpts from what were purported to be German letters and diaries were also published. One diary was said to contain the following entry: "Hans Ritter: October 12. The more one kills, the easier it is. Today participated in the clean-up of the camps of suspects—shot 82."[232] An "official" German order was said to state: "Kill every Soviet Russian; do not stop if you find yourself face to face with an old man or a woman, a little girl or a boy—kill!"[233]

Soviet propaganda also stimulated fear of the Germans by circulating reports about the SS. police division that had been brought to the Leningrad front and that was said to be intended for occupation duty in the city: "General Malwerstedt of the SS. Polizei Division made it perfectly clear that the SS. were going to undertake a gigantic purge of the city, that 400,000 people at least would be killed off or tortured to death right away."[234] After the recapture of Tikhvin in December the Leningrad press reported the finding of mass graves and long rows of gallows, torture chambers, and other evidences of atrocities committed by the Germans against the civilian population.[235]

When starvation set in, it became important for the propaganda to show that there was no hope for better conditions under enemy occupation, that in fact life under German occupation could only be worse than the current privations and hardships. The Germans were described as being ragged and hungry themselves and unable to feed the population. One technique was to publish what were said to be letters from Russians living in the areas of the Leningrad *oblast* that were occupied by the enemy. In November *Leningradskaia pravda* reprinted extracts from such letters: "The Germans take everything they can lay their hands on . . ." "All our young people have been driven by the Germans into concentration camps . . ." "If things go on like this we will all die of hunger."[236] The Germans were portrayed as ill-equipped for the winter. Some were said to have been forced to dress in women's clothes looted from the population. One report says that some captured Germans were paraded in such dresses through the streets of Leningrad.[237]

But hope for a speedy relief of the city was not generally held out in most of the printed propaganda, which, in flagrant contradiction to the above propaganda picture of the Germans, spoke of the enemy as being strong, clever, and well equipped. Not until December did the first signs of real hope appear. On December 10 the Informburo announced the recapture of Tikhvin, which had been preceded a few days before by the liberation of Rostov. On December 11 news of victories on the Moscow front began to arrive. Yet, although this was hailed by the Leningrad press as a sign that the Soviet victory over the Germans was beginning, no promise was made of a speedy change in Leningrad's condition, and the population was warned that a "hard struggle" remained ahead of them and that they would "have to suffer many severe tests."[238]

The propaganda continued to assert that the Party and its chiefs would lead the country to victory and that the nation was rallying around the leadership; but, as before, the population was asked to fight in defense of its own interests and of the fatherland rather than to preserve the regime. There was, of course, a celebration of the October Revolution, during which speeches were made accusing the Germans of trying to "destroy everything won by October," and appeals were made for greater heroism at the front and in the factories.[239] But even Kalinin's letter on that occasion still reminded the Leningraders that they were fighting for their homes, freedom, and families, and made no mention of defending the Soviet system as such.[240]

In Leningrad the radio propagandists became so involved in their propaganda efforts that they cut out all other types of broadcasts. According to one radio official, "It was all agitation from morning till night. Well, there weren't even enough political instructors; there were several hours of radio silence during the day, with only the metronome ticking away, tick, tick, tick. . . . Then they began to say to us: Why spread such gloom and despondency? Couldn't we have at any rate some music? They say that Zhdanov himself said that."[241] But by then many of the musicians were dying of hunger, and the radio committee did not have any food for them.

Maintaining popular morale and cheering up the starving population were, of course, the Party's principal concerns. The prevailing conditions made it increasingly inexpedient to hold mass meetings, which were the favorite technique of the professional propagandists. Instead, it became necessary for the Party agitators to meet with the inhabitants individually or at most in small groups. According to *Leningradskaia pravda*:

The task of the agitators and propagandists, of each Communist and patriot, is to bring a cheerful word into the soul of the masses. A passionate, convinced, and truthful word redoubles the strength, lifts up the weak, inspires those who waver. A discussion, a friendly conversation at the machine, in the dining room, in the shelter, in the corridor of a communal apartment, at the store, must be used to raise the spirit of the people, strengthen their cheerfulness, dispel their doubts.[242]

The Komsomol was also mobilized to uphold morale among the workers. Zhdanov is reported to have told a meeting of Komsomol leaders: "The enterprises have ceased to work; there is no electricity, no water, no food; a second ring of encirclement is being formed, Tikhvin is occupied—it is hard. Your task above all tasks is to work for the welfare of the workers; encourage, inspire, and console all those who suffer. If you manage this assignment, we will thank you for it."[243]

In reality, the influence of propaganda on popular attitudes and morale declined in proportion to the worsening of living conditions and the breakdown of the propaganda media. Not only did the propaganda media reach fewer people, but the population cared even less than before to listen to ideological arguments and patriotic speeches, and was only eager for information that affected its well-being, such as reports on food, fuel, and the possibilities of a breakthrough by the Red Army. The following entry in the diary of a Leningrader is revealing: "The radio says: It is better to die on your feet [facing the enemy]. . . . But we don't want to die at all, neither standing nor lying down. I don't want to think about it."[244] However, more and more people were becoming increasingly convinced of the veracity of the earlier propaganda statements about the Germans.

German propaganda efforts continued to remain ineffective. The failure of the Wehrmacht to capture either Leningrad or Moscow raised doubts in the popular mind about the power of the German army. Furthermore, most Leningraders inevitably blamed the Germans for their suffering. Even the leaflets written for the Germans by Russian deserters were not likely to evoke a favorable response. One such leaflet, for example, promised good treatment, said the German army was undefeatable, denounced the "Jewish-Stalinist" policies of the government, and ended with the words, "Thank Herr Adolf Hitler for his correct policy. Pray to God to give him many years of health."[245] The starving inhabitants of Leningrad had little to thank Hitler for.

Although it was the responsibility of the elite to boost the people's morale, it had little cause for optimism. The failure of the initial German assault on Leningrad in September had only postponed the likelihood of the city's fall. The elite was well aware that unless the German ring around the city was broken soon, Leningrad would be forced to surrender. Information on the precise state of Leningrad's ability to hold out was a closely guarded secret known only to seven persons of the city's leadership; but everybody understood that there remained little food.[246] Referring to two reductions in rations in November, a member of the elite wrote: "The future of Leningrad gives cause for anguish. . . . We are sinking two degrees further into the abyss." And later: "Will there be enough strength to wait until the blockade is lifted? And how many will remain alive to be glad that they survived?"[247] The elite was not only better informed about conditions in Leningrad, but also more concerned over the German threat to Moscow, since it had a greater stake in the survival of the regime. It was thus inevitable that there should be a growing "feeling of fear about the future" among the elite. In November Zhdanov spoke to a meeting of Party leaders assuring them that the Central Committee of the Party and the government would do everything to help Leningrad, but he did not hide from them the gravity of the situation.[248] Party propagandists and political organizers were also informed that the food situation was "extremely bad."[249]

Moreover, the elite's morale was probably greatly shaken by the atmosphere of defeat and panic in Moscow at the height of the crisis and by the loss of contact with administrative centers in the capital. Much of its information about the situation in Moscow was obtained from radio conversations with that city and, no doubt, disseminated by word of mouth. The following conversation took place on October 16 between a girl in Leningrad and her family in Moscow; her father must have been a person of some importance, since, as a rule, the radio could not be used for private conversations.

MOSCOW—MOTHER. Do you have anything to eat, child?
LENINGRAD—DAUGHTER. No, Mother, we have nothing here, we are starving.
MOSCOW—MOTHER. Things are not as yet that bad here; I will try to send you something right away. Ask for your release and go somewhere else.
LENINGRAD—DAUGHTER. No, Mother, I can't do that. All such requests have been refused for a long time. I will have to wait for an order. Are you in danger there, Mother, from the air?
MOSCOW—MOTHER. No, child, not that; but things are terrible as they are.
LENINGRAD—DAUGHTER. Can't you leave?
MOSCOW—MOTHER. I don't know what will happen. Say a few words to Father; he is right here.
FATHER. How are you, my poor child?
LENINGRAD—DAUGHTER (*crying*). What will you do, Father?
MOSCOW—FATHER. We are waiting and looking our fate in the face. The

situation is very sad and uncertain. Anything can happen to us. I have written you that you are to write there [probably an agency that could arrange the daughter's transfer from Leningrad], but it is too late for that. I cannot advise you, for everything I think of today is overtaken by tomorrow's events. Good-by, my child, and don't cry. . . .

MOTHER. My dear child, I don't know what to do. I can barely stand on my feet. It is my sole wish that we shall see each other again. (*Both are crying.*)[250]

Another conversation:

LENINGRAD. Is any one of the superiors there?

MOSCOW. No, we have stopped our operations.

LENINGRAD. Isn't there anybody besides you?

MOSCOW. No, no one is here. They are all already at the station.

LENINGRAD. Has your organization only suspended work, or ceased completely?

MOSCOW. The work is completely stopped.

LENINGRAD. Should I send you material?

MOSCOW. What do you want to send material for when everything is finished?

LENINGRAD (*mumbles an embarrassed farewell*).

MOSCOW (*the sound of a woman crying*).

LENINGRAD (*a radio operator, to her colleague in Moscow*). What is the matter with you?

MOSCOW. There is nothing wrong with me. This is our mood. (*Sound of crying.*)[251]

Officials and technicians whose families resided in Moscow feared the worst for their loved ones. Later the Leningraders spoke of the Moscow panic with some contempt, overlooking the fact that their own steadfastness was dictated at least in part by circumstances and not necessarily by superior character or loyalty.[252]

Despite their various privileges, many members of the elite had to concentrate increasingly on the problem of individual survival, particularly on how to survive the starvation. Many became very weak, others fell ill, and a large number died during the winter of 1941–42. Seventeen thousand Party members alone died during the siege, primarily from starvation and disease.[253] The losses were highest among the rank-and-file members and the lower echelons of officials, who had fewer ration privileges than those in important positions; but even in the higher ranks there were a number who could barely walk about. The fact was that in many instances the slightly superior food rations were insufficient to compensate the elite for the energy it expended in trying to solve overwhelmingly difficult problems.

Promoting rank-and-file members to positions of authority to replace evacuated, mobilized, or sick members was not always successful. According to a Soviet postwar source, "It was found that the *raion* Party committees did not know people well, particularly the rank-and-file workers, and that is why not a few mistakes were made in the selection and promotion of new cadres to responsible positions to replace those who had left for the army. A part of the new Party and economic leaders was found to be unsuitable and had to be replaced."[254] Of course, there were other instances when those promoted proved themselves to be resourceful and energetic, and carried out their new responsibilities most successfully.[255]

It was inevitable that the desperate conditions made some members of the elite give up hope. Party leaders later admitted that "there were, of course, instances when one or another *aktivist* became apathetic, lost his perspective, threw up his hands. By their looks alone they depressed those around them."[256] When this happened, the *aktivists* had to be replaced or were evacuated.[257] It is probable that among the rank-and-file members, such as those working in factories, this apathy was more prevalent than among the leadership. It was particularly hard to set an example of high productivity or to show unwavering enthusiasm and faith on an empty stomach and with shaking knees.

The only escape, evacuation, was limited not only by the poor transportation facilities, but also by the tightness of the control. Unless the elite member was part of a group selected to leave, he had to pull strings in Moscow to be authorized to leave and then again had to struggle to obtain his release from Leningrad. There were, of course, some who were successful, and others who sought to become attached to groups scheduled for evacuation.[258] But even in this period there were members of the elite (including the writer Tikhonov, who then held the rank of regimental commissar), of all categories, who, for various personal reasons, rejected offers of evacuation and chose to remain in Leningrad.[259]

Privileges in matters of rations, fuel, and housing were, of course, influential in keeping some elements of the elite at their posts and working. The elite had a better chance than the population of obtaining food packages from friends or colleagues in Moscow and elsewhere. After the beginning of the siege, these packages became an important factor in the diet of some members of the elite. Owing to its connections and influence the elite was also in a position to resort to all sorts of other means to obtain additional food and fuel, either on a personal basis or in the name of an organization. At least some, if not most, of the officials and employees of the food transportation and distribution system, and of the army quartermaster corps, exploited their positions for their own benefit.[260] According to reports, some women, even highly placed ones, sought to become intimate with such officials in order to obtain food.[261] Nor were some persons in privileged positions above engaging in black-market operations. In fact, as was noted earlier, the black market was supplied and operated largely with the connivance of various members of the elite. Members of the elite were also the black market's best customers.[262]

On the whole, however, the elite did its job and loyally backed the leadership in its decisions. For every member of the elite who despaired or became apathetic there were others who worked with energy, devotion, and a ruthless determination not to surrender. One Party member is reported to have said, "We shall eat bricks, but we will not surrender the city."[263] Despite the bleak outlook for Leningrad's future, the campaign to recruit new members into the Party was fairly successful: in December, for example, some 970 Leningraders joined the Party.[264] Of course, some probably did so in the hope of bettering their living conditions or as a result of pressure by Party organizers. But there were others who joined out of conviction, out of a desire to demonstrate their loyalty to the regime at a time of crisis, or even out of a wish to display defiance to the Germans.

In the end, patriotism, fear of the Germans or of the population, ideological convictions, or simple opportunism all combined to prevent any significant wavering among the elite. Consequently, although the efficiency of the administrative control declined, the leadership, thanks to the sustained efforts of the elite, continued to give the impression that it still had a powerful machine at its disposal with which to impose its will on the population. This greatly influenced the behavior of the Leningraders.

The morale of the population was inevitably very low in this period. After the front was stabilized, the population began slowly to perceive that instead of a German attack, it was probably going to face a protracted and painful siege. The real significance of the siege was made evident to the population by the bombardment and the successive reductions in the food rations. Everybody understood clearly that unless the current food ration was raised, there was no chance of surviving for more than a short time. This was soon confirmed by the rapid increase in the death rate. People repeatedly grasped at hopeful rumors, which reflected their wishful thinking, to the effect that food rations would be increased and that large amounts of food were ready to be shipped to Leningrad.[265] Disappointment in these hopes tended further to undermine morale. Everybody understood equally well that the leadership was highly unlikely to surrender the city voluntarily out of a humanitarian concern for the lives of its inhabitants. Instead, the leadership was expected to fight on at least as long as it could manage to feed the army and the elite.[266]

Consequently, the majority of the population could only look forward to death from starvation, unless the authorities were forced to surrender the city or unless the siege was lifted by the Red Army. Despite various rumors and reports that kept the latter hope alive, rescue seemed unlikely to materialize in time to save hundreds of thousands from dying of starvation, unless, of course, the population was willing to take matters into its own hands. But the population considered itself the victim of a situation it was powerless to change. Rather than make what it would have regarded as the rash choice of attempting to force the authorities' hand, the population became progressively more and more apathetic. In the end, even the "tears froze within the people of Leningrad."[267]

The population's attitudes and expectations were influenced to a considerable extent by its image of the Germans. While in August and September many Leningraders had consoled themselves with the thought that life under the Germans would not be too bad, this opinion altered as the siege dragged on. All kinds of enemy action against the city were at first tolerated, or fatalistically accepted, because they appeared to be short-lived and justifiable in view of the probable fall of the city. But when the German advance stopped, the bombardment gradually came to be regarded as an indication of the German desire to destroy Leningrad.[268] In time, the siege came increasingly to be viewed either as a deliberate German decision to torture the population, or as a sign of the enemy's weakness.[269] Either interpretation caused increasing popular disappointment and hostility toward the Germans.

Yet this growing rejection of the notion of the enemy-liberator did not mean that all Leningraders ceased to hope for a German victory. However, the motive for wanting the Germans to take Leningrad was no longer primarily a political one, but rather the desperate desire to escape death from starvation and bombardment. Whether or not a person held this attitude depended chiefly on how well he expected the Germans to be able to feed the city. There were those who believed that a surrender would improve their situation. Their hopes were sustained by rumors reporting the reopening of stores in occupied areas, and the feeding of deserters and prisoners. School children said: "They say that they [the Germans] captured a boy, fed him till he was full, stuffed his pockets with chocolate, and released him."[270]

But others, influenced by Soviet propaganda and by their increasing hatred of the enemy, doubted that the Germans could or would feed the inhabitants. Preferring a Russian to a German regime, these people accepted the necessity of suffering until the encirclement was broken by the Red Army.[271] The hope that this would happen was strengthened by the fact that there were no indications of the Germans renewing their assault on Leningrad. A captured letter from a girl to her soldier friend read:

Mow the accursed fascist snakes down to the ground. We live here in the heart of the revolution and believe that it cannot get any worse. Our hopes rest with the Red Fleet and the Red Army, which firmly defend Leningrad. Even though we in the city have a hard time, we understand the reason for it and bear the load together with you, with the same desire to win and to drive the enemy from the land.[272]

A man wrote to his brother in the army: "Beat the enemy without mercy, without sparing your strength. Attack him in every position. Defend our dear city of Leningrad. No mercy for the enemy on our holy Soviet soil."[273]

There was also an element of natural local pride in the popular attitude toward the Germans. Some Leningraders were proud of having frustrated the enemy's attempt to capture the city, proud of being the focus of national attention, and proud of hanging on despite desperate difficulties.[274] One disaffected citizen wrote in his diary: "The Leningraders do not know what to do. . . . But with involuntary pride many say that Leningrad is a capital that has never been taken by anybody. The only one in history."[275] For the first time in World War II the undefeated German war machine was meeting its match. The protracted defense of Leningrad was reviving the Russian national self-respect that the early defeats had shaken.

Of course, this did not prevent many Leningraders from criticizing the leadership for its failure to preserve the population from the siege and the subsequent hardships. In this connection one informant reports hearing a woman exclaim, "The scoundrels, they should get a German bomb on their heads!"[276] Some Leningraders accused the leadership of being deliberately insensitive to the suffering of the population and resented the fact that although it was not able to feed the inhabitants, it plagued them with constant demands.[277] Furthermore, few Leningraders felt certain that their sacrifices and privations would be justified in the end, since they believed that their city could not survive the loss of Moscow, and as a result the collapse of the Soviet regime, which in November and December appeared to be imminent.[278] At the same time, under the prevailing conditions few could expect to survive to see the end of the siege. Yet there was no absolute certainty that all of this would occur, and most people preferred not to think about the future. And although some Leningraders were eager to have the siege end, no matter how this came about, others were patriotic or stubborn enough to be reluctant to contemplate the possibility of a voluntary surrender.[279] Thus neither on the question of surrender nor on the attitude toward the leadership was the popular sentiment uniform.[280]

This does not mean that there were no instances of what the Soviet authorities called treasonable activities. But what is surprising is that these instances were so few and that for the most part they were, strictly speaking, nonpolitical in nature. These treasonable incidents involved speculators, looters, robbers, rumormongers, and panicmongers; although the Soviet press labeled these last as German agents, they were probably merely people who were less cautious in their speech than the majority of citizens.

Major bread riots and looting of stores and warehouses, which would not have been surprising, apparently simply did not take place.[281] Public demonstrations demanding the surrender of the city were absent. One informant reports being told that a group of wives of elite and professional people had petitioned the authorities to surrender.[282] This case remained unknown to other informants. However, in November the Leningrad newspapers mentioned "fascist agents" who called for the surrender of the city.[283] Some cases of unrest or strikes among workers, primarily on account of the food shortage, were reported to the Germans by deserters and prisoners of war.[284] Whether they actually occurred is not certain, since the reports were based on hearsay and none of the informants were able to confirm them. Some people, of course, discussed with friends the possibility of revolt by the population when it was driven sufficiently far by despair. They said that the situation might bring about a riot by the women (*babii bunt*), which historically had frequently been the signal for a general rebellion.[285] But the women did not act. The following conversation between some Leningrad women was recorded by a Russian soldier in his diary on November 27, 1941:

At this time the food rations for the last ten days of the month were being issued, and one could hear in the streetcar how the housewives talked about it in great excitement, to the effect that practically nothing was being issued on the basis of the ration cards, and that one could not bear this any longer because one could not live on such rations but only swell up from hunger. One woman said that we should do something about it together. Another woman said: "Do not think that everybody is starving; some have reserves, others get supplies through friends, still others can obtain privileged rations. All of them will say nothing, but we, we will yell a little and that will be the end of this business."[286]

There appear to have been no instances of attempts to harangue the population or to organize public action, nor did any of the informants hear of any organized anti-Soviet groups operating in the city.

An article published by an officer of the secret police describes alleged instances of subversive activities in Leningrad; but, again, few, if any, of these activities could properly be described as political. The writer describes one group made up of children of former Mensheviks and Socialist-Revolutionaries, and headed by the son of the Socialist-

Revolutionary Denisov, which "published on a hectograph leaflets calling for the surrender of the city to the Germans." He also mentions a
sinister gang of former nobles and officers who had succeeded in becoming members of scientific organizations and institutions of higher
learning. "Playing on the food difficulties, these traitors to the fatherland tried to provoke the looting of bread and food stores. On top
of that they planned to murder leading personalities in Leningrad."
Finally:

> During the difficult winter months a counterrevolutionary fascist group,
> made up of persons with dark pasts who had previously been tried for crimi-
> nal offenses, was liquidated. Three of them, who had escaped from jail, were
> living in Leningrad illegally. The group called itself "The Organization for
> the Defense of Hitler's Interests." The members of this group produced
> fascist leaflets calling on the population to give up further resistance to the
> German fascist aggressors. With the objective of undermining the food dis-
> tribution system in Leningrad, the German hirelings manufactured fictitious
> ration cards and, taking advantage of their criminal contacts, stole rations
> from the food stores.[287]

It is clear that the so-called counterrevolutionary groups, if they
existed at all, were few in number and virtually inactive. The few leaflets printed were not widely circulated. Almost none of the informants
or the prisoners of war and deserters mentioned the existence of such
leaflets. In most instances the concern of the "gangs" was obviously
black-market operations or the theft of food, their counterrevolutionary
character being largely an invention of the secret police.

However, the police, assisted by the Komsomol, did carry out some
arrests. In May, *Leningradskaia pravda* published a list of secret
police officers who were decorated for their work in "crushing enemy
agents."[288] The Komsomol guards arrested a considerable number of
people for "violations of revolutionary order and public security"; but
this cannot be taken as a serious indication of extensive political unrest,
since the authorities attributed political motives to all kinds of nonpolitical crimes and misdemeanors.[289] All the available information
indicates that the overwhelming majority of Leningraders remained
politically passive and showed no intention of challenging the authority
of the leadership. Although many people complained and grumbled,
most of them remained "apathetic and completely absorbed in their
personal experiences."[290]

In the eyes of the regime the act that was most clearly anti-Soviet
was desertion. The deserter not only broke all ties with the Soviet
regime and placed himself beyond punishment by the Soviet authorities,
but also became *ipso facto* a tool of the enemy by passing under enemy
control and protection. Actually, although the population was aware

of the political significance of the act of desertion, its motives for deserting were usually entirely nonpolitical. The desperate desire to escape
death by starvation, or the urge to see one's family in the occupied areas,
was a more frequent motive for desertion than the wish to escape Soviet
controls. Desertion for civilians was very difficult because of the tight
security measures in the battle zone and the danger of being shot at
by either side while crossing the lines. Consequently, few civilians
managed to do so. Of the motives of one who did desert it was reported: "In Petersburg he could look forward only to imminent death,
whereas in flight he still had a last bit of hope to save his life. The
situation in Petersburg is hopeless and beyond recovery, and a quick
death from a bullet, be it while fleeing or by execution, is preferable
to a slow and painful death."[291]

The Germans encountered more fugitives and refugees coming from
the immediate battle zone and the suburbs of Leningrad than from the
city proper. In October a German report warned that although there
were far fewer than the expected 100,000 to 200,000 refugees, the stream
of refugees was "constantly swelling."[292] Actually, beginning in November, the number of refugees or deserters rapidly declined. Far greater
opportunity for desertion existed for the soldiers, *opolchenie* men, fortification construction workers, and agents sent behind the German
lines. There is no doubt that there were deserters from all such units.
A German report pointed out that many Soviet agents who dropped
behind German lines deserted:

> Since the choice of agents often depends on the place of origin of that
> person in the various areas [of Russia], one can say of them that there were
> many among them who accepted their assignment only in order to get away
> from the city and to get to their families. Some reported voluntarily to the
> Germans, while the greater part of these people have probably quietly dis-
> appeared among the civilian population.[293]

However, another German report warned of the increasing number of
women and children who were being used by the Soviet authorities for
espionage and sabotage purposes and who were entering the German
lines and loyally attempting to accomplish their missions.[294]

It is thus clear that the overwhelming majority of Leningraders were
"disciplined," as one informant put it.[295] Whether this was entirely or
even primarily due to the efficiency of the administrative and police
controls is open to doubt. Controls alone can hardly explain the absence
of popular rioting, revolt, or looting, which under the circumstances
the leadership would have found difficult to suppress. The explanation
seems to lie rather in the fact that the population of Leningrad never
gave any thought to such action. Strange as it may seem, all the informants whom I interviewed stated that although they believed Lenin-

grad, and even the war, to be lost and had little hope of surviving the siege, they never considered the possibility of taking action against the regime. Indeed, most of them were surprised by the suggestion that they had every reason to revolt: the fact that they had nothing to lose, that they disliked the Communist regime, and that life under the Germans would not necessarily be any worse. Contemporary German estimates of the situation confirm this attitude. Although every German report, based as it was on biased information supplied by prisoners of war and deserters, spoke of increasing popular dissatisfaction and despair in Leningrad, they all concluded that there was little likelihood of revolt.[296]

The fact that not even hunger and despair could provoke the population to riot or to resort to other forms of action appears to have been due to a variety of factors. Chief among these were patriotism, the control exercised by the ration system and the population's complete dependence on the authorities for food, lack of any sense of unity in opposition to the regime, uncertainty about the character and intentions of the Germans, and continuing evidence of the leadership's determination to maintain control. There was also little evidence of marked differences in living conditions between social groups, signs of which might have roused the population. Finally, most Leningraders believed the army to be loyal; therefore, any subversive action on their part would both betray their relatives and friends at the front and have to be taken without the army's support.[297]

Even more remarkable than the absence of riots was the extent to which the social-economic structure survived under such conditions and the degree to which the Leningraders continued to work and perform their duties. It was easy, of course, for people to believe that they were too weak and exhausted to perform the tasks demanded of them. Many Leningraders gave up trying and stayed in bed until they died of hunger and cold. But many others continued to work, to walk for hours to and from work, and to do their jobs. Many dragged themselves to their factories only to die there. In the words of one factory director: "How many workers came to this office saying: 'Chief, I shall be dead today or tomorrow'! We would send them to the factory hospital, but they always died. . . . Out of the 5,000 people we had here, several hundred died. A very large number of them died right here. . . . Many a man would drag himself to the factory, stagger in and die."[298] People went to work knowing that their children or other family members were dying at home. When a person died, his relatives buried him and then returned to work.

Some, of course, were motivated to do so because of the larger rations given to workers. It was of desperate importance for each person to obtain the largest ration possible in order to improve the chances of survival for himself and the members of his family. Driven by hunger and fear for their loved ones, the size of the ration outweighed for most people the effort required to earn it.

Another factor compelling cooperation with the authorities was the widespread desire to remain within an organization, not to be left alone to die without anyone knowing or caring. For many people, the factory or office was a sort of home where one was surrounded by friends and familiar activities, and where one could hope to find a helping hand. In the Soviet system the individual is to a considerable extent identified with his place of work—his shop, office, or work brigade. A good deal of his social life also revolves around his place of employment. He works not only for his employer, but also for the collective, the brigade, or the team to which he belongs and which he thus tends to view as a sort of second family.

There was also a desire to get away from home in order not to have to witness the suffering of one's family. Continuing, systematic work, no matter what its nature, sustained a man's will to live, even though it made inroads into his remaining reserves of physical strength. There was, as one informant said, "nothing else to do but to keep busy."[299] Work kept people from being overwhelmed by their fears and despair. As long as a man worked, he was alive; if he stopped, he was already dead; for his survival appeared to him to depend just as much on his will to work as on the rations he was eating. One citizen described this phenomenon as follows:

What we went through here was a test of character. . . . Not counting the old people, the sick, or those constitutionally in poor health, the first to die among those in normal health were people of weak character, those who gave in morally, who lost the will to work and thought too much of their stomachs. I noticed that when someone gave up washing his neck and ears, stopped going to work, and ate his ration of bread right away and then lay down and covered himself with a blanket, he wasn't long for this world.[300]

Although people died at their machines, in the offices and class-rooms, in the streets and at home, the survivors went on working despite everything. This psychological factor greatly facilitated matters for the leadership. Control measures other than the rationing system were of little or no importance in persuading people to work. People worked not only because the leadership ordered them to do so, but also because they wanted to themselves.[301]

This was also true for Leningraders whose activities did not bear directly on the war effort, such as those engaged in intellectual work. Even in these desperate days they continued their activities. Some secondary schools and trade schools were reopened on November 3, the teachers conducting their classes as well as they could; however, many students dropped out, and most schools closed down in December.[302] Institutes of higher learning remained open, and even gave examinations.[303] Research, literary, and other intellectual institutions continued to function as far as possible; the city's architectural organization, for example, collected blueprints of all the Leningrad landmarks.[304] One informant continued to work on the publication of Pushkin's collected writings; another concerned himself with a study of the Soviet arctic regions.[305] The Writers' and Artists' Unions and remaining members of the Academy of Sciences held meetings and gave lectures.[306]

In general, then, nonconformity in popular behavior was reduced to those areas that dealt with the immediate physical needs of each individual—that is, with food, water, fuel, and light. Each Leningrader sought to solve problems for himself as best he could. In the eyes of the population, the leadership's inability to provide the minimum necessary services and supplies gave each man license to shift for himself within the limits tolerated by the authorities; and since it was a matter of life or death, people did just that. But their activities remained unorganized and isolated. People did not flaunt what they did and took pains not to appear to challenge the authority of the leadership. The leadership, in turn, clearly reserved the right to put a stop to all violations of its regulations as soon as it felt able to do so, and this attitude was understood by the population.

Chapter 8

THE DYING CITY
December 15, 1941–March 1942

FROM A MILITARY point of view December 1941 proved to be a turning point in the war on the eastern front. The German *Blitzkrieg* had collapsed with Hitler's failure to capture either Leningrad or Moscow, and the weakened German forces had to bear the brunt of a general Soviet counteroffensive that came close to destroying the German invasion armies. The Germans were forced to carry out extensive and very costly retreats. Army Group North held out better than the others, but it was forced to retreat from Tikhvin, thus giving up the possibility of carrying out a complete encirclement of Leningrad; moreover, in the subsequent months it was repeatedly placed in a precarious situation by the Soviet offensive, so that for a while it seemed even possible that the siege would be lifted.

In January the Soviet forces encircled Kholm, and in early February they succeeded in cutting off a large German force on the left flank of Army Group North. After several months the encircled forces were freed, but the whole operation proved very costly for the Germans.[1]

In January the Soviet Army attempted to lift the siege of Leningrad by a direct attack north of Lake Ilmen. On January 13 the Second Soviet Assault Army crossed the Volkhov River in the area of Miasnoi-Bor, north of Novgorod, while other forces attacked in the Pogoste area, in an attempt to effect a junction at Liuban on the main rail line to Leningrad. By the end of January, after heavy fighting, the Second Assault Army penetrated some 35 miles into the German-held area and was a scant 10 miles short of Liuban. But the Germans were able to contain this advance as well as the Soviet attacks at Pogoste. In mid-March the Germans succeeded in encircling the Second Assault Army, which then fought on until its complete destruction in June 1942.

Its last commander, Lt. Gen. A. A. Vlasov, who surrendered only in July, later achieved a measure of dubious fame as the head of the German-sponsored Russian Army of Liberation. With the failure of these offensives all hope for the relief of Leningrad in 1942 had to be abandoned.[2]

Meanwhile, the fact that, contrary to all expectations, Leningrad had failed to surrender naturally exasperated Hitler, who consoled himself with accounts of the starvation in the city.[3] He still asserted that the Neva River would form the border between Germany and Finland, and that Leningrad, emptied of its population, would be left to fall into ruin. Although the Germans had neither the planes nor the artillery to destroy the city as Hitler wanted, he still hopefully anticipated Leningrad's collapse after the melting of the Ladoga ice. Nevertheless he was growing impatient with the situation, and no longer being certain of Leningrad's surrender, he began to contemplate a renewed assault on the city. New plans, which the Germans hoped would remove this thorn from their side, were therefore drafted in the summer of 1942.

While the military situation had improved somewhat, the city itself was living through its most trying days. Shrouded in snow and ice, silent except for the noise of gunfire at the front, Leningrad in the winter of 1941–42 resembled a ghost town more than a city still harboring several million inhabitants. Its citizens "lived like arctic explorers, hibernating in darkness and cold, mustering all their will power and firmly determined to put up with everything and survive until the spring brought warmth and light again, sometimes having to summon their last ounce of strength to carry on the daily work for the front and the city."[4] As for the appearance of the city: "Snowdrifts lay in the streets in those days, lumps of ice were slipping from the roofs, the pavements were hidden under layers of frozen snow, dirt was piled up in mounds, the yards were choked up with refuse, the debris of shattered walls lay scattered over the streets. There were bricks, broken barrels frozen into the snow, twisted, broken pipes, shattered window frames, piles of broken glass."[5] Many of the sewage and water pipes froze and burst; it looked as if even the bakeries might have to close down. All public transportation had stopped; the streets, except for an occasional supply or army truck, were empty of vehicles. Nearly every factory was at a standstill.

Yet these same months brought the first real ray of hope for the city. The Soviet counteroffensive reduced the German military threat to Leningrad. More important still, the ice road became firmly established and well enough organized to permit the authorities to increase the level of food rations and to evacuate a substantial part of the noncombatant population. But the effect of the ice road on conditions in the city could only be perceived slowly. A life-and-death race was being run between the improvements that the road provided and the deterioration of the physical condition of the city and its inhabitants.

By mid-December the food and supply situation was so disastrous that the city's survival depended wholly on the ice road. Yet it was by no means clear whether the road would be able to bring in enough to save the city. Inexperience, lack of equipment, very poor road conditions, the great distances involved, the winter weather, and the German air attacks—all these factors continued to prevent the road from fulfilling the transportation plan drafted by the Military Council of the Leningrad Front.[6] However, when Tikhvin was recaptured, the main supply base was moved there, so that the length of the truck road was reduced from 190 miles to 112 miles. The increasing thickness of the Ladoga ice allowed the trucks to drive faster and to carry heavier loads. Nevertheless, in late December the daily amount of supplies carried over the ice road barely exceeded 600 tons instead of the planned 2,000 tons.[7]

At the end of December and in early January various steps were taken to improve the efficiency of the ice road. Tow trucks, fuel dumps, mobile repair teams, and numerous traffic control points were organized. In order to speed up the movement of trucks across Lake Ladoga and reduce their vulnerability to air attacks, six parallel tracks were cleared across the ice.[8]

In mid-January Soviet military successes allowed the authorities to move the main supply bases from Tikhvin to the railroad stations of Voibokalo and Zhikharevo, thus reducing the length of the truck route to 27 and 36 miles, respectively. On January 11 the State Defense Committee ordered the construction of a rail line linking Voibokalo with Lavrovo on the shore of Lake Ladoga, a distance of 22 miles. At the same time, a special truck convoy of 60 three-ton trucks was ordered to carry a daily load of 150 tons of supplies from Voibokalo to Osinovets. The rail link to Lavrovo was completed on February 11, thereby reducing the truck route to the 18-mile stretch across the ice of the lake.[9]

The operation of supplying Leningrad with food was administered from Moscow. To ensure a steady source of supply, certain *oblasts*, *krais*, and republics were ordered to provide specified quantities of food exclusively for Leningrad.[10]

Nevertheless, the ice road was still plagued by bottlenecks: at the loading stations, on the road, and at the unloading points. The single-track rail line between Leningrad and Lake Ladoga was unable to handle the volume of traffic. There was a shortage of railroad engines, as well as of fuel, water, and electric power. Many railroad workers were ill. In the period of December to February, 10,939 railroad workers fell ill and 2,346 died.[11] The tracks were often blocked by snowdrifts, switches were frozen, and there was a shortage of sidings.

The first public order concerning the ice road was not issued until a

month and a half after the road began to operate. On January 5
Zhdanov sent the following letter to the workers of the ice road:

Dear Comrades:

  The front-line truck road continues to operate very badly. Each day it
delivers not more than one-third of the absolute minimum of requirements
for Leningrad and its troops in food and gasoline, requirements that have
already been cut to the bone. This means that the supplying of Leningrad
and of the front constantly hangs by a hair and that the troops suffer terrible
privations. This is even more inadmissible since the supplies for Leningrad
and the front are available. It is clear that it is up to you, the workers of the
front-line truck road, and only up to you, to improve this situation quickly
and to ease the needs of Leningrad and the front.[12]

  On January 9 the Executive Committee of the Leningrad City Soviet
mobilized a part of the population to clear the railroad of accumulated
snow and ice. The plan called for 5,000 persons to work on this task
daily, but because of illness and weather conditions, only 400 to 500
persons reported each day for work.[13]

  To back up Zhdanov's appeal and speed up the traffic, 700 Red Army
political workers and city Party members were sent to the ice road.
The appeal and the political supervision were not without effect. On
the day after the political workers arrived, the number of trucks un-
loaded is said to have doubled, although perhaps this occurred not so
much in reality as on paper.[14] The convoy system was abandoned by
the road administration in favor of a system by which each driver was
required to make two independent trips. To speed up the loading and
unloading, the "best political workers"—that is, NKVD and Party members and Komsomols—were assigned to the staffs of the supply points.
It was decided that the trucks would drive at night with their headlights
on despite German air attacks. In all, some 19,000 people worked on
the ice road.[15]

  At the same time, similar pressure was brought to bear on the October Railroad workers and on the workers who were building the new
lines on the eastern shore of the lake. On January 9 the Leningrad City
Party Committee sent an appeal to the railroad workers asking them
to improve their performance and to assure the uninterrupted transportation of increasing quantities of supplies.[16] A few days later Popkov
stated to a correspondent of *Leningradskaia pravda*:

  I must say that the improvement of the supply of food for the city depends
in many ways on the performance of the October Railroad, at whose head
stands Comrade Kolpakov. One must admit that the railroad has worked
badly and been unprepared to carry out its sacred duty in the matter of
assuring the uninterrupted transportation of food. The comrade railroad
workers and their administrative, Party, and trade-union leaders must bear
very clearly in mind the full extent of the responsibility that rests on their

shoulders. It is unnecessary to explain once again how vital it is to improve the operation of the road in the most energetic manner and the shortest time and to assure within the next day or two the uninterrupted transportation of food into the city. . . . Unfortunately, there are not a few among the railroad workers who have relaxed and forgotten their responsibility toward the workers of the city, particularly among the administrators of the October Railroad and its sections.[17]

These complaints and threats had results. On January 15, for the first time in the two months of its existence, the ice road fulfilled its plan and delivered 2,000 tons of supplies. By the end of January the daily total rose to 3,000 tons.[18] The major portion of these supplies consisted of food, although military equipment, medicine, and fuel were also brought in.*

The October Railroad, however, still made supplying the city a problem. Traffic was constantly interrupted on this single-track line, and only a small amount of freight was moved by each train—the average train load appears to have been only 500 to 700 tons. For a time after Popkov's January criticism, the railroad administration succeeded in doubling the volume of freight moved to Leningrad, but the system soon broke down once more.[19] Zhdanov again appealed to the railroad workers:

Dear Comrades:

Lately the October Railroad has been working badly. Important freight that the workers of the city and Leningrad's industry need most urgently, food, lumber, peat, and other supplies, does not leave the station on time or is held up in transit because the trains come apart, or because they stop to build up steam pressure, or at times simply because train commanders do not issue directives. . . .

The vital interests of Leningrad and the front demand of the railroad workers an immediate improvement in the operation of the line and above all an increase in its traffic capacity, as well as the precise execution of the transport plan. . . .

The Leningrad City Committee of the VKP(b) expects of each of you, comrade railroad workers, unselfish work and high labor discipline.[20]

Once more the October Railroad, despite "great difficulties," managed to improve its performance, at least temporarily, to the point at which it was moving between 1,100 and 1,500 tons of freight per train.[21]

The operation of the ice road continued to improve throughout this period, reaching its peak performance in March. Its success is demon-

---

* In January 78.4 per cent of the 1,771 tons that made up the average daily load of supplies coming into the city consisted of food. In February 72.8 per cent of the 3,380 tons brought in daily was food, and in March 78.3 per cent of the 3,690 tons brought in daily consisted of foodstuffs (Karasev, *Leningradtsy v gody blokady*, p. 183).

strated by the fact that, despite increased rations, it was possible by the end of the winter to accumulate a modest food reserve. At that time Zhdanov is reported as having said, "Now I am rich, I have food for twelve days."[22] In its five months of existence the ice road is said to have delivered to Leningrad a total of 270,900 tons of food and 90,000 tons of other supplies.[23]

Weather conditions and technical difficulties never permitted traffic to flow freely. In February, for example, there were 22 days of snowstorms and blizzards, some halting traffic for several days in a row and blocking the road with snowdrifts over six feet high. To keep the road open the snow had to be continually removed. When the ice weakened in one spot, a new section of road had to be built. Improvements in the control of the traffic and the maintenance of the trucks were made only slowly and after considerable trial and error. Traffic jams continued to be frequent. Truck maintenance was very difficult, especially since all sorts of vehicles, even city buses, were used as trucks. The Leningrad automobile repair plant ceased operations in January because of the fuel and power shortage. New repair shops then had to be organized. Because of the frequent accidents, the enemy shelling and strafing, and the cold, first-aid stations had to be established along the entire length of the ice road, but only "after much dispute."[24] Because the location of the ice road had to be shifted from time to time, over 1,000 miles of road were built in all. These had to be protected by snow fences. Hand shovels were mostly used to keep the roads free of snow. Some 147 bridges were built over fissures in the ice.[25] But in spite of everything in the later stages of the ice road's existence, there were over 400 three-ton trucks on the road each day.[26] Hundreds of trucks were sent from Moscow and other areas of the Soviet Union to speed up the flow of supplies.[27]

German air and artillery fire did considerable damage, but could not halt the traffic, partly because the Germans were unable to bomb or shell with sufficient intensity. The German artillery positions were located 13.6 miles from the ice road, and direct observation had to be carried out at a range of 10 miles. The Germans themselves made the following admission: "In view of the great distance from the German lines [to the ice road] there is little expectation that artillery fire can produce appreciable pressure on the Russians."[28] Thus, although a number of trucks were blown up, and others fell into shell holes, the main loading and unloading points were never destroyed.

Labor control on the ice road was a complicated and difficult problem. The road and its personnel were under the direction of a military road administration, with the trucks organized into battalions. The personnel, although militarized, was often made up of civilian draftees or volunteers from Leningrad.[29] A large number of those who were employed in maintenance, traffic control, or medical services, among whom were many women, had to remain on the ice throughout the entire period of the road's existence. Because the healthiest soldiers had to be sent to the front, the construction battalions were largely made up of convalescent soldiers, who were often not able to perform the hard physical labor demanded of them. In fact, from December to February many of the workers on the road, civilian and military, were sick and weak from hunger and privation.

Control over labor on the supply road was difficult to maintain. The fact that they traveled in convoys ensured that the trucks would arrive together, but it slowed down those drivers who would have been willing to try to make several round trips in a row. When at last the supply bases were moved forward and the convoy system abandoned, each driver was encouraged to make as many round trips as he could without stopping. It was possible, but not easy, to make from two to four trips, although two average round trips meant driving sixteen to eighteen hours a day. Many drivers fell asleep at the wheel or fainted from exhaustion. They were permitted to rest only when they became too exhausted to work. When the railroad was extended as far as the Ladoga, it became possible for each truck to make many more round trips in a day, but even then only if the weather, the condition of the ice, and the enemy bombardment permitted it.[30]

It was difficult to control drivers and loaders who were lazy or who wanted to steal food. Drivers at times dropped one or two sacks of food on the ice and then retrieved them later and sold them on the black market.[31]

The administration and the Party tried several methods to maintain discipline and increase the flow of supplies. There was, of course, the threat of punishment and trial by court-martial for theft and sabotage. There were the ubiquitous Party and police personnel, who had been sent to the road not merely to inspire the workers, but also to keep a check on them. But in view of the extremely difficult and hazardous conditions on the road, the most effective pressure was psychological. The drivers and railroad workers were never allowed to forget that the survival of the city and its inhabitants, including possibly their own families, was up to them and that their friends and neighbors would never forgive them for doing less than their utmost. Thus in his appeal of January 5 Zhdanov wrote:

The heroic defenders of Leningrad, who with honor and glory have preserved our city from the fascist bandits, have the right to demand honest and selfless labor of you.

In the name of Leningrad and of the front I ask you to keep in mind that

you are performing a great and responsible task and are fulfilling an assignment of primary importance to the state and the military.

Everyone on whom the normal operation of the road depends . . . each
at his post, must execute his assignment like a soldier in a forward position.

Do your job, as befits Soviet patriots, honestly, with your heart, without
stinting your strength, in order to organize the transportation of freight to
Leningrad and the front quickly in the amount prescribed by the plan.

The fatherland and Leningrad will never forget your labor.[32]

Popkov's appeal to the October Railroad workers was similar in tone.
And Zhdanov, in his appeal to these workers in February, once more
emphasized this theme:

As a consequence of the bad performance of the railroad men, the transportation of food into Leningrad is continually endangered. Because of this
the population is suffering further privations and hardships.

Because of the irregular and extremely limited import of fuel, the electric
power stations cannot produce the minimum amount of electric power, which
leads to a breakdown in the work of factories and plants. Nor is there electricity for the communal service enterprises, for transportation in the city, or
for the apartments of the city's workers.

The population of Leningrad, which is heroically laboring for the needs
of the front, has the right to demand of the railroad workers honest and selfless work, since the operation of industry and the improvement of the living
conditions of Leningrad's workers depend on their performance.[33]

To reduce theft and laziness, the Party relied in part on organized
social pressure. Culprits were made to appear before "courts for cowards" and to face the criticism of their fellow workers, along with threats
of serious punishment if they did not mend their ways. They were told
such things as, "You will be sent to Leningrad, and we will tell the people
that here is a man who in these times does not want to work for the
fatherland with all his might. Make your excuses to the Leningraders."[34]

Along the road the Party organizations engaged in both mass and
individual propaganda. There were road signs with slogans such as
"The fatherland and Leningrad will never forget your labor," or "Every
two trips provide bread for 10,500 Leningraders."[35] Numerous meetings
were called to discuss Zhdanov's appeals. The Party workers were
mobilized to encourage the multitrip system. The special newspaper
of the ice road, *Frontovoi dorozhnik,* published suggestions of how the
road workers could improve their performance, as well as the names
of the best workers. Medals were handed out. The usual competitions
within and among work brigades and battalions were organized, and
a Red Banner awarded to the winners. When a driver made more than
two trips, a sign was hastily erected at his base saying "Salutations to
the leader of the ice road drivers——, who made —— trips today."[36] Then
the propagandists and Party workers tried to persuade the entire group

to promise to make as many trips. To improve individual performance, signs were pasted in the cabs of trucks whose drivers were careless or had bad driving habits, admonishing the drivers to mend their ways. Because the gasoline was of very poor quality, the drivers had to filter it through cloth themselves before putting it into their trucks. Those who consistently forgot were reminded with signs saying, "Add up how much time you lost by blowing out your gas line on the road and tell the Leningraders the total. Will they forgive your sloppiness?"[37] Drivers were often considerably embarrassed by these signs, which they were not permitted to remove until they had demonstrated that they no longer committed the error. Whether this method of control was widely used is not known; but when it was, it seems to have been effective.

By March the leadership could see that the improved ice road was solving the immediate food problem and had managed to establish a functioning link with the outside. There was no longer any danger that the defense of Leningrad would collapse. At a terrible price Leningrad had survived the worst and was slowly regaining its strength, thanks to the existence of the ice road.

From December 25 to mid-February, bread rations were increased three times, until they nearly matched the rations issued at the beginning of the siege. But to start with these increases did not actually represent a significant improvement in the amount of food issued to the population. As far as most inhabitants were concerned, a real change was only felt after February 15.[38]

The first increase, announced on December 25, allotted an additional 100 grams of bread to workers (who now received 350 grams a day) and 75 grams to all other categories (200 grams a day).[39] The increase came as a surprise to the population, since hardly any of the news media were functioning, and it made a tremendous impression on everybody. One Soviet writer describes meeting a man on that day who had just received his new bread ration at the store and who "while walking, cried, laughed, and held his head in his two hands."[40] People congratulated each other and happily discussed their expectation of further improvements.[41] Those who did not know about the ice road believed that the authorities were expecting a speedy victory, since they were willing to use up the remaining food reserves; while those who knew about the road began to have some faith in its operation. Along with these expectations various happy rumors began to circulate to the effect that the government had prepared mountains of supplies ready to be rushed to Leningrad, or that Stalin had promised all Leningraders sanitarium fare.[42]

But these happy expectations were soon disappointed when the improvement in the bread ration was not matched by a significant in-

crease in other foods. On the contrary, most food staples were no longer
issued or issued only occasionally, so that the increase in the bread ration
had little or no effect on total consumption. In theory, workers were
to receive each month 600 grams of groats, 150 grams of sugar, 75 grams
of vegetable oil or fats, and 300 grams of meat, but in practice many
of these were not regularly available.[43] One Leningrader noted in her
diary on January 11 that she was living exclusively on bread and salt
water, and on January 16 that she cooked glue and that people were
dissolving buttons and making a sort of soup with them.[44]

The authorities continued their desperate attempts to supplement
the food arriving over the ice road with local supplies. Industrial grease
was reprocessed for food, the meat plants made soup out of leftover
bones, soya milk production reached 724.9 tons in December, the production of yeast was organized as a substitute for meat, and flour dust
or food drippings were systematically scraped up in the food-processing
plants. In mid-December the city's Party committee ordered the fishing
trust to catch fish under the ice in the Gulf of Finland and in Lake
Ladoga and to make a daily delivery to the city of between ten and
twelve tons of fish. These efforts produced little result. In all, during
the first quarter of 1942 the city was able to provide from its own resources only 1,229 tons of food.[45]

On New Year's Eve there was a special issue of food, chiefly of
alcoholic beverages, candies, and some fats;[46] but for the vast majority
of the population the rations remained below subsistence level for another month.

The popular attitude toward the ice road was a mixture of hope and
skepticism. There was hope, confirmed later by the further increases in
food rations and by the revived evacuation, because it seemed that the
ice road might save the population; but there was also skepticism because the death rate continued to rise and because the advantages
gained by the road were not expected to last beyond spring. However,
after January 15, when the ice road began to meet its delivery quotas,
the authorities were able to distribute additional food. For example,
on January 18 it was announced that as part of their monthly ration for
January workers would receive about one pound of cereal, office workers half a pound, and dependents a quarter of a pound; while children
under 12 years of age would receive 300 grams of cereal and 75 grams
of fats.[47] A small amount of sugar, which children and dependents received in the form of candy, and some meat rations were also issued.

A new increase in monthly rations was announced on January 24,
consisting of 50 grams of bread for workers, 100 grams for office employees, and 50 grams for dependents.[48] At the same time the quality
of the bread improved somewhat, and some other staples reappeared

in the stores. Unfortunately for the population, this increase coincided with a further deterioration in the food production and distribution system. The bakeries found it increasingly difficult to keep going in view of the electricity and water shortages. During the last week of January work in the baking plants came to a halt because of the breakdown of the water supply.[49] Until the delivery of water could be organized, the Komsomol mobilized boys and girls, who, along with the workers of the bakeries, carried water in pails from the Neva River to the plants to tide them over the crisis.[50] Later, water was pumped from warships anchored along the river.[51] Bread deliveries to the bakery stores became irregular because of these difficulties at the plants and because the supplies had to be transported in hand carts and sleds. Consequently, people had to line up very early in the morning and stand waiting in the severe cold for several hours, and sometimes they waited in vain.

Despite some improvements the rations still fell far short of the population's needs. The wife of a senior political officer wrote her husband in January: "The increase in the bread ration has taken place, but it is not very large. The situation with regard to the food supply is still very bad. We wait and wait for an improvement and will certainly see it."[52]

On February 11 bread rations were increased by a further 100 grams for workers and office workers, and by 50 grams for dependents.[53] This was the last increase, and the new level of bread rations remained constant for another year. But the important factor was that the quality of the bread improved, containing less than 2 per cent of admixtures. Some other foods also became available.[54]

With the increased flow of supplies it gradually became possible to attempt to save at least the more valuable elements of the population. A system of special dietary restaurants, or semisanitariums, was organized in the *raions* and at the more important factories. Upon certification by the medical services, a sick or exhausted worker or employee received at such places a special diet for one or more weeks.[55] Apart from the additional food, the patients were relieved of the necessity to walk to work, stand in line, fetch water and fuel, and other daily tasks that sapped their remaining strength. Members of the elite and industrial workers were the first to benefit from this system. For example, in January and February the Bolshevik Works sent a total of 6,770 employees to the Works' sanitarium for a three weeks' rehabilitation period. Party workers, scientists, and some well-known artists, painters, and writers were sent to the Hotel Astoria, which had been converted into a sanitarium.[56] In many instances this help came too late to save people from death. It was not possible to accommodate all who needed such help, and many workers and ordinary people had to wait until April or May to become eligible for this help.[57]

The average Leningrader, however, lived as before: basically on the official rations to which he was entitled, which until mid-January consisted primarily of bread.[58] Only very few people could secure a steady source of additional food supplies. A larger number, however, through their connections, wealth, or ingenuity, were able to supplement their standard rations at irregular intervals. Of course, everything edible that could be obtained, no matter how unlikely, was eaten. This included all the remaining animals in the city, such as dogs, cats, rats, mice, and sparrows. Leather straps were boiled. One eyewitness, writing in her diary, reports having eaten the following things during that winter: "pancakes made of sawdust, jelly made from carpenter's glue, a moldy bouillon concentrate . . . raw bran, pancakes made from powdered wall-paper glue and containing an insect repellent, and bitter, raw oil cake."[59] As time went on, these delicacies were increasingly hard to come by. Many people became ill from eating such concoctions, and some actually died from them.

Few Leningraders had an opportunity to transfer to jobs that offered larger rations. These jobs usually either involved repugnant tasks or required considerable physical effort. Cutting lumber, working on the ice road, and similar jobs often meant larger rations. However, the increased rations were generally not commensurate with the increased physical effort required, and many workers died as a result of it. It was better to find a job connected in some way with the food production or distribution system, since such jobs gave employees a chance to obtain additional food, usually by illegal means and at the risk of being shot if found out. One Leningrader wrote: "I had luck: I got a job with a meat *kombinat*. I dropped my geological research and instead got more bread as well as quite a lot of rejected blood."[60] Finally, there were certain jobs with the higher police and military administrative organs that were far better supplied with food than any others. The total number of ordinary Leningraders who managed to obtain such jobs was, of course, very limited.

For most people the main source of additional food or extra ration cards was, as before, the gray or the black market. In the various markets the inhabitants constantly tried to sell or barter various personal objects for clothing, food, or fuel. For example, a stove was exchanged for three days' bread ration.[61] The buyers were usually people who either needed certain items of clothing, or could not resist the temptation to acquire valuable objects cheaply. Sometimes the purchaser died as a result of sacrificing his own meager food supplies to his greed. There were also cash transactions. For example, one Leningrader tells of selling his carpet for 600 rubles and buying with the money one kilogram of bread and a bottle of kerosene. Then he tried to sell a pipe, which had been willed to him by a dead colleague; next, his wife managed to barter a bottle of perfume (which people drank for the alcohol) for 200 grams of bread and few cigarettes, and a little later she exchanged some silver spoons for a piece of meat. Other deals involving the exchange of food for valuable objects, such as watches, gold, or even wedding rings, could be made with people who somehow had access to food supplies.[62] The rate of exchange varied with supply and demand. A new pair of women's foreign-made shoes might cost 100 grams of fat or 1,200 grams of bread; a silver spoon of 100 grams weight might cost 250 grams of cereal or flour.[63] According to one account, there were even black marketeers who crossed the Ladoga on foot to bring back food from the other shore for their transactions.[64] Since the speculators primarily bought valuable objects and good clothing, preferably of foreign origin, it seems likely that many of them were either new members of the elite or lower-echelon bureaucrats who had not been able to afford these luxuries before the war. Their customers, those who had such things for sale, would probably be older members of the elite or of the intelligentsia, or thieves.

There was also a growing black market in ration cards that had been stolen or sold by relatives of the dead. The practice of hiding dead members of the family, or at least not reporting their deaths, was widespread in this period. Of course, most people were eager to keep additional ration cards obtained in this way for their own use. Those who sold them were either people who urgently needed a particular food or medicine or some favor, or speculators who had enough to eat themselves and used the cards to acquire valuables and clothes. One former Leningrader tells how he bartered a fur coat of good quality for two ration cards, a worker's and a dependent's, which were good for twenty-one days. The sellers were a "strong, healthy man in a fur-lined leather coat, and his wife, a young, well-dressed woman," who brought their own candle, which was also very valuable, the better to inspect their purchase.[65]

It was natural that under these circumstances an increasing number of desperate and hungry people began to engage in theft and looting; their object was always food, and they either stole the food itself or took any goods that they could sell in order to obtain food. The theft of ration cards, especially from older women and people who collapsed in the streets, became more and more frequent. In December, 24,000 ration cards were lost or stolen.[66] People returning home from the store with their rations were often robbed. In fact, it became so dangerous to carry rations openly that people began to hide them on their persons.

Starving children sometimes simply went up to a person who was leaving a bread store and tried to tear a piece of bread from his hands. One such scene is described as follows: "A woman has thrown a boy, aged about 12, to the ground and is choking him. From his mouth there sticks out a little piece of bread, which he is trying to chew. 'Don't you dare, don't you dare to swallow it! Give back the bread, damn you!' "[67] Or again: "A young boy tore the bread from the hands of a woman and ate it up before her eyes. She beat him with her fists, but she was too weak to take it back and had to watch as her bread disappeared. She cried like a child."[68]

During this period there were also some instances of cannibalism. How often this happened is not known, but all informants report hearing about it or even of having seen evidence of it. Most instances appear to have involved the mutilation or dismemberment of corpses found in the streets, or stored in the morgues, before they were removed to the cemeteries.[69] It was rumored that some of the meat obtained in this fashion was sold in the black market in exchange for more conventional food or resellable objects, but sometimes the despoilers ate it themselves. There were even said to be cases of crazed parents eating their children, and vice versa.[70]

The authorities tried unsuccessfully to put a stop to these activities. Persons caught engaging in them were liable to trial by a military tribunal, which under wartime laws could impose the death penalty for theft and looting, and long prison terms for the other crimes. In April the secretary of the city Party committee, A. A. Kuznetsov, who was also a member of the military council, declared in a speech: "I must say straight off that we shot people for half a pound of bread stolen or withheld from the population."[71] In order to reduce theft of food, the authorities mobilized Party and Komsomol members to keep a watch over the personnel dealing with the transportation and sale of food. The Party sent 3,500 Komsomols to the food stores to keep a check on the sales force and, in addition, established control groups in all stores to ensure that the population would not be cheated. Similar control teams were sent to the food-processing plants, warehouses, and transportation centers. Special Komsomol teams raided food stores, storage facilities, public kitchens, and restaurants in an effort to catch thieves and speculators.[72] Although the authorities tried to enlist the aid of the population in tracking down speculators, as well as thieves and other criminals, the Leningraders generally proved to be uncooperative, except in the case of thieves who attacked people on the streets. Many people, even though they were bitter about the speculators and held them in contempt, were unwilling to denounce to the militia their illegal sources of additional food. Most Leningraders were, in any event, too deeply

absorbed in their individual problems to have any interest or energy left
for spying on others. Moreover, the police organs were too weak and
inefficient to be able to enforce these controls. As a matter of fact, some
Leningraders seemed to resent the attempts of the militia to restrict
black-market operations, since this only complicated their efforts to
find additional food.[73] The population apparently felt that if the authorities were unable to do anything for the starving inhabitants, the
least they could do was leave them alone. As long as the population
was starving, it is doubtful that the authorities could have put a stop
to these activities, since people are willing to run great risks to satisfy
their basic needs. It was only when the food supply in Leningrad increased significantly that the people stopped using the black market
and robberies ceased.

The mortality rate for this period shows what the low level of the
basic food ration cost Leningrad in the winter of 1941–42. The death
rate reached its peak during the first two months of 1942, when the
over-all physical condition of the inhabitants was at its worst, as a result
of the cumulative effect of starvation, cold, and other hardships. Slight
increases in the food rations could not restore weakened bodies in time
to save many. The inhabitants continued to show the effect of these
months of starvation until the summer of 1942.

The actual death rate during this period is a matter of conjecture.
The Soviet authorities never published any statistics, so that all available figures are based on impressions or, at best, semi-informed guesses.
Estimates of the daily death rate at the beginning of January vary between 2,000 and 9,000.[74] During January, as living conditions deteriorated further, this rate increased. According to widespread but uncon-
firmed reports, the daily rate at the end of January, or early in February,
ranged from 12,000 to 20,000; some sources cite estimates of more than
30,000 a day.[75] Soviet historians, basing their information on the Leningrad archives, give the figures for January as 3,500 to 4,000 deaths
registered daily; but of course many deaths went unreported.[76] In the
second half of February the death rate is said to have declined somewhat, but 73,000 persons are officially stated to have died from hunger
during that month.[77] In March the Leningrad undertaker trust alone
buried 89,968 dead, or nearly 3,000 each day.[78]

Inevitably there is a great deal of uncertainty about the total number of civilian deaths during the siege from hunger and illness: "The
death toll from starvation had mounted into staggering figures. Some
said two million, others claimed only half a million. Probably a figure
between seven hundred and fifty thousand and a million would not be
exaggerated."[79] German estimates tended to support the round number
of one million, while an official Soviet commission, which investigated

German atrocities in the Leningrad area, placed the number of civilian deaths for the entire period of the siege at 632,253.[80] The official figure appears to be too low. In September, at the start of the siege, between 2,489,400 and 2,544,000 ration cards were issued to the Leningrad population, and an additional 343,000 ration cards to the persons residing in the city's suburbs.[81] This number did not include several categories of children nor most of the refugees. In March 1943, following the evacuation after September 1941 of 1,081,152 refugees and Leningraders, there remained in the city only 639,900 inhabitants, thus accounting for 1,721,052 persons.[82] Even on the basis of the official number of about 2,887,000 ration card holders in the city and suburbs in September 1941, this leaves 830,000 persons unaccounted for, of whom at most 50,000 were transferred to the armed forces. In reality the total number of civilians, including refugees, in Leningrad in September 1941 probably exceeded 3,000,000; so that at least 1,000,000 to 1,250,000 persons, or about one-third of Leningrad's wartime population, are unaccounted for and may be presumed to have died from the effects of starvation, cold, and illness, most of them during the winter and early spring of 1941–42. A recent Soviet source acknowledges that "over one million Leningraders" perished during the war.[83]

Whatever the precise number of deaths may have been, there is no doubt that it was very high. Although at first men and children succumbed faster than women, the death rate for women increased after January.[84] Soviet medical studies indicate that in 1942 the death rate for infants up to one year of age was 74.8 per cent.[85] A factory director told a foreign correspondent in 1943 that out of his 5,000 workers "several hundred died" during the worst of the famine.[86] An official of the Elektrosila Works wrote that in January and February "people were dying everywhere: in the yard, in the shop, in the canteen, in the street. They walked about all black, sooty, wrapped in rags, leaning on sticks, barely moving their legs. The healthiest, strongest men died."[87] In the Kirov Works alone, despite some special ration privileges, 409 Party members died, mostly from starvation.[88] People were collapsing and dying everywhere, at the hospitals, in the factories and offices, in the streets, at home, while standing in line for food or water, or even while trying to bury another member of the family. People left home to go to the store or to work and never came back, having collapsed or died somewhere on the way. In December and January, because there was no one to come to see how they were, people died at home from simple lack of care, starving to death when they had insufficient strength to go to the store, or freezing when they were unable to light a fire.

Leningrad had become a gigantic charnel house. The occasional glimmers of hope, real or imaginary, that appeared on the horizon were usually swiftly dispelled by the macabre daily procession of thousands of dead and dying. Leningrad resembled some prehistoric mastodon, frozen in its tracks, slowly dying in horrible agony, in darkness, stillness, and falling snow. The enemy was no longer the German army outside the walls; it was inside the city, within each Leningrader, slowly and painfully gnawing him to death.

Diaries of eyewitnesses give us some pictures of those days, pictures that were multiplied thousands of times daily during that winter. The diary of a schoolgirl, Tania Savich, who died in the spring of 1942 from the effects of the winter, contains the following stark entries:

> Jenia died on December 28, 1941, at 12:30 A.M.
> Grandmother died on January 25, 1942.
> Lena died on March 17, 1942.
> Uncle Lesha died on May 10, at 4:00 P.M.
> May 13, at 7:30 A.M., darling Mama died.
> The Saviches are dead, they all died.[89]

The diary of a doctor contained this description, entered in January:

> Having found the room, I entered without knocking. My eyes beheld a horrible sight. A dark room, the wall covered with frost, puddles of water on the floor. Lying across some chairs was the corpse of a 14-year-old boy. In a baby carriage was a second corpse, that of a tiny infant. On the bed lay the owner of the room, K. K. Vandel—dead. At her side, rubbing her chest with a towel, stood her eldest daughter, Mikkau. . . . In one day Mikkau lost her mother, a son, and a brother who perished from hunger and cold. At the entrance, barely standing on her feet from weakness, was a neighbor, Kizunova, her horrified gaze fixed on the dead. She, too, died the next day.[90]

It happened time and again that mothers of little children died, and their bodies remained lying on the beds while the children slowly starved or froze to death from lack of care or because an unscrupulous neighbor had stolen their ration cards.[91] According to a Soviet historian, there were thousands of corpses lying in the streets, on the embankments, and in the houses.[92]

Added to the terror of waiting to die was the horror of the daily struggle for food, each person living with the knowledge that the smallest morsel made the difference between life and death. It was frightening to stand in the bread line and wonder, "Will the bread arrive? Will they issue it? Will there be enough?" It was frightening to be the boy waiting for new ration cards to be issued: "How can I go home without cards? I promised Mother to bring bread. Mother is hungry. Mother has not eaten for two days. Mother will die."[93] It was frightening to stay at home watching a loved one dying or, crazed by hunger, screaming, "I want food . . . I want food!"[94] Mothers had to watch helplessly while their children cried or silently wasted away. A former

Leningrader wrote in his diary at this time: "Death . . . death. . . . Everywhere death. . . . In Leningrad only one thing happens—dying. . . . Leningrad is dying. Slowly and painfully. . . . The city is perishing."[95]

Most survivors seemed to be only a short step behind those they were burying. The inhabitants were either grotesquely swollen with hunger or shrunken to skeletons. Diarrhea with bleeding, and scurvy assumed epidemic proportions, as did heart and respiratory diseases. Women stopped menstruating. Everyone suffered from dizziness; most people could walk only with great difficulty. People were often afraid to sit down lest they should be unable to stand up again.[96]

Two women lead a "dystrophic," holding him up under the armpits. He moves his legs, which are shod in boots, as though they were artificial. His eyes are staring ahead just as if he had been poisoned. The skin of his face is drawn tight. The lips are open, revealing the teeth, which seem lengthened by hunger. The nose has become pointed as if sharpened, and is completely covered with sores. . . . The faces of people are either drawn unnaturally tight and glossy (this is dropsy) or become greenish and knobby. There is not a drop of fat under the skin.[97]

The death rate remained unaffected by the first increases in food rations. The Soviet writer who described the man's joy over the December increase wrote in her diary on January 3: "The explosion of joy that burst out the day when the ration of bread was increased by 75 grams is now only an old memory. The man who cried and laughed from happiness is in the street . . . is probably long since dead."[98]

Like the populace, members of the elite, too, were dying in great numbers. Death among intellectuals was particularly high. As mentioned, 17,000 Party members are said to have perished, mostly from starvation and disease.

However poorly informed the population was about many of Leningrad's problems, it was only too well informed about the death rate. In the absence of official figures, and with people dying all around them, the inhabitants came to believe every rumor, no matter how exaggerated, about the daily number of deaths in the city. These numbers were whispered with the macabre fascination that people often display when discussing a disaster.

The individual Leningrader's expectations concerning his own chance of survival varied. It is certain that some were hopeful that the situation would change significantly before they succumbed. Others expected the worst. Many diaries expressed the wish of the writers to live—"one wants so much, so terribly much, so unbearably to live"—to live until the time when it would be light and warm again.[99] At the same time, most of the writers doubted their chances to survive till summer. With things as they were, there was nothing unnatural or abnormal in a man's saying, "According to my calculation I will live another month and a half."[100] According to reports, many Party and Komsomol members, believing that they were about to die, came to the *raion* committees to turn in their membership cards so they would not fall into strange hands.[101] People would say farewell to each other whenever they met, and this also seemed a natural thing to do.[102] Most of the people whom I interviewed asserted that they did not, at the time, expect to survive. Of course, some refused to believe that this could happen to *them*, but they were in no doubt that it could happen to everyone else.

Inevitably, people became indifferent to death outside their immediate family circles. Everyone was so centered on his own problems that there often remained no interest in what went on even in the next room. One man who lived through the siege reports that he and his wife failed to notice that his neighbor's wife had died and that the surviving family members had moved away; they became aware of it only when the soldier husband came home on leave to find the body of his wife lying on the bed.[103]

In fact, death had none of the usual emotional impact on people. "People had their feelings blunted, and never seemed to weep at the burials. It was all done in complete silence without any display of emotion."[104] The following encounter between two friends took place in the streets of Leningrad during this period:

"Petr Vasilevich, what are you doing?"
"Well, you see." He points with his hand to three small sleds, tied together, one behind the other. On the first lies a big mummy, on the second a smaller one, on the third a suitcase. "That is my wife. Over there is Lucia. And these are my things."
"What are you going to do?"
"I'll have to bury them, I guess; after that I don't know."[105]

In some instances hunger drove people to behave with extreme callousness. One informant describes two such cases: one is of a girl who pulled out her dead father's gold teeth to sell in the black market, and the other is of some children who told him: "We had luck: Papa and Mama died, and we and Grandmother hid their bodies in the attic, and now we have five ration cards for three persons. . . . There is lots of bread."[106]

Alongside the bodies lying in the streets moved a procession of emaciated Leningraders pulling children's sleds or pieces of plywood loaded with corpses on their way to the cemeteries or morgues.

The sight of somebody—man, woman, or child—dragging a child's sled on which lay a dead body wrapped in a blanket or a piece of canvas became a daily commonplace of the winter Leningrad landscape. The spectacle of somebody dying of hunger in a snow-covered street was by no means infrequent in Leningrad. Pedestrians passed by, removed their caps, or muttered a word or two in sympathy, or sometimes did not even stop, since there was no help they could offer.[107]

"Many thousands died quietly every week," so quietly in fact that the authorities had a hard time finding out who was alive and who was dead.[108] It also became a major problem to collect, remove, and bury all of those who died. More and more people were collapsing in the streets and at home; more and more corpses were being abandoned by relatives. According to the testimony of one doctor, in the Moscow *raion* alone about 250 corpses were found every day lying in the streets.[109] The exhausted inhabitants had increasing difficulty in transporting their dead to the morgues or cemeteries, and many did not have the strength to do so.

To help solve the problem of registering the dead, the registration offices, ZAGS, sent representatives to the morgues and cemeteries.[110] To prevent the streets from being choked with bodies, in January the authorities organized special clean-up squads, each of which patrolled certain districts and picked up those who were dead or had collapsed and were in danger of freezing to death. Citizens performing these patrol duties received additional rations of bread and some vodka, as did those who worked in the morgues or transported corpses to cemeteries.[111] Since the patrols went around only once or twice a day and were not too thorough, many corpses remained lying in obscure corners until spring. Often people who died at home were not found for a long time.

There was little that could be done about burials. People were faced with the same choice as before: either themselves to bring the bodies of their relatives and friends to the cemeteries, or to leave them at a morgue, from which they were removed by truckloads to the cemeteries. Burial was nearly impossible; the ground was frozen so hard it had to be dynamited to permit the digging of graves. Generally, the dead were left in a corner of the cemetery to await burial in mass graves. Those who were anxious to obtain individual graves not only had to pay for them at the regular rate, but also had to bribe the gravediggers with considerable quantities of food or with ration cards.[112] Coffins were not provided by the authorities and were usually not available at all; so that most corpses were brought to the cemeteries wrapped in sheets. To ease some of these problems, several factories opened their own cemeteries on factory grounds.[113] On January 7 the Executive Committee of the Leningrad City Soviet expressed its concern over the fact that bodies were left lying about in the cemeteries or were being improperly buried, a practice that created a potential health hazard. The committee, noting that not one of the *raions* had contrived to dig sufficient communal graves, ordered them to bury all corpses and threatened the responsible *raion* authorities with severe punishment if they failed in their task.[114] Actually, no proper burial was possible in many cases until spring.

To many people the struggle not to join the ranks of the dying seemed pointless. Even if they survived the immediate difficulties, even if rations were increased to a subsistence level, they still expected to die in the spring. Despite the harshness of the winter, some Leningraders dreaded the approaching spring even more, partly because they believed it would put a stop to the flow of supplies into Leningrad and partly because they expected terrible plagues to ravage the city. They felt that only the extreme cold had averted the outbreak of widespread epidemics, since it had frozen the corpses and refuse and prevented the pollution of water, but that the spring thaws would bring diseases that the population in its weakened condition could not resist.[115]

Medical services by mid-January were swamped. Hospitals lacked heat and electric light as well as food and medicine. Home visits by doctors were seldom feasible, since there was nothing for them to give to their sick and starving patients. Something, however, had to be done to help the population and in particular to lessen the likelihood that epidemics would sweep the city when the weather moderated. To deal with this problem the city's executive committee and Party committee ordered the vaccination of 1,500,000 Leningraders to be carried out in the period of February through May. Priority was given to workers, office workers, and students. By March 16, 492,209 persons were reported to have been vaccinated.[116] It is not known whether the vaccination program was completed.

Steps also had to be taken to improve sanitary conditions generally and to help people who were too weak or sick to care for themselves. On January 26, therefore, the Executive Committee of the Leningrad City Soviet issued the following decree:

The executive committee of the Leningrad City Soviet of Workers' Deputies wishes to draw the attention of all Soviet, economic, trade union, and social organizations of the city of Leningrad to the necessity for rapidly carrying out urgent measures to improve the sanitation and public services of the population.

The executive committee of the Leningrad City Soviet of Workers' Deputies has decided [here follows a selection of the provisions]:

3. To charge the heads of enterprises, offices, and organizations, the directors of schools, and the commanders of military units and sections with personal responsibility for the sanitary condition and clean-up of houses, yards, and adjacent territories. Directors of enterprises and heads of offices and organizations are to carry out the cleaning up of buildings, yards, and adjacent territories with the help of the workers and employees of their enter-

prises and offices; [directors of schools are to enlist] the help of their students; and commanders of military units or sections are to use military personnel. . . .

5. Within the next days to open for use in each *raion* of the city not less than two steam baths and laundries, and to provide them with fuel and electric power.

To reopen the sanitary decontamination stations, putting into use the shower and washing facilities of the gasproof shelters.

The executive committees of the *raion* Soviets are to give full assistance to the inhabitants in organizing in the basements of houses simple steam baths and washing facilities, and in supplying houses with firewood, bricks, boilers, and kerosene for light to this end.

6. To charge the directors of enterprises with the immediate return to operation of the closed factory steam baths, sanitary decontamination stations, and showers, as well as the washing facilities of the enterprises, for the use of the workers and employees of their enterprises. . . .

11. To charge the executive committees of the *raion* Soviets with supporting and developing the initiative of the Red Cross organization and of the housing collectives in giving medical assistance to sick citizens, and in organizing comradely mutual assistance by citizens (for the purpose of obtaining bread in the stores, securing firewood, cleaning up rooms, receiving hot meals from public kitchens, etc.).

12. To charge the executive committees of the *raion* Soviets with the organization in the house administrations of a sanitation welfare commission, which must unite and organize the work of all commissions, Party activist groups, and tenants in order to establish the basic necessities and cleanliness in the houses.[117]

These provisions reflect the living conditions of the population and the limited means available to the leadership to improve them. The order charged the militia with supervising the execution of these regulations. Violators were to be held "strictly accountable" for breaking the rules on cleanliness and order. Actually, compliance with this order, particularly concerning the cleaning of houses and streets, was very difficult. No clean-up campaign was really feasible in the absence of water, heat, and sewage disposal, especially at a time when most people were too weak to wield shovels, picks, or even brooms.

The order was more effective in procuring medical and social assistance. Various simple measures were taken to help the worst cases among the population. Some hotels and schools were designated as temporary hospitals. The rations of medical personnel were raised sufficiently so that by mid-February some of them could resume visits to the homes of those confined to their beds.[118] Sometimes patients received vitamin tablets, which were easier to ship over the ice road than food because of their small bulk.[119] According to one eyewitness: "The Astoria looks like a hotel now—but you should have seen it then! It was turned into a hospital. Just hell. They used to bring here all sorts of people, mostly intellectuals, who were dying of hunger. Gave them vitamin tablets, tried to pep them up a bit. However, a lot of them were too far gone, and died almost the moment they got here."[120]

In order to help people too weak to care for themselves and who were thus likely to die from neglect, cold, or hunger, the city's Party Committee mobilized the Red Cross and the Komsomol. The initiative for this step came from the Komsomol organization of one of the city's *raions*, which organized a group of 80 members to help care for bedridden persons. The formation of welfare units spread to all the city's *raions*, as well as to the factories, until there were officially 7,300 of such welfare workers.[121]

Every day over 1,000 members of these units worked among the population, and each *raion* provided between 500 and 700 part-time volunteers to assist them.

The members of these detachments solicitously cared for those who were weakened and exhausted, bought food for them on their ration cards, brought water, split firewood, sent the sick to the hospitals and aid stations. The Komsomols of the Vsevolozhskii and Pargolovskii *raions* collected and brought to Leningrad 40 train carloads of pine branches to help fight scorbutic illnesses.[122]

After February 2 an attempt was made to organize in each apartment building a group of nurses' assistants to help sick people, and on February 9 the city Party Committee ordered all Party, industrial, and housing administrations to check all apartments for sick and dead residents.[123] Factories organized teams for the care of sick employees.

The welfare detachments were given considerable authority by the City Soviet. They could move people from one apartment to another and requisition empty apartments better suited for the sick; they assigned orphans to children's homes; and they dealt with individual requests for evacuation. On the request of the welfare units, the city opened special food stores to serve sick people, where the members of the units or of the house commissions could receive rations for their charges without waiting long in line. Each *raion* also opened a public kitchen from which the welfare units could obtain warm food for the persons in their care. An attempt was made to organize in each apartment house one public room where the residents could warm themselves and obtain hot water.

In practice, it was not possible to carry out these efforts on the necessary scale. For each person receiving help, there were many more who received none. According to one Soviet source, the Red Cross and Komsomol arranged for regular home care for only 38,000 persons.[124] Since the Komsomol help was not widely available, it is clear that many people had to rely on friends and neighbors rather than on the Komsomol and Red Cross. At least two informants asserted that they had never heard of such activities.[125] The available sources do not indicate what criterion, if any, was applied in determining who would receive this assistance.

Help was also needed for orphans and for children whose parents were unable to care for them. From December on, the number of orphaned children in the city grew daily at an alarming rate. The existing children's homes were soon swamped. Various measures were taken to remedy this situation. Some factories and *raion* organizations opened new children's homes.[126] During the first half of 1942, eighty-five new children's homes were organized and equipped largely from donations collected from the population. These homes eventually cared for some 30,000 young children, while teen-age orphans were sent to trade schools.[127]

On February 8 the city's executive committee, acting on directives issued by the Council of People's Commissars of the USSR, ordered all kindergartens and day nurseries to remain open on a 24-hour basis and to board 70 per cent of the children enrolled with them.[128] Somewhat earlier, on January 19, the city's Party Committee had directed that 30 dining halls be opened for the use of school children 8 to 12 years old whose parents had difficulties in feeding them at home.[129] Some 30,000 school children were said to have made use of these dining halls.

In the children's homes, the orphans received somewhat better food, vitamins, and limited medical care, and the *raion* authorities saw to it that these homes were provided with firewood.[130] The privations the children had undergone can be guessed at from the following description of an orphanage in February 1942:

All of them, without exception, pressed close to the stove, and, like fledglings, sank their heads into their shoulders, let the sleeves of their dressing-gowns trail below their wrists, and with tears fought one another for a place near the stove. . . . The children's generally depressed spirit showed not only in their outward appearance, but in the whole of their psychological behavior. Everything enervated them, everything was difficult for them. . . .

For a long time the children refused to take off their breeches, felt boots, frocks, and caps, although the room was quite warm. Stealthily they would lie down in bed in their dresses, their stockings, their breeches. . . .

It was distressing to see the children at the table at mealtimes. They ate their soup in two stages—first the broth, then the rest of the contents. Porridge or fruit jelly they spread on their bread. Some of the bread they broke up in microscopically small fragments, which they hid in matchboxes. The children would often leave their bread to the last as the daintiest dish of all and eat it after they had disposed of their earlier courses. They did this with such enjoyment that it sometimes took them hours to eat a piece of bread, which in the process they examined as if it were some unaccountable wonder.[131]

During this period nearly all the remaining utilities and services ceased to operate. The water and sewage pipes were frozen; electricity was unavailable and public transportation nonexistent. According to *Leningradskaia pravda,* by the spring of 1942 only nine houses in the Frunze *raion* still had functioning water and sewerage facilities.[132] The banks closed because they had no electric lights. The newspapers appeared irregularly, and the public-address system suffered frequent stoppages.[133] There was still mail service; but it was poor, partly because there were not enough workers to sort out mail and partly because the exhausted mailmen and volunteers found it very difficult to make deliveries.[134]

With the improvement in the food supply system in January, the leadership made an attempt to solve the fuel and power problems, and to provide at least the key installations of the city with a more regular supply of firewood. One of the first steps was to legalize and control the removal and distribution of wooden structures. On January 26, by the order of the Executive Committee of the Leningrad City Soviet mentioned above, it was decided:

9. In order to improve the population's supply of firewood, to authorize the executive committee of the *raion* Soviets to begin immediately to take apart dilapidated wooden buildings (houses, barns) and all sorts of wooden structures owned by the state, as well as communal ones, according to address lists agreed on with the Executive Committee of the Leningrad City Soviet.[135]

This order did not extend to wooden houses still in use. It appears that most of the wood thus obtained went for the use of bakeries, various institutions, and industrial installations rather than to the general public.[136]

It is not clear why the leadership was so conservative in this measure, and why it had acted with such delay. Possibly one reason was simple bureaucratic reluctance to disregard the rules of "Soviet legality" and face the problem of dismantling "socialist property." Even in this emergency bureaucratic and accounting procedures were preserved. When the order was put into effect, the dismantling of buildings had to proceed according to a plan controlled by the highest city authority, the Executive Committee of the Leningrad City Soviet. Of course, the labor for these operations was provided by the benefiting agencies or enterprises, or by the citizens of the *raion.*

The cautious dismantling of wooden structures could not possibly provide sufficient fuel for industry and the electric power stations. Yet it was imperative to maintain a minimum output of electric power and to revive Leningrad's industry as soon as possible. Therefore, the remaining resources around the city had to be exploited in an effort to obtain additional fuel. According to the secretary of the Leningrad Party committee, A. A. Kuznetsov:

It was decided to organize the cutting of firewood in the suburban zone and to exploit the internal resources of the city. Three thousand Leningrad workers, the overwhelming majority of them women, took up saws and axes and went off to cut firewood. Under difficult conditions, with insufficient housing and food, the workers stubbornly learned the profession of lumber-jack, which was new to them. . . . If at the start the average output amounted to 1.1 cubic meters per person per day, it reached 5.5 cubic meters per day by the end of 1942, with the norm set at 2.6 cubic meters.[137]

The undertaking was by no means voluntary. The workers had been mobilized for this task by "an appeal of the Leningrad Party organiza-tion and of its leader, Comrade Zhdanov."[138] An attempt was also made to dig for peat, which was probably a nearly hopeless task in view of the cold. As a rule each enterprise, factory, or agency (even hospitals) sent its own lumber-cutting crew, composed of its own employees.[139] Only such a method could ensure that each would obtain its share of the fuel.

The Party organization, and particularly the Komsomol, took an active part in implementing these measures. It was claimed, probably with some exaggeration, that in response to the executive committee's order of January 26 "thousands" of Komsomols were mobilized to dig peat and cut lumber:

On the appeal of the Party thousands of Komsomols went out to bring in lumber and peat. . . . But it is not enough to have obtained peat and lumber, to have brought it to Leningrad quickly; it is also necessary to use each kilogram of fuel correctly and intelligently. The creative mind of the Komsomol must be directed to converting the power systems to the use of peat and firewood, and to taking the initiative in developing small power stations and factory power installations.[140]

Actually, these measures did not provide sufficient fuel to keep the electric power stations or much of industry going. Since there was no housing for the workers and only primitive tools, the task of cutting down trees in the middle of winter would have been extremely arduous under normal circumstances, particularly for inexperienced women. But these people were all weak from starvation. Even additional rations could not help them to achieve much. Furthermore, the boilers of the electric power stations could be converted to the use of peat and wood fuels only with great difficulty, and even then the results were not very satisfactory. Consequently, additional fuel had to be obtained from out-side. According to Popkov: "In February 1942 the Military Council of the Leningrad Front decided to organize the importation of coal into the city via Lake Ladoga. 1,500 Leningraders were sent to transport the coal; under difficult conditions, they brought in, in two months, over 25,000 tons of coal."[141] The Council of People's Commissars sent to the ice road 200 trucks from Moscow and Gorki for the sole purpose of carrying coal to Leningrad.¹⁴² The effect of these measures became noticeable only very slowly.

When the Germans were pushed back in December, it became possible to rebuild the Volkhov hydroelectric station, which had been dismantled in 1941, and use it for Leningrad. Consequently, toward the end of January the Elektrosila Works received orders to help in the reconstruction of the station and to send there a number of skilled workers and engineers. The generators that had been evacuated to the east in the fall were brought back in February; but the station did not begin to provide electric power for Leningrad (by means of an underwater cable across Lake Ladoga) until the fall of 1942.¹⁴³

It was apparently also in January that the authorities were able to start improving Leningrad's radio and telephone communications with the outside. A telephone cable was laid across the ice, thus linking the city directly with the rest of the country; although at times power failures and German bombardment still interrupted communications.¹⁴⁴

The order of January 26 benefited the population very little, since, as has been pointed out, most of the fuel obtained in this manner went for official use. The inhabitants continued to steal wood from abandoned houses and to break up fences and sheds. In the diary of a Soviet writer there is the following entry for January 25: "Just now a crowd fell upon the wooden fence of the hospital and tore it up for fuel."¹⁴⁵ Also, as before, people burned furniture—either their own or pieces taken from empty apartments—and tore up flooring and all other wood they could find. When people froze to death, it was generally not because of any total lack of firewood, but because of their inability, in their extreme weakness, to chop it up into usable form.

To most people the long-standing prohibitions against taking wood for fuel, whether from trees, fences, abandoned or demolished houses, or unused apartments, seemed just another example of leadership's callousness or inefficiency. Why should the trees in the parks be carefully preserved while many Leningraders were freezing? Yet taking wood from any of these sources was officially classified as theft. Since, however, the authorities did not generally interfere, the population simply continued to use illegal means to keep warm.

With regard to water, as before the population got it from whatever source was available: from the river and the canals, from broken water mains, or from the few taps that still functioned. Since the exhaustion of the inhabitants made it very difficult to procure water, few people shaved, or washed themselves or their clothing; whatever water was available was used primarily for drinking and cooking. The population continued to use all the previous methods to dispose of garbage and excrement. Since the authorities made no attempt to control or organize the means by which people procured water or disposed of sewage and garbage, the population necessarily fell back on its own devices.

The population found the hardships imposed by the shortage of electric light, fuel, water, and transportation demoralizing and difficult to bear. Not only did these shortages make additional inroads on the slender remaining strength of the inhabitants, but everyone feared that at some moment he would no longer be able to find fuel or lamp oil and might freeze to death in darkness. A Soviet writer wrote in her diary on February 3: "Never before has life in Leningrad seemed to me to be so painful. Our two oil wicks are a real torture. One's longing for light is like one's longing for bread."[146] It was frustrating to find a demolished or abandoned home and lack the strength to climb into it, or to obtain a piece of lumber and find oneself too weak to drag it home. It was a minor tragedy to spill some of the small amount of water that one was attempting to carry home after one had walked far in order to obtain it. Nevertheless the citizens could still sometimes look at their problems with wry humor. In a Soviet war novel, written by a Leningrad writer, a woman consoled her friends at a water hole in the Neva River with the remark: "We are well off. Can you imagine the Americans with their skyscrapers if they had to carry water up to the seventieth floor? They would have given up right away."[147]

For the leadership in Leningrad, the primary objective was, of course, the defense of the city. And here the leadership could begin to be cautiously optimistic. The German defeat before Moscow and the liberation of Tikhvin, for the time being at least, eliminated the threat of a complete encirclement of Leningrad. The ice road was operating increasingly better. It looked as though the Volkhov offensive might break the German ring. The only problem was whether Leningrad could survive until its expected rescue.

According to one source, after the Tikhvin victory in December Zhdanov is reported to have sent to the Party organizations an enthusiastic letter, in which he promised that the relief of Leningrad would take place in the immediate future.[148] There is no doubt that the leadership, both in Moscow and in Leningrad, was jubilant. Indicative of the mood was the following intercepted radio conversation between Moscow and Leningrad:

MOSCOW. Things will be better. Here things are already much better. Have you been reading the newspapers?

LENINGRAD. Yes, I have, and I feel wonderful about the good news.

MOSCOW. Hold out! As far as food goes, there will be a big improvement soon. We are taking important steps here in this respect. It won't be long—then things will be well with you too.[149]

This conversation was apparently hinting not only at increased shipments of food for Leningrad, but also at an offensive to break the German siege. An appeal to the population of the occupied areas around Leningrad, issued in early 1942 in the name of the Leningrad *Oblast* Party Committee and the Military Council of the Leningrad Front, declared:

The hour of your liberation from the horrible, bloody yoke of the German fascist occupiers is approaching. The heroic Red Army is victoriously developing its advance on all fronts, mercilessly beating the enemy. Hitler's robber plans to capture Moscow and Leningrad and enslave the peoples of the Soviet Union have collapsed. Before Moscow, Leningrad, Tula, Kalinin, and Rostov, the beaten fascist hordes have met their fate. . . .

Every day more and more *raions* of the Leningrad *oblast* are being liberated by the Red Army and returned to the dear Soviet family.

Soon the Red Army will come to you too. Like beaten dogs the defeated and retreating fascist bands will soon march past you.

Dear comrades! Prepare a worthy welcome for the Red Army.[150]

Above and beyond the hope of a military rescue, the Red Army successes had already brought about two important changes in the situation. First, it was now unlikely that the Germans would be able to mount a new attack on Leningrad in the immediate future. Second, the shortening of the supply road to Leningrad could be expected to bring about a substantial increase in the volume of supplies reaching the city.

In March the hopes of driving the Germans away from the Leningrad area were disappointed. The danger of a renewed German attempt to capture the city, or complete its encirclement, remained. But the operation of the ice road ensured that the defending forces would be fed and could be reinforced by fresh troops from the outside. The ice road also permitted resumption of the industrial and civilian evacuation, so that even if the Germans captured the city, much valuable personnel and equipment would escape them. By re-establishing a direct link between Leningrad and the power of the Soviet State, the ice road also strengthened the position of Leningrad's leadership vis-à-vis the population. The leadership was in a better position to resist any possible popular pressure for a surrender of the city. It is probable, however, that the leadership did not allow itself to worry too much about this; it knew that the key element in its control system was the army, and as long as the latter remained loyal and the Germans were kept at bay, it had every chance of preserving its controls inside Leningrad.

It was natural, therefore, that the leadership should consider it essential to give every priority to preserving the strength of the defending armed forces. Since the food shortage, the industrial stoppages, and the absence of replacements had dangerously weakened the Red Army forces around Leningrad, it was inevitable that the first benefits from the operation of the ice road would accrue to them rather than to the civilian population. Consequently, the rations of the troops were increased before those of the civilians, and by larger amounts. The first increase occurred, according to German reports, on or about December 15, when, in addition to their daily ration of 500 grams of bread, the soldiers received some sugar, fats, meat, and vodka.[151] On January 21, again earlier than the increase in civilians' rations, the army rations were further increased to 800 grams of bread, as compared with the 350 grams that the city workers were receiving.[152]

The defending forces also began to receive help in the form of equipment and reinforcements delivered over the ice road. Gasoline, medical supplies, ammunition, spare parts, and even tanks began to arrive in increasing quantities. In return, Leningrad sent troops across Lake Ladoga to reinforce the Red Army units that were attacking from the east. There the troops could be re-equipped and properly fed while they were helping to relieve the city. Some fresh forces arrived to replace them.[153]

In addition to hunger and cold, the population had to suffer the constant strain of the unrelenting German bombardment. Although the Germans did not renew their air attacks until April, artillery bombardment not only continued, but constantly increased. In January, 2,696 artillery shells exploded in the city, in February, 4,771, and in March, 7,380, making a total of 20,817 shells in the period of December through March, and a total of 519 Leningraders killed and 1,447 wounded.[154] During the same period, the effectiveness of Leningrad's civil defense sharply declined. As noted earlier, by December the civil defense organization had become largely inoperative because of the lack of water and the exhaustion and death of its members.

On January 26, after the second increase in the food ration, the Executive Committee of the Leningrad City Soviet attempted to revive the civil defense organization. The committee ordered the population "to re-establish immediately in all enterprises, official schools, houses, communal quarters, and other places of public use the watch hours of the janitors and the round-the-clock civil defense watch of the members of the self-defense groups."[155] In view of the conditions and the high death rate it was not possible for the population to comply with this order. Several months were to pass before the inhabitants had sufficiently recovered and the weather had moderated enough to permit the groups to re-form and operate effectively again.

Leningrad's industry in this period was faced with almost insurmountable problems. The shortages of fuel, water, and power for industrial use and the exhaustion of the workers had become critical in

December and became even worse in January and February. German artillery fire also caused serious disruptions. By January only 21 per cent of the factories had glass in their windows, the windows of other factories being boarded up. In 63 per cent of the factories there was no electric light, and 78 per cent had no ventilation; so that in some factory shops the concentration of harmful fumes and smoke was ten to fifteen times the authorized peacetime level.[156] As a result many enterprises closed down. According to the director of the Kirov Works:

> On December 15 everything came to a standstill. There was no fuel, no electric current, no food, no streetcars, no water—nothing. Production in Leningrad practically ceased. We were to remain in this condition until the first of April. It is true that food began to come in in February across the Ladoga ice road. But we needed another month before we could start any regular kind of output at the Kirov Works.[157]

Some factory shops continued to operate after a fashion, either by switching to hand-manufacturing methods, or by managing to obtain a very limited amount of electric or steam power. They were able to produce small amounts of munitions, mines, and hand grenades; they sometimes repaired guns, electric motors, and tanks, or did other "odd jobs."[158] For the most part, however, the factories used this period of idleness to make repairs in their machines and buildings, collect scrap iron, clean up the shops and surrounding areas, and send workers to dig peat or cut lumber.

Nevertheless, by juggling supplies, material, and labor, the leadership managed to obtain some vital parts and repairs. For example, according to the secretary of the Party committee of the Stalin Works: "In February the shops were not heated. It was cruelly cold. The temperature in the shops was the same as out-of-doors; the workers' hands were so cold that they would stick to the part they were working on. The Party committee called the Communists in and informed them of an urgent order. The factory had to work, no matter how. And the people worked and performed miracles."[159]

But even in factories and shops that remained in operation, no continuous production was possible on account of the frequent interruptions in the power supply and the shortage of lubricants, raw material, or spare parts, as well as the fact that the workers had to stop work constantly to rest.[160] Because industry could no longer operate on the basis of a predetermined general plan, the role of the local industrial administration was enlarged; many decisions had to be left to Leningrad's leadership and to individual managers. This development became increasingly marked as time went on. According to a Soviet history of the Elektrosila Works, "Leningrad's industry in 1942 and 1943 was not planned by the central body. Leningrad was a sort of autonomous eco-

nomic unit, planning and carrying out its own plan. The City Committee of the Party, Comrade A. A. Zhdanov personally, and his closest
assistants, A. A. Kuznetsov and Ia. F. Kapustin, daily directed the work
of the factory and helped it."[161]

Local directives generally took precedence when an industrial estab-
lishment had to produce for local needs. In other cases, though, particularly when the items being produced were needed elsewhere, the local
administration and Leningrad's leadership still took their instructions
from Moscow. The regular administrative channels and procedures
continued to remain largely in force. At least throughout January, Leningrad's harassed industrial managers were still bombarded from Moscow with requests for annual reports, accounts, and inventories, and still
told what to send to the "mainland." The following radio conversation
is fairly typical of the early days of January:

MOSCOW. Comrade Romanov, when will you have the yearly report and accounts ready?
LENINGRAD. I cannot say today. My secretary is ill, Slaviaskii is ill, and my
courier is ill.
MOSCOW. That, of course, is very bad, but you must see to it that this matter
does not drag on.
LENINGRAD. I cannot do everything, you have to admit. I will see what can
be done but it will take time.[162]

Leningrad's managers asked Moscow for money, for instructions, for
permits to evacuate personnel.[163]

It has been noted that one of industry's chief problems was the condition of the workers. In one major factory, illness caused 55 per cent
of the workers to be absent in January, 61 per cent to be absent in February, and 59 per cent in March.[164] Many of the remaining workers
were so weak as to be unable to perform much work. For example, in
one factory, workers are said to have had to tie themselves to the tanks
they were repairing because they feared they would fall off when they
became dizzy from hunger.[165] Workers kept fainting or falling asleep.[166]
When the Elektrosila Works sent skilled workers and technicians to
assist in the reconstruction of the Volkhov power station, they were so
weak that they could not stand during the trip and had to be laid on
the floor of the trucks.[167] It was obvious that even if most of industry
had not been forced to a standstill for other reasons, the condition of
the workers would have prevented it from operating.

To conserve the energy of the workers it became necessary to reduce
the daily work hours from eleven or twelve to eight. In order to reduce
absenteeism and avoid the long walks to and from work, which sapped
the workers' remaining strength, many factories organized dormitories
for their employees and also arranged for them to receive their rations
at the factory. In February some factories managed to set up small

clinics, where the most valuable of the sick workers received some medical attention and extra food. The factories could also heat some parts of their buildings, and some provided washing facilities.[168]

Control over labor was still predominantly exercised by means of the ration card and canteen coupons. When the authorities urgently needed the completion of a specific task, such as the repair of damaged tanks, the workers selected were sometimes issued the front-line rations that soldiers received, and additional labor was recruited with promises of more food. At times the administrators ensured the fulfillment of the required quota by withholding the canteen coupons for the workers' dinner until the prescribed work norm was met.[169]

Aside from the inducement of food, the authorities lacked any effective controls over absenteeism, at least until it became possible to visit the homes of absent workers. Threats were of no avail. Each individual worker decided whether he felt strong enough to walk to work, or whether he would forego for a while the advantage of using the factory canteen and stay at home to rest; if he chose the second alternative, he could use the time to try to obtain something in the black market. The standard rule requiring medical certificates for absences was generally simply overlooked. Doctors had too many desperately ill or dying patients to have time to issue such certificates. For the same reason it was not possible to enforce the law against tardiness. The administration had to be satisfied if the workers managed to drag themselves to the factories at all.

The leadership and the Party organizations, of course, continued their propagandistic activities among the workers to induce them to higher productivity and to preserve morale. The Party organizations, and particularly the Komsomol, were, as always, supposed to inspire the workers not only by propagandizing, but also by setting an example of high performance, energy, and initiative. In the words of one secretary of the city Party Committee:

Much attention is paid to making the vanguard role of the Communists more significant. In a whole series of factories there is not one among the Communist producers who does not fulfill the production norm. By their personal example of courage and devotion the Communists carry along with them the non-Party people, inspire them to perform glorious deeds. . . .
The Bolshevik word, spoken and printed, is a powerful source of political influence on the masses, for uniting and mobilizing Soviet peoples. Wherever the Party organizations have been able to organize effective political agitation the struggle for the fulfillment of production orders, for overcoming difficulties, is the most successful.[170]

The same author cited some specific and successful examples of Party propaganda among workers. These included the public reading of the correspondence between the secretary of a factory shop and former employees serving with the Red Army, in which the latter urged the workers to do their utmost for the front. In many other factories socialist competitions were organized between shifts. Elsewhere the leading or best workers were encouraged by the Party organizations to propagandize their fellow workers. In critical areas, such as cutting lumber, digging peat, producing vital industrial goods, or increasing the volume of traffic on the October Railroad, the Komsomol, as was seen, was ordered to play a leading role in solving the difficulties and in setting an example to others.[171]

It is probable that on a very limited scale these efforts had some success. But they could not overcome the food shortage and its consequences, or the fuel and power problem. Leningrad's labor was not capable of a sustained large-scale effort. Yet a large proportion of the workers continued to go to work, not only because they wanted the larger rations, but because they sought the company of their fellow workers rather than remain in cold, dark rooms alone, and because many were motivated by the will to live and believed that if they did not keep busy they would die.

The improvement in the ice road now made it possible to resume industrial evacuation. Stocks of needed materiel, machinery, and personnel were sent to the east, although only equipment light enough to be carried on trucks could be moved.[172] The amount of machinery that was evacuated in January and February does not appear to have been very large. Not until the spring, or even summer, were enough transportation facilities available to permit the large-scale removal of factory equipment. As was seen, apart from equipment, many more skilled workers and technicians were evacuated to help operate new factories in the east.[173] Soviet war industry could ill afford to dispense with the skill of Leningrad's workers. In the period of January 22 to April 15, 66,182 factory and office workers were transferred.[174] This evacuation, by depleting the local pool of trained workers, hindered the reactivation of the city's industry in the spring.

In view of the food shortage, it was highly desirable to remove from the city as many as possible of the inhabitants who were not essential to its defense. In December one-third of the population was made up of nonworking women, children, and old people. Consequently, on December 6, the Military Council of the Leningrad Front authorized the evacuation of civilians over the ice road and ordered that by December 20, 5,000 persons be evacuated daily from the city.[175]

Accordingly, on December 25 the Council for Evacuation, part of the Council of People's Commissars of the USSR, ordered the Leningrad *Oblast* Executive Committee to establish an evacuation center in Tikhvin large enough to handle 3,000 to 4,000 people at a time.[176] Later the transshipment points, feeding points, and other facilities were moved farther west, to the railway station of Zhikharevo, and then to Lavrovo, Kabona, and Lednevo on Lake Ladoga.

Since the evacuation depended on the operation of the ice road, it could not be systematized until the road itself was properly organized. In the beginning the truck traffic was too irregular and limited to provide transportation for many people. Only old women, children, and those too weak to walk traveled on trucks, while others had to cross the ice on foot or skis. Many died in the attempt. Consequently, the rate of evacuation fell far short of the planned level, and only 36,118 persons were evacuated in the period of December 6 to January 22.[177]

With improvements in the operation of the ice road and the shifting of the railhead from Tikhvin to Voibokalo, it became possible to speed up the flow of evacuees. On January 22 the State Defense Committee ordered the evacuation of 500,000 Leningraders and put A. N. Kosygin, the deputy chairman of the Council of People's Commissars of the USSR, in charge of the operation. This high-level decision gave to the evacuation of Leningrad a priority character it had lacked so far. The transportation of evacuees began to improve. A number of buses were sent from Moscow.[178] Special medical aid posts were established along the route where the evacuees could warm themselves or receive medical assistance. The evacuees were taken by train to the shore of the lake; from there they went by truck to the other side, and then were taken on by train to their destination. But even at best, the trip was not without great danger. Since there were few buses, most evacuees had to travel in open trucks—and the temperature reached forty degrees below zero. The ice road was frequently shelled and strafed by the Germans, as were the transfer points. Trucks were often lost in the blizzards or fell through holes in the ice. Under these circumstances, to arrive frostbitten was one of the less tragic outcomes of the trip.[179] Of course, evacuation by air continued to be open to select elements of the population throughout this period.

Each person authorized to leave Leningrad was permitted to take 40 lb. to 60 lb. of baggage, which he had to bring to the station himself.[180] He had to turn in his ration card, to prevent it from winding up on the black market, and received in exchange a special food ration that was to feed him on the trip. Upon arrival at the other side of Lake Ladoga, the evacuee was fed and received further rations for the rest of the trip.[181]

For various reasons, not everyone was eager to leave even now. Pride, the feeling of obligation toward those who remained behind, or fear of conditions elsewhere still made many Leningraders hesitate to ask for permission to leave. For example, in one radio conversation, a Leningrader told Moscow that the situation had become "a little worse."

Yet he replied to Moscow's question "Do you perhaps want to come to us?" with the answer "No, I am doing very well here."[182] There were those who were so weakened by hunger that they did not expect to survive the trip and preferred to die at home.[183] Some did not wish to abandon various friends and relatives who could not leave. Some said: "In Leningrad we can expect an improvement. In the rest of the country, where we would be without homes, they will have, or they already do have, the same hunger, the same disruption of living conditions."[184] One woman noted in her diary that although she was so ill that she thought she might die, she still did not want to leave, and that when finally persuaded to do so, she was ashamed of her decision.[185]

The authorities were determined to remove all nonessential residents and put pressure on those who asked to remain in Leningrad for various reasons. One informant felt too weak to undertake the trip and even obtained a medical certificate to this effect. Yet the administration of the institute where she was employed disregarded the certificate and "strongly hinted that a refusal could mean her arrest and forcible deportation to Siberia."[186] This threat was sufficient to persuade the informant to leave. In other cases recalcitrants were called before the NKVD or were arrested and forcibly evacuated.[187] Those who refused to leave, moreover, were in danger of losing their ration and apartment privileges. The authorities were, in other words, prepared to enforce their evacuation orders.

Yet those who were eager to leave were on the whole very patient in waiting for their turn. There was, of course, some resentment against a system of selection that gave the elite evacuation priority over the people and organizations precedence over individuals. But, in general, people accepted the necessity for some sort of priority system, and, besides, there was little choice for the individual but to wait his turn. Unauthorized evacuation was both difficult and dangerous, since it was tantamount to desertion. A young worker, who later deserted to the Germans, gave this description of the method by which he managed to leave:

On January 21, 1942, in exchange for my ration card, my landlady obtained a pass to Lake Ladoga for me from a friend at the Military Medical Academy. The pass was not accepted at the control point. I went back a little way, then climbed over a fence, and took the passenger train to the Ladozhskoe station on Lake Ladoga. From there I traveled by truck, across the lake to Zhikharevo, and then by train to Volkhovstroi. There were no document checks up to that point. I was traveling with my landlady and her child. I went on by train to Vologda via Tikhvin-Babaevo. I received food on the strength of my release certificate, because I pretended to have lost my evacuation authorization.[188]

Tight controls were obviously maintained only at the exits from Leningrad. From there on it was possible to bluff one's way to the interior, provided one had some valid-looking documents. Yet it is unlikely that any significant number of Leningraders resorted to illegal methods of leaving the city. It was at best feasible only for single and relatively strong persons, since so many difficulties could arise in making the attempt. Furthermore, the population appeared to have had an exaggerated notion of the extent and thoroughness of the controls and knew little about how the evacuation actually proceeded. Consequently, it took a person of considerable initiative or daring to risk leaving without proper authorization.

The authorities did succeed in the end in evacuating the planned number of residents from the city. In January 11,296 left, in February 117,434, and in March 221,947; so that altogether 554,000 persons were evacuated over the ice road in the period of November to mid-April.[189]

Since the amount of baggage that could be taken along was very limited, the evacuee had in effect to leave most of his possessions behind. Some people, particularly the intelligentsia, could receive authorization to seal their apartments until their eventual return. But most people felt that in a war of long duration there was little hope of ever recovering their possessions. Consequently, many evacuees tried to sell some or all of their belongings before leaving, usually for cash. This could be done in the market or at official purchasing centers that had been set up for this purpose.[190] Of course, only those who were wealthy, by Soviet standards, had something worth selling. The rest of the population frequently had to accept the loss of all their meager possessions in exchange for the salvation offered by the evacuation.

The rising death rate and the extremely difficult living conditions had an inevitable effect on the leadership's control over the population. This control had seriously weakened by December. The regular police organs had become increasingly inoperative. Regulations concerning registration of and surveillance over people living in apartment houses were no longer enforced. Beginning in January, the leadership attempted to reassert its authority.

On January 13 Popkov denounced all black-market speculators, thieves, and other criminals, and demanded that energetic steps be taken to put a stop to their activities:

> We must also take the most effective measures in the struggle with all sorts of disorganizers of the food-supply system, with thieves and marauders who resort to all sorts of tricks in order to loot food and to wax fat on the people's sufferings. Thieves, speculators, and marauders will be mercilessly punished according to wartime laws. The Leningrad Soviet is certain that in the struggle with these enemies of the people, whose deeds are assisting our foreign enemies, the German fascist cannibals, the state and legal organs will receive the widest support and assistance. The society of our city . . . must participate most actively in uncovering and capturing marauders, thieves, and speculators.[191]

Shortly thereafter the Executive Committee of the Leningrad City Soviet issued an order reinstating the previously existing checks on apartment residents and the other security measures that had been put into force at the start of the war. In addition to ordering that all buildings should again be guarded by gatekeepers or janitors, the committee gave the house administrations ten days in which to make up their staffs to the normal number and "to re-establish the regular working hours of the *upravdoms,* passport registrators, bookkeepers, and other workers responsible for receiving new tenants."[192] The militia, reinforced by Komsomol guard units, was ordered to supervise the proper execution of this and other orders. But in practice the surviving police force was in no position to carry out these directives.

Because of the famine it had been impossible for the authorities to keep in check the ever-growing number of robberies and other crimes. Only after rations were increased did it become possible to re-establish tighter controls. On February 9 the commanding officer of the Leningrad garrison announced:

Lately there have been noted in the city of Leningrad instances of violations by individual citizens of revolutionary discipline and of the wartime rules established by the military authorities. Enemy elements exploit these conditions in order to carry out their subversive work.

The Military Council of the Leningrad Front has charged me with the maintenance of revolutionary order in the city of Leningrad and has placed under my orders the troops of the NKO [People's Commissariat of Defense] stationed on the territory of the Leningrad garrison, the Worker Peasant Militia, the destruction battalions, and the troops of the NKVD.[193]

The order instituted a tighter curfew, by which all members of the population, except for those who were able to secure new passes issued by the garrison commander, were prohibited from being out of doors after eleven o'clock at night. Effective police control was not re-established until April, when the city's militia was reinforced by replacements from Moscow.[194]

In order to combat speculation on food, and particularly to prevent the black-market sale of ration cards and the use of ration cards of dead Leningraders, the administration frequently invalidated the cards in use and issued new ones. Thus, whereas previously ration cards had been valid for a month at a time, they were now frequently issued only for two weeks or less. This also permitted the authorities to check on absenteeism, since a person whose work entitled him to a high ration card could not hope to stay at home and use it for any length of time. Furthermore, these frequent registrations enabled the city's administration to obtain a more accurate idea of the death rate in the city.[195]

The authorities also took steps to solve another problem faced by the population, the shortage of money, which was caused by the closing of the banks and the shutting down of many enterprises and offices. Salaries were paid infrequently or with delay. It has been pointed out above that evacuees needed cash and wanted to dispose of the possessions they had to leave behind. The authorities' answer to all of these problems was to open purchasing centers where people could sell clothing, furniture, household goods, and similar objects in their possession.[196] These centers also took advantage of the unique opportunity to acquire for the Public Library and the Academy of Arts and Sciences the various private libraries that evacuating intellectuals and scholars had to leave behind.[197] It is probable that art objects were also sold and bought, although people would have been more likely to sell them to speculators, from whom they could receive a larger return than at the government stores.

Disrupting as they did every phase of life, the difficulties brought about by the siege seriously interfered with the dissemination of news and propaganda. According to the secretary of the Leningrad City Party Committee, "In the Vyborg *raion*, for example, the only loudspeaker in operation was in the office of the secretary [of the *raion* Party committee]."[198]

The printing and distribution of newspapers became even more irregular than before, so that most people were unable to obtain copies. The newspapers posted on the bulletin boards of various buildings and factories, as well as at certain street corners, were often put up only after one or two days' delay. Most of the population lacked the energy to seek them out, anyway. It was for this reason that most people found out about the increase in the food ration in December only when they went to buy bread.

The population was kept informed largely by word-of-mouth propaganda, the dissemination of which became one of the principal functions of the Party propagandists.

Mass forms of propaganda work could not be employed. The characteristic trait of agitation in the period of the hunger blockade was individual discussion.

The agitator came to the apartment of a Leningrader. With simple, sincere words he helped people to whose lot had fallen unheard-of trials to realize that without steadfastness, without moral fortitude, it would be impossible to defend Leningrad.

The agitator became the link between the population of the city and the "mainland," since with rare exceptions radios did not work either in the enterprises or in the homes.

The agitators received all important news from the Party *raion* committees.[199]

Because of the importance attributed by the authorities to propaganda and indoctrination of the population, the maintenance of a corps of full-time agitators, even at this desperate stage, was considered to be fully justified. It was the job of the agitators to disseminate the news among the population, or at least among the workers and employees of key enterprises. The mechanics of this process in the Vyborg *raion*, for example, were as follows:

Here, at six o'clock each morning, a watch of lecturers and consultants of the *raion* agitation point [*raiagitpunkt*] was assembled in order to write down the contents of the radio broadcasts. From eight to nine they assembled the agitators and instructed them. For the timely instruction of the *aktivs* and the benefit of the agitators, the *raion* Party committees also called the Leningrad TASS office, from which they received short verbal reports on the latest news. This information was reproduced and sent by courier to the enterprises and apartment buildings.[200]

In December, special Komsomol propaganda teams were organized by the city and *raion* Komsomol committees. They led discussions among workers on such themes as "Let us overcome all difficulties in order to be victorious over the enemy," "On the prohibition of the unauthorized departure of workers and office workers from enterprises of the defense industry," and "On the food situation in Leningrad."[201]

Fortunately for the Leningrad propagandists, the war news during this period was very good. There was naturally much ado over the Tikhvin victory, since it gave hope for the possible relief of Leningrad. The Red Army successes on the Moscow front were given full play in Leningrad;[202] mass meetings were held in the factories and institutions, and many congratulatory messages were sent to the government and to the people of Moscow.[203]

Soviet successes in the Leningrad area, which gave rise to hopes that the blockade would be lifted, were reported in detail only for a short time in December.[204] During the next two months Soviet communiqués reported many Red Army successes on various parts of the front, but reports about operations in the Leningrad area became increasingly vague.

Nevertheless, the official military estimates of the prospects for Leningrad were optimistic. The general propaganda theme was that the Germans had suffered heavy losses in their attempt to recapture the city and had been forced to pass to the defensive.[205] A Soviet officer wrote: "The situation has changed. We know the enemy is still strong—to underestimate this would be criminal—but our forces, while advancing, inflict blow after blow on the fascists, annihilating their manpower and equipment, and will continue to do so as long as the German occupiers have not been completely destroyed."[206] Similar sentiments were expressed by the Military Council of the Leningrad Front in an order-of-the-day to the troops.[207]

Popkov and other leaders also expressed cautious optimism in connection with the operation of the ice road. They made it clear that they considered that the worst was over, since the Germans would not be able to force an unconditional surrender on the city. They pointed out, moreover, that as Leningrad regained its strength, the likelihood of a successful new German assault declined.

Under the circumstances it was inevitable that many rumors circulated among the population. When military victories occurred, the rumors almost always became optimistic. In December, after the successes at Tikhvin and Moscow, "people began to expect the relief of Leningrad to follow shortly upon these victories."[208] Some people cried for joy, others embraced; everybody excitedly discussed the news. People began to feel that Leningrad would survive if only they could manage to hold out a little longer. The relief of Leningrad by the Red Army was rumored to be only a matter of weeks away, two months at the most.[209]

But when the official news remained vague, the population began to be skeptical about Soviet military successes, at least insofar as the Leningrad war zone was concerned. According to one informant, Popkov's New Year's message failed to hold out any hope for the immediate future.[210] In January and February, except for occasional flurries of hopeful rumors, the population became increasingly convinced that there was no prospect for the speedy relief of Leningrad; they received some encouragement, however, from rumors that large amounts of food were on the way to the city.[211]

Nor did the population expect to be rescued by the Germans, a possibility that some people had entertained earlier. The failure of the Germans to take Leningrad and Moscow, their winter retreats, and the inactivity on the Leningrad front lent support to the Soviet propaganda assertions that the Germans were relatively weak and unprepared for winter. It was rumored, for example, that the Germans were unable to bomb Leningrad because they could not use their gasoline in the prevailing cold.[212] But then when the Soviet victories did not lead to the relief of Leningrad, some people began to doubt whether the Germans were as weak as Soviet propaganda alleged.

While most Leningraders did not expect the Germans to try to take the city during the winter, this did not mean that they believed all danger of attack had passed. Those who mistrusted Soviet reports of military successes, or who doubted that Leningrad would be relieved before spring, expected a renewed German assault on the city with the coming of warmer weather. They feared that all the sacrifices made by the Leningraders would be in vain and that a renewed German attack would overcome the defenders.[213]

Soviet propaganda, meanwhile, was profiting from the military retreats of the Germans to issue fresh and more authentic-sounding anti-German material. Reports of German atrocities from escaped prisoners of war, partisans, and liberated civilians were given wide circulation. Much was made of alleged German atrocities in Tikhvin. In other stories the Germans were reported to have burned a number of civilians in their houses, blown up others, beaten women and children to death, and so forth.[214] Every Soviet citizen was urged to feel an unwavering hatred of the Germans and to seek merciless revenge. This propaganda campaign went into high gear when on January 6 Molotov sent to the Allies and neutral nations a long catalogue of the German atrocities and crimes committed in the Soviet Union.[215] In February a published statement by German prisoners of war denouncing German mistreatment of captive Russian soldiers and civilians lent credence to the campaign.[216] The Germans, so Soviet propaganda asserted, were more than enemies: they were sadistic monsters who wanted not only to enslave Russia, but to torture and destroy its people.

Soviet propaganda continued to appeal to the pride of the inhabitants and to their sense of duty to persuade them to bear the privations of life in Leningrad and carry on their work. In the words of *Leningradskaia pravda*:

> Nevertheless, under conditions of encirclement it is inevitable that privations and misfortunes affect the weak and give birth to depression among the timid. It is to Leningrad's honor that such people are few among us. But no matter how few they are, one must remember that provocateurs and fascist agents take advantage of our difficulties, try to sow doubts, disbelief, and defeatism, and try to exploit such people.[217]

A frequent device to stiffen morale was to award large numbers of medals. A typical occasion was the decoration of 607 workers on January 14, 1942, and that of 79 civil defense workers two days later.[218] A *Leningradskaia pravda* editorial discussing the awards declared:

> The 607 wonderful fighters of the labor front as well as the courageous fighters of the MPVO have set examples of great service to the fatherland and to our beloved city. Their awards are at the same time awards to all the heroic defenders of Leningrad for achievements in fighting and working.
>
> Our entire country is watching with admiration how, with unequaled steadfastness, with utter selflessness and iron will, the Leningraders are defending their city. Adding to the fine revolutionary traditions of their city, the Leningraders set an example to all Soviet people of courageous service to the fatherland.[219]

Appeals to the pride and sense of responsibility of the workers generally used the theme that whoever failed in his duty bore direct responsibility for the continued suffering of the population or for the difficulties of the soldiers at the front. The kinship between the soldiers and the civilians was further emphasized by visits of delegations of civilians to the front and of soldiers to the factories. The civilians were supposed to inspire the troops to fight harder, and the soldiers to induce the workers to produce more weapons. The civilian delegations, carefully selected from among various social groups, collected gifts such as guitars, handkerchiefs, tobacco, razors, and hand-knitted winter clothes from the inhabitants and brought them to the troops. Such trips to the front involved considerable danger, since not only did the civilians run the risk of being killed by German planes and guns, but there was also a chance that in their undernourished condition they might freeze to death on the way.[220]

The available sources suggest that the earlier propaganda campaign picturing Leningrad as the focal point of the attention and concern of the entire Soviet Union was no longer stressed. Probably the battle of Moscow drew public attention away from Leningrad. Leningrad's fate, moreover, did not appear to be so much in doubt as it had earlier.

The Party and the leadership naturally tried to gain prestige from the improvements in living conditions. The leadership, for example, took full credit for the organization of the ice road, but no blame for any of its failures. Thus on January 13 Popkov explained the reasons for the ration difficulties since the beginning of the siege, and then went on to say:

> The delivery of food into the city under conditions of a nearly total blockade was successfully organized as a result of the great work carried out by the Leningrad Party and Soviet organizations under the leadership of Comrade Zhdanov, who literally did not for an hour leave without attention, without his personal direct control, the problem of providing the city with food.
> The government is showing the greatest concern for Leningrad and has taken all steps to provide Leningrad with the necessary food stocks.[221]

Whereas up to this time the leadership and the Party had assumed none of the blame for the suffering of the population, from mid-January on they were quick to claim credit for the various decrees that were intended to ease the living conditions of the Leningraders and to point to these measures as evidence of their "concern for the people." The Party, for example, loudly proclaimed its role in organizing the care of the sick and weak in their homes, and made a great ado over this demonstration of solidarity and Soviet concern for the common man.

The citizeness Rybakova wrote to the Priorskii *raion* committee of the Komsomol, the first one to organize welfare detachments: "I am ill and have not been able to move from my bed for two months. The girls cut firewood and cleaned up the room, all in a comradely fashion, but most of all they raised the morale of the invalid. I am moved to tears. In what other country could this have happened? I thank you, and I will not forget the help shown to me. Many thanks for the Stalinist concern for the people."

The Komsomol detachment of the Primorskii *raion* alone, composed of 80 persons, visited 13,810 apartments, and helped over 75,000 Leningraders. Comrade Zhdanov highly praised the work of the welfare detachments. In his words, in those days they "consoled, encouraged, and inspired the Leningrad population."[222]

The military successes quite naturally accrued to the prestige of the Party and the leadership. These victories appeared to bear out the leadership's prediction that the Germans would inevitably be defeated in the end, thereby justifying the decision to defend Leningrad at all costs.

It is, however, probably correct to say that Party and leadership propaganda operations were actually at their lowest point during most of this period. They lacked the means to communicate with the masses. Fortunately for the authorities, the improvements in both the military situation and the food situation obviated to some extent the necessity for a mass propaganda effort.

During this period of Leningrad's greatest difficulties, the authorities still encouraged some intellectual and artistic activities and maintained in operation a number of institutions of higher learning. A few secondary schools apparently also tried to keep going. To keep these schools open was extremely difficult in view of the shortage of fuel and electricity. Few students had enough strength or persistence to attend classes. In one secondary school, upper classes opened on January 15 with 70 students. Classes lasted only half an hour each. There was no heat, the inkwells were frozen, and students kept fainting from hunger. Schools tried to help their students. For New Year's, for instance, the children were given a party and a show, and received some extra food and candy.[223]

Artists still held occasional meetings and congresses. A joint meeting of Leningrad writers, artists, scientists, and academicians was held in January, despite the fact that there was no heat in the meeting hall.[224] In early February a two-day congress of Baltic writers was held. The delegates slept in the meeting hall and on the second day burned their chairs to keep the small stove going.[225]

Most of the elite, as was pointed out, suffered like the rest of the population. Those in the middle and lower echelons were increasingly unable to cope with the situation; many of them were dying. Fortunately, the leadership's demands on the managers and technicians declined during most of this period because of the virtual stoppage of industrial activity and the almost total breakdown of all services and utilities. Nevertheless, the strain on the managerial and administrative personnel who were still at work was heavy. There was so much to be done and so little to do it with, even when the problem merely consisted in keeping a part of one's employees alive and some elements of the enterprise or institution going. Many administrators worked themselves into a state of collapse by attempting this nearly impossible task. Like the workers, many of them lived at their offices, to be on hand for the constant emergencies and to save themselves the effort of going to and from work. Some of them were too exhausted and weak to go anywhere else, anyway.[226]

The attitude of the elite was a mixture of hope and despair. Although they did not expect a German assault, the rapid dying-off of the population led many members of the elite to believe that they, too, would not survive and that only a quick military solution by the Red Army could avert a total collapse of the city.[227]

Some of the ups and downs of hope and despair can be seen from the diary of a well-known Soviet writer, Vera Inber:

January 3. They say (and it is true) that everywhere, in Tikhvin, in Volkhov, in Murmansk—particularly in Murmansk—there stand trains with food. There lie mountains of crates with the sign "For Leningrad Only!" People are talking of this with enthusiasm, with emotion. It is reported that there is everything there, including fruit.
Leningrad lives on the last remnants of its strength. This straining of all efforts to the limit can be felt in everything. . . . What will happen if they fail to bring in food in the immediate future?

January 4. How tired one is of all this excitement, of this perpetual tension in which one lives. When will the suffering of Leningrad finally end? I have the impression that if the siege is not broken within ten days, the city will not be able to hold out.

January 5. They say that we have taken Mga. But who has heard this?

January 7. It is asserted that Gen. Meretskov's troops [54th Army] will be in Leningrad on January 10.

January 25. The situation is catastrophic.[228]

There is no doubt, as Soviet sources later admitted, that there were Party members who became "apathetic, lost their perspective, and gave up."[229] At the end of February an editorial in the *Leningradskaia pravda* denounced the views of those members of the elite who maintained that under the prevailing conditions "no great things could be undertaken."[230] More than one member of the elite hinted or asked Moscow outright to be permitted to leave Leningrad.[231]

But not everybody was equally depressed. The higher echelons of the elite probably remained more resolute and determined than the

lower ones. The majority of the intercepted radio messages in this
period, although often complaining of illness among the Leningrad
staffs, usually dealt with business and administrative problems in efficient and resolute tones.

In an effort to preserve the morale of the Party activists, some *raion*
organizations held meetings in spite of the difficulties involved in such
undertakings:

> When the activist is left to himself he can become despondent, apathetic,
> but then the *raion aktiv* meets, and each one sees how much strength there is
> in our *raion* Party organization, each mentally compares his own work with
> that of other comrades, and each is involuntarily braced.
> Particularly memorable is the *aktiv* that met in January, at a very difficult
> time. Several hundred activists assembled precisely on time in one of the
> halls of the *raion*.
> Each felt the need to get together, to exchange ideas, to consult with
> each other on how best to solve the difficult problems facing the city.[232]

The rest of this article made it clear that this was the only meeting
held in January and that even later in the year the group never met
more than twice a month.

As before, the Party continued to recruit new members and promote
others to positions of responsibility to fill the vacancies left by those
who died or were evacuated. Thus, in December, 970 new members
were recruited, in January 795, in February 615, and in March 728.[233]

Except for the relatively few who gave in to despair and became
apathetic, the elite did its job and stood by the leadership. During the
blackest part of this period, some of the elite, as was seen, feared the
worst, either a surrender to the Germans or a popular revolt. However,
the survival of the Soviet regime appeared more and more probable in
the light of the military victories. The elite therefore had every reason
to remain loyal and active. Furthermore, no one wanted to forego the
privileges attached to elite status. These privileges also served as an
inducement in the recruitment of new members.

From the viewpoint of the population no period of the siege of
Leningrad was so full of horror and despair as were these winter months.
That under these conditions the city would suffer from a morale problem that was completely beyond the authorities' ability to solve or
control is self-evident. A letter written in February by a Leningrad
woman to her husband in the army is typical of the civilian mood:

Dear Pavlik:

> How are you and how is your health? In your last letter you wrote that
> you are getting horsemeat. Well, that is not bad at all—we envy you. L. Yu
> is also having a bad time with food. A few days ago they got a goat, which
> they keep next to the bathroom. Things are worse for us, but they have prom-
> ised us that the situation will be better shortly. We shall wait. A small glim-

mering is noticeable. We already receive 300 grams of bread. I have already written you that Mother died. . . . Pavlik, I sometimes feel so hopeless that at night when I go to sleep I ask myself whether I will be able to get up next morning. I am very weak. You cannot imagine how I look—only skin and bones, a living skeleton. I think now that we are going to receive food, that we might not die of hunger after all, but the organism is so weak that it is susceptible to every illness, and I therefore expect various plagues such as cholera and typhus in spring and am sure I shall be among the first to fall ill from something. It would be best therefore to leave Leningrad now, but this is impossible for us. The evacuation of Leningrad is at present being carried out, but only the families of officers are leaving. Pavlik, can't you arrange this for me? Pavlik, it seems to me now that I would give anything just not to be here. It's true that there's no knowing in advance whether the food situation might not be worse where one is sent than here, but I think that there one can buy—at least for a lot of money—lots of potatoes. . . .

These are all dreams. I think I will soon join Mama. I have not been to see Lesha. It is too far and I have no strength to walk, although I would like to know how he is. I have written but received no reply.[234]

Despite increases in rations in February the number of deaths and sick people seemed to grow, and many diaries expressed the belief of their writers that they would not survive.[235]

In their despair many Leningraders now became increasingly hostile to the Germans and fell to blaming them for the terrible living conditions. According to reports, it was not uncommon to hear the complaint "They are sitting warm and well fed in their bunkers and letting us perish here from hunger."[236] After picturing those warm, well-fed Germans sadistically gloating over the tortured city, people rejoiced to hear that Germans in other areas were dying by the thousands from the cold.

The population did not expect to be saved even if the city did surrender to the Germans, because, as a German report noted, people were quite sure that the Germans would not be able to feed the population.[237] People feared that a German attack on the city would completely disrupt the food supply and distribution system. Most Leningraders, moreover, felt convinced that the city would be swept by plagues in the spring, and a German occupation would do nothing to avert this danger: "The question of whether the Germans will succeed in taking Leningrad is seldom raised. It is generally held that an occupation of the city will not be able to remove this acute threat."[238] For most people the Germans did not represent a desirable alternative to their present life, as even German reports made clear.[239]

The fact that the Leningraders had less interest in being rescued by the Germans increased their reliance on the city's authorities and reduced to some extent the motivations for nonconformist political behavior. After all, the choice in a besieged city was very limited: either to revolt and surrender the city to the enemy, or to remain loyal to the leaders of the defense. It is clear, at any rate, that for the most part the population was too concerned with its immediate problems to worry much about the Germans. Although conditions could have been expected to stimulate the spread of oppositionist sentiments, this was not the case.

In fact, there arose a fairly widespread feeling that all the death and suffering would not have been in vain. National and local pride appear to have played a role in producing this attitude, at least among the intelligentsia. Thus some said, "It is horrible, but nevertheless it is better than a victory by the Germans—the old merciless enemies of everything Russian."[240] People felt pride in the fact that they lived in the "Hero City." One man who did not expect to live more than a month said, "I am so proud. How Leningrad is holding out! How Leningrad is holding out!"[241] Another person wrote in her diary: "Let our children and our children's children never forget about the blockade of Leningrad, let them never forget how we suffered for victory."[242] Similarly, one informant, who expected to die shortly from hunger, was very indignant because Popkov had stated that Leningrad would not be surrendered. He felt that one should not even mention surrender, that Leningrad was too precious a city to be turned over to the Germans, no matter what the cost.[243]

The fact that most Leningraders were in favor of continuing the defense of the city did not mean that they were uncritical of the leadership, and to a lesser degree of the elite. The inhabitants were often quite bitter about the inability of the leadership to protect them from the worst consequences of the siege and about the real or imaginary privileges granted to the elite. In the absence of any immediate substantial improvements, it was natural for some people to blame the leadership openly for lack of concern for the inhabitants, as well as for insufficient imagination and initiative. An example of this attitude is reported as follows:

> Horrible, how horrible! . . . The greatest crime and treason lies in the fact that the civilian population was simply not taken into consideration, that from the start nothing was done to save it, that the time was passed up when much could have been done to help it, that the city was brought to this condition. Couldn't they have dropped medicine? Some kind of vitamins? Condensed foods or dry vegetables? After all they yelled about food laboratories and factories! And now — nothing. Absolutely nothing. Five months of nothing. They build a track over the Ladoga, but this is just taking place now! And then not to help the population, but in order to continue the struggle. . . . Much, very much could have been done, but human life is worthless with us. What is the use of talking? . . . They save themselves, only themselves, at any price.[244]

One informant recalls how when he saw a man collapse in the street and lie there unable to rise, the man exclaimed, "This is how far we got under Stalin!"[245]

Typical of the jealousy felt toward the elite is this statement made to the friend of a former Leningrader:

> They feed their own. Any way they can, depending on rank. They deliver to the home of one man a monthly package, another they help to tide over with a special food issue, to a third they slip an extra ration card. Others are simply flown by plane out of the encirclement. Do you think that members of the NKVD or the city Party committee are starving? Or that they might be dying? I can cite you here and now with ease hundreds of names of our kind, among them important scholars, who have died up to now. But can we find at least one more or less important Party member who died of hunger? You won't find a single one![246]

Some elements of the population were convinced that the evacuation system favored the elite, and naturally they resented this. They were bitter, too, at realizing that most of the large-scale black-market operators were members of the elite or were connected with it.

Yet these attitudes did not represent in the political sense a challenge to the leadership's authority. Naturally, some people grumbled a great deal. The reassurances that the leadership published in the press or broadcast in propaganda announcements were received with mistrust. Many people doubted whether they would be alive by the time the promised help arrived. But this popular resentment and criticism was not on any high emotional level. Dreading the future, physically exhausted, bending every effort merely to solve the daily problem of survival, most Leningraders could scarcely avoid becoming totally apathetic or indifferent to anything that did not affect their immediate life. In the words of a German report based on information given by deserters and German agents: "Because of the lengthy period of starvation the population is physically so weakened that it is apathetic to everything. The people have only one desire, which is to see the end of starvation as soon as possible."[247] Most Leningraders did not even bother to voice their bitterness or resentment. When someone did complain, others noted with surprise that there should be anyone left with enough energy and interest to do so.[248]

For most Leningraders in this period the unit of immediate importance remained the family or the group of fellow workers. Within each family there was a certain division of labor in procuring the various essentials and sharing the available food, fuel, water, and medicine. Family members usually tried to take care of each other and often made great sacrifices for one another; parents sometimes sacrificed their lives for their children. Outside the family group popular cooperation and mutual assistance were less evident. People were, of course, hindered by the fact that there was little anyone could do for anyone else. Social contact outside of the home or place of employment was very difficult, and the problem, for example, of finding out the fate of a friend or colleague who had not been heard of for some time was considerable, unless he lived in the immediate vicinity. If a person did succeed in tracking down a friend and found him dying of hunger, there was usually no way of helping. Occasionally people gave dying friends their own daily ration—a useless gesture since it made little difference in the fate of the "dystrophic"—or tried to arrange to have them admitted to a hospital or sanatorium.[249] There were, of course, exceptional cases of people who did all they could to assist their fellow men. Not all those who had food reserves took advantage of their good fortune to enrich themselves on the black market; in fact, these people often went out of their way to help friends or even strangers.[250] But cooperation was frequently placed on a mercenary basis simply because people could not afford to give away any of the strength or material goods they had left if they wished to remain alive.

As in the immediately preceding period, it would not have been unreasonable to expect riots and other disturbances, considering what life in Leningrad was like. The remarkable fact was that they did not occur. There are no reports, for example, of attempts by desperate civilians to attack food warehouses, bakeries, or food trucks. The same people who stole food for themselves, who might even commit murder for it, or who were half insane from hunger or fear for their loved ones patiently stood in line for hours on end waiting for their daily rations. Even on the days when no bread was issued, no group or mass acts of desperation were reported.

Similarly, there were no riots or disorders in connection with the mass dying of the inhabitants. There are no indications that people became hysterical, or that they publicly denounced the authorities or sought revenge for the death of loved ones. As noted earlier, there was not even loud grieving. The dead were abandoned or buried, and the inhabitants remained passive.

Most of the inhabitants patiently waited their turn to be evacuated. There were no instances of people attempting to force the authorities to evacuate them out of turn, no demonstrations, no cases of people storming evacuation trucks or trains—despite the fact that many feared they would be unable to survive unless their turn came quickly.

There were no public political acts, such as demonstrations, public demands for surrender, or marches on the Smolny Institute. There were no attacks by individuals or groups on *raion* administrative or Party offices, or on individual leaders or members of the elite, despite the general belief that they were better off than the people.

It is significant that none of the available diaries, letters, interrogations, memoirs of participants, or interviews with informants indicates that any sort of mass action was even considered by the inhabitants. Speculations that some Leningraders had expressed earlier about the possibility of a revolt by some element of the population do not appear to have continued during this period.

Not only was the population completely dependent on the authorities for its rations, but it lacked the emotional drive and the energy to riot. There was no hysteria; there was only quiet despair, or quiet hope that the situation would improve. There were also still many people left who were willing to support the authorities and to do their best to help in defending their beloved city.

Chapter 9

THE FORTRESS CITY
March 1942–January 1943

Wﾘﾟﾟ ﾟﾟﾟ ﾟﾟﾟﾟﾟﾟ of spring, the Germans made new plans for their campaign in Russia. In his Directive 41 of April 5, 1942, Hitler once again decided to try to capture Leningrad, although he made the undertaking conditional on German successes in the Crimea and Caucasus.¹ It was decided that the Eighteenth Army would be reinforced by the Eleventh, commanded by General Field Marshal Erich von Manstein, as soon as it had completed the capture of Sevastopol. The objective of the planned Operation "Nordlicht" was for the Germans to cross the Neva River and effect contact with the Finns east of Leningrad, thereby establishing a close ring around the city. This was to be followed by an assault on Leningrad. At the same time Hitler still hoped to achieve the surrender of the city by intensive aerial and artillery bombardment, for which purpose some 800 heavy artillery pieces were to be concentrated around Leningrad.² The offensive was scheduled to begin on September 14.

Following the fall of Sevastopol in July, elements of the Eleventh Army and all the heavy siege artillery were transferred to Leningrad. At the same time the Eighth Air Corps was assigned to support the forthcoming operation. But the German plans were upset by two events. First, part of the major element of the Eleventh Army had to be diverted to support the operations in the south. Second, the Soviet command, well aware of the build-up on the Leningrad front and anxious to lift the siege, launched its own offensives on August 27 in the Siniavino-Mga sector and at Tosno and Uritsk. During the following month the Germans had to fight hard to keep their hold on Leningrad, especially near Lake Ladoga, where the Russian forces achieved deep penetrations. Although these penetrations were contained and eventually destroyed, with heavy losses to the Red Army, the battle absorbed all the resources of the Eighteenth Army and elements of the Eleventh, with the result that the planned offensive had to be abandoned. The subsequent crisis in the Stalingrad-Caucasus area forced the transfer there of the Eleventh Army units from Leningrad. By mid-October the Leningrad front was therefore substantially the same as in the spring. From then on the Germans had to pass completely to the defensive in this sector.[3]

In the last two months of 1942 the over-all military situation began to change in favor of the Soviet Union. The Soviet offensive at Stalingrad was launched on November 19 and was followed by other offensives in the northern Caucasus and in the region of Kursk. These operations developed into a general Soviet winter offensive along the entire front, during which the Germans lost heavily in men and materiel and were forced to retreat in many sectors of the front.

The Soviet High Command also drew up new plans for breaking the blockade of Leningrad. These plans called for a simultaneous attack by the Leningrad and Volkhov forces in the area immediately south of Lake Ladoga, where the German Eighteenth Army held a ten-mile-wide, heavily fortified strip of territory. The Soviet forces advancing from east and west were to effect a junction and then drive south in an attempt to roll up the right flank of the German positions encircling Leningrad.[4]

The attack began on January 12. The Soviet forces operated with two armies and elements of a third against some six German divisions entrenched in a series of strong points. The Soviet units made slow but steady progress, and on January 18 a junction of the attacking armies was effected. At the same time, the city of Schlusselburg was taken. The German blockade was broken and a narrow corridor, between five and six miles wide, along the southern shore of Lake Ladoga was occupied by the Soviet forces. Further attempts to widen this corridor failed despite numerous Soviet attacks.[5]

Thus, despite a great effort the Red Army was unsuccessful in its attempt to lift the blockade of Leningrad completely. The city remained under German fire for another year. But the liberated corridor, although very narrow and harassed by German artillery fire, permitted the re-establishment of a direct rail link to Leningrad.

In March 1942 Leningrad began its slow climb to recovery. As the pulse of life quickened, the city gradually regained strength and became the strong fortress it should have been a year earlier, capable of withstanding a further year and a half of siege and every German attempt to destroy it. This recovery was not accomplished without the investment of a great deal of energy on the part of the authorities, and exertion and suffering on the part of the population. As the flow of supplies into the city increased, it was not too difficult to restore the major

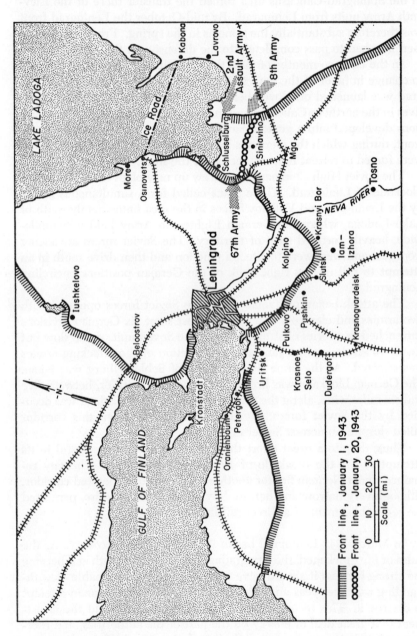

THE SOVIET BREAKTHROUGH, JANUARY 1943

mechanical elements of the industrial and municipal operations. But to revive the human element was slower and more painful. The Leningraders often could not keep pace with the duties imposed upon them. Nor was it possible to eradicate the memories of the past winter, or the fear of the next one.

Improvement in living conditions came about only very slowly. Although the ice road and, later, boat traffic on Lake Ladoga provided the city with a steady and increasing flow of supplies, the total amount of food and goods available to the population remained limited. The new ration level would have been sufficient to sustain the citizens fairly well in normal times, but was not enough to ensure a speedy recovery from the preceding hardships. The death rate remained high, particularly throughout May. Furthermore, many of the subsequent improvements and the preparations for another winter of siege were made dependent on the population's own efforts, no easy task in view of the exhaustion of the inhabitants. The realization that they would largely have to bring about their own salvation added to their anxieties, as did the intensified aerial and artillery bombardment and the threat of a new German assault.

After mid-February, food and other supplies became increasingly available; for at the same time that the capacity of the Ladoga transportation system increased, not only did the size of the population decrease (through deaths and evacuation), but local food sources were being systematically developed and exploited. As far as the population was concerned, the improvement came about only by degrees, since the leadership gave priority to the needs of the army and the building up of reserves.* Even at their best the supplies available to the population remained, on the whole, below their presiege level.

The bread ration instituted on February 11 remained in force throughout the remainder of the year. The major changes were in the quality of the bread and in the increasing availability of other staples.† But there were many foods that always remained in short supply, and there were frequent interruptions in the availability, for example, of cereals for young children, lamp oil or kerosene, matches, and cigarettes.

---

* On April 8 Leningrad had on hand 8,057 tons of flour, 442 tons of soya, 1,687 tons of cereal, 302 tons of fish, 1,794 tons of butter, 846 tons of vegetable oil, and 3,117 tons of sugar (Karasev, *Leningradtsy v gody blokady,* p. 208).

† In April the official monthly food ration for workers and technicians was set at 1,800 grams of meat, 500 grams of fish, 2,000 grams of cereal, 800 grams of fat, and 900 grams of sugar; office workers: 1,000 grams of meat, 400 grams of fish, 1,500 grams of cereal, 400 grams of fat, and 500 grams of sugar; dependents: 600 grams of meat, 250 grams of fish, 100 grams of cereal, 200 grams of fat, and 400 grams of sugar; and children: 600 grams of meat, 250 grams of fish, 1,200 grams of cereal, 400 grams of fat, and 500 grams of sugar (Karasev, *Leningradtsy v gody blokady,* p. 237).

Special food issues were made on holidays such as May Day, when increased amounts of meat, millet, dried peas, fish, and sugar, as well as some wine and vodka, were issued.[6] When the ice road melted in April, a temporary drop in the food ration occurred until boat traffic could be resumed on Lake Ladoga, but by June rations were larger than before.[7] During the summer the available food reached its highest level, owing in part to the local cultivation of vegetables.[8] The bread issued ceased to contain the previous admixtures, although white bread was only available to children and invalids.[9] The city's food reserves continued to grow month by month.[*] A substantial part of the canned goods distributed to the army and the civilians was of foreign origin—from America, New Zealand, or Australia.

The ration system preserved the earlier scale of preferential treatment by granting the largest ration increases to the workers and technicians and the smallest to unemployed persons. Workers in key or difficult occupations, such as the transportation system, sometimes received larger rations.[10] The improved conditions also permitted a certain amount of upgrading of some white-collar workers, whose work could now be regarded by the authorities as having greater social value. Teachers, for example, began to receive workers' rations in April.[11] Ration differentials were observed even in the distribution of such scarce items as matches. On March 5, for example, two boxes of matches were issued to workers and white-collar workers, while dependents received only one box.[12]

The authorities now took steps to speed up the recovery of the productive elements of the population and save those in the second and third stages of distrophy. On April 21 a chain of 153 special dietary restaurants was instituted for the purpose of providing special meals for those selected to use them.[13] The selection was made at local clinics by a commission composed of a doctor and representatives from the *raion* soviets and trade unions. The meals gave the recipients a daily amount of food that was somewhat larger than the regular workers' ration and considerably larger than that of dependents.[†] Priority in the use of the restaurants was given to workers and other useful persons, who were allowed to eat in them for two to four weeks depending on their physical condition. Consequently, only a small section of the population benefited from this system. According to Soviet sources, some 200,000 to 260,000 Leningraders used these restaurants; but of these, 69 per

---

[*] For example, by July 1 the city had 28,393 tons of flour, and on October 1 there were 55,440 tons of flour (Karasev, *Leningradtsy v gody blokady*, p. 258).

[†] The total food issued in the three daily meals amounted to 500 grams of bread, 30 grams of butter or fat, 50 grams of meat, 40 grams of sugar or candy, and some groats or semolina (GD [97]).

cent were workers, 18.5 per cent were office workers, and only 12.5 per cent were dependents, although these last had received the smallest rations during the winter and had suffered most from hunger.[14] The special dietary restaurants were discontinued on August 1. From July 6 on, there were regular restaurants in operation, at which registered persons, especially workers, could receive all their meals on the basis of their ration cards.[15]

School children were offered hot meals at their schools. This announcement sharply increased attendance; on May 3 the number of students at one school jumped from 70 to 547.[16]

In view of the vitamin deficiency of the inhabitants, large-scale consumption of the pine needle infusion described earlier was encouraged by the authorities during the spring and summer: "Thousands of our children and youngsters went out to collect these fresh twigs and there wasn't a factory canteen, a school, a government office—in fact there was hardly a place in Leningrad where there weren't buckets of this liquid, and everybody was urged to drink of it as much as he could. It didn't taste particularly good, but people drank gallons and gallons of it."[17]

To supplement the imported rations and to provide some reserves of food, the Executive Committee of the Leningrad City Soviet decided to have the population cultivate individual garden plots. Consequently, on March 19 the committee issued an order instructing the executive committees of the *raion* Soviets of workers' deputies to organize private and collective vegetable gardens; the order was to be acted upon at once, and the *raion* committees were to work in conjunction with the factory trade-union committees (*Fabzavkom*), the trade unions (*Mestkom*), and the house organs.[18]

The execution of the order involved rather complex administrative operations. The city authorities set aside over 17,000 acres of land for these gardens.[19] On the basis of rules drafted by the executive committee, seed packages were sold only to the unions of the people who were making use of the scheme, and to factories and various institutions. The Department of Local Industry was ordered to produce gardening tools, which were sold to the population,[20] and people were to be given lectures on gardening. The order provided for the conversion of school grounds and land belonging to various health institutions into vegetable gardens and for the sale of soil and seeds for the indoor raising of vegetables. The executive committees of the *raions* were charged with directing and controlling the development of the individual plots.

Plots and supplies were allotted to organized groups, such as institutions, factories, offices, and schools; people living in apartments were also divided into groups, some by house and some by block, the allotments in the latter case being subdivided into individual or family plots.

The plots were located within the city in parks, gardens, empty lots, and open fields, or in the suburbs. The army and many of the factories and larger enterprises or institutions developed auxiliary farms outside the city, which were cultivated for the benefit of the entire group.[21] To what extent the rather cumbersome administrative arrangement interfered with the project is not known, but it was well designed to bring into evidence many bureaucratic roadblocks and inefficiencies.

According to Soviet sources, 270,000 Leningraders received individual garden plots.[22] However, the total of vegetables harvested in 1942 was only between 60,000 and 76,000 tons, a substantial part of the crop remaining in the hands of the individuals and organizations that grew it.[23] Additional vegetables were issued during the summer in the restaurants and factory canteens.[24]

The whole undertaking suffered very much from the population's lack of experience. For example, school children diligently weeded up carrot plants. Because of the poor water supply, the lack of tools and fertilizer, and so forth, many people failed to grow the expected vegetables on their plots. One eyewitness reported that most cabbages had grown "enormous, absurd leaves, of little or bitter taste," which even the horses would not eat.[25] Many of the amateur gardeners found it hard to perform the arduous work required of them. Part of the harvest had to be stored away by the individual inhabitants for the winter months, in case it became necessary to reduce the rations then. Nevertheless, the campaign did enrich the diet of many Leningraders with some vitally needed fresh vegetables. In addition the population gathered and ate wild sorrel, grass, and nettles, all of which helped to counter the effects of scurvy.[26]

Popular participation was unquestionably eager, since this campaign was of immediate and direct benefit to the participants, especially after the authorities told the population, "You'll eat as much as you've planted; don't expect anything from outside."[27]

In addition to developing individual plots, the authorities expanded the cultivation of vegetables and wheat in the remaining unoccupied collective farms of the region.[28] The largest part of the food grown on the farms was reserved for the armed forces and official organizations rather than being distributed through the ration system. Nevertheless, some of this produce did reach the population via the open market. For example, it is reported that in April and May some milk could be obtained in the open market in exchange for bread, at the rate of half a liter of milk for the equivalent of two days' bread rations of a dependent.[29] Since this exchange was legal, it indicates how severe the food shortage of the peasants was.

The cultivation of all the nonindividual gardens required labor from the respective operating agencies and from manpower especially drafted for the purpose, including some 7,000 Komsomols. The city also mobilized some 5,000 school children and sent them to work on the farms during the summer, thus combining health benefits for the children with useful labor for the state.[30] At harvest time the authorities drafted over 10,000 Leningraders for obligatory labor in the fields.[31]

The usual socialist competition was also instituted, the most productive farms or schools receiving from the *raion* executive committees certificates and some monetary rewards. The temporary farm labor was kept under control by threatening to send home those whose performance was poor, thus depriving them of the benefits of their work.[32] These threats and incentives were not always sufficient to overcome the reluctance of some Leningraders to be separated from their families, their dread of the physical demands of the work, and their fear, justified at times, of losing their jobs during their absence. It did not improve matters that in some areas near the front lines the gardeners were often shelled by the Germans.[33]

Despite many improvements, the food supply remained tight and continued to be one of the main objects of popular concern. The morale of the Leningraders tended to fluctuate substantially in direct proportion to the available rations or their expectations concerning future supplies. Those who had believed in the rumor that Stalin had personally ordered unlimited quantities of food to be sent to Leningrad were of course disappointed.[34] Even a year later, despite further improvement, a driver told a foreign correspondent: "It's good to be heroes, but we could all do with a spot of ordinary quiet living . . . It's a lot better; I get six hundred grammes of bread. Not enough, really, considering what we Leningrad people have gone through."[35]

The barter markets remained important sources of food and other supplies for the population. Despite the increases in rations, these markets continued to be quite active throughout the rest of the year, although prices or exchange rates declined somewhat.[36] In addition to such food items as potatoes and meat, the open market continued to serve as a major source for clothing, cigarettes, matches, spirits, and kerosene and other fuels.[37] The quality of many items was very low, as is evident from the fact that in October the city's school children were ordered to collect maple leaves in the parks for use as a substitute for tobacco.[38]

The records also indicate that the theft of food, ration cards, and similar items continued, although on a reduced scale. There were frequent thefts of vegetables from garden plots and farms, forcing the authorities to introduce a five years' prison sentence for such offenses. Theft of food from state-owned supplies for resale on the black market continued to be punishable by death.[39]

The slowness of the improvement in the amount and quality of food

certainly delayed the physical recovery of the inhabitants. From March
through July dystrophy continued to predominate in Leningrad, and
thousands died every day from its effects. According to official figures,
89,968 people were buried in March and 102,497 in April, the number
of deaths slowly declining to 6,885 in September.[40] Many more were
so weak as to be unable to walk. Of those evacuated, many died en
route and others required hospitalization. One doctor noted that in
March many workers were unable to perform heavy labor because they
were "completely exhausted and in advanced stages of scurvy."[41] The
Soviet writer Fadeev, who visited Leningrad in the last days of April,
reported that his stepsister was "in a very poor condition."

> I had known her as a handsome woman in the full bloom of physical
> maturity. Before me was almost an old woman, withered, with puffy eyelids,
> darkened face, and swollen legs. Her dark, smoothly combed hair was heavily
> streaked with grey. . . . Her delicate hands had coarsened and become
> rough: the knotted hands of a manual worker.
> The first thing she told me was that owing to physical weakness she had
> had to give up, only a few days before, the responsibility for the apartment
> building [where she had held the post of civil defense warden].[42]

The same author also observed that many people in the streets were
obviously suffering from various stages of exhaustion:

> There were still many emaciated faces to be seen. Now and then one
> came across people sitting on the steps in front of a building or wandering
> about on spindly legs, people who were so dried up in appearance, whose
> faces were so dark, that one could see that it was doubtful whether they could
> be saved. . . . Sometimes two elderly people helped a third along; some-
> times it was a wife who took an enfeebled husband by the arm.[43]

In view of their weakness, the inhabitants continued to worry, particularly in March and April, about the possible outbreak of epidemics.
One eyewitness wrote in her diary: "At this moment the fate of Leningrad is being decided for this spring: Will we have epidemics, or will
we manage to avoid them? One is left breathless at the thought that
typhus or dysentery could ravage Leningrad. Who would escape it and
who would care for the sick?"[44]

In April and May a number of cases of typhus occurred. But no
infectious diseases reached epidemic proportions because of the energetic measures taken by the administration.[45] The weakened Leningraders easily fell victim to various less serious respiratory and in-
testinal diseases, from which many had not the strength to recover.
In March an attempt was made to issue antidysentery pills to the population, but this measure apparently was not very effective.[46] Subsequently, the head of the Leningrad Health Department told a foreign
correspondent: "In the hospitals, the death rate among adults was

high throughout the summer of 1942 because of the aftereffects of the famine."[47] In order to overcome the shortage of physicians and other medical personnel, 200 doctors and 900 nurses were sent by Moscow to Leningrad.[48] The death rate declined after the summer was over because of the improvement in living conditions and the elimination, by death or evacuation, of many of the most weakened inhabitants.

The city authorities knew, of course, that no local administrative measures could be successful without the preservation and expansion of the supply road. The leadership therefore devoted a great deal of attention to its operation, with the particular aim of eliminating its defects and the desperate improvisations that had so often characterized it to date. The traffic on the ice road reached its greatest volume in March as a result of the successful construction of a railway branch line from Zhikharevo to Kabona and Lednevo, thereby shortening the truck road to the 18-mile stretch across the ice of Lake Ladoga.[49] At the same time the transshipment of supplies, road maintenance, traffic control, and all other aspects of the road's operation were greatly improved. But the spring thaw was near and with it the end of the ice road.

The ice began to melt in the last days of March. Numerous bridges were hastily flung up over the widening cracks in the ice. The flooding of the road and the crumbling of the ice caused many accidents and sharply reduced the road's capacity. On April 15 heavy trucks had to be barred from the road, and only light trucks with continually decreasing loads could be used. All traffic finally came to a halt on April 24.[50] From then on all supplies had to reach Leningrad by water.

The organization of the water transportation system on Lake Ladoga was not the crash program that the development of the ice road had been. Instead, the Leningrad leadership had given it careful thought and planning. The problems were a shortage of usable vessels, poor harbor facilities, and insufficient storage space.

Actually, most ships on Lake Ladoga were in the service of the defense fleet. The remainder were for the most part too small to cross the lake safely. Of 70 available ships and two barges, only ten were suitable. To obtain sufficient shipping capacity the authorities arranged for the transfer to the lake from the Gulf of Finland of a number of fishing motorboats and river steamers, some of which had to be dismantled first and then rebuilt on the shore of the lake. Most of them were moved by rail, since the Germans held one bank of the Neva River. Leningrad's shipyards were ordered to build 11 metal barges with a freight capacity of 600 tons each, which were then sent to Lake Ladoga by rail in sections and assembled upon arrival; and 31 wooden barges of 385 tons each were built at Siastroi.[51]

In July and August, by order of the State Defense Council, a number of river boats were sent to the Ladoga from other parts of the Soviet Union.[52] At the same time, preparations were made to improve the harbor, storage, and road facilities. Several harbors were developed on both shores of the lake, the main ones being Kabona and Osinovets; development of these facilities continued throughout the summer. The transport flotilla was placed by the Military Council of the Leningrad Front under the administrative control of the Ladoga naval command and the Northwest State River Shipping Administration. The change from the army-controlled single administration for the ice road to the naval-civilian dual administration for the lake shipping was due in part to the difference in technical know-how between the two operations and in part to the transfer of responsibility for the defense of the supply road from the army to the Ladoga naval flotilla.

According to Soviet sources,[53] on April 19 the military council approved a transport plan for the Ladoga shipping that provided for the daily delivery of 4,200 tons of supplies and the daily evacuation from Leningrad of a minimum of 3,000 people and 1,000 tons of freight. On May 22, one month after the ice road became inoperative, the first ship arrived on the west shore of Lake Ladoga.*

The initial daily deliveries fell well short of the plan, because the ice on the lake did not completely melt until mid-June and the Germans subjected the harbors and shipping to intensive bombardment. Nevertheless, the volume of freight moved daily increased from 1,500 tons in May to 3,500 tons by the end of June. Ship construction and improvement of harbors and roads further expanded the volume of traffic. On July 15 a new transport plan required the daily delivery of 7,000 tons of freight and the evacuation of 10,000 persons. In October, shipments reached their peak with a monthly total of 150,000 tons, after which they continued to decline, owing to bad weather, until the end of November, when the lake froze over again.[54] German efforts to interfere with the traffic failed to halt the flow of supplies to Leningrad, in spite of some large raids by as many as 40 to 60 planes.†

It was fortunate that the improved supply line allowed the authorities to lay in substantial food reserves while at the same time reducing

---

* According to these sources, the freight capacity of the new ships built by spring 1942 amounted to 22,000 tons. Other construction required the building of 70 kilometers of corduroy roads, 100,000 square meters of storage space, and an eventual total of 27 quays and 25 kilometers of rail lines; extensive earth-moving operations were also necessary.

† During 1942 the Germans were said to have flown 100 sorties against the Ladoga shipping and facilities and to have dropped 300 bombs. Fifteen sunken ships were subsequently raised. Some sources claim that there were 142 daylight and 27 night raids in 194 days and 6,370 bombs dropped (*Propaganda i agitatsiia*, No. 3 [1943], cited in *LVOVSS*, I, 306; *LP*, Jan. 19, 1947; Saparov, pp. 238–41).

the size of the population that remained in the city. For although during the fall of 1942 the authorities had made extensive preparations to build a new ice road for the coming winter, the arrival of warmer weather greatly restricted the operation of the road. The first truck column did not manage to cross until December 23. Operating conditions remained poor all winter, and the road had to be closed by March 30, 1943. An attempt was made to lay a railroad track across the ice, a project that is reported to have been completed in mid-January 1943, but this line was never used. Fortunately, the Soviet breakthrough along the shore of Lake Ladoga in January 1943 opened for Leningrad a direct railroad line to the interior and relieved it of its complete dependence on the ice road.[55]

Food alone could not have revived Leningrad from its prostration. It was the improvements in the supply of fuel, power, and water and the revival of parts of the transportation system that actually brought about the rebirth of the city as a functioning and organized whole.

As a result of the efforts to develop local sources of peat and to import both peat and hard coal from outside, it became progressively possible for some of the electric power stations and factories to resume operations, but only on a limited scale. Most of the peat came from bogs that before the war had not been regarded as having economic importance. Nevertheless, at the cost of great effort from the exhausted and untrained workers, a limited amount of peat from local sources was kept in constant supply throughout the remainder of the siege. A quantity of hard coal from the Petchora and Vorkuta fields also reached Leningrad. Coal shipments during 1942 amounted to over 108,000 tons.[56] On April 25 the State Defense Committee ordered the construction of a liquid fuel pipeline, 18 miles long, across Lake Ladoga. The pipeline was completed on June 18 and somewhat eased the strain on the shipping facilities by providing Leningrad with over 32,000 tons of oil and gasoline.[57]

Despite these efforts, the total amount of fuel obtained was barely sufficient to keep some of the electric power stations and industrial plants going. None of it could be spared for the civilian population. The industrial fuel problem remained in a state of constant crisis, always necessitating the most stringent economies.[58]

Electric power was reserved primarily for the use of industry, the transportation system, and essential utilities. Thus, although additional electric power became available in the fall of 1942, when Leningrad was reconnected with the Volkhov hydroelectric station, most Leningraders did not receive any electricity in their homes during 1942.

One of the immediate results of the electric power stations' resuming operation was the partial revival of the streetcar service.[59] When, on

April 15, the first streetcar went by, people cried and cheered; eye-witnesses noted that for a while riders were even unusually polite to each other.[60] With trucks and other transportation in short supply, streetcars were used to move goods and supplies within the city. But before this could be done, the population had to clear the streets of the ice, snow, and rubbish that had accumulated there.

This measure was considered urgent by the administration for two other reasons. It was obviously essential to prevent the spread of epidemic diseases, which the accumulation of rubbish and filth littering the city made a potential danger. Moreover, in order to revive some of the public services and utilities and to repair the water and sewage systems, the streets and yards had to be cleared.

Earlier attempts at cleaning up the city had failed. It had been impossible to carry out the executive committee's order of December 12, 1941, in the particularly difficult conditions of those days.[61] Apparently the administration realized this and did not seriously press the matter. No systematic, general mobilization of the city's population had taken place, although the order was based on the obligatory labor decree. Later in the winter some factory workers had been employed in clean-up work in and around their enterprises, but no city-wide effort was made. According to a Soviet historian, the present order was issued by the State Defense Committee on February 2 and instructed the Leningrad authorities to clean up the city.[62] A partial mobilization, organized at places of employment and by the housing committees, was carried out on March 8 in an attempt to meet this order.[63] But an insufficient number of persons reported for work, and the exhausted workers accomplished little of a task that in peacetime had required a force of 20,000 workers and a great deal of equipment. According to the *Leningradskaia pravda* editorial of March 26:

> Up to now the clean-up campaign of the city has been completely unsatisfactory. The snow and dirt have been removed from less than half of the city's houses. Some streets are still impassable to pedestrian and vehicular traffic because of piles of heaped-up ice. In many places the storm sewers are blocked by rubbish. Because of this, in some places water has accumulated and is threatening to flood basements and lower floors. Hundreds of yards with neglected garbage pits have become real sources of infection.[64]

The city's executive committee realized that if "the urgent measures for cleaning up the city and preventing the spread of epidemic diseases" were to be carried out, further steps would have to be taken. On March 25, therefore, the committee issued an order mobilizing the entire population.[65] On the basis of the obligatory labor decree, all men between the ages of 15 and 60 and all women between 15 and 55 years of age, with the usual exceptions, were to work on cleaning up the city in the period of March 27 to April 8. Employees of inoperative enterprises and offices were to work an eight-hour shift each day, other employees two hours in addition to their regular hours, and housewives and students six hours.

To make sure everyone participated, the executive committee ordered every able-bodied citizen to carry on him the mobilization and work certificate issued by the *raion* authorities; these certificates were to be "the only documents certifying to the fulfillment of obligatory labor for places of permanent employment as well as for places of residence."[66] As a further safeguard, severe punishment was threatened for anyone failing to carry out his assigned share of work.[67] The Leningrad press gave this warning: "Anyone who attempts to avoid doing his civic duty not only violates state discipline, violates the rules of socialist community life, but is also a dangerous disorganizer, a parasite who helps the enemy."[68]

The administration was obviously concerned about public morale and uncertain of how the public would respond to this demand. It is possible that the leadership had tried to avoid carrying out this mobilization as long as it could, until the threat of disastrous epidemics outweighed all other considerations. In March it was still difficult to assess the physical and mental state of the inhabitants, but it was obviously generally very poor. The task, which one eyewitness described as being like "trying to clean up the North Pole if it were covered with refuse,"[69] would have required a formidable effort under the most favorable conditions. Since there was no mechanized equipment available, all the work had to be done by hand. In this instance the leadership had to turn to a population most of whose members could barely walk, and require it to accomplish this task with the simplest hand tools and with little equipment to carry away the ice and refuse.

As usual the Party resorted to a propaganda campaign. It mobilized its members to push, propagandize, cajole, and control the population. Some 12,000 special wall newspapers and an "enormous quantity of posters and slogans" were produced and displayed. Party agitators resorted to the time-honored Soviet technique of propagandizing the achievements of the "advanced workers"; workers were continually exhorted to greater efforts; and socialist competition was encouraged between work brigades.[70] The Party and the elite were also instructed to set an example by doing some work themselves, as well as to organize and control the work of others.[71] The Komsomol organized numerous shock brigades from among its members who were to set an example for the population and do some of the most difficult work, including the clean-up of civil defense slit trenches that had served as temporary morgues or rubbish dumps during the winter.[72]

As a matter of fact the authorities appear to have concentrated on this campaign most or all of the control methods available to them. The stick and the carrot were equally in evidence, although the carrot consisted largely of intangible future benefits: freedom from epidemics, water, public transportation, better living conditions. There is no indication that any direct material inducements were offered. Some of those mobilized for the campaign were rewarded by being allowed to visit a public steam bath, 25 of such baths having been reopened in March.[73] The report of April 17 of the Leningrad executive committee stated that the *raion* executive committees were asked to send in lists of the names of their best workers, to whom the city Soviet awarded official citations.[74] Some of those who failed to do their duty were tried by their neighbors in so-called "comradely courts" and were fined.[75]

If one is to believe official Soviet claims, the work of 300,000 citizens, a majority of whom were women, for a period of twenty days, resulted in the removal of 1,000,000 tons of refuse, trash, ice, and snow from 12,000 courtyards and over 32,000,000 square feet of streets, which would be 352 pounds per person per day.[76] What this meant in practice can be judged from the following description, which is typical of accounts given in many other diaries:

> There were housewives and school children and educated people—professors, doctors, musicians, old men, and women. One turned out with a crowbar, another with a shovel, another with a pickaxe; someone had a broom, somebody else a wheelbarrow; another came with a child's sled. Some of them hardly had the strength to drag their legs. Five people would harness themselves to a child's sled and pull and pull, for they had no strength left to do more.[77]

Under the circumstances this was a remarkable achievement, but since the city had over 200,000,000 square feet of streets and yards, this meant that the major part of Leningrad's streets was still not cleared of ice and snow.

The repair of the water and sewage systems, which accompanied the clean-up campaign, was not finished by the original deadline. On April 9 *Leningradskaia pravda* wrote:

> Much still remains to be done. Although the houses, streets, squares, and embankments have been cleared of great amounts of trash, ice, and filth, work has not been completed in all *raions*. The city has not yet been put into proper sanitary condition.
> This is why the Executive Committee of the Leningrad City Soviet has extended the period of mobilization of the population for the cleaning of the city to April 15.[78]

The same editorial noted that work on repairing water and sewerage facilities was even further behind schedule, and that a water shortage would make it difficult to keep the houses and people clean. It complained further:

The administration of the Vodokanal bureau of the Leningrad executive committee, headed by Comrade Zinoviev, is fulfilling its assignment in an unsatisfactory manner. The bureaus that were organized under the *raion* executive committees for the restoration of water and sewerage facilities are still not properly staffed, lack the proper technical leadership, and therefore cannot manage the entire task with which they are charged. The chairmen of the executive committees of the *raion* Soviets must now give special supervision to the water and sewerage installations in the *raions* and complete the restoration of these facilities in all houses with the utmost speed.[79]

Actually, the repair campaign, despite large-scale assistance by the mobilized population, never did achieve the prescribed objectives within the set time. On April 17 the city's executive committee reported that the major part of the clean-up campaign had been successfully completed and thanked all the participants. At the same time, however, it directed the *raion* executive committees to complete the clean-up of the remaining houses and yards by April 25.[80] Despite its shortcomings, the clean-up campaign went a long way toward helping Leningrad return to normal, in both appearance and activity, and it considerably boosted popular morale. Of course, the frequent breakdowns of the water, sewage, and garbage collection systems, as well as the bombardment, soon covered many streets again with litter and rubble.[81]

Meanwhile, the population continued to struggle with the fuel shortage. Local resources of firewood were totally insufficient to supply individual homes in addition to municipal and military needs. In the spring the population received occasional allocations of wood from bomb-damaged wooden homes and structures; but in order to get the wood, people had to dismantle and transport it by their own efforts.[82] They had managed to survive the preceding winter by stealing wood and burning furniture, but such methods would hardly serve again. By midsummer, therefore, the leadership was confronted with the very serious problem of how to lay in sufficient reserves of firewood for the coming winter.

The failure of the Volkhov offensive and uncertainty about how successful the fall offensive would be, as well as the decision to transform Leningrad into a fortress city, led the leadership to expect that it would have to face a second winter of siege. Having barely survived the first one, the city's authorities had no intention of allowing a repetition of that winter's appalling conditions. This time plans were made to prepare the city as thoroughly as the local forces and materials would permit. Firewood, therefore, had to be obtained entirely from local sources. Unless this problem was solved—that is, unless the houses were adequately heated—inevitably the water and sewage pipes would freeze again, thereby renewing the danger of widespread epidemics.

The cutting of firewood was therefore continued throughout this period. Some 21,000 Leningraders were mobilized for this purpose.[83] But the work lacked the incentives of the vegetable-growing campaign, so that the authorities had to rely on propagandistic appeals and threats of harsh punishments. Considerable amounts of firewood were cut on the east side of Lake Ladoga by the local population there, which was mobilized for the purpose, and by work brigades sent out from Leningrad.[84]

The results of the peat-digging campaign were fairly modest. On July 14 *Leningradskaia pravda* published an appeal by the joint city and *oblast* Party committees to the peat workers. In it, the committee noted that only one month remained in the peat-working season and that the daily quota of 8,500 tons of peat was not being met. The appeal continued: "Leningrad cannot count now on fuel brought in from outside. The supplying of the city with fuel depends on you, on your untiring and sacrificial labor. Whether there will be water and light in the city, whether the factories and plants will work, whether the streetcars will run, depends on you. Each of you must clearly understand what responsible work you are doing."[85]

The appeal condemned the lack of discipline among the workers and demanded of the Party, trade-union, and Komsomol organizations that they develop "mass socialist competition" among the workers and make wider use of Stakhanovite methods.

Despite these efforts, the supplies of firewood and peat were still not sufficient to meet the city's needs. On August 25 the city executive committee was forced to announce: "The firewood procured in the suburbs does not cover the fuel requirements of the enterprises, schools, hospitals, steam baths, and laundries, or the minimum needs of the population. The possibility of obtaining further fuel is very limited."[86] Once again, therefore, the administration left it up to the initiative of the industrial enterprises to obtain additional fuel through their own efforts. In September the enterprises were authorized to mobilize a part of their work force for woodcutting in the suburban forests, after coordinating these operations with the lumber trust. Even so, fuel remained critically short for the rest of the year, and woodcutting had to continue throughout the winter.[87]

In the face of these difficulties, the Leningrad authorities very sensibly sought the fuel they needed in the city proper by systematically demolishing wooden buildings. This undertaking required the mobilization of the entire able-bodied population for a month beginning in

September. On August 25 the Executive Committee of the Leningrad City Soviet announced:

Under the conditions prevailing in Leningrad, since it is not possible to supply fuel fully in a centralized fashion to the enterprises, offices, and population of the city, firewood procured by the population itself is the basic and principal source for satisfying the city's needs in fuel. . . . Under these circumstances the only way of obtaining additional fuel is by tearing down for firewood some of the wooden buildings located in the city itself, and first of all those in the southern and southwestern *raions*.[88]

Consequently, the committee ordered workers and white-collar employees to work on this project during their "free time and days of rest," while the unemployed Leningraders had to join work brigades organized by the administrations of their apartment houses. The order read as follows: "Every able-bodied citizen is obligated to prepare during the month not less than four cubic meters [5.2 cubic yards] of firewood, of which two cubic meters will be retained for his own use. People who have fulfilled the set norms are to be excused from further work on the preparation of firewood."[89] The houses to be torn down were to be listed by the chairmen of the *raion* executive committees, who, together with the Leningrad Housing Administration, also had to provide new quarters for "all citizens whose houses [were] to be torn down."[90] In this fashion both the population and the administration benefited from the measure, which in addition helped reduce the fire hazards in the city by eliminating highly inflammable wooden structures. The allotment of two cubic meters of fuel for the citizen's private use was not so generous that it met all his needs, and to obtain even this minimum he had to provide an equal amount for the city. The wood was transported by hand or by streetcar, as were most other commodities in the city. Some 9,000 wooden houses were eventually torn down by the population and cut up for firewood.[91] This obviously required the resettlement of a considerable number of people. Despite precise orders and procedures, some *raion* administrations showed a definite lack of concern about providing new quarters for these dispossessed citizens and were criticized for it in the press. The basic incentives for this work consisted in warning the citizens that only those who participated would be warm in winter, and that those who did not fulfill the prescribed norm would be made to work for long periods of time.[92]

The campaign actually continued after the month of mobilization and was pursued in a less intense and less general fashion throughout the winter; but the results fell short of the total needs. Consequently, the authorities were unable to ensure the proper heating of Leningrad, and the population was again obliged to resort to independent, and in the strictest sense illegal, actions to supplement their authorized firewood rations. Furthermore, the inhabitants still had to expect that in the coming winter they would be forced, as before, to live in one room, crowded around a single stove, and that at least some breakdowns in the availability of water and sewerage facilities would be inevitable.[93]

The supply of water to the population continued to improve slowly throughout the summer. The availability of electric power permitted the water-pumping stations to resume operation, while the warm weather thawed out the frozen water pipes. Although the water and sewage systems were partly put back into operation, resumption of normal service was prevented by the fact that numerous pipes had broken as a result of bombardment or freezing. During the summer, particularly in August, intensive efforts were made to repair the water and sewage systems. The plan was to have enough water pressure to provide water up to the third floor of the apartment houses.[94] But at least most Leningraders no longer had to obtain their water from the Neva or the canals.

The extensive repairs that were made fell short of the ambitious target set by the administration. Many houses remained without water for the rest of the year; even a year later, following another intensive repair campaign, 20 per cent of the water pumped was still being lost because of breaks in the pipes. Moreover, the water was still not very safe to drink throughout 1942.[95] For the remainder of the siege it was a constant race between the repair work and the new damage inflicted by German artillery fire. Nevertheless, the water situation was considerably eased both for the inhabitants and for industry.

The operation of the sewage system was similarly improved, to the extent that most refuse did not have to be thrown into the streets and yards as it had been in the winter. Of course, the system could continue to operate only if the pipes could survive the freezes of the next winter without breaking, which state of affairs the authorities were not completely successful in achieving.

Repairs to housing in preparation for another winter of siege began during the summer. The damage to houses resulting from the German bombardment and the winter cold had been extensive and threatened to become worse as time went on. By spring the majority of houses had damaged roofs and broken windows. Many buildings that were still in use had shell holes.[96]

The winterization of houses was obviously of great interest to all Leningraders and was bound to involve a large number of those who remained in the city. The technique used to carry out this campaign offers an excellent example of many Soviet campaigns, in which the population was usually asked, and made, to lift itself by its own boot straps. The opening gun was apparently a lengthy article by Popkov, chairman of the Executive Committee of the Leningrad City Soviet, which was published in the local press on August 11. He gave detailed and precise technical instructions to the inhabitants on how to prepare their houses for the winter, such as ordering newspapers to be wrapped around water pipes, windows to be boarded up, and so forth.[97]

A number of features of the winterization campaign were obligatory. The kitchens of the houses had to be heated (in order to prevent the freezing of water pipes), and the house committees were told to enforce this order. All tenants living on the upper floors of apartment houses had to move to empty apartments on the lowest three floors either in their own or in neighboring houses (again to prevent the freezing of water and sewage pipes, at least up through the third floor). No temporary stoves could be installed in apartments without the inspection and approval of the fire department, the homemade stoves of the preceding year having been responsible for many fires. The whole winterizing operation had to be accomplished with the material on hand. According to Popkov, one needed "only initiative and alertness to find and use" the necessary supplies, an assertion that was not very helpful when it came to solving the practical problems of carrying out the order.[98]

On the day following the publication of Popkov's article, it was announced, hardly to anyone's surprise, that the Kuibyshev *raion* of Leningrad had challenged the inhabitants of the October *raion* to a socialist competition in winterization and general improvement of the living facilities of their *raions*.[99] The challenge—which had been issued, as was usual in such cases, by the Party "*aktiv* of enterprises, offices, and houses" of the *raion*—was of course accepted the next day. The city's administration and Party organization hastened to give official approval to the launching of a city-wide competition, in which, of course, all *raions* were assumed to be eager to participate. On August 17 the executive committee announced that the vital task of preparing the city for another winter of siege required the "combined efforts of the Soviet, Party, and Komsomol organizations, with the active participation of the entire population of the city of Leningrad." "In order to support the initiative of the workers of the Kuibyshev *raion*," the executive committee announced the rules of the city-wide competition and the prizes to be awarded. The first prize was 100,000 rubles, to be distributed to the best workers of the winning *raion*. The *raion* winning second place would receive 75,000 rubles, and the third 50,000. Another 50,000 rubles were set aside for the best workers of the other *raions*.[100] Since this campaign ran concurrently with several other campaigns, it must be presumed that there was hardly an idle person left in Leningrad.

On October 13 it was announced that as a "result of widespread mobilization" the campaign was a great success: 872,900 square feet of roofing and 48,064 stoves were said to have been repaired, 220,000 chimneys cleaned, nearly 6,000,000 square feet of windows glassed or covered with plywood, and 304 miles of water pipes insulated. In all, 6,131 buildings had been completely prepared for winter. Several *raions* failed to finish on time. They were told to complete their work by November 1. A continuing competition on the best winterizing of houses was ordered for the rest of the winter, and another one was organized on the best use of living space. Supervision over the work was entrusted to the "political workers in each house," whose task it was to inspire the inhabitants and to make sure that everyone participated and at least attempted to keep his living quarters in repair.[101]

The fact that continuing campaigns were organized suggests that many houses were still inadequately prepared for winter when the original campaign came to a close. Much of the work was probably of poor quality. Subsequent complaints about breakdowns support this assumption. Apparently, too, the inhabitants were sometimes reluctant to move to other apartments and, as before, tended to use only one room, the most suitable for their purpose, with insufficient regard for the proper heating and maintenance of the building as a whole. The fuel shortage obviously made it very difficult for people to obey the instruction to keep two stoves going, one in the room they lived in and one in the kitchen.

The administration was determined to prevent the illegal and chaotic behavior of the population that had prevailed the previous winter in regard to housing. On November 3 the Executive Committee of the City Soviet made it illegal to saw wood in apartments and on staircases, or to throw trash and filth out of windows or in places not set aside for this purpose. Violators of these and other housing rules were subject to fines of up to 100 rubles or 30 days in jail, while those who used parts of buildings for fuel were to be given stiffer sentences.[102] A combination of threats, rewards, appeals to self-interest, and other controls was thus all resorted to at once, in an effort to make living conditions in the houses at least bearable, if not comfortable.

The authorities ordered industry to assist the population in this undertaking with skilled labor, tools, and some manufactured goods. But as is so often the case in the Soviet Union, the one-track drive to achieve a specific goal was carried out at the expense of other and often equally vital measures. The bureaucratic industrial management, seeking the usual 100 per cent achievement of planned goals and being goaded by the Party organs to do its utmost, did so at its own expense. Thus while the factories faithfully carried out the orders to help the population winterize their homes, some enterprises failed to do much about their own preparations for the winter.

In a number of enterprises there are plans for preparations for winter, but they are far from having been realized. Thus in the factory directed by Comrade Kolesnikov a plan was drafted way back in June, but up to now it has largely remained only a plan—nothing more! The limits set for the moving of machinery and the repair of water pipes, electric power plants, and stoves have been violated, moved further back. What is the value of plans like these? . . .

It is essential to arrange for the heating of production space and workers' buildings, repair roofs, fix doors and vestibules, put in double windows, and put glass in or cover up windows.[103]

Each new campaign called for so much concentrated effort that there remained little energy or interest for the continuation of the old. Thus despite all the triumphant claims made in October, Popkov had to admit by January 1, 1943, that there were numerous breakdowns of water and sewage facilities. According to his account of the situation, "the successes had gone to some people's heads, and many leaders became unconcerned; they ceased to watch, to care about the conditions in the houses." "There are also cases," he continued, "of people who are only concerned with show, with the percentages."[104]

The surviving Leningraders were on the whole inclined to do no more than was absolutely required of them. The attempts to winterize or repair damage to homes or improve the use of living space were only partly successful, precisely because each individual Leningrader preferred to devote his energy to improving his own quarters rather than the building as a whole. Most people were reluctant to invest material and effort in more ambitious schemes. In view of the continuing bombardment, some people did not see much sense in the constant efforts to repair damage in the city. "Some workers show harmful sentiments when they explain their lack of flexibility by referring to the difficulties of wartime conditions, saying in effect: 'Why repair or fix things up since the war is still on?' This is why we still have certain shortcomings in the operation of a number of industrial and municipal enterprises and offices."[105]

Although the sum total of improvements represented a considerable advance over what conditions had been the winter before, the Leningraders were still subject to a great deal of anxiety and want. In addition, the population had to live and work under the great physical and mental pressure that continuing German bombardment and renewed threats of an enemy attack entailed.

The winter had partially paralyzed both belligerents along this sector of the front. Many defense measures and installations in Leningrad had fallen into disuse. When with the coming of spring the danger of a renewed German assault on the city became obvious, it was clear that the authorities needed to take all necessary measures as soon as possible to prepare the city for the worst. In late May, apparently, a decision was taken to transform Leningrad into a military or fortress city (*voennyi gorod*).[106] On July 5 the Military Council of the Leningrad Front passed a resolution to evacuate most of the nonessential population, to fortify many streets, to militarize most of the remaining inhabitants, and thus to transform the city into an "impregnable fortress."[107] To achieve this naturally required large-scale popular participation and consequently a tightening of administrative controls over the population.

One important measure that had to be taken immediately was the construction of fortifications inside and outside of the city. Apart from having deteriorated, the fortifications that had been built so hastily a year before were insufficient for present purposes. The emergency forced the authorities to resort to the usual expedient of mobilizing large masses of the inhabitants. Except for a few innovations, the decree, issued on May 31 by the Executive Committee of the Leningrad City Soviet, was very similar to the one issued on August 29, 1941.[108] It provided for a mobilization of the population by the executive committees of the *raion* Soviets on the basis of the obligatory labor decree, to be carried out between June 1 and June 4, inclusive. The order, however, was not published in the press until June 3, and it is unlikely that it had been announced over the radio, since many private and public radios were still out of commission.

The new decree provided for a ten-hour workday and a payment of ten rubles per day for those who fulfilled the norm and twelve rubles for those who overfulfilled it. This not only represented an increase in the pay scale over the earlier campaigns, but had the novel feature of an incentive payment for overfulfillment of the daily norm. What those who failed to meet the norm were to be paid was not stated. Under the first order, mobilized factory and office employees had received their previous average daily wage, but the 1942 order temporarily removed them from the regular payrolls and gave them the same pay as everybody else. A particular incentive for the defense work was the authorities' offer to feed the workers and put them in the highest ration category, in addition to which they would receive a daily bonus of 100 grams of bread.

The most significant new feature of the 1942 order was the control system that it introduced. The order itself carried only the somewhat obscure statement: "All mobilized persons are to be issued booklets in which to keep an account of how much obligatory labor they have carried out."[109] The significance of this idea was elaborated several days later in *Leningradskaia pravda*:

All persons mobilized for defense construction work are issued a special booklet in which the results of their labor will be marked. This booklet is for every construction worker a sort of testimonial of his *political conscientious-ness* [*soznatelnost*, italics mine], a proof of the degree of his participation in the defense of his beloved city. The construction chiefs must concern them-selves with the best organization of the work, with the correct assignment of labor forces, with *the fulfillment and overfulfillment of assignments by all the construction workers* [italics in the original].[110]

Since the situation was less desperate than a year earlier, the au-thorities had time to be selective about the mobilization and to institute methods for obtaining high productivity from the workers. Fewer per-sons were mobilized for this undertaking than in August 1941. The work extended for a period of over two months. In July, in particular, a systematic effort was made to fortify the city proper by barricading or walling up windows in cellars and lower floors and by erecting new tank traps, pillboxes, gun emplacements, and street barricades through-out the city.[111] Most of the construction workers were, of course, women, although some military personnel also participated, perhaps because certain positions had to be ready for instant use.[112] In prepara-tion for possible street fighting a number of buildings and installations were again mined.[113]

To man the defenses in preparation for the expected new German attack, the earlier military training of the civilian population was re-sumed on March 10.[114] The compulsory universal military training instituted in 1941 had been largely discontinued during the winter because of the cold and starvation.[115] The local press now made it clear that at any moment the population could be called upon to fight the invading Germans.[116] Nevertheless, during the next two or three months the population was generally still too weak and exhausted to do any serious training. On August 12 the Party committee ordered all Party, Komsomol, administrative, and trade-union personnel, male and female, to pass a 110-hour training program in street fighting. Factory workers were armed and organized into units that were eventually assembled into 52 battalions.[117] According to one source, each worker received a card certifying to his position as a soldier of Leningrad's interior de-fense.[118]

Some of the Leningraders who underwent military training were subsequently sent into the armed forces. But the majority were left to serve as part of the interior defense forces on a stand-by basis. During the spring and summer of 1942 the army also received substantial re-inforcements from the outside, over Lake Ladoga.[119] Although neither the defenses nor the militarized civilians were put to the test by a German assault, it appears that on the whole Leningrad was far better prepared to resist attack by the fall of 1942 than a year earlier.

About this time national attention in the Soviet Union was focused on the German summer offensives on the central and southern fronts.

To the dismay of many Soviet citizens the Germans appeared not only to have recovered from the winter defeats, but to have sufficient strength to threaten once more the existence of the Soviet Union. On July 25, for example, *Leningradskaia pravda* wrote: "The German fascist monsters are advancing on Rostov-on-the-Don and Stalingrad. A serious danger is threatening our country."[120] The successes of the Germans at Stalingrad and in the Caucasus were reminiscent of their campaign the preceding year, during which they had overcome the strongest resistance the Red Army could offer. On November 6 Kuznetsov declared: "The danger that threatens our country has increased today. The enemy is advancing on the Grozny and Baku oil fields; he threatens to capture Stalingrad and to cross the Volga; he tries to seize the Black Sea coast. The fascist leaders have not abandoned their plans to seize Moscow and Leningrad."[121] Thus neither the threat to Leningrad nor to the Soviet Union as a whole appeared to have diminished. Only the subsequent Soviet victory at Stalingrad changed the picture.

The renewal of German aerial bombardment of Leningrad in April and the subsequent increase in the volume of artillery fire, including 16.5-inch guns, also required the rapid revival and reorganization of Leningrad's civil defense, much of which had ceased to exist during the winter months. During the winter, 8,000 civil defense workers were transferred to the armed forces, 4,247 died, and others were evacuated; so that by March the city's civil defense organization had only 5,000 members.[122]

Orders to repair and rehabilitate the air raid and chemical warfare shelters were issued simultaneously with the start of the clean-up campaign in March 1942. Part of the reason for the urgency appears to have been a genuine fear on the part of the leadership that the Germans would use poison gas against Leningrad.[123] Consequently, on April 9 *Leningradskaia pravda* issued a reminder to its readers: "The siege condition, air attacks, and artillery bombardment make it a duty for each Leningrader to remember the absolute necessity of . . . constantly strengthening the antiaircraft and antichemical defenses of the city. One of the foremost tasks in the next days is to put into combat readiness all air raid and chemical shelters."[124]

More important still was the reorganization of the civil defense system. Earlier attempts at reorganization, such as the order of January 26 described in Chapter 8, had apparently borne little fruit. Additional dislocation continued to occur as a result of the evacuation of the civilian population. By April, elements of the Komsomol were mobilized to expand the civil defense units, and people were recruited in factories and institutions. With the improvement in living conditions, it was also possible to revive self-defense groups in apartment houses. On August 1 there were 14,600 defense workers in civil defense battalions, 45,000 in factories and major institutions, and 57,000 in self-defense groups.[125] On August 8, by order of the military council, the civil defense system was reorganized. Control over civil defense sectors was taken away from the chiefs of the militia in each sector, and instead 35 militarized civil defense battalions were formed.[126] But this still did not meet Leningrad's civil defense needs. The problem was finally solved by the leadership in a very simple and direct manner: everybody was ordered to become a member of the civil defense organization. On August 27 the chief of the Leningrad civil defense, acting on instructions from the Military Council of the Leningrad Front, issued an order:

1. To draft the entire population between the ages of 14 and 60 to carry out civil defense duties and to participate in an obligatory manner in defending the city from fires and the results of air attacks and artillery bombardment by the enemy. In view of the above, all citizens capable of performing civil defense duties are to be listed in the membership of the civil defense groups of the civil defense house organizations.

2. To direct the civil defense groups to carry the full responsibility for civil defense and fire fighting resulting from aerial bombardment or artillery fire, which they are to combat with their own strength and means. . . .

4. To give to the command posts of the block civil defense organizations the right to enlist during working hours a part of the workers and employees of small enterprises and institutions located within the block for civil defense duty and fire prevention of homes and public buildings upon the sounding of the alert.[127]

In all, by order of the military council, 300,000 Leningraders were to participate in self-defense groups.[128]

Although the order did not list any penalties for failure to register with or serve in the civil defense organizations, its is probable that the penalties were in fact severe. The civil defense organization thus managed to cover the entire city. Numerically, at least, the new civil defense organization was quite formidable, and once there was enough water and food, it was fairly competent to deal with the damage inflicted by the Germans. By December there were officially 21,357 persons in the civil defense battalions, 52,527 in factories and large institutions, and 228,000 in apartment houses.[129]

From the available sources it would appear that the administration did not attempt to reimpose strict observance of all the civil defense regulations upon the population. In particular the police gave up insisting that people go into shelters or stay off the streets during artillery bombardments.[130] Since the Germans in general shelled only one specific target or city district at any given time, forcing the population to seek shelter on a city-wide basis would only have disrupted life in Leningrad and played into the hands of the enemy. The population appears to have been only too willing to ignore the standing orders to take shelter, and eventually the administration legalized this practice. On December 8, 1942, for example, it authorized the movement of handcarts and sleds on the streets during alerts. On February 4, 1943, streetcars caught in a district under fire were ordered to discharge their passengers; apparently this had previously been optional.[131]

It was of course vital to the city to resume industrial operations, but this could only be done slowly. Many factories had been severely damaged during the winter and had to have extensive repairs before they could operate efficiently. Preference was naturally given to factories engaged in war production, such as the remaining shops of the Kirov Works, which resumed operation in April.[132] Operations could be conducted only on a small scale, because of shortages of labor, raw material, and fuel, and because of German artillery fire. One Soviet eyewitness describes the Kirov Works as exhibiting "immense buildings deserted and split, plunged into darkness, the window frames glistening with humidity . . . a pile of destroyed freight cars, piles of coal, and the heavy chimneys of the factory blasted by shells."[133] Officially, fifty factories that had been closed down were reopened in April, seven more in May, and eighteen in June; but their output was very limited.[134] The available labor force was but a fraction of that of the preceding year. The Kirov Works had only about 2,000 workers instead of over 30,000, and the Voroshilov Works some 5,000 instead of 20,000. Many factories had only a few hundred workers instead of the thousands who had worked there earlier.[135] This was of course a measure of the losses suffered by the population during the winter and of the extensive evacuation. Following the completion of the evacuation, Leningrad's industry had only one-third of its prewar machinery and workers left.[136]

Shortages of raw material and fuel were so severe that some factories were forced to curtail production soon after resuming operations.[137] Other factories, as before, were often forced to resort to all sorts of substitute materials, with a corresponding decline in the quality of the goods produced. In casting iron, for instance, factories had to use peat or bricks made of coal dust and tar. One casting shop found in May that 96 per cent of its castings were defective.[138] When the city's wooden houses were broken up for fuel, all metal fixtures were carefully collected by the *raion* Soviets to be melted down for munitions.[139] In addition to these difficulties, the factories had to procure much of their own fuel and other industrial materials, help feed their workers, and repair their plants, as well as assist the population and the authorities in repairing the winter and bomb damage throughout the city.

The enemy bombardment added substantially to the difficulties, making it advisable to decentralize production. In all, the German bombardment destroyed 840 industrial installations and damaged 3,000 others.[140] The director of the Kirov Works explained:

The way we kept the place going is by having decentralized it. The important thing is not to hold up production, not to lose too many machine tools and too many people if and when there is a direct hit. That's the principle on which we work. We have divided the work into small units, with only a corner of each workshop or quarter of a workshop taken up with people and machinery, and this section as far as possible protected against blast and splinters.[141]

Yet despite all their precautions, the factories and the workers continued to suffer severely from German fire. During the war the Kirov Works suffered hits by 770 bombs and 4,419 shells.[142] Some workers broke under the strain and required periodic stays at rest homes. Moreover, the protective arrangements interfered with production.

The authorities acted with great energy in reviving industry and apparently accepted no excuses for failure from the industrial managers, who had to make constant improvisations to keep their plants going. In May *Leningradskaia pravda* complained: "Still not all enterprises in Leningrad are working equally well. There are some that not only fail to fulfill their obligation to produce more than the plan, but even fall short of the plan itself. The leaders of these enterprises point to the [prevailing] conditions, to the difficulties created by the war; they only talk about the plan, but take no steps to achieve its fulfillment and over-fulfillment."[143]

In view of the local difficulties and shortages, it is probable that the city's leadership gained further direct control over industry, since a considerable amount of planning, at least, had to be done at local level. Subsequently, the secretary of the Leningrad City Party Committee wrote that in 1942: "The City Party Committee stepped even closer to the leaders of industry: it actively influenced the work on and completion of orders for the needs of the Leningrad front; it checked directly through the *raion* committees and the primary Party organizations on the realization of the plan; and it struggled for the correct cooperation [of industry] and better distribution of labor and material resources."[144] Nevertheless, the control was far from total. Moscow demanded that some items be produced for use outside of Leningrad, and it also continued to decide the question of industrial evacuation from the city.[145]

As time went on, an increasing number of factories resumed work, at least on a limited scale. The Elektrosila Works, for example, received electric power again in the fall of 1942 and began to operate on the basis of a comprehensive production plan.[146] By mid-1943, despite the shortages, Leningrad's industry had made an extraordinary recovery:* in

---

* The value of Leningrad's industrial output rose from 1.4 billion rubles in 1942 to 2.5 billion rubles in 1943, as against 14.1 billion rubles in 1940 (Karasev, *Leningradtsy v gody blokady,* p. 277).

addition to producing a major part, if not all, of the ammunition requirements of the Leningrad front, as well as some heavy weapons, it also
manufactured various items for other areas of the Soviet Union.[147]

The leadership's success in reviving Leningrad's industry was due in
large measure to its ability to mobilize and control the necessary industrial labor force. To obtain the necessary labor, the leadership relied on
volunteers and on its power, under the decree of February 13, to mobilize elements of the population for war work.

The mobilization probably began in the last days of April or early
May and mainly involved women and adolescents. It is possible that
some younger girls volunteered, since some went to work at the age of
14.[148] The decree of February 13 permitted young people 16 to 18 years
of age to be inducted for work in trade and industrial schools, which in
many instances amounted to sending them as apprentices into the factories or to putting them to work on the railroad.[149] Some older people
were probably also drafted.

In October the labor mobilization decree was amended to extend
the age of women liable to the draft from 45 to 50.[150] Most of the people
working in the transportation system and on the Ladoga had been
drafted; the stevedores were chiefly disabled soldiers and "Leningrad
workers who had been ordered by the Leningrad Party organization to
do this work." The female coal-unloading brigades, for example, were
composed of girl students and women white-collar and textile workers
sent there by the Komsomol. [151] It is doubtful whether many of them
had volunteered for this dirty and difficult assignment.

In addition to the labor draft, the industrial labor force was supplemented in November 1942 by the authorized transfer of office workers
to the production line.[152] The authorities showed far more consideration to this class of employees than to the housewives and young girls
they drafted. The order made the following provisions: "when possible"
workers should be transferred to factories near their places of residence
and in the same ministry as their present places of employment; young
people or those who had worked in factory production before should
be transferred first; and new workers should receive their previous
salaries for the first three months, regardless of the work they did, which
in many instances amounted to unskilled low-paid labor. The decree
exempted from the transfer persons with higher or secondary "special"
education, those under 16 or over 50 years of age, and pregnant women.
The authorities obviously wished to preserve the morale of the office
workers and to disrupt administrative work as little as possible. Otherwise the Smolny would certainly have echoed with cries of anguish from
hard-pressed managers and factory directors.

To train the new workers, most of whom were women, the factories and unions organized numerous technical classes and study circles.[153] It is probable that the quality of the initial production was poor in many instances; but in time the women (who now made up 70 to 80 per cent of the industrial labor force) learned to work fairly efficiently.[154]

There are also indications that local controls and planning were far from efficient and that considerable bureaucratic confusion and mismanagement persisted. Despite the acute shortage of skilled labor, there was no real centralized organization to control the distribution of labor until February 1943.[155] As a result, while the administration was drafting unskilled workers into industry and struggling to increase production, trained workers from factories that had been forced to curtail production, or had closed down, were sometimes drafted into the army or sent to cut firewood, instead of being transferred to other factories.[156] Another indication of the lack of control is the fact that plant managers sometimes fired workers illegally—for example, workers drafted for firewood-cutting or agricultural work, war veterans, or family members of men in the armed services. Most of these inconsistencies were not eliminated until the end of 1942 or early 1943.*

If production was to be maintained at a high level and if the plans were to be fulfilled, strict labor discipline was essential. The administration hastened to indicate to the workers that, with the improvement in living conditions and the resumption of industrial operations, it would reimpose the old rules concerning tardiness, absenteeism, failure to fulfill the norms, and the like. Since most violations were punishable by severe jail sentences, if not worse, the Leningraders could not afford to ignore the regulations once the authorities had made it clear that they would insist on their observance. Thus, according to an eyewitness, the dispensary in one factory was prohibited by the management from issuing more than ten medical excuses each day, regardless of the number of workers who should have been let off.[157] Nevertheless, in many factories one-third of the workers were absent from May through July because of illness.[158] With the continuing use of factory dormitories and the resumption of public transportation, tardiness was no longer so easily excused, although it is probable that some allowances were made when the delay was due to such causes as enemy bombardment.[159] The Party, management, and trade unions were directed to check on the fulfillment by workers of the individual production pledges that they made during socialist competitions.[160]

---

* On September 24, 1942, for example, the Leningrad City Executive Committee prohibited factories from hiring workers to replace those mobilized for agricultural work or for cutting firewood; on February 2, 1943, factories were prohibited from firing invalid veterans, and on March 28, 1943, factories were ordered to give preference to dependents of military personnel (*Sbornik ukazov,* pp. 97–98, 194).

One of the easiest methods used by the authorities to punish culprits and display them as an object lesson to others was to try them, condemn them to several months or years of hard labor, and then send them to work in the same factory where they had worked before, but for no pay and for prison rations.

Other methods to encourage high productivity included the time-honored socialist competitions. A competition could be organized between shops or shifts in the same plant, or between different factories or organizations. Once launched and pushed by the Party, the competition spread to all levels of industry or transportation, as the case might be, and was developed at national level. No factory, shop, or worker could avoid participating in it. The anniversary of the October Revolution was traditionally marked by a special competition, and this year was no exception.[161] As usual, the most successful competitors were given as a reward a Red Banner, some enterprises receiving their prizes from the State Defense Committee and some from the Presidium of the Supreme Soviet.[162]

Among other methods used to raise labor productivity was a system under which individual workers opened a so-called "personal revenge account," or "vengeance account." A similar system had been developed in the army. Each manufactured item that a person produced over and above the plan was entered into such an account.[163]

During the summer of 1942 a movement called the "Two Hundred Percenters" is said to have developed among the stevedores, whom other workers were consequently urged to emulate. Overfulfilling the daily production norm by 200 per cent meant in this case unloading 20 to 25 tons of supplies per day from the arriving ships.[164]

Of course, it was much easier for enterprises or individual workers to subscribe to these competitions or obligations, or to promise to fulfill and overfulfill the plan, than actually to do so. The authorities were only too well aware of this problem and tried to provide inducements and bring pressure to bear in order to avoid receiving empty promises.

The competition can develop into a senseless business if it is reduced only to the undertaking of obligations. Obligations must be immediately accompanied by their realization. If you said "I shall do it," keep your word.

From now on, a check on the effectiveness of competitions cannot be postponed for any length of time. The results of the work of each person must be constantly held up to the view of all, in order that the entire collective may know who is ahead, who is falling behind.[165]

Public praising and shaming, which had been used before, was resumed as soon as conditions allowed. Comments on the performance of individual workers were posted on factory bulletin boards, published in newspapers, or mentioned in public meetings and speeches.[166] It

would have taken a peculiarly insensitive or foolhardy person to ignore
a warning such as the following, which was posted on the factory bulletin board: "Shame! Shame that a highly skilled riveter like Comrade
Gusev should have failed so miserably in the task which our comrades
at the front were expecting him to fulfill without fail. We expect him
to pull himself together in the future. The Editorial Board."[167] The
public shaming of delinquent workers, whether of individuals or of
groups, could develop into such a harassment campaign that few dared
to ignore it, particularly when compared with the public praise, rewards,
and sometimes medals heaped on the leading workers.

There were also material incentives for increased productivity. Pre-
miums were paid for overfulfillment of production.[168] Cash prizes were
awarded to the winners of various socialist competitions, as was seen
above in connection with the winterization campaign. Other forms of
rewards, usually unofficial, may have included preferential treatment
for the better workers and their families in connection with the use of
rest homes, extra food rations or better meals in the canteens, promo-
tions to administrative or supervisory positions, and so forth.

The earlier propaganda theme stressing that it was the patriotic duty
of each citizen to produce as much as possible for the war effort, and
that the successful outcome of the siege depended on such efforts, continued unabated. Production failures were described not merely as
causing loss to the "state" or "plan," but as having a direct effect on
local military operations or on the survival and well-being of fellow
Leningraders.[169] There also reappeared the "gratitude and pride"
theme, which pictured the city as the focus of attention both of Stalin
personally and of the nation as a whole.

The available evidence indicates that this labor control system was
generally effective. The press published a substantial list of enterprises,
offices, and individuals who had overfulfilled the production plans in
varying degrees.[170] There were also many failures, but under the circumstances even modest successes were impressive.

During the late spring and the summer of 1942 the authorities decided to anticipate the hardships of another winter of siege by evacuating a substantial proportion of the remaining population. Whereas
at the beginning of 1942 there remained in the city 2,282,000 people,
of whom 700,000 were dependents, by April 554,186 of these had been
evacuated over the ice road and by air.[171] On April 19 the Military
Council of the Leningrad Front directed that an additional 3,000 persons were to be evacuated daily from the city. Actually, some delay
occurred while the ice was breaking up on Lake Ladoga, but from
May 27 to July 31 an additional 338,545 Leningraders were said to have
been evacuated. Women with two or more children, persons living on

pensions, invalids, trade-school students, orphans, students, teachers,
artists, and other persons in similar categories were evacuated on a
compulsory basis. In July it was announced that 1,100,000 people remained in the city, and that it had been decided to reduce the population to 800,000 by evacuating a further 300,000 nonessential residents.
The mass evacuation was to be completed by August 15 and was to
proceed at an average rate of 10,000 persons daily. The actual rate of
evacuation fell somewhat short of this goal, since between August 7
and August 15, for example, only 46,000 people were evacuated. Among
the remaining population there were 274,000 workers and employees
of various industries, of whom 86,000 were employed in defense industries.[172] Actually, it would appear that the Leningrad population
was not reduced to the planned 800,000 until 1943, but it was probably
under one million by mid-August 1942. According to Soviet sources,
the population in May 1943 was down to about 637,000.[173]

In a speech on November 6, 1942, Kuznetsov, the secretary of the
Leningrad City Party Committee, said: "There now remains in the city
the minimum population essential for work on the immediate needs of
the city's economy. Only the working population remains. Much work
has been carried out on the evacuation of the population; the majority
of the industrial enterprises have been evacuated. Offices and enterprises that are not essential to a front-line city have been reduced."[174]

The evacuation of industrial enterprises and machinery also continued. Of the 333 Leningrad enterprises of national or republic importance, 133 (including 92 of the largest plants) had been completely
evacuated by summer 1942. On July 20 the State Defense Committee
ordered the Military Council of the Leningrad Front to evacuate 23,467
industrial machines of various types. Actually, by November 1942,
28,426 machines are said to have been evacuated, as well as large quantities of raw material and semifinished goods.[175] In all, 292,900 metric
tons of industrial freight were shipped out.[176] At this time much of the
equipment earmarked in 1941 for removal from the city was finally sent
away, much the worse for wear after having spent nearly a year standing in the city's railroad freight yards.[177] Thus by the end of the evacuation there remained in Leningrad 175 major industrial enterprises that
could operate in a limited fashion.[178]

Considerable ingenuity was shown in many instances during the
evacuation. For example, a great deal of rolling stock, which was
urgently needed elsewhere, had been trapped in Leningrad by the siege.
When Moscow ordered the evacuation of some of this stock, it was
moved across Lake Ladoga on three specially built barges, which were
presumably used to transport supplies on their return trips. About 150
locomotives and a "large number" of freight cars were evacuated in this

way. Tank cars had their wheels removed and were then floated across the lake.[179]

This phase of the evacuation was by far the best organized and controlled, and proceeded at a fairly even and rapid rate. The evacuees suffered fewer hardships than before because of the milder weather and the better-organized transportation and reception systems. As before, the destination of the evacuees was determined by the authorities, who also provided the food, the transportation, and all the other facilities on the trip.

The inhabitants continued to have mixed feelings about the evacuation. Undoubtedly some people were only too happy to escape from the city or to have their families removed to a safer place. Many were certainly afraid of a repetition of the starvation of the previous winter. But Soviet sources report that there were also many people who felt that the improved conditions made their departure less desirable in view of the probable food shortages elsewhere and the dangers and hardships of the trip.[180] And there were also those who owing to family ties, local pride, or habit preferred to remain in Leningrad regardless of the consequences.

The authorities, however, made it very difficult to avoid being evacuated. On September 29 a decree of the Presidium of the Supreme Soviet made the willful avoidance of compulsory evacuation, in the case of people living near the front, punishable by five to eight years' imprisonment.[181] Since the evacuation was compulsory for many categories of persons, various excuses were offered to the evacuation and housing committees, as well as to the heads of organizations, by people wishing to be taken off the evacuation lists. Some women said, "My husband has forbidden it, and he is in the army on the Leningrad front"; others argued that to live as an evacuee they needed "lots of money," which they did not have. Women with two or more children, who were in the compulsory evacuation category, went to work in the factories to avoid evacuation. One Soviet historian claims that German propaganda was seeking to encourage the residents to remain in the city in order to wreck the evacuation program.[182] It is uncertain how many people succeeded in having their evacuation orders changed; but it is likely that most of those who were ordered to leave did so despite their reluctance.[183] Only when the unity of the family was threatened, particularly when children were involved, did people disregard the advice given them by the authorities to leave. Moreover, this was possible only in cases when the parents had some freedom of choice. For example, when the question of sending school children to summer agricultural camps arose, it was found that some parents were afraid to be separated from the children lest something happen to them. Some parents also feared that their children would be suddenly evacuated from Leningrad once they were assembled in the camps.[184]

Although illegal avoidance of evacuation orders was rarely, if ever, attempted, it is apparent that despite pressure from the authorities many people who had a choice chose to remain and resisted within permissible limits suggestions that they leave. Some indications of this can be gleaned from the fact that despite the government's boast that only those who were necessary to the defense of Leningrad were allowed to remain, an undetermined, but substantial, number of children, housewives, and older persons were still left in the city by the end of the year.[185]

Taken as a whole, all these measures undoubtedly increased the city's battleworthiness. The remaining population was to a large extent militarized. Most people wore some sort of uniform. An increasing flow of war materiel manufactured in Leningrad's factories reached the front, thereby helping to prepare for the offensive of January 1943. Although the precise degree of effectiveness of these defense measures cannot be determined, since no German offensive against the city actually developed, they seem to have been fairly efficient. Despite the intensification of the artillery bombardment, the renewal of aerial attacks, and the reduced size of the population, the Germans failed to halt the city's gradual recovery.

The primary objective of Leningrad's leadership remained, as it always had been, the effective defense of the city, no matter at what cost to the inhabitants. But whereas this objective could not be achieved without some regard for the needs of the people, the leadership was at the same time forced to rely heavily on local resources. The measures taken by the leadership fell roughly into three categories. In the first were those necessary to preserve the life of the remaining population, to improve living conditions, and as a result to revive Leningrad as a functioning entity. In the second category came the measures necessitated by the renewed enemy threat and the decision to transform Leningrad into an impregnable fortress. Finally, following upon the realization that the siege would last for a long time, there were the measures designed to avoid a repetition of the disastrous conditions of the previous winter.

Under the prevailing conditions, most of these measures had to be carried out with only very limited help from outside. The city's leadership was given directions from Moscow, but had to rely largely on its own ingenuity and local resources to accomplish the prescribed objectives. In its turn, the leadership tended to use the same methods on the lower administrative personnel, accepting few excuses for failure, and leaving it up to them to improvise ways of complying with orders from above. The result was an attempt at intensive utilization of locally available material and human resources; this in turn meant not only that increasing burdens had to be placed upon the people, but also that the administration had to tighten its controls over the population.

This was simplified to some extent by the fact that many of the objectives of the administration, especially measures designed to improve or safeguard living conditions, coincided with interests of the inhabitants, who were therefore quite willing to cooperate. This did not necessarily mean that all Leningraders displayed uniform zeal in their tasks, or that they were equally interested in fulfilling orders that were not directly concerned with living conditions. To maintain or develop the proper discipline, the administration needed to create among the people the proper attitude and at the same time to indicate that it was ready and able to punish all violators.

Each of the mass campaigns described above was therefore accompanied by a large-scale propaganda operation in which hundreds of propagandists, Party workers, and officials, as well as the press and radio, participated. Moreover, as always, propaganda had to help maintain high popular morale and preserve the rituals of Soviet public political behavior. The propaganda techniques that were used were all very familiar to Soviet citizens. The enemy, as before, was described as being brutal and monstrous.[186] There was a renewal of the exchanges of messages between Leningrad and other cities in the Soviet Union.[187] The usual appeals to patriotism and local pride were made; wide publicity was given to outstanding individual achievements on the war and labor fronts. Individuals or small groups were awarded medals, although a disproportionately large number of these seem to have been awarded to the elite. At the end of the year, furthermore, the Presidium of the Supreme Soviet created the Leningrad Defense Medal, which was to be awarded to all active participants in the city's defense.[188] There were the usual public pledges and resolutions with regard to production, and these were promoted by some 10,000 full-time Party agitators.[189] School children wrote to the soldiers at the front asking them how many Germans they had killed, presumably in order to stimulate them to fight harder; war heroes were sent on lecture tours to factories to encourage the workers to produce more arms; and the Leningraders were constantly reminded that their liberation depended first of all on their own efforts.[190]

Some indication of the progressive normalization of life in Leningrad can be obtained from the reappearance of various political rituals that had been discontinued during the winter. Thus May Day was celebrated with only a few proclamations, some flags, and a series of speeches given over the radio by various leaders and celebrities, some of whom were sent to Leningrad from Moscow for the purpose. "But in spite of the fact that all institutions and industrial establishments continued to work, the people of Leningrad regarded the day as a holiday. . . . No meetings of any sort and no extra duties had been fixed for the evening, in order to make it possible to observe the Leningrad workers' traditional holiday, even if it was only at home."[191]

By mid-June conditions had so far improved that the leadership did not hesitate to join the nation-wide campaign designed to elicit popular support for the signing and ratification of the Soviet treaty of alliance with England and the United States. Public approval of the ratification of the treaty was expressed in numerous "well-attended meetings and discussion groups that met in the factories and plants, in the trenches and dugouts at the front, in the gun emplacements and on the ships of the Baltic fleet, in the offices and houses."[192]

Improvements in over-all conditions led to a resumption of large-scale propaganda and morale-building operations and a significant increase in the number of propagandists.[193] The radio resumed limited operation over the public-address system, newspapers became more widely available, and club meetings, lectures, and other group activities were held again.[194] In the fall of 1942 a number of theaters and motion-picture houses were reopened. On April 8 the Leningrad Philharmonic began to play over the radio again, and on the next day it gave a public concert, at which Shostakovich's Seventh Symphony, the so-called Leningrad Symphony, was performed with great fanfare.[195]

On the whole the propaganda was not unduly optimistic and did not mislead the population to any marked degree about the dangers and difficulties facing it. The Leningraders were promised neither a speedy victory nor a painless winter. On the contrary, they were repeatedly told that the military situation around Leningrad was grave and that even the minimum of winter comforts could be obtained only at the price of an immediate maximum effort. The propaganda spoke on the whole in calm and resolute tones. There was no repetition of the alarm and near-panic of the preceding year. From August 1942 on, the propaganda tried to make everybody who remained in the city feel that he was regarded and must regard himself as a soldier and maintain discipline accordingly. Everyone was to say with pride that he was a defender of Leningrad.[196]

Of course, the authorities had to have the power to enforce their demands upon the population, particularly the mass mobilization orders. The leadership also had to demonstrate that it was capable of enforcing those rules and regulations that because of previous conditions had become inoperative. For the average Leningrader the tightening of controls was demonstrated not only by the flood of orders and directives from the top, but particularly by the revival of the supervisory activities of the various enforcement agencies and systems.

The existing police agencies were expanded and reinforced.[197] Several orders were issued embodying changes in the duties of the housing committees, watchmen, and other administrative and supervisory personnel in apartment buildings; one of the functions of these personnel had been to keep a close watch over the activities and movements of the inhabitants, and this duty was renewed. Once again overnight visitors had to register and explain their presence. There were frequent document checks in the streets, and all exits of the city were under close police guard.[198]

The authority of the militia was further expanded. In the past, exit permits for people leaving Leningrad had been issued by the militia, who first checked with the evacuation committees to determine whether the applicants had obtained the proper authorization for the trip. In the summer of 1942, when some Leningraders began to go on business trips, the militia was given the additional power to determine not only whether the applicant had the proper authorization, but also whether the trip as a whole was justified.[199] The growing power of the militia was also apparent in a new wave of arrests and deportations, which swept up various persons whom the authorities considered to be unreliable or undesirable, either because of their past record of behavior or because of their national origin.[200] The population was reminded by the press and the propagandists that enemy agents lurked everywhere and that a good citizen had to be discreet, cautious, and suspicious of everything that was not completely orthodox.[201] The increasing numbers and activity of the police organs demonstrated to the population that the authorities were ready and able to enforce their decisions and punish offenders. The control problem was also simplified by the reduced size of the population and the removal of potential troublemakers.

Administrative enforcement and controls depended for their success, of course, on the behavior and attitude of the administrative and Party elite. The leadership's demands on the elite were hard to satisfy. The technological and administrative elite were particularly hard-pressed. They were forcefully reminded that the primary criterion of success was the fulfillment and overfulfillment of production goals. For example, the following "horrible" example of an engineer turned "German agent" was reported in the press: "Outwardly this engineer conducted himself quite like a Soviet person; he was verbally working on fulfilling the production program, he shouted about the need to increase the assistance to the front, but at the same time he sabotaged production, lowered the quality of defense goods."[202] The press also published from time to time the names of successful and unsuccessful administrators.

It is fairly evident that most of the normal Soviet bureaucratic practices survived despite all changes. Careers were made just as well, if not better, under war conditions as in peacetime, and Leningrad's elite did not lack careerists. There was more than one instance of people who were "only concerned with show, with the percentages."[203]

The Party and the Komsomol continued their previous recruiting drive for new members. On November 8 the Leningrad Komsomol organization was authorized by the Central Committee of the Party to accept for membership applicants as young as 14, a measure designed not only to increase the Party's membership, but to extend its control over the teen-agers who were working in industry. According to a Soviet source, 20,508 teen-agers, most of whom were employed in industry, joined the Komsomol between April and November of 1942; so that despite the evacuation of some 20,000 members during this same period, the total Komsomol membership in November 1942 stood at 27,316 (as against a prewar membership of 226,722), most of whom were new to the organization. A year later there were 47,301 Komsomols in the city.[204] Of the 27,316 Komsomol members in November 1942, 21,280 were girls, a reflection of the total composition of the industrial labor force. Women also formed nearly half of the Party members. By June 1943 the Leningrad Party organization had 30,768 full members and 16,667 candidate members, most of whom had joined during the war.[205] In this way the number of persons affiliated with the Party constituted about 14 per cent of the city's population, and a year later, when the total population was 560,000, the proportion of Party and Komsomol members rose to 17 per cent.

The Leningrad elite no doubt suffered new disappointments and anxieties when the Soviet forces not only failed to smash the enemy, but allowed the Germans to prepare for a new offensive on Leningrad and make further advances in the south. In general, however, the concern that the elite felt in 1942 was a far cry from its despair and fear in the preceding year. The elite could not fail to have more confidence in the leadership, which had brought the city through the worst without collapsing and which was obviously prepared to carry on for as long as Leningrad remained besieged.

The elite, and in particular the Party and the administrative bureaucracy, took advantage of their positions to acquire as many benefits as circumstances allowed. Some of those who were suffering from the effects of the winter, or who feared the prospect of another one, probably managed to arrange to be transferred out of Leningrad. It is obvious that many members of the Leningrad elite were anxious to get away from the city and its constant dangers and hardships, at least for a little while. It was not too difficult to find some official pretext, in conjunction with the local authorities or the head office in Moscow, for going on a trip. One Soviet writer, for example, made two air trips to Moscow in the spring and summer of 1942 and further excursions during 1943.[206] The elite abused the privilege of the so-called business trip so flagrantly that the authorities were forced to step in and regulate these trips. Two decrees of the Council of People's Commissars of the USSR were published, on June 26, 1942, and November 2, 1942, restricting the freedom of bureaucrats and officials to travel on so-called missions (*komandirovkii*) and giving the militia veto power over such trips.[207]

Nevertheless, the elite continued to evade the restrictions and to make use of loopholes in the regulations to go on leave. It was not until March 1943 that the Leningrad leadership took some measures to restrict this illegal behavior:

Despite the order of the Presidium of the Supreme Soviet of the USSR of June 26, 1942, canceling regular and special leaves during wartime, there have lately been requests addressed to the Executive Committee of the Leningrad City Soviet by the chairmen of the executive committees of the *raion* soviets, by administrative heads, and by department officers for leave for themselves as well as for their subordinates.

Along with this there has become established the illegal practice of granting staff members leave in the guise of sending them on missions, and in a whole number of cases they were paid the cost of the trip, per diem, and the housing cost.[208]

The elite continued also to benefit from the general improvement in conditions, particularly with regard to food. Not only did the administration upgrade the ration category of some of the lower echelons of the bureaucracy and of the intelligentsia, but the elite also continued to receive food parcels and other gifts from friends and associates in Moscow and elsewhere.[209] The improved communications with the outside and the greater travel opportunities allowed at least some elements of the elite to keep in touch with their evacuated families, and to help or visit them, a privilege largely denied to the rest of the population. The privileges enjoyed by the elite brought at least some of its members another advantage. Having sent their wives to safety, they found it easy to acquire friends among the young women who had remained in the city; some of the liaisons thus formed apparently continued after the end of the siege. Popkov is reported to have told the foreign correspondents the following joke in 1944: "The evacuated wives, for instance, learning of what was going on in Leningrad, took as their slogan: 'Death to the foreign invaders!' But when the wives returned, the girls who had taken their places adopted as their slogan: 'Now we go underground to become partisans and continue the struggle secretly.' "[210]

The heroic and tragic period of the siege had come to an end by August 1942. From then on, despite its frequent crises and constant dangers, life in Leningrad assumed a semblance of normality, and the elite had, as seen above, both time and opportunity to revert to its bureaucratic habits and techniques. But it, too, was becoming somewhat war-weary. Nevertheless, even if some elements of the elite became less inspired and enthusiastic than the leadership wished, the group as a whole remained sufficiently loyal and energetic to back up the leadership's commands. Most objectives ordered by the administration were reached, if not always within the prescribed time or with the required thoroughness.

After the horror of the winter's famine, most Leningraders were too engrossed by the daily struggle for life, and too relieved to have survived, to concern themselves unduly with the general military situation in the Soviet Union or matters beyond the immediate future. Popular interest remained absorbed in local conditions and developments, this localism being greatly encouraged by the isolation that the siege imposed upon Leningrad. In April and May the Leningraders generally did not believe the Germans to be capable of an immediate assault upon the city, and the concern over the military situation was therefore less absorbing than that over shortages and health problems.[211]

The military consideration uppermost in most people's minds remained the question of Leningrad's relief. Militarily, hopes for such relief were dim. The official communiqués were noncommittal and limited to the usual inventories of enemy casualties and losses of equipment.[212]

Then, at the end of May, the situation seemed to take a turn for the worse, dispelling popular optimism about Leningrad's safety from a new German assault. The June and July orders mobilizing the population for the construction of fortifications and barricading of streets and buildings were disheartening. Another sharp reminder that the Leningraders still had to face a long siege, with all its accompanying privations and dangers, came when the official campaign to prepare the city for another winter of siege opened on August 11. The thought of having to live through a second winter of siege under intensified artillery and air bombardment was for many people a terrifying prospect. There was no certainty that the miracle of the ice road could be repeated, or that the food and fuel situation would not sharply deteriorate as during the preceding winter. As a consequence of the strain under which the

Leningraders lived, their physical exhaustion, and their inability to see an end to their suffering, there was a great deal of war-weariness and apathy among the people. Others, however, longed for action, no matter how extreme, just to put an end to the siege. Thus one woman is reported to have said: "It would be better to fall upon the enemy with bared chests; to die to the last man or to throw them back. One cannot go on living like this; this is no life."²¹³

Yet despite people's impatience to end the siege, it seems that a German victory was never widely regarded by the population as a desirable solution for Leningrad's difficulties. Not only were the Leningraders influenced by tales of German atrocities, descriptions of which were given almost daily by Soviet propaganda, but they also feared, as previously, any disruption of their precarious living conditions. Although some were prepared to pay any price to escape from Leningrad, others, as one deserter reported in May, were "'afraid that they would be mistreated or tortured on the German side."²¹⁴ Furthermore, many Leningraders had come to hate the Germans as a result of their previous suffering and losses.

On the whole, as before, popular morale was directly affected by living conditions, and most of all, after the winter of starvation, by the food situation. Since military developments affected these conditions, military developments also had an effect on popular morale. Yet at the same time the population was proud of what it had suffered. Like all survivors of a battle or of a disaster anywhere in the world, the Leningraders felt that the experience they had shared in the preceding winter set them apart from other people, and it made them see their deeds in a heroic light. There was, as noted by a foreign correspondent, "a slight aloofness towards Moscow, a feeling that, although this was part of the whole show, it was also in a sense a separate show, one in which Leningrad had largely survived thanks to its own stupendous efforts."²¹⁵

After the dangers, horrors, and sufferings of the winter, all subsequent developments appeared something of an anticlimax. The siege increasingly assumed the aspect of an unpleasant routine. There were certainly some Leningraders who felt that their preceding heroism entitled them to something better than the treatment they continued to receive. Views like these, reinforced by the estrangement from Moscow that the enforced isolation of the city fostered, tended to breed resentment against the central authorities for their failure to help Leningrad and for their continuing defeats at the hands of the Germans.

The attitude of many Leningraders toward the local leadership was also shaped by the latter's continuing demands on the exhausted population. Such acts as the refusal of plant managers to allow more than a prescribed number of workers to take medical leave, regardless of how sick they were, or the fact that workers were discharged and then drafted for woodcutting details were naturally resented. Some Leningraders who were ordered to perform physical labor beyond their capabilities or who were made to work in places subjected to German artillery fire were also bitter. The leadership's increased prestige with the population, which was largely based on the fact that the regime had survived and had organized the ice road, was counterbalanced to a certain extent by its failure to save those who had died during the winter and by its inability to effect the relief of Leningrad. Yet the Leningraders were also perfectly well aware that the leadership was more firmly in control than a year before and that despite its shortcomings it remained the only source of authority capable of guiding the population.[216]

From the strictly political standpoint, popular behavior presented no control problem for the authorities. The survival of the regime through the winter, the seemingly successful defense of Leningrad, and the tightening of police controls, as well as the growing popular dislike and distrust of the Germans, combined to ensure popular obedience to authority. The available material gives little indication of any oppositionist activity except for a few instances of desertion and an announcement that several NKVD officers were decorated for their part in maintaining discipline: "These splendid *Chekists* [NKVD] ensured revolutionary order in the besieged city, extirpated with an iron hand the enemy filth, and rendered harmless the spies and agents that the enemy sent over to us in an effort to cause panic in our ranks."[217]

It may be assumed that although the increased controls made Leningraders more cautious in their speech than during the winter, they nevertheless had greater freedom of speech than before the war, partly because of a feeling that they had demonstrated their loyalty during the preceding winter, and partly because of the difficulty the administration had in completely cowing a populace that had lived, and continued to live, in such close proximity with danger and death. The improvement in conditions increased social cohesion, which had suffered a serious setback during the starvation period. The evacuation streamlined the remaining population, so that nearly everyone participated in the city's life and defense. An *esprit de corps* developed, common when people are faced by danger for a long period of time. The experience shared by the Leningraders had created a bond between them that established a basis for mutual assistance.

Although the authorities still found it necessary to put defense requirements ahead of individual safety, continuing, for example, to operate factories directly exposed to enemy artillery fire, human life had become valuable again, after having been so terribly cheap during the preceding months. This was undoubtedly a factor contributing to popular solidarity. Yet, at the same time the population frequently disregarded the civil defense regulations. In fact, some people took pride in being under enemy fire. A year later a foreign correspondent noted seeing in the Kirov Works a woman whose eyes showed "great weariness" and a "touch of almost animal terror"; but when he asked another girl whether she wanted to transfer to a less exposed factory, he was told, "No, I am a Kirov girl and my father was a Putilov man."[218]

The ability of the administration to re-establish and expand its controls over the population in this period is not surprising, since the authorities remained the only source of help available to the population. If the authorities had failed to organize improvements in conditions, or if conditions in the late spring of 1942 or later that year had again deteriorated as they did in the fall of 1941, it is conceivable that the exercise of administrative controls in Leningrad might have been seriously impaired or might even have collapsed.

But the worst fears of the population—an epidemic or a breakdown in the importation of food—were not realized. Instead, the leadership, at the same time that it stepped up its demands on the population and tightened discipline, was able to increase food rations, improve living conditions, evacuate many of the people, and take further measures to prepare the city for a long siege. No matter how demoralized the inhabitants were by the enormous losses they had sustained during the winter, and no matter how disappointed to find that the war was by no means over, they had little choice but to obey the authorities' demands. Since most of these demands were fairly sensible and of direct or indirect benefit to the city and its inhabitants, there was considerable incentive for the population to carry them out. Actually, the most significant obstacles to the effective exercise of administrative controls were the occasional breakdown of people in responsible positions and the frequent loss of highly trained personnel, as well as fairly widespread apathy and war-weariness among Leningraders in general. None of the various means employed to overcome these problems—threats, incentives, propaganda, and so forth—was completely successful.

Nevertheless, by fall of 1942, Leningrad was in fairly good condition to stand the siege until the Germans were finally driven back in January 1944. Life in the city involved hardship and danger, and there was no certainty of final victory; but despite everything the city was infinitely better prepared for war than a year earlier. Leningrad had finally become a fortress city and was prepared to play its role in Soviet strategy. Costly as it was for the defenders to hold out, the city was a dagger in the sides of the Germans and pinned down forces that were vitally needed by the enemy to hold his crumbling fronts elsewhere in the Soviet Union.

*

The news of the Red Army's breakthrough on January 18, 1943, was greeted with great joy by the city's population. There were numerous public celebrations, which continued until the arrival in Leningrad on February 7 of the first train bearing military supplies, food, and official delegations from Moscow.[219] The military successes led many people to expect a speedy termination of the siege. In the words of a captured letter from Leningrad: "Our joy at learning about the breakthrough was boundless. Everybody had tears of happiness in his eyes. Now all live in the hope that the hateful Germans will actually be driven away. Then life will be easier."[220]

Living conditions in the city did indeed improve. Food was more plentiful. The vegetable growing campaign, for example, produced a harvest of 60,000 tons from individual gardens as compared with 26,000 tons in 1942, and the farms grew an additional 75,000 tons.[221] The people received their full food rations, part of which consisted of imported canned meats and fats, and the children occasionally received American chocolate.[222]

Some much needed consumer goods, such as toothbrushes, lighters, soap, sewing needles, and even toilet water, became available in the stores. Firewood was brought in from the eastern shore of Lake Ladoga, where it was cut by a work force of some 10,000 Leningrad women.[223] The electric and water services were restored to a considerable extent. In the fall of 1943 a concerted effort was made to repair damaged buildings, roofs, and windows. Motion-picture houses and theaters were open to entertain the war-weary Leningraders.

As a result of the improved conditions and communications with the outside, Leningrad's leaders sought to increase the city's industrial output. In order to increase the labor force in the defense industries, the authorities transferred to it large numbers of workers from nonessential jobs and in the fall brought back to the city some evacuated workers.[224] By order of the State Defense Committee, Leningrad's industry began to produce machinery and equipment needed for the restoration of factories in the areas liberated from the Germans. The authorities sought to increase labor productivity by 15 to 40 per cent, making the exhausted inhabitants work in shifts of ten to twelve hours and subjecting them to a barrage of propaganda.

Despite improvements, life in Leningrad during 1943 continued to be both hard and dangerous. The Germans intensified the artillery bombardment of the city and subjected it to frequent air attacks. Six thousand Leningraders were killed or wounded in the factories or on the streets.[225] Some of Leningrad's factories were exposed to the most concentrated bombardments of the war. During September, the German fire became so intense that the city authorities were forced temporarily to close motion-picture theaters and schools and to prohibit unnecessary public gatherings.

In the fall, the Soviet High Command initiated preparations for a major offensive on the Leningrad front. With reinforcements from outside, the Soviet forces built up a substantial superiority over the Germans in both numbers and fire power. The attack was launched from the Oranienbaum area on January 14, in conjunction with attacks on the Volkhov and Novgorod fronts. Next day the Leningrad forces began an assault along the entire front. After fierce fighting, the Red Army captured Krasnoe Selo on January 19, then Pushkin, Slutsk, Mga, Gatchina, and finally Krasnogvardeisk on January 26. The Germans were forced to retreat all along the front, leaving behind the heavy artillery pieces with which they had bombarded Leningrad. On January 27, to the sound of 24 salvos from 324 guns, Zhdanov and General Govorov made the long-awaited announcement: "In the course of the fighting a task of historic importance has been achieved: the city of Leningrad has been completely freed from the enemy's blockade and from the enemy's barbarous artillery bombardment."[226] The city celebrated that night with fireworks, laughter, and a few tears.

On January 26, 1945, in recognition of its heroism, the Presidium of the Supreme Soviet of the USSR awarded the city of Leningrad the Order of Lenin, and 470,000 of its citizens received a medal "For the Defense of Leningrad." Unquestionably they had earned it.

Chapter *10*

Conclusions

A PROTRACTED SIEGE had not been foreseen by either side. It came about largely as a result of a deliberate change in the strategic objectives of the Germans in their Russian campaign. They made a decision to besiege Leningrad just at the moment when a concentrated assault on the city, it seems, would have brought certain success. The Soviet leaders, who rightly assumed Leningrad was a major objective of the German invasion, did not anticipate either the rapid approach of the Germans or the reluctance of the victorious enemy to exploit his immediate chance of capturing the city. They therefore made no preparations for a prolonged siege. Hence most steps taken by the city's authorities in the first six months of the war were emergency measures devised in response to the growing threat to the city.

On the whole, these measures were quite sensible and very similar to those taken in England after the outbreak of the war, particularly after Dunkirk. In both cases one finds the emergency construction of fortifications, the hurried raising of volunteer defense units, preparations to defend factories, the fear of enemy agents and saboteurs, the hurried organization of civil defense measures, and civilian evacuations.* In Leningrad, as in England, enemy aliens and persons with suspicious backgrounds were often interned. In both places there was food and fuel rationing. The German advance on Leningrad, like the

* The parallel between the British Local Defense Volunteers (later Home Guard), armed with shotguns and old rifles, and the *opolchenie*, for example, is obvious enough. Had the Germans carried out "Operation Sea Lion" in 1940, however, it is doubtful whether the British volunteers, despite their high morale and determination, would have been of greater military worth than the *opolchenie*. During that year Lord Beaverbrook, the British Minister for Aircraft Production, had taken measures to defend individual factories against land attacks. The British population had been alerted to watch out for spies and saboteurs, and "Cooper's Snoopers," so named after the Minister of Information, Duff Cooper, had caused the arrest and trial of various persons for alleged defeatism.

Dunkirk evacuation, provided a great impetus to the construction of shelters and slit trenches and to extensive popular participation in civil defense activities. The authorities in both places were by no means certain that they could prevent an enemy invasion, and consequently both appealed to the population to participate in a last-ditch stand, which in England was epitomized by the slogan "You can take one with you." In both Leningrad and England emergency measures often conflicted with one another and suffered in their execution both from bureaucratic dogmatism and from exaggerated enthusiasm on the part of local authorities and excited amateurs.

Despite many similarities, however, there were also great differences between the reactions of England in 1940 and Leningrad in 1941. These differences arose out of the totalitarian character of the Soviet regime, the techniques of Soviet administrative control and the degree to which they were employed, and the cultural and social factors that conditioned the responses of the Soviet population.

The decision of the Soviet leadership to prolong the defense of Leningrad as long as possible was justifiable from the military point of view because the fall of the city would have constituted a severe strategic, economic, and moral loss to the Soviet regime. The leaders took the stand that there would be no voluntary surrender of the city; its loss would be excusable only if it fell to an overwhelming German assault. In making this decision the Soviet leaders were prepared to accept for the city's population far greater loss and suffering than would probably have been regarded as justifiable by Western standards. It is doubtful whether Western governments would have been able or willing to require their soldiers and civilians to continue to resist enemy attack under conditions of actual starvation. The Soviet authorities apparently were not influenced by such considerations. They accepted the death of about one-third of Leningrad's population as a necessary price to pay for the contribution that the continuing defense of the city made to the over-all Soviet defense effort. While they never questioned their right to demand such sacrifices of the Leningraders, since from their point of view the rights and welfare of the population were subordinate to the interests of the state and of the Party, they had some doubts about how much privation the inhabitants were willing to bear and at what point the city's defense would collapse. These doubts were partly the product of the deeply rooted distrust that the leadership felt, even before the war, concerning the political loyalty of the population. The complex and overlapping Soviet administrative and political control systems, by which the authorities sought to control and direct the behavior of each person, were in effect perfectly designed for a permanent state of siege. It is not surprising, therefore, that when war came there was little need to tighten administrative controls or to undertake a major administrative reorganization.

The political leadership ensured the retention of its powers by preserving the supremacy of the Party and the police over all levels of governmental, military, and administrative machinery. Although some further concentration of power occurred during the war as a result of the organization of the State Defense Committee and of the military councils, the Party leadership kept control of these organizations by supplying most of the members. The authority of Party officials, from the city government level down to that of the political organizers in apartment houses, remained undiminished throughout the war.

The war also made little change in the inefficiencies inherent in the highly centralized decision-making process and in the methods of implementing decisions. The extreme degree of control that the Moscow authorities exercised over all decisions became a real handicap to Leningrad's leadership. Although the latter included some very prominent Party leaders, such as Zhdanov and Voroshilov, most of their decisions, even minor ones, still had to be initiated, or at least approved, by the central leadership in Moscow—despite the fact that Moscow was often not in a position to assess the real situation in Leningrad. Thus Stalin reprimanded Zhdanov for organizing a defense council in the city and insisted on changing its membership. The State Defense Committee had to approve the decision to convert a bottling plant in Leningrad to the production of Molotov cocktails. When the wife of a medical officer applied for permission to leave Leningrad, the Evacuation Committee of the USSR passed on the case. The various commissariats in Moscow continued to issue instructions on how Leningrad was to use its industrial resources and which enterprises were to be evacuated.

These practices tended to deprive the city's leaders of initiative and limited their ability to make effective use of local facilities and resources. For example, despite the critical shortage of firewood during the winter of 1941–42, the Leningrad authorities did not organize either the production of emergency stoves or the tearing down of wooden buildings for fuel, although these measures would have saved many people from freezing to death. Similarly, in the fall of 1941 much industrial machinery was dismantled for evacuation by order of the authorities in Moscow, although it was impossible to get it out of the city.

The lower echelons of the Party and bureaucracy generally proved unwilling to show initiative. Their main concern was to demonstrate the proper degree of zeal and loyalty, with little regard for the effectiveness of their activities. The emphasis on the "fulfillment and overfulfillment of plans" and the preoccupation with keeping up appearances were fully in accord with the usual means by which the local Soviet administrative and Party bureaucracies measured success and demonstrated their loyalty to the central leadership. The rush to join the *opolchenie* and other military units was partly motivated by eagerness to demonstrate political attitude. In some instances the determination of the lower echelons of the bureaucracy to prove their loyalty interfered with the leadership's plans, as in the evacuation, when officials, in order to demonstrate the political reliability of the population and their own control of the situation, discouraged people from leaving the city.

The Soviet leadership and administration had been accustomed since the Revolution to regard the population as a source of manpower that could be drawn upon at will to perform any unexpected or urgent task. The population had in fact been used in this way for a variety of purposes: organizing mass demonstrations, assisting on the land at harvest time, constructing railroads and canals, and developing new industrial centers in Siberia. In this sense the administrative controls over the population had been geared for total mobilization even before the German attack. Consequently, under conditions of war emergency the authorities felt completely free to require the citizens to perform any task no matter how difficult or dangerous. Mobilization was either "voluntary," as in the case of the *opolchenie*, or obligatory, as in the construction of fortifications. The authorities also looked on general mobilization as a symbolic expression of national unity and a test of popular support of the regime. In this way, the leadership tried to overcome emergencies and technological shortcomings by the lavish use of manpower. Similarly, it compensated for administrative inefficiencies and lack of foresight by making the population as a whole responsible for the solution of various problems such as civil defense.

One of the shortcomings of the system was its inefficient use of manpower. There was considerable disregard of the capacities of the people mobilized and much misuse of skilled personnel. The administration did not hesitate to mobilize physically unsuitable people, including older men, women, and even children, to perform the most arduous or dangerous tasks. The large numbers of trained workers and Party officials who were taken into the *opolchenie* deprived industry and the control system of vitally needed skilled personnel. Other people with valuable qualifications were used to dig trenches or for other purely physical work. There were conflicting demands for manpower in the various projects instituted. For example, mobilization for the *opolchenie* and fortification construction interfered with civil defense requirements and the military training of the population. These in turn interfered with industry's efforts to increase production of military goods. The result was a chaotic situation in which the local administrative and control agencies appeared to pursue several contradictory goals simultaneously. The system placed severe burdens on the administrators who were responsible for the execution of the tasks, and it inflicted considerable and often unnecessary hardships on the people. In the end, of course, despite the inefficient use of labor, the sheer weight of the manpower used ensured the completion of the prescribed tasks.

The response of the Leningraders to the leadership's demands and their behavior under extreme stress were, of course, the most dramatic and heroic features of the siege. The discipline and devotion to duty displayed by the people in the face of terrible privations and losses appear to have exceeded the most optimistic hopes of the leaders, who had several reasons to lack confidence in the steadfastness of the citizens. They suspected, for example, that various elements in the population were either politically disaffected, or not averse to a German conquest of the city. These elements probably never formed a majority, for the city's population contained a relatively high proportion of Party members or sympathizers, and it had a strong tradition of local patriotism. Nevertheless, the number of disaffected persons, while fluctuating in response to circumstances, appears to have been far from negligible.

Another factor behind the leaders' distrust was the lack of confidence that many people felt either in the ability of the authorities to prevent the eventual surrender of Leningrad or in the survival of the Soviet regime as a whole, especially during the fall of 1941, when Moscow was under attack. Some people wondered whether their sacrifices were worth while if they could not prevent ultimate defeat.

Finally, there was uncertainty about how long the population, and especially its demoralized elements, would remain passive and obedient to the leaders' demands when they found themselves and their families dying from hunger or the bombardment. Yet one of the most striking facts about the behavior of Leningrad's population is the absence of any overt form of unrest or protest.

The behavior of the Leningraders was the result of a combination of factors, of which at least some were peculiar to Soviet conditions and to Leningrad. One of these was Leningrad's geographic location, which reduced the ability of the population to escape from the city. It was relatively easy for the authorities to control the movement of civilians across Lake Ladoga and in the front-line areas. The population, which could not leave the city without official permission, was entirely dependent on the leadership for food, since the authorities controlled and operated the city's sole source of supplies.

Another factor contributing to popular docility was an ingrained habit of obedience to the authorities. The Leningrader was conditioned to subordinate his rights and interests to those of the community or the state, and to make personal sacrifices for the benefit of the community when called upon to do so. He was also used to the sight of the elite and the "socially useful" getting preferential treatment and to the lack of special consideration given to women.

There was, furthermore, no prior experience of political freedom or initiative; there were no political groups, slogans, or programs to consolidate whatever incipient opposition to the regime may have existed. The Soviet citizen had no sense of group interest in opposition to the authorities. Twenty-four years of Communist controls and the systematic destruction of most of the actual or potential forms of opposition had left the population incapable of independent political action. The Germans, being foreign invaders and, moreover, making no attempt to engage the population's political interest, provided no ideological alternative to the Soviet regime.

The Stalinist terror system had created a fear of denunciation and an atmosphere of mutual distrust among the citizens, so that few people were willing to voice any criticism of the authorities. The disaffected Leningrader did not conceive of himself as one of a like-minded group, but as an isolated individual confronting a ruthless and all-powerful state. Even during the most difficult period of the siege, the city administration and leadership succeeded in preserving at least the appearance of an integrated and effective authority and gave no indication of relinquishing any of its powers. The Leningraders believed the army to be loyal to the regime, or at least to its patriotic duty, and could not expect an insurrection from that quarter.

Disaffected or demoralized Leningraders, therefore, believing that resistance to the authorities was not only fruitless but suicidal, never translated their attitudes into action. Instead they looked to others to bring about a change in the situation. Before they learned what the invaders were like, they expected the Germans to solve their problems; but they did not think it advisable or desirable to risk their own chances of "liberation" by actively assisting the Germans in the conquest of the city. Later they hoped that either "the women" or the army would take the initiative in forcing the leadership to surrender Leningrad. Since the individual Leningrader did not believe he could either resist the authorities or change their decisions, he had to choose between submission or flight. Consequently, the only form of disobedience that appealed to such people was defection to the Germans. In Leningrad, as was mentioned, opportunities to escape were few. Hence the vast majority chose submission.

Later in the siege, the deterioration of living conditions tended to increase dependence on the authorities, who used the ration card as an effective instrument of control, and thereby further encouraged political conformity. Moreover, hunger, cold, and physical weakness produced emotional apathy rather than rebelliousness among the inhabitants and tended to concentrate each person's attention and energy on the problems of day-to-day survival.

Within the Soviet system, strong unifying influences were at work. Social life in the Soviet Union was highly collectivized, and the great majority of Soviet citizens were integrated into an active community. The Leningrader shared his apartment with other families and, together with the other residents of his apartment house, was required to share in various community projects under the leadership of the Party activists and the housing management. At his place of employment he usually belonged to a work brigade or a shop or an office group, which in turn was a part of a larger organization encompassing the entire office or enterprise. His professional, social, and recreational activities were also organized. The social groups gave the individual Leningrader a sense of belonging to a larger unit than his immediate family and to some extent substituted for his family. They gave him moral support, a sense of security, and various forms of assistance in time of need. It was natural, for example, that a worker should ask his factory director to arrange for his burial or to secure medical help for his family. The residents of an apartment house often helped those too weak to care for themselves. By fulfilling his obligations both at work and at home, a man ensured for himself and his family the continuing benefits of membership in the various collective groups. The organization of collective activities continued even in the worst period of the siege.

Another factor, closely related to the above, was the will to live, which often took the form of a desire to remain active. Many Leningraders feared to die alone, or to remain isolated and helpless in their rooms, where hunger, cold, and despair seemed most oppressive. They came to believe that they would die if they stopped being active or could no longer remain on their feet. This, like the desire to remain in good standing with neighbors, co-workers, and organizers, gave people an incentive to work.

An important role in maintaining discipline was also played by various attitudes that the inhabitants held. Among these were patriotism, local pride, growing resentment of the Germans, reluctance to betray the soldiers defending the city (many of whom were themselves from Leningrad), and unwillingness to see so much suffering serve no purpose. Soviet propaganda helped to foster such feelings.

There was inevitably considerable paralysis of economic activities during the winter of 1941–42 as a result of shortages and the poor physical condition of the people. The functioning of a large modern city like Leningrad proved especially vulnerable to the breakdown of electric power, which, in conjunction with the food shortage, brought most of the city's productive activities to a halt and caused additional breakdowns in other essential services.

From the point of view of the mere preservation of life, only the food supply proved to be critical, since the Leningraders managed to deal with the other shortages by individual expedients. The city itself was not without resources, and the citizens managed to find limited quantities of fuel and water, to improvise sources of light, and to make special arrangements for garbage disposal. Thus when the authorities could not satisfy the people's basic needs, the Leningraders resorted to self-help and independent activities. Inevitably, this led to a certain amount of illegal or nonconformist behavior, such as black marketing, hiding the bodies of the dead, stealing ration cards or fuel, and even cannibalism. These activities, however, remained limited, partly because of the individual's continuing dependence on the authorities for food and guidance, and partly because few people had the means to avail themselves of illegal sources of supply. Irregular activities neither seriously challenged the authority of the administration nor significantly disrupted the social structure. Since the irregularities were devoid of any political or ideological content, the leadership had no difficulty in suppressing them as soon as it was able to improve the supply situation and repair some of the utilities.

On the whole, the population of Leningrad showed a high degree of adaptability to adverse conditions and a remarkable capacity to bear privations. This was undoubtedly due in part to the fact that the Leningraders, like most other inhabitants of the Soviet Union, were used to harsh living conditions and to fluctuations in the availability of food and other goods and services. The population, therefore, accepted the necessity of a more primitive existence and showed considerable initiative in solving living problems. Popular ingenuity, of course, could not overcome the food shortage once local resources were exhausted. In the vital matter of food, only the ice road saved Leningrad from total collapse.

It appears that in general the administrative and control system in Leningrad was effective even under extreme conditions. Considerable credit for this is probably due to the determination and energy of the leadership. It also seems that the Soviet system had been successful, more so indeed than the leaders were willing to believe, in molding the attitudes and responses of Soviet citizens. In Leningrad, when firm leadership and habits of disciplined behavior were combined with patriotism, they produced a degree of steadfastness and devotion to duty that astonished not only the leadership but even the Leningraders themselves.

The siege is recorded in Soviet histories as one of the glorious events of World War II, and indeed there can be no doubt that Leningrad earned its title of "Hero City." Today the Party takes pride in the siege as a demonstration of its successful leadership. Surviving Leningraders, however, usually prefer to forget the horrors of the siege, which remind them only too vividly that the city's title was paid for with the lives of those dear to them.

NOTES

NOTES

For full titles and publication data see the Bibliography. Bracketed numbers refer to the German documents listed on pp. 349–54. The following abbreviations are used:

BSE   *Bolshaia sovetskaia entsiklopediia.*

GD   German documents.

IMT   *The Trials of the Major War Criminals Before the International Military Tribunal.*

LP   *Leningradskaia pravda.*

LS 1–7   Interviews conducted by the author with people who were in Leningrad during the war.

LVOVSS   *Leningrad v Velikoi Otechestnennoi Voine Sovetskogo Soiuza.*

NMT   *Trials of War Criminals Before the Nuremberg Military Tribunals.*

OZAOT   *Osnovnye zakonodatelnye akty o trude rabochikh i sluzhashchikh.*

NOTES TO CHAPTER ONE

1. For the history of Leningrad, I consulted *BSE*, XXIX (1954), 517–24; Mikhailov, pp. 200–205; and GD [112]; for the geography of the city, Mikhailov, pp. 200–205; and Shabad, p. 151.

2. *BSE*, XXIV (1953), 533.

3. *Ibid.*, p. 524.

4. For the history of the negotiations, see Mannerheim, pp. 294–300; Anderson, pp. 169–70; *Finnish Blue Book*, pp. 49–50; Tanner, pp. 5–88; *Documents on German Foreign Policy*, pp. 628–29.

5. Degras, pp. 325, 336; Woodward and Butler, pp. 228, 350–51, 558, 577.

6. Sontag and Beddie, p. 78.

7. *Ibid.*, p. 107.

8. For the text of the Soviet treaties with Estonia, Latvia, and Lithuania, see Shapiro, II, 210–14.

9. *Finnish Blue Book*, pp. 49–56.   11. Degras, pp. 421–23.

10. *Pravda*, Nov. 3, 1939.   12. Mannerheim, p. 370.

13. Kripton MS; Kripton, *Osada Leningrada*, pp. 19–31.

14. A. A. Kuznetsov, speech before the Leningrad Soviet, in *O gazifikatsii Leningrada*, pp. 14, 24–25.

15. Karasev, "Leningrad v period blokady," p. 10, n. 46.

16. Kripton, *Osada Leningrada*, p. 26; Werth, p. 69; LS 2.

17. Castro Delgado, p. 62.

18. Pospelov, pp. 276–78; Garthoff, p. 41.

19. Voroshilov, p. 20.   21. *Civil Defense*, p. 97.

20. LS 3, 4.   22. Sirota, "Borba," p. 120.

23. *OZAOT*, p. 5; see also Meisel and Kozera, pp. 356–58.

24. Meisel and Kozera, pp. 361–62.

25. *Ibid.*, pp. 363–64.

26. *OZAOT*, p. 17.

27. Karasev, *Leningradtsy v gody blokady*, p. 127.

28. Degras, p. 489.

NOTES TO CHAPTER TWO

1. Halder MS, IV, 126–28.

2. Bor, p. 204.

3. GD [8].

4. Halder MS, VI, 42, entry for March 30, 1941.

5. Mannerheim, p. 405.

6. For the Finnish-German negotiations, see *NMT*, X, 407, 982–83, 998–99; Mannerheim, pp. 406–8; Erfurth, pp. 30, 32.

7. Reinhardt, p. 122.

8. Blau, pp. 38, 41.

9. Reinhardt, p. 122.

10. The description of the campaign is based on the following sources: Reinhardt, pp. 122–26; Halder MS, IV; Manstein; Assmann; Tippelskirch; *BSE*, XXX, 357–62; Mannerheim; Erfurth; Telpukhovskii; *LVOVSS*, I; and Anders.

11. Halder MS, VI, 168, entry for June 24, 1941.

12. *Politicheskoe obespechenie*, p. 10.

13. Halder MS, VI, 212.

14. Halder, *Hitler als Feldherr*, p. 40.

15. Karasev, *Leningradtsy v gody blokady*, p. 101.

16. Mannerheim, pp. 416–17.

17. Soviet sources state that on the left flank of the Soviet defenses there remained at that time only token units totaling no more than 10,000 men (Karasev, "Leningrad v period blokady," p. 4; *LP*, Nov. 12, 1941).

NOTES TO CHAPTER THREE

1. Hilger and Meyer, p. 336.

2. Halder MS, VI, 162, entry for June 22, 1941.

3. GD [8].
4. *Ibid.*
5. Kripton, *Osada Leningrada*, pp. 51–52.
6. GD [89].
7. "Secret Speech," pp. 43, 46.
8. Werth, p. 83; Fischer, p. 183; Kripton, *Osada Leningrada*, pp. 43–44; LS 1, 3, 4.
9. *Pravda*, June 23, 1941.
10. LS 3, 4; Fischer, pp. 180–81; Kripton, *Osada Leningrada*, p. 43; Polzikova-Rubets, p. 12.
11. *LVOVSS*, I, 8–10.
12. Karasev, *Leningradtsy v gody blokady*, p. 34.
13. *Ibid.*, p. 35; Likhomanov, p. 5.
14. Sirota, "Borba," p. 122.
15. Kripton, *Osada Leningrada*, pp. 48–49; LS 2, 3, 4.
16. *LVOVSS*, I, 11.
17. *Ibid.*, p. 15.
18. Kripton, *Osada Leningrada*, p. 81.
19. Reinhardt, p. 132.
20. *Biulleten*, No. 27, July 14, 1941; and No. 31, Aug. 22, 1941.
21. Pavlov, pp. 13–14.
22. LS 3, 4; Bogdanovich, XXI, 212.
23. Fischer, pp. 184–85.
24. *BSE*, XXX (1954), 358; Avvakumov, p. 194. Werth, pp. 110–11 mentions a figure of 400,000. Karasev, *Leningradtsy v gody blokady*, pp. 70–71, places the number of persons mobilized for construction work in July and August at one million persons.
25. Karasev, *Dokumentalnye materialy*, p. 148.
26. Tikhonov, pp. 12–13.
27. *LVOVSS*, I, 37–38.
28. Avvakumov, p. 194.
29. Kripton, *Osada Leningrada*, pp. 102–5, and Kripton MS.
30. Polzikova-Rubets, p. 19.   33. LS 6.
31. Bogdanovich, XXI, 212.   34. LS 3.
32. Likhomanov, pp. 9–10.   35. Likhomanov, p. 10.
36. Kripton, *Osada Leningrada*, p. 78.
37. *LVOVSS*, I, 401–2.
38. Telpukhovskii, p. 85.
39. Lauterbach, pp. 48–49; Golikov, p. 31; Saparov, p. 12; Fineberg, p. 12; Karasev, *Leningradtsy v gody blokady*, p. 73.
40. Karasev, *Leningradtsy v gody blokady*, pp. 47–48.
41. *Ibid.*, pp. 38–41; Beliaev and Kuznetsov, pp. 17–18.
42. *BSE*, XXXI (1955), 79.
43. Sirota, "Voenno-organizatorskaia rabota," p. 22.
44. Stalin, p. 14.
45. *LVOVSS*, I, 20–21.
46. LS 3, 4.
47. Kripton, *Osada Leningrada*, pp. 85–89.
48. Bogdanovich, XXI, 204.   50. LS 2–4, 7; Shcheglov, p. 12.
49. Ketlinskaia, p. 174.   51. GD [79].
52. Likhomanov, pp. 6–7; *LP*, July 5, 1941; Avvakumov, p. 183.

53. *Partiinoe stroitelstvo,* No. 13 (1942), quoted in *LVOVSS,* I, 190.

54. *BSE,* XXX (1954), 358.

55. Sirota, "Voenno-organizatorskaia rabota," p. 22; Khudiakova, p. 12; Likhomanov, p. 8.

56. Beliaev and Kuznetsov, pp. 18–24.

57. *BSE,* XXXI (1955), 80. Moscow is reported to have had 120,000 volunteers.

58. Werth, p. 110.

59. Komar, p. 58.

60. Beliaev and Kuznetsov, p. 23, state that out of 12,000 volunteers in the Vyborg *raion* only 5,418 were accepted by July 7; in the Kalinin *raion,* 6,358 out of 8,911 volunteers were accepted; and in the Petrograd *raion,* 3,012 out of 3,323.

61. Karasev, *Leningradtsy v gody blokady,* p. 42; Beliaev and Kuznetsov, pp. 25–31.

62. Karasev, *Leningradtsy v gody blokady,* p. 42; Beliaev and Kuznetsov, pp. 41, 45; Skomorovsky and Morris, p. 141; *Propaganda i agitatsiia,* No. 13 (July 1942), cited in *LVOVSS,* I, 182.

63. *The New York Times,* June 5, 1956; Sirota, "Voenno-organizatorskaia rabota," p. 22; Beliaev and Kuznetsov, p. 43.

64. Beliaev and Kuznetsov, p. 43; Dymshits, p. 35.

65. Beliaev and Kuznetsov, pp. 26–30.

66. *LVOVSS,* I, 46–50.

67. *Propaganda i agitatsiia,* No. 13 (July 1942), cited in *LVOVSS,* I, 181.

68. GD [8].

69. LS 1–4, 6.

70. LS 3, 4; Bogdanovich, XXI, 204.

71. Karasev, *Leningradtsy v gody blokady,* p. 74; Beliaev and Kuznetsov, p. 31.

72. Karasev, *Leningradtsy v gody blokady,* pp. 75–77.

73. Beliaev and Kuznetsov, pp. 33–37.

74. Karasev, *Leningradtsy v gody blokady,* pp. 77–78; Beliaev and Kuznetsov, p. 39.

75. Karasev, *Leningradtsy v gody blokady,* pp. 48–49; Beliaev and Kuznetsov, pp. 39–40; Sheverbalkin, p. 42.

76. GD [88]; GD [63], Sept. 18, 1941.

77. *LVOVSS,* I, 253; Werth, p. 110; Komar, p. 58; Beliaev and Kuznetsov, pp. 56–100.

78. Werth, p. 168; Lauterbach, p. 50.

79. Werth, p. 111.

80. *Ibid.,* p. 107; Golikov, p. 31; speech by A. A. Kuznetsov on November 6, 1942, cited in *LVOVSS,* I, 253; *Propaganda i agitatsiia,* No. 13 (July 1942), cited in *LVOVSS,* I, 181.

81. LS 1, 2; Raus, pp. 149–51.

82. Sirota, "Voenno-organizatorskaia rabota," p. 17.

83. GD [63], Sept. 25, 1941.

84. Werth, p. 111; Kripton, *Osada Leningrada,* pp. 90–92; Beliaev and Kuznetsov, p. 100.

85. Sirota, "Voenno-organizatorskaia rabota," p. 20; Zhdanova, p. 9.

86. Sirota, "Voenno-organizatorskaia rabota," p. 21; Khudiakova, p. 9; Zhdanova, p. 9.

87. Osipova, p. 93.
88. Karasev, *Leningradtsy v gody blokady*, p. 78; Sirota, "Voenno-organizatorskaia rabota," p. 24; *LVOVSS*, I, 193.
89. Karasev, *Leningradtsy v gody blokady*, p. 79.
90. *Ibid.*, pp. 58–59.
91. Dymshits, p. 111.
92. *LP*, June 27, 1941, cited in *LVOVSS*, I, 11.
93. *Biulleten*, No. 27, July 14, 1941.
94. GD [8].
95. Meisel and Kozera, pp. 366–67.
96. "O poriadke podgotovki nasileniia k protivovozdushnoi i protivokhimicheskoi oborone i poriadok organizatsii grupp samozashchity na territorii RSFSR," July 2, 1941, cited in *Khronologicheskoe sobranie zakonov*, pp. 334–35.
97. *Biulleten*, Nos. 28–29, July 29, 1941.
98. *LP*, July 29, 1941, cited in *LVOVSS*, I, 15–16.
99. *Propaganda i agitatsiia*, Nos. 23–24 (1942), cited in *LVOVSS*, I, 275.
100. Karasev, *Leningradtsy v gody blokady*, p. 88.
101. *Ibid.*
102. LS 1; Bogdanovich, XXI, 205–6; Werth, p. 133.
103. Karasev, *Leningradtsy v gody blokady*, p. 87; Sirota, "Voenno-organizatorskaia rabota," p. 27.
104. Karasev, *Leningradtsy v gody blokady*, p. 87; *Propaganda i agitatsiia*, No. 20 (October 1942), cited in *LVOVSS*, I, 241; Sirota, "Borba," p. 121.
105. Karasev, *Leningradtsy v gody blokady*, pp. 87–88.
106. *Ibid.*, p. 88.
107. Tregubov, pp. 10–11; Sirota, "Borba," p. 121.
108. Karasev, *Leningradtsy v gody blokady*, p. 84; Tregubov, p. 11.
109. Karasev, *Leningradtsy v gody blokady*, pp. 86–87.
110. *Ibid.*, pp. 83, 89.
111. *Ibid.*, p. 52.
112. *LP*, Aug. 22, 1941, cited in *LVOVSS*, I, 45.
113. GD [6], No. 1, Oct. 1, 1941; Dymshits, p. 27.
114. Sirota, "Borba," p. 122.
115. Polzikova-Rubets, p. 21; Fischer, p. 186.
116. Sirota, "Borba," p. 122.
117. Bogdanovich, XXI, 205; Komar, p. 86; LS 1.
118. Karasev, *Leningradtsy v gody blokady*, p. 84.
119. LS 5; Inber, *Leningrad*, p. 21; Bogdanovich, XXI, 205.
120. Kripton, *Osada Leningrada*, p. 80.
121. Bogdanovich, XXI, 205.
122. *Biulleten*, Nos. 28–29, July 29, 1941.
123. Voznesensky, p. 47.
124. *Ibid.*, pp. 21–22.
125. *Ibid.*, p. 19.
126. *LP*, July 4, 1941, cited in *LVOVSS*, I, 173.
127. *Ibid.*, June 22, 1942, cited in *LVOVSS*, I, 173.
128. Karasev, *Leningradtsy v gody blokady*, p. 55.
129. *LP*, June 22, 1942, cited in *LVOVSS*, I, 174.
130. *Ibid.* For other instances, see Komar, p. 58; Werth, p. 71.

131. Karasev, *Leningradtsy v gody blokady*, pp. 50, 51.
132. *Ibid.*, p. 51.
133. *LP*, July 24, 1941, cited in *LVOVSS*, I, 6–7.
134. *Partiinoe stroitelstvo*, No. 13 (1942), cited in *LVOVSS*, I, 192.
135. Komar, p. 58.
136. Karasev, *Leningradtsy v gody blokady*, p. 52.
137. Skomorovsky and Morris, p. 25.
138. Karasev, *Leningradtsy v gody blokady*, p. 56; *Partiinoe stroitelstvo*, No. 13 (1942), cited in *LVOVSS*, I, 192–93.
139. *Partiinoe stroitelstvo*, No. 13 (1942), cited in *LVOVSS*, I, 193.
140. *Velikii gorod Lenina*, p. 61; Sitnikova, p. 94.
141. Karasev, *Leningradtsy v gody blokady*, p. 57.
142. *Pravda*, June 27, 1941.
143. Sinitsin, pp. 38, 43.
144. Kripton, *Osada Leningrada*, pp. 67–68; GD [63], Sept. 25, 1941; LS 3, 4.
145. *LP*, June 24, 1941, cited in *LVOVSS*, I, 7.
146. *Ibid.*, May 5, 1943, cited in *LVOVSS*, I, 328.
147. Avvakumov, p. 219.
148. Sitnikova, p. 92.
149. *LVOVSS*, I, 195.
150. *LP*, May 5, 1943, cited in *LVOVSS*, I, 328; *Velikii gorod Lenina*, p. 63.
151. LS 1, 3, 4.
152. Werth, p. 71; GD [80]; GD [81].
153. GD [27]; see also Fischer, p. 186.
154. Saparov, pp. 150–51; Karasev, "Leningrad v period blokady," p. 8, n. 28; Karasev, *Leningradtsy v gody blokady*, p. 94.
155. Komar, p. 59. For what happened to the Kirov equipment, see Werth, p. 113; GD [22].
156. Voznesensky, p. 34.
157. Karasev, "Leningrad v period blokady," p. 8, n. 28; Karasev, *Leningradtsy v gody blokady*, p. 94.
158. Karasev, *Leningradtsy v gody blokady*, p. 56.
159. Sitnikova, pp. 90–91; Komar, p. 58.
160. Polzikova-Rubets, pp. 28–29; LS 1, 3–5; Karasev, "Dokumentalnye materialy," p. 149.
161. Karasev, *Leningradtsy v gody blokady*, pp. 92–95.
162. *BSE*, XXX (1954), 358; Karasev, *Leningradtsy v gody blokady*, p. 94; Sirota, "Borba," p. 126.
163. Karasev, *Leningradtsy v gody blokady*, pp. 81, 90f.; Shcheglov, p. 12; Dymshits, p. 60.
164. *Biulleten*, Nos. 28–29, July 29, 1941.
165. Karasev, "Dokumentalnye materialy," p. 149.
166. Karasev, *Leningradtsy v gody blokady*, pp. 91f., 94.
167. *Ibid.*, p. 94; Likhomanov, p. 12.
168. Karasev, *Leningradtsy v gody blokady*, p. 92.
169. Bogdanovich, XXI, 207.
170. Polzikova-Rubets, p. 29.
171. Kripton, *Osada Leningrada*, p. 134; LS 3, 4, 6; GD [27].
172. LS 2, 6; Osipova, p. 96; Bogdanovich, XXI, 206.

173. Likhomanov, p. 13.

174. Bogdanovich, XXI, 206f.; Polzikova-Rubets, p. 29; GD [27]; LS 1, 3, 4; Shcheglov, p. 12.

175. Polzikova-Rubets, p. 38.

176. Bogdanovich, XXI, 209; Pavlov, p. 42; LS 3, 4.

177. Bogdanovich, XXI, 206–7.

178. GD [64].

179. LS 1–4, 6.

180. Osipova, p. 93; Bogdanovich, XXI, 206–7.

181. LS 6.

182. LS 3, 4; Kripton MS.

183. Bogdanovich, XXI, 209–19.

184. LS 1–3, 5, 6; Kripton, *Osada Leningrada*, p. 69; Osipova, p. 93; Bogdanovich, XXI, 209–10.

185. LS 3, 4; Bogdanovich, XXI, 207.

186. Ketlinskaia, pp. 37–41; Chakovskii, pp. 81, 84; GD [27].

187. LS 1–6; Dinerstein and Goure, pp. 199–201.

188. Bogdanovich, XXI, 201; Ketlinskaia, pp. 17–26.

189. Ketlinskaia, *passim*.

190. GD [8].

191. Karasev, *Leningradtsy v gody blokady*, p. 94.

192. GD [8]; Osipova, pp. 92–93; Werth, p. 128; Kripton, *Osada Leningrada*, p. 129; LS 1–5.

193. Karasev, *Leningradtsy v gody blokady*, p. 91.

194. *Sbornik zakonov SSSR* (1945), pp. 129-30.

195. *Pravda*, June 26, 1941.

196. *LP*, June 28, 1941, cited in *LVOVSS*, I, 12.

197. Meisel and Kozera, p. 365.

198. Sinitsin, p. 34.

199. Karasev, *Leningradtsy v gody blokady*, pp. 55, 57, 83, 88.

200. Sirota, "Voenno-organizatorskaia rabota," p. 27; LS 2.

201. Kripton MS; LS 2, 5; Avvakumov, p. 260.

202. Sirota, "Voenno-organizatorskaia rabota," p. 27.

203. *Ugolovnyi kodeks RSFSR*, p. 55.

204. *LP*, July 31, 1941, cited in *LVOVSS*, I, 16–17.

205. LS 1–5; Kripton, *Osada Leningrada*, p. 53; Werth, p. 128; Shcheglov, pp. 8, 25.

206. Vishnevskii, pp. 335–404.

207. LS 1–4, 6; Werth, p. 128; Bogdanovich, XXI, 200.

208. Werth, p. 128.

209. *Propaganda i agitatsiia*, No. 14 (1942), cited in *LVOVSS*, I, 184–85.

210. GD [6], No. 1, Oct. 2, 1941.   212. GD [47]; GD [55].

211. GD [47]; GD [55].   213. LS 1, 3, 4.

214. *Propaganda i agitatsiia*, Nos. 23–24 (1942), cited in *LVOVSS*, I, 272–73.

215. Likhomanov, pp 5, 9.

216. *LVOVSS*, I, 272–75; Avvakumov, pp. 223–24; Dymshits, p. 123.

217. Stalin, p. 13.   219. Werth, p. 125

218. *Pravda*, July 6, 8, 1941.   220. LS 3, 4, 6.

221. *LVOVSS*, I, 5, 22, 27, 29f.

222. *LP*, July 6, 1941, cited in *LVOVSS*, I, 23.

223. *LVOVSS*, I, 37; Dymshits, p. 13.
224. *Pravda*, July 3, 1941, cited in *LVOVSS*, I, 20.
225. *Na zashchitu Leningrada*, July 20, 1941, cited in *LVOVSS*, I, 29.
226. *Pravda*, June 23–August 21, 1941.
227. *LVOVSS*, I, 19, 23.
228. *Nazashchitu Leningrada*, July 22, 1941, cited in *LVOVSS*, I, 28.
229. Stalin, p. 10.
230. *LP*, Aug. 13, 1941, cited in *LVOVSS*, I, 35.
231. Stalin, p. 16; *Pravda*, June–August 1941, *passim*; *LVOVSS*, I, 9, 17.
232. Bogdanovich, XXI, 201.   234. LS 3, 4; Shcheglov, p. 8.
233. LS 3, 4.   235. Osipova, p. 93.
236. Avvakumov, p. 226.
237. Karasev, *Leningradtsy v gody blokady*, p. 83.
238. *LP*, June 28, 1941, cited in *LVOVSS*, I, 13.
239. Avvakumov, p. 201
240. *Sbornik zakonov SSSR* (1956), p. 395.
241. *LP*, Aug. 10, 1941, cited in *LVOVSS*, I, 33.
242. Sitnikova, p. 89.
243. *LP*, Aug. 10, 1941, cited in *LVOVSS*, I, 33.
244. LS 2.
245. *LVOVSS*, I, 33–34; Shcheglov, pp. 9, 11.
246. Fainsod, p. 232.
247. Avvakumov, p. 227; Likhomanov, p. 40.
248. *Pravda*, Nov. 21, 1943.
249. *Ibid.*, June 24, 1943.
250. *Partiinoe stroitelstvo*, No. 13 (1942), cited in *LVOVSS*, I, 190.
251. Werth, pp. 113–14; *Partiinoe stroitelstvo*, No. 13 (1942), cited in *LVOVSS*, I, 190; Komar, p. 61.
252. Ketlinskaia, pp. 527–28.
253. GD [64].
254. *Ibid.*
255. GD [27]. A similar judgment was made by Kripton (MS).
256. Karasev, "Leningrad v period blokady," p. 15; Cherniavskii, p. 89; Sirota, "Borba," p. 131.
257. *Biulleten*, Nos. 28–29, July 29, 1941.
258. *Ibid.*; see also *LVOVSS*, I, 119.
259. Karasev, "Leningrad v period blokady," p. 15.
260. Fischer, p. 184.   262. GD [64].
261. GD [8].   263. LS 6.
264. Osipova, p. 92.
265. *Ibid.*
266. *Ibid.*, p. 94.
267. Kripton, *Osada Leningrada*, pp. 65, 67; Bogdanovich, XXI, 208–10; LS 1, 3–5, 6.
268. Werth, p. 81.
269. LS 3, 4; Kripton, *Osada Leningrada*, pp. 117–18.
270. Kripton, *Osada Leningrada*, p. 65.
271. *IMT*, VIII (1947), 337.   273. GD [75].
272. GD [64].   274. LS 1, 3, 5; Kripton MS.
275. Osipova, p, 93.
276. GD [8].

277. Kripton, *Osada Leningrada,* p. 65.
278. *Ibid.,* p. 72.
279. *Ibid.,* p. 54.

NOTES TO CHAPTER FOUR

1. In addition to the sources indicated in Chapter 2, n. 10, the description of the military operations in this chapter is based on Zydowitz; Hubatsch; and Kardel.
2. Blau, p. 70.
3. *IMT,* XV (1948), 329–30.
4. Muggeridge, p. 448.
5. Halder, *Hitler als Feldherr,* p. 41.
6. Halder MS, VII, 77–78.
7. Mannerheim, pp. 426-27.   9. GD [110].
8. Halder MS, VII, 83.   10. Reinhardt, p 133.
11. *Ibid.*
12. GD [111].
13. Halder MS, VII, 109.
14. Liddell-Hart, *The Other Side of the Hill,* p. 278.
15. Bor, p. 209.

NOTES TO CHAPTER FIVE

1. Lt. Gen. M. Khozin, *Leningradskaia pravda,* Nov. 12, 1941, cited in GD [67].
2. GD [36].
3. *LP,* Aug. 21, 1941, cited in *LVOVSS,* I, 41.
4. *Ibid.,* Sept. 2, 1941, cited in *LVOVSS,* I, 59.
5. GD [88]; Avvakumov, p. 187.
6. LS 1, 2; Kripton, *Osada Leningrada,* p. 133; GD [5].
7. Komar, p. 60.
8. Werth, p. 112.
9. Order No. 270, Staff of the High Command of the Red Army, Aug. 16, 1941, Anti-Kom. 116/56.
10. GD [36].   13. GD [86].
11. GD [37].   14. GD [7].
12. GD [39].   15. GD [86].
16. GD [101]. The reference is to *LP,* Dec. 3, 1941.
17. GD [28].
18. GD [68].
19. *Propaganda i agitatsiia,* Nos. 23–24, 1942, cited in *LVOVSS,* I, 276; *Politicheskoe obespechenie,* p. 34.
20. GD [68].
21. GD [62].
22. David J. Dallin, *Soviet Espionage,* p. 248.
23. Beliaev and Kuznetsov, p. 35.
24. *LP,* Aug. 22, 1941, cited in *LVOVSS,* I, 43.

25. Saparov, p. 17; Sirota, "Voenno-organizatorskaia rabota," p. 19; Shcheglov, p. 26.

26. Polzikova-Rubets, p. 37; Gruzdev, p. 37.

27. Werth, pp. 128–29.

28. GD [43]; GD [76]. GD [92] reports the capture of workers from three different defense plants all mobilized on September 18.

29. GD [117].

30. Karasev, *Leningradtsy v gody blokady*, pp. 105–6; Komar, p. 60; Sirota, "Voenno-organizatorskaia rabota," p. 25.

31. Sirota, "Voenno-organizatorskaia rabota," p. 25.

32. Fadeev, p. 77.

33. Karasev, *Leningradtsy v gody blokady*, pp. 105, 121; Beliaev and Kuznetsov, p. 38.

34. Sirota, "Voenno-organizatorskaia rabota," p. 24.

35. LS 1; Kripton, *Osada Leningrada*, p. 134.

36. LS 3, 4.

37. *Biulleten*, No. 36, Sept. 30, 1941.

38. Werth, p. 118.

39. Komar, p. 63.

40. GD [6], No. 5, Oct. 19, 1941; *ibid.*, No. 6, Oct. 31, 1941; *ibid.*, No. 7, Nov. 14, 1941; Karasev, *Leningradtsy v gody blokady*, pp. 125–26.

41. GD [6], No. 5, Oct. 19, 1941.

42. Werth, p. 102.

43. Lauterbach, p. 49; Sirota, "Voenno-organizatorskaia rabota," p. 24; Karasev, *Leningradtsy v gody blokady*, pp. 123–24.

44. Sirota, "Voenno-organizatorskaia rabota," p. 29; Werth, p. 112.

45. Grechaniuk, p. 258.

46. Karasev, *Leningradtsy v gody blokady*, p. 127.

47. *Biulleten*, Nos. 34–35, Sept. 15, 1941.

48. Karasev, *Leningradtsy v gody blokady*, pp. 123–24.

49. Dymshits, p. 147.

50. GD [6], No. 4, Oct. 9, 1941; GD [19]; GD [63], Jan. 22, 1942.

51. Kripton, *Osada Leningrada*, p. 133; LS 1, 3, 4; Pavlov, p. 15.

52. GD [1]; GD [3].

53. Bogdanovich, XXI, 211.

54. Karasev, *Leningradtsy v gody blokady*, pp. 143, 147; Sirota, "Borba," p. 123.

55. Halder MS, VII, 85, 103, 217; GD [91].

56. Lauterbach, p. 54; Odintsov, p. 87.

57. Karasev, *Leningradtsy v gody blokady*, p. 145; Sirota, "Borba," p. 124.

58. *Atlas ofitsera*, p. 196; Sirota, "Borba," p. 124.

59. Karasev, *Leningradtsy v gody blokady*, pp. 147, 151; Tregubov, pp. 10–11; Sirota, "Borba," pp. 123–24.

60. *Atlas ofitsera*, p. 196; Sirota, "Borba," p. 124; BSE, XXX (1954), 360. Khudiakova, p. 27, places the number of incendiary bombs dropped on Leningrad in 1941 at 67,078.

61. Karasev, *Leningradtsy v gody blokady*, p. 146.

62. *Ibid.*, p. 149; Inber, *Leningrad*, pp. 27–50, 283; Markevich, p. 7; Tregubov, pp. 10–11; Sirota, "Borba," p. 123.

63. Karasev, *Leningradtsy v gody blokady*, p. 149.

64. Tregubov, pp. 10–11; Sirota, "Borba," p. 123.

65. Karasev, *Leningradtsy v gody blokady,* pp. 143–49; Karasev, "Leningrad v period blokady," p. 7; Dymshits, p. 112.

66. Fischer, p. 186.

67. *Pravda,* March 3, 1944; Werth, p. 162.

68. Dymshits, pp. 112, 143; Khudiakova, p. 54. According to other sources the Badaev warehouses were destroyed on Sept. 10 (Pavlov, p. 54).

69. Among those listed in the sources were the Gostinnyi Dvor, the Lenin Flour Mill, food storage areas No. 1 and No. 10, a margarine factory, etc. GD [99]; GD [98]; GD [6], No. 9, Dec. 4, 1941; GD [65]; Mikhailov, p. 205; LS 2 reported destruction of the Parkhovskie food storage areas. *Atlas ofitsera,* p. 196, describes heavy damage to several areas of the city that were known to house food supplies.

70. Karasev, *Leningradtsy v gody blokady,* p. 140.

71. Khudiakova, p. 27.

72. *Pravda,* March 3, 1944; Kniazev, p. 65; Karasev, *Leningradtsy v gody blokady,* p. 146; Sirota, "Borba," p. 126.

73. *BSE,* VIII (1951), 414; *LP,* July 11, 1942, cited in *LVOVSS,* I, 196.

74. Inber, *Leningrad,* pp. 31–32.

75. Pavlov, pp. 44, 48; Karasev, *Leningradtsy v gody blokady,* p. 108.

76. LS 1–4.

77. Kripton, *Osada Leningrada,* p. 152; Kripton MS; LS 1–5.

78. Kripton MS; LS 3, 4.

79. LS 1–4; Kripton MS.

80. LS 1–4; Dymshits, p. 145.   82. Dymshits, p. 144.

81. Bogdanovich, XXI, 217.   83. *Ibid.,* p. 148.

84. Kripton, *Osada Leningrada,* pp. 147, 150–51; LS 1, 3, 4.

85. Dymshits, pp. 144, 147.

86. LS 1–5; Skomorovsky and Morris, p. 45; Karasev, *Leningradtsy v gody blokady,* p. 153; Dymshits, pp. 127, 147.

87. Karasev, "Leningrad v period blokady," p. 7.

88. Komar, p. 61.

89. Inber, *Leningrad,* p. 25; *Biulleten,* No. 37, Oct. 1941; Pavlov, p. 36; Dymshits, p. 146.

90. Sinitsin, pp. 35–36; Avvakumov, pp. 203–4.

91. Komar, pp. 58–59; Werth, p. 113; LS 7.

92. LS 7.

93. Werth, p. 113; Komar, pp. 58–59; GD [1].

94. *LP,* Sept. 16, 1941, cited in *LVOVSS,* I, 72.

95. GD [6], No. 5, Oct. 19, 1941; GD [43].

96. *LP,* Oct. 21, 1941, cited in *LVOVSS,* I, 86.

97. Karasev, "Leningrad v period blokady," p. 8; Werth, pp. 72, 118.

98. Dymshits, pp. 145–46.

99. Werth, pp. 117–18.

100. *Ibid.,* p. 72.

101. Karasev, "Leningrad v period blokady," p. 8.

102. Dymshits, p. 146.

103. Karasev, *Leningradtsy v gody blokady,* p. 137.

104. Sirota, "Borba," p. 134.

105. *BSE,* XXIV (1953), 526.

106. Karasev, *Leningradtsy v gody blokady,* p. 139.

107. *Ibid.,* pp. 137, 139.

108. *Ibid.*, pp. 91–93.

109. *Ibid.*, p. 132; Chakovskii, p. 43; Werth, p. 65.

110. Sirota, "Borba," p. 132.

111. Saparov, p. 35.

112. Pavlov, p. 30; Saparov, p. 40.

113. Karasev, *Leningradtsy v gody blokady*, p. 132.

114. Sirota, "Borba," p. 133.

115. Karasev, *Leningradtsy v gody blokady*, p. 93.

116. *Ibid.*, pp. 91, 94.

117. Karasev, "Leningrad v period blokady," p. 14.

118. Dymshits, p. 143.

119. Pavlov, p. 42.

120. Karasev, "Leningrad v period blokady," p. 8; *LP*, Oct. 3, 1941.

121. Karasev, "Leningrad v period blokady," p. 9; Karasev, *Leningradtsy v gody blokady*, p. 163; Polzikova-Rubets, pp. 27–28; LS 2.

122. Karasev, "Leningrad v period blokady," p. 9; Karasev, *Leningradtsy v gody blokady*, p. 164.

123. *BSE*, VIII (1951), 486.

124. GD [36]; Tikhonov, p. 7.

125. Pavlov, pp. 16–17.

126. *LVOVSS*, I, 140, 200; Sirota, "Voenno-organizatorskaia rabota," p. 20.

127. Sirota, "Voenno-organizatorskaia rabota," p. 20; *LVOVSS*, I, 71.

128. GD [90].

129. Pavlov, pp. 15–16.

130. Karasev, *Leningradtsy v gody blokady*, p. 105.

131. Pavlov, p. 16.

132. *Ibid.*

133. *Ibid.*, pp. 16–17.

134. Sinitsin, p. 35.

135. *Ibid.*

136. GD [86].

137. Sirota, "Voenno-organizatorskaia rabota," p. 18; see also Saparov, p. 17, and *BSE*, XXVI (1954), 146. According to Sirota, Molotov and Malenkov were in Leningrad in September 1941, while according to *BSE* and Saparov they were there in August. The article on Molotov in *BSE*, XXVIII (1954), does not mention his presence in Leningrad.

138. GD [93].

139. Sirota, "Voenno-organizatorskaia rabota," p. 24.

140. Karasev, *Leningradtsy v gody blokady*, pp. 105–6.

141. Sirota, "Voenno-organizatorskaia rabota," p. 24.

142. *Ibid.*; Karasev, *Leningradtsy v gody blokady*, p. 104.

143. Komar, p. 60.

144. GD [87].

145. *Pravda*, June 24, 1943, cited in *LVOVSS*, I, 341; *Partiinoe stroitelstvo*, No. 13 (1942), cited in *LVOVSS*, I, 192.

146. GD [38]; Karasev, *Leningradtsy v gody blokady*, pp. 105, 155.

147. *Biulleten*, No. 36, Sept. 30, 1941.

148. *LP*, Aug. 26, 1941, cited in *LVOVSS*, I, 54; Karasev, *Leningradtsy v gody blokady*, p. 105.

149. LS 1–5; Avvakumov, pp. 21–22; Karasev, *Leningradtsy v gody blokady*, p. 154.

150. Karasev, *Leningradtsy v gody blokady*, p. 155.

151. *Ibid.*, p. 156.

152. GD [59]; GD [6], No. 1, Oct. 2, 1941.

153. GD [59]; GD [6], No. 4, Oct. 9, 1941.

154. Karasev, *Leningradtsy v gody blokady,* p. 141; Panfilov, p. 12.

155. GD [98].

156. *Propaganda i agitatsiia,* No. 14 (1942), cited in *LVOVSS,* I, 184–88.

157. Karasev, *Leningradtsy v gody blokady,* p. 154.

158. Tikhonov, p. 6; *LP,* Sept. 2, 1941, cited in *LVOVSS,* I, 60; and Nov. 12, 1941, cited in *LVOVSS,* I, 104; *Propaganda i agitatsiia,* No. 14 (1942), cited in *LVOVSS,* I, 184–87; and Nos. 23–24 (1942), cited in *LVOVSS,* I, 275.

159. Tikhonov, p. 6.

160. *LP,* Sept. 2, 1941, cited in *LVOVSS,* I, 60.

161. *Propaganda i agitatsiia,* No. 14 (1942), cited in *LVOVSS,* I, 185–86.

162. *Ibid.,* p. 186.

163. *LP,* Aug. 22, Aug. 27–Sept. 1, 1941, cited in *LVOVSS,* I, 43–55.

164. *Ibid.,* Sept. 2, 1941, cited in *LVOVSS,* I, 59–61.

165. *Ibid.,* Sept. 16, 1941, cited in *LVOVSS,* I, 71.

166. LS 3, 4; Kripton, *Osada Leningrada,* p. 135.

167. Fineberg, pp. 7–8. This theme was repeated in *LP,* Aug. 27, Sept. 19, 1941, cited in *LVOVSS,* I, 55, 76.

168. *LP,* Sept. 28, 1941, cited in *LVOVSS,* I, 81–82.

169. Fineberg, p. 7; *Velikii gorod Lenina, passim; LP,* Aug. 22, 1941, cited in *LVOVSS,* I, 43.

170. *LP,* Aug. 28, 1941, cited in *LVOVSS,* I, 57.

171. *Ibid.,* Sept. 16, 1941, cited in *LVOVSS,* I, 59.

172. *Ibid.,* Sept. 20, 1941, cited in *LVOVSS,* I, 77.

173. GD [68].

174. *LVOVSS,* I, 59.

175. *LVOVSS,* I, 74; Polzikova-Rubets, p. 34; *Velikii gorod Lenina,* pp. 12–16.

176. *LP,* Sept. 11, 1941, cited in *LVOVSS,* I, 68–70.

177. Kripton, *Osada Leningrada,* p. 138; LS 2.

178. Kripton MS.

179. *LVOVSS,* I, 254; Werth, p. 129; Lauterbach, p. 52.

180. LS 1–4, 6; Kripton MS; Bogdanovich, XXI, 217.

181. Osipova, p. 100.

182. Kripton, *Osada Leningrada,* pp. 142–43.

183. LS 2; Kripton, *Osada Leningrada,* p. 143.

184. *LP,* Sept. 24, 1941, cited in *LVOVSS,* I, 80.

185. *Ibid.,* Sept. 7, 1941, cited in *LVOVSS,* I, 64.

186. *Ibid.,* Sept. 24, 1941, cited in *LVOVSS,* I, 80.

187. GD [2].

188. Inber, *Leningrad,* pp. 26–27.

189. *LP,* Sept. 24, 1941, cited in *LVOVSS,* I, 81.

190. Kripton MS.   192. LS 2.

191. LS 1–5; Kripton MS.   193. Kripton MS.

194. Karasev, *Leningradtsy v gody blokady,* p. 127.

195. *Ibid.,* pp. 127–28; Khudiakova, pp. 53–54; Sirota, "Borba," pp. 130–31.

196. Karasev, *Leningradtsy v gody blokady,* pp. 128–29.

197. *Ibid.,* p. 120.

198. Pavlov, p. 43.

199. Karasev, *Leningradtsy v gody blokady*, pp. 120–28. In July the consumption of flour had been 40,000 tons and in August 44,800 tons.

200. LS 1–5; "The Surgeons of Leningrad"; GD [83]; GD [6], No. 2, Oct. 6, 1941; GD [2], Sept. 10, 1941; Kripton, *Osada Leningrada*, p. 226.

201. Karasev, *Leningradtsy v gody blokady*, p. 120.

202. *Ibid.*, p. 129.

203. *Ibid.*; *LVOVSS*, I, 119.

204. Karasev, *Leningradtsy v gody blokady*, p. 130. Pavlov, p. 50.

205. Lauterbach, p. 48.   208. Pavlov, p. 48.

206. Inber, *Leningrad*, p. 18.   209. Sirota, "Borba," p. 136.

207. Werth, p. 111.   210. *Ibid.*, p. 44.

211. *Ibid.*

212. Karasev, *Leningradtsy v gody blokady*, p. 129.

213. *Ibid.*; GD [85]; *LP*, Jan. 13, 1942, cited in *LVOVSS*, I, 118; Sirota, "Borba," p. 134.

214. Karasev, *Leningradtsy v gody blokady*, p. 130.

215. *Ibid.*; GD [6], No. 5, Oct. 19, 1941; *ibid.*, No. 6, Oct. 31, 1941.

216. Pavlov, p. 49.

217. *Ibid.*, pp. 43, 107; Karasev, *Leningradtsy v gody blokady*, p. 128.

218. Sirota, "Borba," p. 133.

219. Karasev, *Leningradtsy v gody blokady*, p. 132.

220. Pavlov, p. 92; Karasev, *Leningradtsy v gody blokady*, p. 132.

221. Sirota, "Borba," p. 136.

222. *Biulleten*, No. 37, Oct. 14, 1941; LS 1–5; *LP*, Oct. 10, 1941.

223. GD [84]; GD [30].

224. Bogdanovich, XXI, 204; Kripton MS.

225. Dymshits, p. 148.

226. LS 1–5; Kripton, *Osada Leningrada*, p. 165; Polzikova - Rubets, p. 64.

227. *Biulleten*, Nos. 34–35, Sept. 15, 1941.

228. Kripton, *Osada Leningrada*, p. 178.

229. Dymshits, p. 149.

230. LS 3, 4, 7; GD [17].

231. LS 7.

232. Karasev, *Leningradtsy v gody blokady*, p. 137.

233. Pavlov, pp. 47–48.

234. Karasev, *Leningradtsy v gody blokady*, p. 137.

235. GD [2].

236. *Biulleten*, No. 36, Sept. 30, 1941.

237. LS 1–5.

238. Inber, *Leningrad*, p. 22; Kripton MS; LS 2–5; Fadeev, pp. 38–42.

239. LS 1–5; Karasev, *Leningradtsy v gody blokady*, p. 139.

240. *Biulleten*, No. 36, Sept. 30, 1941.

241. LS 1–5; Polzikova-Rubets, p. 34; Dymshits, p. 125.

242. Inber, *Leningrad*, pp. 16–17; Werth, pp. 130, 133; Dymshits, p. 146.

243. LS 3, 4.

244. LS 1–5; Kripton MS.

245. Kripton, *Osada Leningrada*, p. 147; GD [6], No. 5, Oct. 19, 1941.

246. Dymshits, p. 145.

247. LS 2–6.

248. LS 1, 3, 4; Kripton, *Osada Leningrada*, pp. 69–70; GD [6], No. 1, Oct. 2, 1941.
249. LS 2–4.
250. GD [88].

NOTES TO CHAPTER SIX

1. Goerlitz, p. 401.
2. *NMT*, X, 1097–98.
3. GD [4].
4. GD [9].
5. *NMT*, XI, 563.
6. GD [9].
7. *IMT*, VIII (1947), 113.
8. *Ibid.*, I (1947), 58.
9. *Ibid.*, XIII (1948), 482.
10. *Ibid.*, XXXIV (1949), 426.
11. Goerlitz, p. 402.
12. *New York Times*, Nov. 9, 1941.
13. *Ibid.*
14. Halder MS, VII, 217.
15. Bartz, p. 105.
16. Lauterbach, p. 49; Fadeev, p. 96.
17. Odintsov, pp. 42–43.
18. GD [25].
19. Goerlitz, p. 402.
20. The information contained in this paragraph is based on Dinerstein and Goure, pp. 166–69.
21. *Ibid.*, pp. 177–205.
22. *Ibid.*, pp. 169–71.
23. *LP*, Nov. 6, 1941, cited in *LVOVSS*, I, 98.
24. Karasev, *Leningradtsy v gody blokady*, pp. 133–34.
25. *LVOVSS*, I, 109.
26. The operations described in this paragraph are based on Karasev, *Leningradtsy v gody blokady*, pp. 140–43; Shcheglov, pp. 84–231.
27. Halder MS, VII, 153–64; GD [42].
28. Dinerstein and Goure, pp. 171–76.

NOTES TO CHAPTER SEVEN

1. Fadeev, p. 37.
2. *LP*, Jan. 13, 1942, cited in *LVOVSS*, I, 118.
3. GD [29].
4. *LP*, Oct. 22, 1941, cited in *LVOVSS*, I, 90.
5. *Ibid.*, Nov. 12, 1941, cited in *LVOVSS*, I, 104.
6. Fadeev, pp. 41–42.
7. Werth, p. 81.
8. Mannerheim, p. 443.
9. Pavlov, p. 94.
10. Karasev, *Leningradtsy v gody blokady*, p. 134.
11. Sirota, "Borba," p. 134.
12. Avvakumov, p. 221; *Propaganda i agitatsiia*, No. 20 (October 1942), cited in *LVOVSS*, I, 236; *Pravda*, March 3, 1944; Saparov, p. 50; Tikhonov, p. 37.
13. Sirota, "Voenno-organizatorskaia rabota," p. 29; Karasev, "Leningrad v period blokady," p. 22.
14. Karasev, *Leningradtsy v gody blokady*, p. 171.

15. Saparov, pp. 54–77; Avvakumov, p. 206; Pavlov, p. 122; Sirota, "Borba," p. 145.

16. Karasev, "Leningrad v period blokady," p. 22.

17. Saparov, pp. 52f., 105.

18. Karasev, "Leningrad v period blokady," p. 22; Karasev, *Leningradtsy v gody blokady*, p. 171.

19. Saparov, p. 53; Fineberg, pp. 59–60.

20. Pavlov, p. 104.

21. Karasev, *Leningradtsy v gody blokady*, p. 175.

22. GD [63], Apr. 24, 1942; Saparov, pp. 75, 96; Sirota, "Borba," p. 145.

23. Sirota, "Borba," p. 134.

24. Karasev, *Leningradtsy v gody blokady*, p. 175.

25. Saparov, p. 99; Karasev, "Leningrad v period blokady," p. 23.

26. Sirota, "Borba," p. 145.

27. Karasev, *Leningradtsy v gody blokady*, pp. 180, 183.

28. Saparov, pp. 100f.; Karasev, *Leningradtsy v gody blokady*, p. 176.

29. Karasev, *Leningradtsy v gody blokady*, p. 132; Pavlov, pp. 95–96.

30. *LVOVSS*, I, 119; Karasev, *Leningradtsy v gody blokady*, p. 134.

31. Pavlov, p. 107.

32. GD [85].

33. Karasev, *Leningradtsy v gody blokady*, p. 134.

34. Pavlov, p. 53.

35. Sirota, "Borba," p. 136.   37. Pavlov, pp. 51, 53.

36. *Ibid.*   38. Saparov, p. 49.

39. Karasev, "Leningrad v period blokady," p. 16.

40. Pavlov, p. 54.

41. *Ibid.*, p. 78.

42. *LP*, Nov. 12, 1941, cited in *LVOVSS*, I, 104.

43. *LVOVSS*, I, 119.

44. Karasev, *Leningradtsy v gody blokady*, p. 135.

45. *LVOVSS*, I, 119; Karasev, *Leningradtsy v gody blokady*, p. 136; Khudiakova, p. 55; Sirota, "Borba," p. 135; LS 1, 3–5.

46. Werth, p. 155.

47. *Biulleten*, No. 38, Oct. 27, 1941.

48. LS 1, 3, 4.

49. Dymshits, p. 156.

50. Kripton, *Osada Leningrada*, p. 178; GD [100], Dec. 24, 1941; Karasev, *Leningradtsy v gody blokady*, p. 194.

51. Dymshits, p. 126.

52. *Ibid.*, p. 181.

53. According to GD [100], Dec. 24, 1941, a dog sold for 300 rubles and a cat for 200.

54. Bogdanovich, XXI, 206–8; Inber, *Leningrad*, p. 44; Polzikova-Rubets, pp. 64, 69; Werth, p. 132; LS 1–5; Kripton, *Osada Leningrada*, p. 165; Dymshits, pp. 155, 161.

55. Fadeev, p. 24.

56. Dymshits, p. 291.

57. LS 1, 5; GD [99].

58. GD [52]; Inber, *Leningrad*, p. 79; LS 5.

59. Pavlov, p. 62.

60. *Biulleten*, Nos. 45–46, Dec. 30, 1941.

61. Inber, *Leningrad*, p. 89.
62. GD [77].
63. Dymshits, p. 182.
64. *Ibid.*, p. 153.
65. Werth, p. 116.
66. *Ibid.*, p. 131; LS 1–5; GD [100], Dec. 24, 1941; Pavlov, p. 115.
67. LS 3, 4.
68. Werth, pp. 21–22.
69. Polzikova-Rubets, p. 63.
70. Pavlov, p. 63.
71. Polzikova-Rubets, p. 15; Tikhonov, p. 35.
72. Pavlov, pp. 116–17, 137.
73. LS 1–5; Skomorovsky and Morris, p. 19; GD [100], Dec. 24, 1941; Kripton, *Osada Leningrada*, p. 174.
74. Dymshits, pp. 192–93.
75. *Ibid.*, p. 193.
76. *Ibid.*, p. 160.
77. *Ibid.*, p. 193.
78. Kripton, *Osada Leningrada*, p. 183.
79. Karasev, "Leningrad v period blokady," p. 18; Pavlov, p. 110.
80. Tur, pp. 10–18.
81. Karasev, "Leningrad v period blokady," p. 18; Pavlov, p. 112.
82. Karasev, "Leningrad v period blokady," p. 19; Pavlov, p. 111.
83. Karasev, *Leningradtsy v gody blokady*, p. 184; Petrovskaya, pp. 210–11.
84. Sirota, "Borba," pp. 149–50.
85. Inber, *Leningrad*, pp. 64–75; Ketlinskaia, pp. 474–75; LS 1–4; Fadeev, pp. 136f.; Tikhonov, p. 28; Karasev, "Leningrad v period blokady," pp. 13, 18–19.
86. Sirota, "Borba," p. 150.
87. Fischer, p. 118.
88. Fadeev, p. 137.
89. Ershov, pp. 284–89.
90. Karasev, *Leningradtsy v gody blokady*, p. 135; LS, 1, 3, 4.
91. Kripton MS.
92. Inber, *Leningrad*, p. 50; LS 1–5; Petrovskaya, p. 211.
93. Werth, p. 73.
94. Dymshits, pp. 132f., 183, 244.
95. Karasev, *Leningradtsy v gody blokady*, p. 157.
96. Inber, *Leningrad*, p. 51; Werth, p. 80; Polzikova-Rubets, p. 96; LS 1–5; Karasev, *Leningradtsy v gody blokady*, p. 186; Dymshits, p. 321.
97. Karasev, *Leningradtsy v gody blokady*, p. 157.
98. LS 1–5; Inber, *Leningrad*, p. 51; Werth, p. 80; Dymshits, pp. 184, 320.
99. Karasev, *Leningradtsy v gody blokady*, p. 137.
100. *Biulleten*, No. 37, Oct. 14, 1941.
101. Karasev, *Leningradtsy v gody blokady*, p. 137.
102. *Biulleten*, Nos. 39–40, Nov. 12, 1941.
103. Karasev, *Leningradtsy v gody blokady*, p. 137.
104. *Ibid.*, p. 138.
105. *Ibid.*; *Propaganda i agitatsiia*, No. 20 (October 1942), cited in *LVOVSS*, I, 242.
106. *BSE*, IX (1951), 44.
107. *Biulleten*, Nos. 41–42, Nov. 29, 1941; Karasev, *Leningradtsy v gody blokady*, p. 139.
108. Karasev, "Leningrad v period blokady," p. 13.
109. Karasev, *Leningradtsy v gody blokady*, p. 139; *LP*, Nov. 20, 1941.
110. *Biulleten*, Nos. 45–46, Dec. 30, 1941.
111. Karasev, "Leningrad v period blokady," p. 12.

112. *Ibid.*, p. 13.
113. *Ibid.*, pp. 12–13.
114. Werth, p. 114.
115. Dymshits, p. 115.
116. Fadeev, p. 11; LS 1–5; Kripton, *Osada Leningrada*, p. 190.
117. LS 1–5; Kripton MS; Fadeev, pp. 11–16, 44. Dymshits, pp. 290, 292.
118. Dymshits, p. 290.
119. *Ibid.*, pp. 115–16.
120. *Biulleten*, Nos. 43–44, Dec. 18, 1941.
121. LS 1–5; Fadeev, p. 11; Petrovskaya, p. 200.
122. *Biulleten*, Nos. 41–42, Nov. 29, 1941.
123. *LP*, Dec. 12, 1941, cited in *LVOVSS*, I, 114.
124. Beltiugov, p. 156.
125. LS 2; Fineberg, p. 25; GD [104]; GD [6], No. 5, Oct. 19, 1941;
GD [63], Jan. 14, 1942.
126. GD [63], Jan. 14, 1942.
127. GD [63], Dec. 14, 1941; GD [41]; GD [17]; LS 2; Werth, p. 80.
128. LS 2; GD [63], Jan. 14, 1942.
129. GD [6], No. 6, Oct. 31, 1941.
130. GD [71]; GD [117]; GD [63], Jan. 14, 1942; LS 2.
131. GD [117].
132. GD [34]. These letters all dated from the first half of December;
Dymshits, p. 320.
133. GD [15]; GD [64]; GD [66].
134. GD [72].
135. GD [68].
136. GD [12].
137. *Ibid.*
138. GD [87].
139. GD [69].
140. GD [116].
141. GD [104].
142. *Biulleten*, No. 36, Sept. 30, 1941; *BSE*, IX (1951), 289.
143. Propaganda i agitatsiia, No. 20 (October 1942), cited in LVOVSS,
I, 241; Sirota, "Voenno-organizatorskaia rabota," p. 26.
144. *LP*, Nov. 27, 1941, cited in *LVOVSS*, I, 108.
145. Sirota, "Voenno-organizatorskaia rabota," p. 25.
146. Karasev, *Leningradtsy v gody blokady*, p. 157; Sirota, "Voenno-
organizatorskaia rabota," p. 25.
147. Karasev, *Leningradtsy v gody blokady*, p. 220.
148. GD [6], No. 6, Oct. 31, 1941; *ibid.*, No. 7, Nov. 14, 1941.
149. *Biulleten*, Nos. 45–46, Dec. 30, 1941.
150. GD [114]; GD [6], No. 9, Dec. 4, 1941; *Pravda*, Mar. 3, 1944.
151. *BSE*, XXIV (1953), 524; Gibbons, p. 9; Sirota, "Borba," p. 127.
152. Lauterbach, p. 57.
153. Werth, p. 49; Gibbons, p. 9; Lauterbach, p. 27.
154. *New York Times*, Apr. 4, 1956; Interview of Strezhelkovskii, chairman of the city's executive committee, by Mr. Hans Heymann, member of
the U.S. Housing Delegation, which visited the USSR in 1956. Mr. Heymann
kindly made this interview available to me.
155. *Pravda*, March 3, 1944.
156. *Ibid.*
157. LS 1–4; Chakovskii, pp. 223–32; Dymshits, p. 125.
158. *USSR Information Bulletin*.
159. *Soviet News* (London), Oct. 29, 1945.
160. Kniazev, p. 64.
161. *Atlas offitsera*, p. 196.
162. Fadeev, pp. 44–45; LS 1, 2.
163. Dymshits, p. 116f.

164. Kripton, *Osada Leningrada,* p. 154; Werth, pp. 53, 55, 74.
165. *Biulleten,* Nos. 41–42, Nov. 29, 1941.
166. Kripton, *Osada Leningrada,* pp. 180–87. Dymshits, p. 151.
167. *Biulleten,* Nos. 43–44, Dec. 18, 1941; *LP,* Dec. 2, 1941.
168. GD [3]; GD [6], No. 5, Oct. 19, 1941; Tikhonov, p. 120; Fineberg, p. 25; Karasev, "Leningrad v period blokady," pp. 9–10.
169. Karasev, *Leningradtsy v gody blokady,* p. 158.
170. Karasev, "Leningrad v period blokady," p. 9.
171. Avvakumov, p. 203; Tikhonov, pp. 18–19; Kripton MS.
172. Karasev, "Leningrad v period blokady," p. 10.
173. Skomorovsky and Morris, p. 30.
174. *LP,* Jan. 1, 1942, cited in *LVOVSS,* I, 291; Avvakumov, pp. 73, 204; Dymshits, p. 159.
175. Inber, *Leningrad,* p. 87.
176. Karasev, "Leningrad v period blokady," p. 13; Werth, pp. 71, 114; *LP,* Apr. 18, 1942, cited in *LVOVSS,* I, 153–54.
177. GD [101], taken from an editorial in *LP,* Dec. 3, 1941.
178. *LVOVSS,* I, 2.
179. LS 7.
180. GD [11], Dec. 19, 1941, 19.30 hrs.; *ibid.,* Dec. 20, 1941, 13.15 hrs.; *ibid.,* Dec. 29, 1941, 11.30 hrs.; Komar, p. 65.
181. GD [11], Jan. 4, 1941, 13.50 hrs.
182. Dinerstein and Goure, pp. 195–98.
183. *LP,* Oct. 5, 1941, cited in *LVOVSS,* I, 83–84.
184. *Ibid.,* Oct. 29, 1941, cited in *LVOVSS,* I, 194.
185. *Partiinoe stroitelstvo,* No. 13 (1942), cited in *LVOVSS,* I, 194.
186. Werth, p. 72.   188. Dymshits, pp. 155, 157.
187. Tikhonov, p. 18.   189. White, p. 104.
190. Werth, p. 114.
191. *Biulleten,* Nos. 39–40, Nov. 12, 1941.
192. Werth, p. 74.
193. Kripton MS.
194. GD [98].
195. GD [119]; GD [77]; Komar, p. 63; Werth, p. 115; Dymshits, p. 157.
196. Karasev, "Leningrad v period blokady," p. 18.
197. Dymshits, p. 160.
198. Tikhonov, p. 120; Komar, p. 63; Avvakumov, p.205; Werth, p. 115.
199. *LVOVSS,* I, 104.
200. Saparov, pp. 265–66; Dymshits, pp. 153, 155.
201. Werth, pp. 73, 115.
202. Karasev, *Leningradtsy v gody blokady,* p. 133; Werth, p. 113.
203. Werth, p. 113.
204. Komar, pp. 58–59.
205. GD [11], Dec. 17, 1941, 13.30 hrs.
206. Werth, p. 113.
207. GD [94]; Polzikova-Rubets, p. 60; LS 3–5.
208. GD [14].
209. Karasev, "Leningrad v period blokady," p. 24; Karasev, "Dokumentalnye materialy," p. 149.
210. GD [11], Dec. 19. 1941, 19.10 hrs.
211. Polzikova-Rubets, p. 60; LS 3-5, 7.

212. Inber, *Leningrad*, p. 44; Werth, pp. 22–23.
213. Dymshits, p. 160.
214. GD [95].
215. *LP*, Nov. 12, 1941, cited in *LVOVSS*, I, 104.
216. Dymshits, p. 168.
217. *Ibid.*, pp. 168–69.
218. Sirota, "Voenno-organizatorskaia rabota," p. 20; Werth, p. 21; Inber, *Leningrad, passim.*
219. Polzikova-Rubets, p. 147.   221. LS 5.
220. *Sbornik ukazov*, pp. 127–28.   222. Dymshits, p. 124.
223. Chakovskii, p. 54.
224. *Biulleten*, Nos. 43–44, Dec. 18, 1941.
225. Polzikova-Rubets, p. 73; LS 2–4.
226. Dymshits, p. 125.
227. Fadeev, pp. 38–40.
228. *LP*, Oct. 21, 1941, cited in *LVOVSS*, I, 86.
229. Dinerstein and Goure, pp. 172–74, 178–79; Dymshits, p. 151.
230. *LP*, Nov. 12, 1941, cited in *LVOVSS*, I, 104.
231. *Ibid.*, Dec. 11, 1941, cited in *LVOVSS*, I, 111; and Sept. 20, 1941, cited in *LVOVSS*, I, 77.
232. *Ibid.*, Oct. 27, 1941, cited in *LVOVSS*, I, 96.
233. *Ibid.*, Oct. 30, 1941, cited in *LVOVSS*, I, 96–97.
234. Werth, p. 129.
235. *LP*, Dec. 27, 1941, cited in *LVOVSS*, I, 116–17.
236. *Ibid.*, Nov. 12 1941, cited in *LVOVSS*, I, 104.
237. GD [57]. This is not confirmed by the informants.
238. *LP*, Dec. 11, 1941, cited in *LVOVSS*, I, 111.
239. *Ibid.*, Oct. 29, 1941, cited in *LVOVSS*, I, 94–96.
240. *Ibid.*, Nov. 7, 1941, cited in *LVOVSS*, I, 99.
241. Fadeev, p. 40.
242. *LP*, Dec. 11, 1941, cited in *LVOVSS*, I, 111.
243. Karasev, *Leningradtsy v gody blokady*, p. 190.
244. Dymshits, p. 150.   248. Pavlov, pp. 38–39.
245. GD [45].   249. Dymshits, p. 128.
246. Pavlov, p. 101.   250. GD [29].
247. Inber, *Leningrad*, pp. 44, 53.   251. *Ibid.*
252. White, p. 94.
253. Sirota, "Voenno-organizatorskaia rabota," p. 31.
254. *Ibid.*, p. 21.
255. Werth, pp. 190–222; LS 7.
256. *Partiinoe stroitelstvo*, No. 13 (1942), cited in *LVOVSS*, I, 192.
257. *Ibid.*; *Pravda*, June 24, 1943, cited in *LVOVSS*, I, 192.
258. GD [11], Jan. 11, 1942, 08.35 hrs.; *ibid.*, Dec. 18, 1941, 10.30 hrs.; Bogdanovich, XXI, 207.
259. LS 3, 4; GD [11], Jan. 9, 1942, 17.10 hrs.; *ibid.*, Jan. 7, 1942, 14.40 hrs.
260. Karasev, *Leningradtsy v gody blokady*, p. 193.
261. LS 2; Petrovskaya, p. 211.
262. Karasev, *Leningradtsy v gody blokady*, pp. 192-93.
263. Kripton MS.
264. Sirota, "Voenno-organizatorskaia rabota," p. 31; Karasev, *Leningradtsy v gody blokady*, p. 204.

265. Dymshits, pp. 152, 159.
266. LS 2–4.
267. Fadeev, p. 42.
268. Kripton, *Osada Leningrada,* pp. 152, 174; LS 1, 3, 4.
269. LS 1, 3, 4; Kripton MS; Bogdanovich, XXII, 208.
270. Polzikova-Rubets, p. 79.
271. LS 3, 4; GD [6], No. 6, Oct. 31, 1941.

272. GD [18].   276. LS 3.
273. GD [16].   277. LS 3–5.
274. Kripton MS; LS 3, 4.   278. LS 1–5.
275. Bogdanovich, XXII, 204.   279. LS 3–5.

280. LS 1–5; Kripton, *Osada Leningrada,* p. 174; Skomorovsky and Morris, p. 19.
281. Kripton, *Osada Leningrada,* pp. 205–6; Pavlov, p. 115.
282. Kripton MS.
283. *LP,* Nov. 12, 1941, cited in *LVOVSS,* I, 104.
284. GD [99]; GD [84].
285. LS 3, 4.
286. GD [17].
287. *Propaganda i agitatsiia,* No. 14 (1942), cited in *LVOVSS,* I, 187–88.
288. *LP,* May 23, 1942, cited in *LVOVSS,* I, 166 .
289. Sirota, "Voenno-organizatorskaia rabota," p. 27.

290. Dymshits, pp. 155, 169.   293. GD [84].
291. GD [10].   294. GD [40].
292. GD [113].   295. LS 3.

296. For example, GD [49]; GD [63], Oct. 13, 1941; *ibid.,* Nov. 24, 1941; GD [6], No. 5, Oct. 19, 1941.
297. LS 1–7; GD [63], Jan. 1, 1942.

298. Werth, p. 73.   300. Fadeev, p. 17.
299. LS 3, 4.   301. Dymshits, pp. 149-60.

302. Fadeev, p. 62; Polzikova-Rubets, p. 50; Karasev, *Leningradtsy v gody blokady,* p. 157.
303. Inber, *Leningrad,* pp. 40–50.
304. Werth, p. 49.
305. LS 1, 3, 4.
306. Inber, *Leningrad,* p. 51; Karasev, *Leningradtsy v gody blokady,* pp. 216–17.

NOTES TO CHAPTER EIGHT

1. Tippelskirch, pp. 246–47; Bartz, pp. 104–5.
2. For a description of the military operations, see Anders, pp. 74–75; Tippelskirch, pp. 246–50; *BSE,* XXX (1954), 361; *LVOVSS,* I, 255.
3. Picker, p. 65.
4. Tikhonov, p. 112.
5. *Ibid.,* p. 39.
6. Saparov, pp. 99–101, 108; *Propaganda i agitatsiia,* No. 9 (May 1942), cited in *LVOVSS,* I, 162.
7. Karasev, *Leningradtsy v gody blokady,* pp. 176, 180.

8. *Ibid.*, pp. 178, 181; Saparov, pp. 109, 116.

9. Karasev, *Leningradtsy v gody blokady*, p. 181; Saparov, pp. 116–21, 140–45.

10. Khudiakova, pp. 79–81.

11. Saparov, p. 178.

12. *Frontovoi dorozhnik*, Jan. 19, 1942, cited in *LVOVSS*, I, 119.

13. Karasev, *Leningradtsy v gody blokady*, p. 178.

14. Saparov, pp. 105–7; Karasev, *Leningradtsy v gody blokady*, pp. 181–82.

15. Saparov, p. 114; Karasev, *Leningradtsy v gody blokady*, p. 179.

16. Avvakumov, p. 207.

17. *LP*, Jan. 13, 1942, cited in *LVOVSS*, I, 118–19.

18. Saparov, pp. 107, 121; Avvakumov, p. 207; Tikhonov, p. 38.

19. *LP*, Feb. 25, 1942, cited in *LVOVSS*, I, 143; Avvakumov, p. 207.

20. *LVOVSS*, I, 142–43.

21. *LP*, Feb. 25, 1942, cited in *LVOVSS*, I, 143; and Mar. 3, 1942, cited in *LVOVSS*, I, 144.

22. Karasev, *Leningradtsy v gody blokady*, p. 183.

23. Saparov, p. 215; Sirota, "Borba," p. 148.

24. Saparov, p. 167.

25. *Ibid.*, pp. 155–62, 182.

26. GD [63], Apr. 24, 1942.

27. Khudiakova, pp. 108–9.

28. GD [56].

29. Kripton MS.

30. Saparov, pp. 101, 107–8; Fineberg, p. 38; Karasev, *Leningradtsy v gody blokady*, p. 182.

31. Saparov, pp. 85, 101, 125.

32. *LVOVSS*, I, 119–20.

33. *Ibid.*, pp. 142–43.

34. Saparov, p, 138; for another trial scene, see Dymshits, p. 264.

35. Saparov, p. 132.

36. *Ibid.*

37. *Ibid.*, p. 133.

38. Werth, pp. 74, 81, 114; Kripton, *Osada Leningrada*, p. 208; GD [82].

39. *LVOVSS*, I, 119.

40. Inber, *Leningrad*, p. 48.

41. LS 3, 4; Kripton, *Osada Leningrada*, p. 191; Polzikova-Rubets, p. 80; Dymshits, p. 160.

42. Kripton, *Osada Leningrada*, p. 212; Inber, *Leningrad*, p. 56; GD [63], Mar. 19, 1942.

43. GD [108]; Chakovskii, p. 74; GD [105]; GD [63], Jan. 22, 1942.

44. Dymshits, p. 161.

45. Karasev, *Leningradtsy v gody blokady*, pp. 196–97.

46. *Ibid.*, p. 83; Dymshits, p. 160.

47. *LP*, Jan. 18, 1942.

48. *LVOVSS*, I, 119.

49. LS 3, 4; GD [102]; Werth, p. 93; GD [63], Mar. 19, 1942; Khudiakova, p. 74.

50. Inber, *Leningrad*, pp. 62–63; Skomorovsky and Morris, p. 132; White, pp. 99–100; Dymshits, p. 223.

51. Dymshits, p. 224; Sirota, "Borba," p. 138.

52. GD [78].

53. *LVOVSS*, I, 119; Kripton, *Osada Leningrada*, p. 208.

54. Karasev, *Leningradtsy v gody blokady,* p. 237; Khudiakova, p. 113.
55. Karasev, *Leningradtsy v gody blokady,* p. 195; Kripton, *Osada Leningrada,* pp. 204–5; Avvakumov, p. 208; LS 1–5.
56. Karasev, *Leningradtsy v gody blokady,* p. 195; Werth, p. 21; Sirota, "Borba," p. 140.
57. Fadeev, p. 45; Sirota, "Borba," pp. 140–41.
58. Dymshits, pp. 161, 322.   60. Filippov, pp. 112–13.
59. *Ibid.,* p. 322.   61. Dymshits, p. 159.
62. Bogdanovich, XXII, 216–37; LS 3, 4; Karasev, *Leningradtsy v gody blokady,* p. 193; Polzikova-Rubets, p. 98.
63. Kripton, *Osada Leningrada,* pp. 201–2.
64. Dymshits, pp. 298–99.
65. Bogdanovich, XXII, 220–21.
66. Pavlov, p. 62.
67. Bogdanovich, XXII, 231.
68. GD [27]. See also Kripton, *Osada Leningrada,* p. 195.
69. LS 1–5; Kripton, *Osada Leningrada,* p. 203; Bogdanovich, XXII, 236; GD [102]; Petrovskaya, p. 211.
70. Bogdanovich, XXII, 237; GD [27]; GD [102]; Kripton, *Osada Leningrada,* p. 203; LS 1–5; Petrovskaya, p. 211.
71. Karasev, *Leningradtsy v gody blokady,* p. 193.
72. *Ibid.*; Sirota, "Borba," p. 139.
73. GD [120].
74. GD [105] puts the death rate at 2,000–3,000 daily; GD [102] puts the rate at 6,000 daily; Kripton, *Osada Leningrada,* p. 205, estimates it at 9,000–10,000 daily.
75. GD [60]; GD [46]; GD [102]; Kripton, *Osada Leningrada,* p. 205; LS 2, 6.
76. Karasev, *Leningradtsy v gody blokady,* p. 184; Khudiakova, p. 57.
77. GD [58]; GD [19]; Sirota, "Borba," p. 150.
78. Karasev, *Leningradtsy v gody blokady,* p. 185.
79. Lauterbach, p. 51.
80. Karasev, *Leningradtsy v gody blokady,* p. 185.
81. *Ibid.,* p. 120.
82. *Ibid.,* p. 286; Pavlov, p. 150.
83. Kniazev, p. 65.
84. LS 1–5; Werth, p. 50; Karasev, *Leningradtsy v gody blokady,* p. 184.
85. Novoselskii, pp. 2–3.
86. Werth, p. 73.
87. Komar, p. 66.
88. Sirota, "Voenno-organizatorskaia rabota," p. 31.
89. Karasev, *Leningradtsy v gody blokady,* p. 185; Dymshits, p. 256.
90. Karasev, *Leningradtsy v gody blokady,* p. 185.
91. Dymshits, p. 134.
92. Karasev, *Leningradtsy v gody blokady,* pp. 188–89.
93. Filippov, p. 230.
94. *Ibid.,* p. 228.
95. Bogdanovich, XXII, 217–19.
96. *Ibid.,* XXII, 219, 236–37; GD [107]; Werth, p. 50; Dymshits, pp. 223, 323.
97. Inber, "Leningradskii dnevnik," p. 47.

98. *Ibid.*, pp. 56–67.
99. Dymshits, pp. 137, 162, 322.
100. Kripton, *Osada Leningrada*, p. 200.
101. Karasev, *Leningradtsy v gody blokady*, p. 186.
102. Bogdanovich, XXII, 235; Werth, pp. 73, 116.
103. Bogdanovich, XXII, 231.   106. Filippov, pp. 112–13.
104. Werth, p. 50.   107. Fadeev, p. 4.
105. Bogdanovich, XXII, 217.   108. Werth, p. 131.
109. GD [32]; Karasev, *Leningradtsy v gody blokady*, p. 189.
110. Inber, *Leningrad*, p. 50.
111. GD [32]; Bogdanovich, XXII, 227; Dymshits, p. 112.
112. LS 3, 4.
113. Chakovskii, p. 86; Inber, *Leningrad*, pp. 46–59; Werth, p. 115; GD [63], Apr. 24, 1942.
114. Karasev, *Leningradtsy v gody blokady*, p. 189.
115. GD [20]; Petrovskaya, p. 225.
116. Karasev, *Leningradtsy v gody blokady*, pp. 198–99.
117. *Biulleten*, Nos. 3–4, Feb. 27, 1942, cited in *LVOVSS*, I, 127–28.
118. Kripton, *Osada Leningrada*, p. 209; LS 1–4.
119. Skomorovsky and Morris, p. 19.
120. Werth, p. 21.
121. Karasev, *Leningradtsy v gody blokady*, pp. 190–91; Sirota, "Borba," p. 152.
122. *Propaganda i agitatsiia*, No. 20 (October 1942), cited in *LVOVSS*, I, 241.
123. Sirota, "Borba," pp. 150–51; Likhomanov, p. 22.
124. Sirota, "Voenno-organizatorskaia rabota," p. 26.
125. LS 3, 4.
126. *LP*, Feb. 3, 1942, cited in *LVOVSS*, I, 133.
127. Karasev, *Leningradtsy v gody blokady*, p. 192.
128. *LP*, Feb. 10, 1942, cited in *LVOVSS*, I, 139.
129. Karasev, *Leningradtsy v gody blokady*, p. 192.
130. Chakovskii, pp. 194–243; Fadeev, p. 52.
131. Fadeev, p. 52.
132. *LP*, Oct. 13, 1942, cited in *LVOVSS*, I, 214.
133. Inber, *Leningrad*, pp. 53, 61, 71.
134. Polzikova-Rubets, pp. 100–101; Dymshits, pp. 307–9.
135. *LVOVSS*, I, 127.
136. Werth, p. 88; Fadeev, p. 16; Karasev, *Leningradtsy v gody blokady*, pp. 212, 279.
137. *Partiinoe stroitelstvo*, Nos. 9–10 (May 1945), cited in *LVOVSS*, II, 10.
138. *Propaganda i agitatsiia*, No. 20 (October 1942), cited in *LVOVSS*, I, 230.
139. LS 2; Skomorovsky and Morris, p. 32.
140. *LP*, Feb. 6, 1942, cited in *LVOVSS*, I, 136.
141. *Pravda*, Mar. 3, 1944.
142. Karasev, *Leningradtsy v gody blokady*, p. 213.
143. *BSE*, IX (1951), 44.
144. Chakovskii, p. 102; White, p. 99.
145. Inber, *Leningrad*, p. 61.

146. Inber, "Leningradskii dnevnik," p. 188.
147. Ketlinskaia, p. 509.
148. Kripton, *Osada Leningrada,* p. 192.
149. GD [31].
150. *LVOVSS,* I, 346–47.
151. GD [63], Jan. 1, 1942; *ibid.,* Jan. 14, 1942.
152. Sirota, "Borba," p. 148.
153. Sirota, "Voenno-organizatorskaia rabota," p. 29; GD [106]; GD [63], Jan. 22, 1942; GD [103].
154. Karasev, *Leningradtsy v gody blokady,* p. 219.
155. *LVOVSS,* I, 128.
156. Karasev, *Leningradtsy v gody blokady,* p. 214.
157. Werth, p. 114.
158. *Ibid.;* GD [54]; Komar, p. 65; GD [63], Jan. 22, 1942; Lauterbach, p. 66; Karasev, *Leningradtsy v gody blokady,* p. 214; Dymshits, pp. 159–61.
159. *Partiinoe stroitelstvo,* No. 13 (1942), cited in *LVOVSS,* I, 195.
160. Dymshits, pp. 159–61.
161. Komar, p. 69.
162. GD [11], Jan. 2, 1942.
163. *Ibid.,* Jan. 9, 1942; *ibid.,* Jan. 11, 1942.
164. Karasev, *Leningradtsy v gody blokady,* p. 124.
165. Saparov, p. 119.
166. Dymshits, pp. 157, 159, 161.
167. Komar, pp. 22, 67.
168. Gibbons, pp. 16–19; Ketlinskaia, pp. 529–31; GD [61]; Werth, p. 115; Karasev, *Leningradtsy v gody blokady,* p. 195.
169. Ketlinskaia, pp. 572–73.
170. *Propaganda i agitatsiia,* Nos. 3–4 (February 1942), cited in *LVOVSS,* I, 131.
171. *LP,* Feb. 6, 1942, cited in *LVOVSS,* I, 135–36; Karasev, *Leningradtsy v gody blokady,* p. 215.
172. GD [11], Jan. 17, 1942.
173. Werth, pp. 71, 113; GD [11], Dec. 20, 1941.
174. Karasev, *Leningradtsy v gody blokady,* p. 200.
175. *Ibid.,* p. 199.
176. GD [118].
177. Kripton, *Osada Leningrada,* p. 212; Karasev, *Leningradtsy v gody blokady,* p. 199; LS 3, 4; Pavlov, p. 150.
178. Karasev, *Leningradtsy v gody blokady,* p. 200.
179. Saparov, pp. 147–50; Skomorovsky and Morris, p. 55; LS 2–4.
180. GD [70]; LS 2–5.
181. Skomorovsky and Morris, p. 56; LS 2–5.
182. GD [11], Jan. 7, 1942.
183. LS 5.
184. Kripton, *Osada Leningrada,* p. 215.
185. Dymshits, pp. 161–63.
186. LS 5.
187. Kripton, *Osada Leningrada,* p. 218; Bogdanovich, XXII, 238; LS 5.
188. GD [108].
189. Pavlov, p. 150.
190. LS 3, 4; Bogdanovich, XXII, 225; Fadeev, p. 26.

191. *LP*, Jan. 13, 1942, cited in *LVOVSS*, I, 119.
192. *LVOVSS*, I, 128.
193. *LP*, Feb. 10, 1942, cited in *LVOVSS*, I, 138–39.
194. Dymshits, p. 175; GD [121].
195. Kripton, *Osada Leningrada*, p. 197; GD [35].
196. Bogdanovich, XXII, 225.
197. LS 3, 4.
198. *Propaganda i agitatsiia*, Nos. 23–24 (1942), cited in *LVOVSS*, I, 278.
199. *Ibid.*
200. *Ibid.*
201. Karasev, *Leningradtsy v gody blokady*, p. 204.
202. *Pravda*, Dec. 10, 12, 13, 1941; *LP*, Dec. 10, 1941, through March 1942; Dymshits, p. 159.
203. GD [13]; *Pravda*, Dec. 14, 1941.
204. *LP*, Dec. 21, 1941, cited in *LVOVSS*, I, 111–12; *Pravda*, Dec. 22–27, 1941.
205. *LP*, Feb. 23, 1942, cited in *LVOVSS*, I, 139–42.
206. *Ibid.*, p. 142.
207. *Ibid.*
208. LS 3.
209. LS 3, 4; Kripton, *Osada Leningrada*, p. 212; GD [63], Mar. 19, 1942.
210. LS 3.
211. Dymshits, pp. 159, 161.
212. LS 3, 4; Polzikova-Rubets, p. 89.
213. GD [102]; Kripton, *Osada Leningrada*, p. 212.
214. Werth, p. 81; *LP*, Dec. 27, 1941, cited in *LVOVSS*, I, 116–17.
215. *Pravda*, Jan. 7, 1942.
216. *Ibid.*, Feb. 5, 1942.
217. *LP*, Dec. 11, 1941, cited in *LVOVSS*, I, 11.
218. *Ibid.*, Jan. 14, 1942, cited in *LVOVSS*, I, 111, and Jan. 16, 1942, cited in *LVOVSS*, I, 122.
219. *Ibid.*, Jan. 16, 1942, cited in *LVOVSS*, I, 122.
220. Inber, *Leningrad*, pp. 86–88.
221. *LP*, Jan. 13, 1942, cited in *LVOVSS*, I, 118.
222. *Propaganda i agitatsiia*, Nos. 23–24 (1942), cited in *LVOVSS*, I, 278.
223. Polzikova-Rubets, pp. 84–92.
224. Gruzdev, p. 12.
225. Inber, *Leningrad*, pp. 80–81.
226. *Ibid.*, p. 82; Fadeev, p. 38; Bogdanovich, XXII, 215.
227. GD [11], Jan. 7, 1942; GD [44]; Dymshits, pp. 134–37.
228. Inber, *Leningrad*, pp. 50–51, 52, 61f.
229. *Partiinoe stroitelstvo*, No. 13 (1942), cited in *LVOVSS*, I, 192.
230. *LP*, Feb. 27, 1942.
231. GD [11], Dec. 9, 1941.
232. *Partiinoe stroitelstvo*, No. 13 (1942), cited in *LVOVSS*, I, 191.
233. Sirota, "Voenno-organizatorskaia rabota," p. 31; Karasev, *Leningradtsy v gody blokady*, p. 204.
234. GD [20].
235. Dymshits, pp. 134, 137, 163.

236. GD [102].
237. GD [63], Jan. 22, 1942; GD [32].
238. GD [32].
239. GD [63], Jan. 22, 1942; GD [61].
240. Kripton, *Osada Leningrada*, p. 198.
241. *Ibid.*, p. 200.   245. LS 2.
242. Dymshits, p. 136.   246. Bogdanovich, XXII, 235.
243. LS 3.   247. GD [19].
244. Bogdanovich, XXII, 226.   248. Bogdanovich, XXII, 226.
249. *Ibid.*, 228–34; LS 3, 4; Dymshits, pp. 135–37.
250. LS 3, 4; Filippov, p. 113; Werth, p. 22.

NOTES TO CHAPTER NINE

1. Blau, p. 121.
2. Greiner, p. 405; Manstein, pp. 290–94.
3. For the history of the 1942 military operations, see Manstein, pp. 293–300; Greiner, pp. 407–13; *LP*, June 22, 1943, cited in *LVOVSS*, I, 339; Tippelskirch, p. 290; Zhilin, p. 156; Kardel, pp. 38–56.
4. Vasilev, p. 26.
5. *Ibid.*, pp. 26–28; Karasev, *Leningradtsy v gody blokady*, pp. 272–74; Tippelskirch, p. 329; Zhilin, p. 222; Iarkhunov, *passim*.
6. Fadeev, pp. 9–10, 21.
7. GD [121]; GD [23].
8. GD [53]; GD [26]; GD [97].
9. Skomorovsky and Morris, p. 117.
10. *Ibid.*
11. Polzikova-Rubets, p. 108.
12. *LP*, Mar. 5, 1942.
13. Karasev, *Leningradtsy v gody blokady*, pp. 237–38; Khudiakova, p. 114.
14. Avvakumov, p. 209; P. Popkov, "Leningrad v dni Otechestvennoi Voiny," *Propaganda i agitatsiia*, No. 220 (October 1942), cited in *LVOVSS*, I, 236; Sirota, "Borba," p. 141.
15. Karasev, *Leningradtsy v gody blokady*, p. 238.
16. *Ibid.*, p. 239; Polzikova-Rubets, p. 113; *LP*, May 5, 1942.
17. Werth, p. 162.
18. *LP*, Mar. 28, 1942, cited in *LVOVSS*, I, 154–55.
19. Karasev, *Leningradtsy v gody blokady*, p. 240.
20. Fineberg, p. 66; Polzikova-Rubets, p. 124.
21. Polzikova-Rubets, pp. 120–21.
22. *Propaganda i agitatsiia*, No. 20 (October 1942), cited in *LVOVSS*, I, 237; Avvakumov, p. 209.
23. *Pravda*, Mar. 20, 1944; Karasev, *Leningradtsy v gody blokady*, p. 245.
24. Sirota, "Borba," p. 141.   26. Dymshits, pp. 140, 351.
25. Inber, *Leningrad*, p. 139.   27. Inber, *Leningrad*, p. 139.
28. *LP*, Dec. 31, 1942, cited in *LVOVSS*, I, 285.
29. Fadeev, p. 25.
30. Polzikova-Rubets, pp. 113–38; Karasev, *Leningradtsy v gody blokady*, p. 243.

31. Karasev, *Leningradtsy v gody blokady*, p. 245.

32. Polzikova-Rubets, pp. 130–31, 138.

33. *Biulleten*, No. 19 (1942) cited in *Sbornik ukazov*, p. 104; Polzikova-Rubets, p. 122; Komar, p. 68.

34. Polzikova-Rubets, p. 111.

35. Werth, p. 17.

36. Fadeev, p. 25; GD [63], Apr. 24, 1942; GD [51]; GD [26].

37. Fadeev, p. 25; GD [63], Apr. 24, 1942; GD [51]; GD [23]; GD [26].

38. Polzikova-Rubets, p. 141.

39. Fadeev, pp. 24–25; Polzikova-Rubets, pp. 125, 129–31; Werth, p. 164; *LP*, May 31, 1942.

40. Karasev, *Leningradtsy v gody blokady*, p. 236.

41. Fischer, p. 189.   43. *Ibid.*, pp. 18–19.

42. Fadeev, pp. 45–46.   44. Inber, *Leningrad*, p. 101.

45. *Ibid.*, p. 109; GD [49]; GD [33]; LS 2.

46. *LP*, Mar. 4, 1942.   48. Sirota, "Borba," p. 152.

47. Werth, p. 162.   49. GD [24]; Saparov, p. 187.

50. Saparov, pp. 189–211.

51. *Ibid.*, pp. 221–32; Karasev, *Leningradtsy v gody blokady*, pp. 255–56.

52. Khudiakova, p. 116.

53. Saparov, pp. 221–32; GD [97]; "Severozapadnyi vodnik" Nov. 19, 1942, cited in *LVOVSS*, I, 363.

54. Karasev, *Leningradtsy v gody blokady*, p. 256; Saparov, p. 277.

55. Saparov, pp. 309–24; Tikhonov, p. 83; Ryzhak, "Rol zheleznykh dorog v sovremennoi voine," *Krasnaia zvezda*, Sept. 9, 1945; Dymshits, pp. 440–41.

56. Khudiakova, p. 122.

57. Karasev, *Leningradtsy v gody blokady*, p. 256; Khudiakova, p. 121.

58. *LVOVSS*, I, 238, 293, 323.

59. *Prapaganda i agitatsiia*, No. 20 (October 1942), cited in *LVOVSS*, I, 237.

60. Fadeev, pp. 16–17; Werth, p. 55.

61. *LP*, Dec. 12, 1941, cited in *LVOVSS*, I, 114.

62. Sirota, "Borba," p. 150.

63. *LVOVSS*, I, 150; Karasev, *Leningradtsy v gody blokady*, p. 226; Likhomanov, p. 25; Dymshits, pp. 139, 321–22.

64. *LP*, Mar. 26, 1942, cited in *LVOVSS*, I, 151.

65. *Biulleten*, Nos. 5–6 (1942), cited in *LVOVSS*, I, 149–50.

66. *Ibid.*, p. 150.

67. *LP*, May 29, 1942.

68. *Ibid.*, Mar. 26, 1942, cited in *LVOVSS*, I, 151.

69. Inber, *Leningrad*, p. 102.

70. *Propaganda i agitatsiia*, Nos. 23–24 (1942), cited in *LVOVSS*, I, 279.

71. *LP*, Mar. 26, 1942, cited in *LVOVSS*, I, 151.

72. Karasev, *Leningradtsy v gody blokady*, p. 227.

73. Polzikova-Rubets, p. 103; *LP*, Mar. 3, 1942; Sirota, "Borba," p. 152.

74. *LP*, Apr. 17, 1942, cited in *LVOVSS*, I, 153; Dymshits, p. 140.

75. Dymshits, p. 140.

76. *LP*, Apr. 17, 1942, cited in *LVOVSS*, I, 153.

77. Fadeev, p. 7.

78. *LP,* Apr. 9, 1942, cited in *LVOVSS,* I, 151.

79. *Ibid.,* p. 152

80. *Ibid.,* Apr. 17, 1942, cited in *LVOVSS,* I, 152–53.

81. Dymshits, p. 140.

82. Fadeev, p. 11.

83. Karasev, *Leningradtsy v gody blokady,* p. 257.

84. *LP,* Nov. 24, 1942, cited in *LVOVSS,* I, 373; Werth, p. 161.

85. *Ibid.,* July 14, 1942, cited in *LVOVSS,* I, 197.

86. *Ibid.,* Aug. 26, 1942, cited in *LVOVSS,* I, 208.

87. *Ibid.,* Sept. 1, 1942, cited in *LVOVSS,* I, 210; and Jan. 1, 1943, cited in *LVOVSS,* I, 243.

88. *Ibid.,* Aug. 26, 1942, cited in *LVOVSS,* I, 208.

89. *Ibid.*

90. *Ibid.*

91. Sirota, "Borba," p. 127.

92. *LP,* Sept. 1, 1942, cited in *LVOVSS,* I, 210; and Aug. 26, 1942, cited in *LVOVSS,* I, 208.

93. *LVOVSS,* I, 281.

94. *LP,* Aug. 11, 1942, cited in *LVOVSS,* I, 204; Aug. 12, 1942, cited in *LVOVSS,* I, 206; and Aug. 17, 1942, cited in *LVOVSS,* I, 207; Avvakumov, p. 217; Tikhonov, p. 66.

95. Polzikova-Rubets, pp. 153–54; Werth, p. 162.

96. Tikhonov, p. 49.

97. *LP,* Aug. 11, 1942, cited in *LVOVSS,* I, 204–6.

98. *Ibid.,* p. 204.

99. *Ibid.,* Aug. 12, 1942, cited in *LVOVSS,* I, 206.

100. *Ibid.,* Aug. 18, 1942, cited in *LVOVSS,* I, 207; Likhomanov, pp. 35–37.

101. *Ibid.,* Oct. 13, 1942, cited in *LVOVSS,* I, 212–13; and Oct. 30, 1942, cited in *LVOVSS,* I, 217; Avvakumov, p. 217; *Propaganda i agitatsiia,* No. 20 (October 1942), cited in *LVOVSS,* I, 238.

102. *Biulleten,* No. 23 (1942), cited in *Sbornik ukazov,* p. 120.

103. *LP,* Sept. 24, 1942, cited in *LVOVSS,* I, 211.

104. *Ibid.,* Jan. 1, 1943, cited in *LVOVSS,* I, 289.

105. *Ibid.,* May 1, 1943, cited in *LVOVSS,* I, 324.

106. *LVOVSS,* I, 168.

107. Inber, *Leningrad,* p. 125; Avvakumov, p. 209; Karasev, *Leningradtsy v gody blokady,* p. 254.

108. *LP,* June 3, 1942, cited in *LVOVSS,* I, 168.

109. *Ibid.*

110. *Ibid.,* June 7, 1942, cited in *LVOVSS,* I, 171.

111. Inber, *Leningrad,* pp. 125–27; Fadeev, p. 26; Karasev, *Leningradtsy v gody blokady,* p. 249.

112. Polzikova-Rubets, pp. 132–33; GD [96].

113. GD [84].

114. Karasev, *Leningradtsy v gody blokady,* p. 250.

115. Sirota, "Voenno-organizatorskaia rabota," p. 25.

116. *LP,* July 23, 1942, cited in *LVOVSS,* I, 198; and Aug. 7, 1942, cited in *LVOVSS,* I, 202–3.

117. Karasev, *Leningradtsy v gody blokady,* pp. 249, 251.

118. Komar, pp. 67–68.

119. GD [63], Apr. 24, 1942; GD [48]; *LVOVSS*, I, 253; Dymshits, p. 351.

120. *LP*, July 25, 1942, cited in *LVOVSS*, I, 199.

121. *LVOVSS*, I, 249.

122. Karasev, *Leningradtsy v gody blokady*, p. 252.

123. Komar, pp. 67–68; GD [96].

124. *LP*, Apr. 9, 1942, cited in *LVOVSS*, I, 152.

125. Karasev, *Leningradtsy v gody blokady*, p. 253.

126. *Ibid.*, p. 252.

127. "Order of the Chief of the Leningrad PVO No. 6," *LP*, Aug. 27, 1942, cited in *Sbornik ukazov*, pp. 39–40.

128. Karasev, *Leningradtsy v gody blokady*, p. 252.

129. *Ibid.*, p. 253.

130. Werth, *passim;* Fadeev, pp. 22, 24.

131. *Sbornik ukazov*, p. 40.

132. Werth, p. 114; Saparov, p. 257.

133. Inber, *Leningrad*, 201.

134. Karasev, *Leningradtsy v gody blokady*, p. 229. The Germans estimated that fifteen to twenty were in operation in March and April. GD [58]; GD [63], Apr. 24, 1942; GD [21].

135. GD [21]; GD [52]; GD [63], Apr. 24, 1942; GD [26].

136. Kniazev, p. 64.

137. GD [52]; GD [26].

138. Fadeev, pp. 81–82; Chakovskii, p. 438; *Propaganda i agitatsiia*, No. 20 (October 1942), cited in *LVOVSS*, I, 231; GD [115].

139. Fineberg, p. 20.   141. Werth, p. 116.

140. Kniazev, p. 64.   142. Kniazev, pp. 59–64.

143. *LP*, May 24, 1942, cited in *LVOVSS*, I, 167.

144. *Pravda*, June 24, 1943, cited in *LVOVSS*, I, 342.

145. Komar, p. 69; Karasev, *Leningradtsy v gody blokady*, p. 276.

146. Komar, p. 69. For other plants, see Inber, *Leningrad*, p. 225; *Propaganda i agitatsiia*, No. 20 (October 1942), cited in *LVOVSS*, I, 230; *LP*, Dec. 31, 1942, cited in *LVOVSS*, I, 284.

147. Werth, p. 109.

148. GD [74]; Saparov, pp. 280–282; Werth, pp. 60–61.

149. Meisel and Kozera, p. 369.

150. "Decree of the Presidium of the Supreme Soviet of October 10, 1942," *Sbornik ukazov*, p. 97.

151. Saparov, pp. 264–65, 280.

152. "Decision of the Council of People's Commissars of November 4, 1942, No. 1768," cited in *Sbornik ukazov*, pp. 95–96.

153. Karasev, *Leningradtsy v gody blokady*, p. 229.

154. GD [115]; Karasev, *Leningradtsy v gody blokady*, p. 230; Dymshits, pp. 354–55.

155. *Sbornik ukazov*, p. 103.

156. GD [52].

157. Fischer, p. 189.

158. Karasev, *Leningradtsy v gody blokady*, p. 237.

159. *Propaganda i agitatsiia*, No. 20 (October 1942), cited in *LVOVSS*, I, 238.

160. *LP*, May 24, 1942, cited in *LVOVSS*, I, 167.

161. Avvakumov, p. 210.
162. *LP*, May 23, 1942, cited in *LVOVSS*, I, 165; *Propaganda i agitatsiia*, No. 18 (September 1942), cited in *LVOVSS*, I, 222.
163. *Propaganda i agitatsiia*, Nos. 23–24 (1942), cited in *LVOVSS*, I, 277.
164. Saparov, pp. 268–69; Karasev, *Leningradtsy v gody blokady*, p. 231.
165. *LP*, May 24, 1942, cited in *LVOVSS*, I, 167.
166. Saparov, pp. 265, 315.
167. Werth, p. 121.
168. *Partiinoe stroitelstvo*, No. 13, (1942), cited in *LVOVSS*, I, 195.
169. Karasev, *Leningradtsy v gody blokady*, p. 232.
170. *Propaganda i agitatsiia*, No. 18 (September 1942), cited in *LVOVSS* I, 221–22; *Partiinoe stroitelstvo*, No. 13 (1942), cited in *LVOVSS*, I, 195; *LP*, Nov. 24, 1942, cited in *LVOVSS*, I, 373.
171. Sirota, "Borba," p. 149.
172. The material in this paragraph has been taken from Karasev, *Leningradtsy v gody blokady*, pp. 199–200, 254–57, 280; Likhomanov, pp. 37–38.
173. Sirota, "Borba," p. 153; Karasev, *Leningradtsy v gody blokady*, p. 286.
174. *LVOVSS*, I, 256.
175. Karasev, *Leningradtsy v gody blokady*, pp 257–58.
176. Khudiakova, p. 120.
177. Werth, p. 113.
178. Karasev, *Leningradtsy v gody blokady*, p. 257.
179. Saparov, pp. 257–58; Khudiakova, pp. 120–21.
180. Likhomanov, p. 38.
181. *Sbornik ukazov*, pp. 34–35.
182. Karasev, *Leningradtsy v gody blokady*, p. 262.
183. Polzikova-Rubets, pp. 116–17.
184. *Ibid.*, p. 122.
185. *Ibid.*, p. 117; Werth, *passim;* Karasev, *Leningradtsy v gody blokady,* pp. 239, 263.
186. *LVOVSS*, I, 255, 397; *Propaganda i agitatsiia*, No. 20 (October 1942), cited in *LVOVSS*, I, 367–72.
187. *LP*, May 2, 1942, and Oct. 18, 1942, cited in *LVOVSS*, I, 156–57, 225; Avvakumov, p. 196.
188. *LP*, July 11, Aug. 22, Dec. 10, 24, 1942, cited in *LVOVSS*, I, 196, 219, 280, 281–82.
189. Avvakumov, p. 226.
190. Polzikova-Rubets, pp. 104–6, 160; *LP*, Jan. 7, 1943, cited in *LVOVSS*, I, 295–96.
191. Fadeev, pp. 33–34.
192. *LP*, June 20, 1942, cited in *LVOVSS*, I, 171–72.
193. Karasev, *Leningradtsy v gody blokady*, p. 263.
194. *Propaganda i agitatsiia*. No. 20 (October 1942), cited in *LVOVSS*, I, 238; Avvakumov, p. 226; *LP*, May 2, 1942, cited in *LVOVSS*, I, 157; Fadeev, p. 20.
195. Inber, *Leningrad*, p. 139; Tikhonov, pp. 23–24.
196. Werth, *passim*.
197. GD [121]; Dymshits, p. 177.

198. GD [96]; Polzikova-Rubets, p. 167; GD [50]; GD [63], Nov. 30, 1942.

199. Decision of the *Sovnarkom* of the USSR of June 26, 1942, cited in *Sbornik ukazov*, pp. 99–102; Decision of the *Ispolkom* of the City of Leningrad of March 17, 1943, *Biulleten Lengorsoveta*, No. 7–8 (1943), cited in *ibid.*, pp. 98–99.

200. GD [73]; Kripton, *Osada Leningrada*, p. 217.

201. *Propaganda i agitatsiia*, No, 14 (1942), cited in *LVOVSS*, I, 188.

202. *Ibid.*

203. *LP*, Jan. 1, 1943, cited in *LVOVSS*, I, 289.

204. Karasev, "Vozrozhdenie goroda-geroia," p. 120.

205. Karasev, *Leningradtsy v gody blokady*, pp. 263, 280; Karasev, "Vozrozhdenie," p. 120.

206. Inber, *Leningrad*, pp. 110–17, 129–37, 226.

207. *Sbornik ukazov*, pp. 99–102.

208. *Biulleten Lengorsoveta*, No. 7–8, cited in *Sbornik ukazov*, pp. 98–99.

209. Inber, *Leningrad*, pp. 101, 117.

210. White, p. 108

211. Fadeev, p. 14; GD [63], Apr. 25, 1942.

212. *Pravda*, Mar. 1–June 1, 1942, *passim*.

213. Inber, *Leningrad*, pp. 225–26.   215. Werth, p. 70.

214. GD [52].   216. LS 2–4, 6.

217. *LP*, May 23, 1942, cited in *LVOVSS*, I, 166.

218. Werth, pp. 61, 120.

219. Karasev, *Leningradtsy v gody blokady*, pp. 272–75; Dymshits, pp. 439–41.

220. GD [109].

221. Karasev, *Leningradtsy v gody blokady*, p. 286; Werth, p. 164.

222. Werth, p. 87; GD [109].

223. Werth, p. 161.

224. Karasev, *Leningradtsy v gody blokady*, pp. 279–80, 300.

225. *Ibid.*, p 297.

226. *Ibid.*, p. 309.

BIBLIOGRAPHY

American Council of Learned Societies. Gosudarstvennyi plan razvitiia narod-nogo khoziastva SSSR na 1941 god. Baltimore, Md.: Universal Lithographers, no date.

Anders, Gen. Wladyslaw. Hitler's Defeat in Russia. Chicago: Henry Regnery Co., 1953.

Anderson, Albin T. "Origins of the Winter War: A Study of Russo-Finnish Relations," World Politics, VI, No. 2, January 1954.

The Anti-Stalin Campaign and International Communism, comp. Russian Institute, Columbia University. New York: Columbia University Press, 1956.

Assmann, Kurt. Deutsche Schicksalsjahre. Wiesbaden, Germany: Eberhard Brockhaus, 1950.

Astakhov, F. A. "The Soviet Air Force," Sloviane, No. 8, August 1947.

Atlas offitsera. Moscow: Glavnaia Topograficheskaia Administratsiia, 1947.

Avvakumov, S. I. (ed.) Geroicheskii Leningrad, 1917–1942. Leningrad: Ogiz. Gospolitizdat, 1943.

———. Leningrad v Velikoi Otechestvennoi Voine Sovetskogo Soiuza (LV-OVSS). I, II, June 22, 1941, to March 24, 1944. Leningrad: Ogiz. Gospolitizdat, 1944.

Bartz, Karl. Als der Himmel Brannte. Hannover, Germany: Adolf Sponholtz Verlag, 1955.

Beliaev, S., and P. Kuznetsov. Narodnoe opolchenie Leningrada. Leningrad: Lenizdat, 1959.

Beltiugov, Col. V. G. "Proryv blokady Leningrada," Vazhneishie operatsii Velikoi Otechestvennoi Voiny, 1941–1945, ed. P. A. Zhilin. Moscow: Voennoe Izdatelstvo Ministerstva Oborony SSSR, 1956.

Biehl, Max. "Binnenwanderung in der Sowjetunion," Zeitschrift für Geo-Politike, No. 11, November 1954.

Biulleten Leningradskogo Soveta Deputatov Trudiashchikhsia. Leningrad, 1941–42.

Blau, George E. The German Campaign in Russia: Planning and Operations, 1940–1942. Dept. of the Army Pamphlet No. 20-261a, Washington, D. C., March 1955.

Bogdanovich, A. "Ia-grazhdanin Leningrada," Novyi zhurnal (New York), XXI, XXII, 1949.

Bolshaia sovetskaia entsiklopediia, 2d ed. (Moscow), 1950–58.

Bor, Peter. Gespräche mit Halder. Wiesbaden, Germany: Limes Verlag, 1950.

Buxa, Werner. Weg und Schicksal der 11 Infanterie Division. Kiel, Germany: Verlag Hans-Henning Podzun, 1952.
Castro Delgado, Enrique. J'ai perdu la foi à Moscou. Paris: Gallimard, 1950.
Chakovskii, Aleksandr. Eto bylo v Leningrade. Moscow: Sovetskii Pisatel, 1953.
Cherniavskii, U. G. "Obespechenie gorodov prodovolstviem v gody Velikoi Otechestvennoi Voiny," *Istoriia SSSR*, No. 4, 1959.
Civil Defense in Western Europe and the Soviet Union (U.S. Congress, Committee on Government Operations, Fifth Report). Washington, D.C.: Government Printing Office, 1959.
Dallin, David J. "Reorganizatsiia Krasnoi Armii," *Sotsialisticheskii Vestnik*, No. 4, February 25, 1941.
————. Soviet Espionage. New Haven, Conn.: Yale University Press, 1955.
Degras, Jane (ed.). Documents on Soviet Foreign Policy. III. London: Oxford University Press, 1953.
Dinerstein, Herbert S., and Leon Goure. Two Studies in Soviet Controls. Glencoe, Ill.: The Free Press, 1955.
Documents on German Foreign Policy. Ser. D, V. Washington, D. C.: Government Printing Office, 1953.
Dymshits, A., et al. (eds.) Podvig Leningrada, dokumentalno-khudozhestvennyi sbornik. Moscow: Voennoe Izdatelstvo Ministerstva Oborny SSSR, 1960.
Encyclopædia Britannica, XIII (1958), "Leningrad."
Erfurth, Waldemar. Der Finnische Krieg, 1941–1944. Wiesbaden, Germany: Limes Verlag, 1950.
Ershov, Lt. Col. V. "Rabota NKVD v gospitaliakh vo vremia voiny," *Novyi zhurnal*, XXXVII, 1954.
Fadeev, A. Leningrad v dni blokady. Moscow: Sovetskii Pisatel, 1944.
Fainsod, Merle. How Russia Is Ruled. Cambridge, Mass.: Harvard University Press, 1953.
Filippov, B. "Petrograd-Leningrad," *Grani*, No. 10, 1950.
Fineberg, J. (ed.). Heroic Leningrad. Moscow: Foreign Languages Publishing House, 1945.
The Finnish Blue Book. New York: J. B. Lippincott Co., 1940.
Fischer, Louis (ed.). Thirteen Who Fled. New York: Harper and Brothers, 1949.
Garthoff, Raymond L. Soviet Military Doctrine. Glencoe, Ill.: The Free Press, 1953.
Gibbons, John. The Epic of Leningrad. London: Daily Worker League, 1944.
Goerlitz, Walter. History of the German General Staff, 1657–1945. New York: Frederick A. Praeger, 1953.
Golikov, S. Vydaiushchiesia pobedy sovetskoi armii v Velikoi Otechestvennoi Voine. Leningrad: Gospolitizdat, 1954.
Govorov, Leonid Alexandrovich. V boiakh za gorod Lenina. Leningrad: Voenizdat Narodnogo Komissariata Oborony, 1945.
Grechaniuk, N., V. Dmitriev, F. Krinitsyn, and Iu. Chernov. Baltiiskii Flot. Moscow: Voennoe Izdatelstvo Ministerstva Oborony SSSR, 1960.
Greiner, Helmuth. Die Oberste Wehrmacht Führung, 1939–1943. Wiesbaden, Germany: Limes Verlag, 1951.
Gruzdev, Ilia Aleksandrovich. Rodnaia zemlia. Leningrad: Leningradskoe Gazetno-zhurnalnoe i Knizhnoe Izdatelstvo, 1944.

Halder, Franz. Diary, IV, VI, VIII (manuscript in the possession of the author).

——. Hitler als Feldherr. Munich: Münchener Dom Verlag, 1949.

Hilger, Gustav, and Alfred G. Meyer. The Incompatible Allies. New York: The Macmillan Co., 1953.

Hubatsch, Walter. 61. Infanterie-Division. Kiel, Germany: Verlag Hans-Henning Podzun, 1952.

Iarkhunov, V. M. Cherez Nevu. Moscow: Voennoe Izdatelstvo Ministerstva Oborony SSSR, 1960.

Inber, Vera. "Leningradskii dnevnik," *Deviatsot dnei,* 1948.

——. Le Siège de Leningrad. Translated from Russian by Doussia Ergaz. Paris: Albin Michel, 1946.

Kalmykov, V. A. (ed.) Oni srazhalis za Leningrad. Leningrad: Leningradskoe Gazetno-zhurnalnoe i Knizhnoe Izdatelstvo, 1946.

Karasev, A. V. "Dokumentalnye materialy o trudiashchikhsia Leningrada v gody blokady," *Istoricheskii arkhiv,* No. 6, November–December 1956.

——. Leningradtsy v gody blokady. Moscow: Izdatelstvo Akademii Nauk SSSR, 1959.

——. "Leningrad v period blokady, 1941–1943," *Istoriia SSSR,* No. 2, 1957.

——. "Vozrozhdenie goroda-geroia," *Istoriia SSSR,* No. 3, 1961.

Kardel, Hennecke. Die Geschichte der 170 Infanterie-Division. Bad Neuheim, Germany: Verlag Hans-Henning Podzun, 1953.

Katerli, E., V. Ketlinskaia, and A. Pazi (eds.). Leningrad, 1944. Leningrad: Leningradskoe Gazetno-zhurnalnoe i Knizhnoe Izdatelstvo, 1944.

Ketlinskaia, Vera. V osade. Moscow: Izdatelstvo IsKVLKSM "Molodaia gvardiia," 1948.

Khronologicheskoe sobranie zakonov, ukazov presidiuma verkhovnogo soveta i postanovlenii pravitelstva RSFSR 1935–1945. IV. Moscow: Gosizdat Iuridicheskoi Literatury, 1949.

Khudiakova, N. D. Vsia strana s Leningradom (1941–1943). Leningrad: Lenizdat, 1960.

Kniazev, S. P. "Kommunisty Leningrada v borbe za vostannovlenie goroda," *Voprosy istorii KPSS,* No. 1, January 1961.

Kochakov, B. M. Ocherki Istorii Leningrada 1895–1917. III. Moscow-Leningrad: Izdatelstvo Akademii Nauk SSSR, 1956.

Komar, E. G. Arsenal energovooruzheniia. Leningrad: Ogiz. Gospolitizdat, 1945.

Kripton, Konstantin. Manuscript (written at the request of the author).

——. Osada Leningrada. New York: Chekhov Publishing House, 1952.

Kuznetsov, A. A. O gazifikatsii Leningrada. Leningrad: Lenizdat, 1945.

Latvian-Russian Relations—Documents. Compiled by Dr. Alfred Bilmanis. Washington, D. C.: The Latvian Legation, 1944.

Lauterbach, Richard E. These Are the Russians. New York: Harper and Brothers, 1944–45.

Leningradskaia pravda, June 1941–January 1943.

Liddell-Hart, B. H. The German Generals Talk. New York: William Morrow and Co., 1948.

——. The Other Side of the Hill. London: Cassell and Co., Ltd., 1951.

Likhomanov, M. I. "Massovo-politicheskaia rabota Leningradskoi partiinoi organizatsii v pervyi period Velikoi Otechestvennoi Voiny," *Voprosy istorii KPSS, uchenye zapiski,* No. 289, 1960.

LVOVSS. *See* Avvakumov, Leningrad.

Mannerheim, Marshal. The Memoirs of Marshal Mannerheim. Translated by Count Eric Levenhaupt. London: Cassell and Co., Ltd., 1953.

von Manstein, Generalfeldmarschal Erich. Verlorene Siege. Bonn, Germany: Athenäum Verlag, 1955.

Markevich, N. "Ia Leningradets," in Gorod geroi. Kuibyshev: Ogiz. Kuibyshevskoe Izdatelstvo, 1942.

Meisel, James H., and Edward S. Kozera. Materials for the Study of the Soviet System. Ann Arbor, Mich.: George Wahr Publishing Co., 1950.

Mikhailov, Nicholas. Soviet Russia: The Land and Its People. New York: Sheridan House Publishers, 1948.

Muggeridge, Malcolm (ed.). Ciano's Diplomatic Papers. London: Odhams Press Ltd., 1948.

Mushnikov, A. N. Baltiitsy v boiakh za Leningrad, 1941–1944. Moscow: Voennoe Izdatelstvo Ministerstva Oborony SSSR, 1955.

New York Times, June 1941–January 1943.

Novoselskii, S. A., article in *Gigiena i sanitariia,* No. 7-8, 1946.

Odintsov, Col. Gen. G. F. "Artilleriia v boiakh za gorod Lenina," *Artilleriiskii zhurnal,* No. 11, November 1945.

O gazifikatsii Leningrada: Materialy IX sessii Leningradskogo gorodskogo Soveta Deputatov Trudiashchikhsia 18–19 July, 1945. Leningrad: Lenizdat, 1945.

Osipova, L. "Dnevnik kollaborantki," *Grani,* No. 21, 1954.

Osnovnye zakonodatelnye akty o trude rabochikh i sluzhashchikh. Moscow: Gosizdat Iuridicheskoi Literatury, 1953.

Paget, R. T. Manstein. London: William Collins, 1951.

Panfilov, A. Geroicheskii oreshek. Moscow: Voennoe Izdatelstvo Ministerstva Oborony SSSR, 1958.

Pavlov, D. V. Leningrad v blokade, 1941. Moscow, Voennoe Izdatelstvo Ministerstva Oborony SSSR, 1958.

Petrovskaya, Kyra. Kyra. Englewood Cliffs, N.J.: Prentice-Hall, Inc., 1959.

Pevzner, G. Iu. (ed.) Zashchitniki Leningradskogo neba. Leningrad: Leningradskoe Gazetno-zhurnalnoe i Knizhnoe Izdatelstvo, 1943.

Picker, Henry. Hitler's Tischgespräche, 1941–1942. Bonn, Germany: Athenäum Verlag, 1951.

Politicheskoe obespechenie velikoi pobedy pod Leningradom. Leningrad: Voenizdat Narodnogo Komissariata Oborony, 1945.

Polzikova-Rubets, Kseniia Vladimirovna. Oni uchilis v Leningrade. Leningrad: Gosizdat Detskoi Literatury, 1948.

Pospelov, P. N., *et al.* (eds.) Istoriia Velikoi Otechestvennoi Voiny Sovetskogo Soiuza, 1941–1945. Moscow, Voennoe Izdatelstvo Ministerstva Oborony SSSR, 1960.

Pravda, June 1941–January 1944.

von Raus, Erhard. "Im Tor nach Leningrad," *Wehrwissenschaftliche Rundschau,* III, March 1953.

von Reinhardt, Gen. Oberst a.D. Hans. "Der Vorstoss des XXXXI. Panzer-Korps im Sommer 1941 von Ostpreussen bis vor die Tore von Leningrad," *Wehrkunde,* III, March 1956.

von Rohwer, Jürgen. "Die Sowjetische U-Bootwaffe in der Ostsee 1941–1945," *Wehrwissenschaftliche Rundschau*, X, October 1956.

Rudel, Hans Ulrich. Stuka Pilot. Dublin: Euphorian Books, 1952.

Ryzhak, Lt. Col. S. "Rol zheleznykh dorog v sovremennoi voine," *Krasnaia zvezda*, September 9, 1945.

Saparov, A. Doroga zhizni. Leningrad: Leningradskoe Gazetno-zhurnalnoe i Knizhnoe Izdatelstvo, 1949.

Sbornik ukazov, postanovlenii, reshenii, rasporiazhenii i prikazov voennogo vremeni, 1942–1943. Leningrad, Leningradskoe Gazetno-zhurnalnoe i Knizhnoe Izdatelstvo, 1944.

Sbornik zakonov SSSR i ukazov presidiuma verkhovnogo soveta SSSR. Moscow, Gosizdat Iuridicheskoi Literatury, 1945.

———, 1938–1956. Moscow, Gosizdat Iuridicheskoi Literatury, 1956.

"Secret Speech of Khrushchev Concerning the 'Cult of the Individual,' Delivered at the Twentieth Congress of the Communist Party of the Soviet Union, February 25, 1956," in *The Anti-Stalin Campaign and International Communism*, ed. Russian Institute, Columbia University. New York: Columbia University Press, 1956.

Shabad, Theodore. Geography of the USSR. New York: Columbia University Press, 1951.

Shapiro, Leonard. Soviet Treaty Series. I, II. Washington, D.C.: Georgetown University Press, 1950, 1951.

Shcheglov, Dm. V opolchenie. Moscow: Voennoe Izdatelstvo Ministerstva Oborony SSSR, 1960.

Sheverbalkin, P. R. "Kommunisty-organizatory narodnoi vooruzhennoi borby v tylu vrazheskoi armii," *Voprosy istorii KPSS, uchenye zapiski*, No. 289, 1960.

Sinitsin, A. M. "Chresvychainye organy sovetskogo gosudarstva v gody Velikoi Otechestvennoi Voiny," *Voprosy istorii*, No. 2, 1955.

Sirota, F. I. "Borba Leningradskoi partiinoi organizatsii za sokhranenie zhizni naseleniia goroda v period blokady," *Voprosy istorii KPSS, uchenye zapiski*, No. 289, 1960.

———. "Voenno-organizatorskaia rabota Leningradskoi organizatsii VKP(b) v pervyi period Velikoi Otechestvennoi Voiny," *Voprosy istorii*, No. 10, 1956.

Sitnikova, T. A. "Kommunisty Vyborgskogo Raiona Leningrada v glave trudovogo geroizma rabochikh v period blokady goroda," *Voprosy istorii KPSS, uchenye zapiski*, No. 289, 1960.

Skomorovsky, Boris, and E. G. Morris. The Siege of Leningrad. New York: E. P. Dutton & Co., Inc., 1944.

Sontag, R. J., and J. S. Beddie (eds.). Nazi-Soviet Relations, 1939–1941. New York: Didier, 1948.

Sosnovy, Timothy. The Housing Problem in the Soviet Union. New York: Research Program on the USSR, 1954.

Stalin, J. O Velikoi Otechestvennoi Voine Sovetskogo Soiuza. Moscow: Ogiz. Gosizdat Politicheskoi Literatury, 1947.

"The Surgeons of Leningrad," *Time* Magazine, XLI, April 5, 1943.

Tanner, Väinö. The Winter War. Stanford, Calif.: Stanford University Press, 1957.

Telpukhovskii, B. S., F. S. Korotkov, A. V. Mitrifanov, and A. M. Samsonov (eds.). Ocherki istorii Velikoi Otechestvennoi Voiny 1941–1945. Moscow, Izdatelstvo Akademii Nauk SSSR, 1955.

Tikhonov, Nikolai. The Defence of Leningrad. London: Hutchinson & Co., Ltd., no date.

von Tippelskirch, Kurt. Geschichte des Zweiten Weltkriegs. Bonn, Germany: Athenäum Verlag, 1951.

Tregubov, M. "Krasnoznamennaia MPVO Leningrada," *Za Oboronu*, No. 2, 1946.

The Trial of the Major War Criminals Before the International Military Tribunal. Nuremberg, Germany, 1947–1949.

Trials of War Criminals Before the Nuremberg Military Tribunals. X, XI. Washington, D.C.: Government Printing Office, 1950, 1951.

Tur, A. F. "Rasstroistva pitaniia i drugie zabolevaniia u deteii Leningrada v 1941–1943," *Pediatriia*, No. 4, 1944.

Ugolovnyi kodeks RSFSR. Moscow: Gosizdat Iuridicheskoi Literatury, 1953.

USSR Information Bulletin, Washington, D.C., January 29, 1949.

Vasilev, Maj. Gen. A. V. Borba za Leningrad v Velikoi Otechestvennoi Voine, 1941–1945. Moscow: Izdatelstvo "Znanie," 1959.

Velikii gorod Lenina. Moscow: Ogiz. Gosudarstvennoe Izdatelstvo Khudozhestvennoi Literatury, 1942.

Vishnevskii, Vsevolod. "U sten Leningrada," *Deviatsot dnei*, 1948.

Voroshilov, K., *et al.* The Red Army Today. (Speeches Delivered at the Eighteenth Congress of the C.P.S.U.(B.), March 10–21, 1939.) Moscow: Foreign Languages Publishing House, 1939.

Voznesensky, Nikolai A. The Economy of the U.S.S.R. During World War II. Washington, D.C.: Public Affairs Press, 1948.

Werth, Alexander. Leningrad. London: Hamish Hamilton, 1944.

White, William L. Report on the Russians. New York: Harcourt, Brace & Co., 1945.

Wood, William W. Our Ally: The Russian People. New York: Charles Scribner's Sons, 1950.

Woodward, E. L., and Rohan Butler (eds.). Documents on British Foreign Policy, 1919–1939. 3d Ser., V. London: H.M. Stationery Office, 1952.

Zentner, Kurt. Nur Einmal Kannte Stalin Siegen. Hamburg: Gruner Verlag, 1952.

Zhdanova, T. A. Krepost na Neve. Moscow: Gosizdat Politicheskoi Literatury, 1960.

Zhilin, P. A. (ed.). Vazhneishie operatsii Velikoi Otechestvennoi Voiny 1941–1945. Moscow: Voennoe Izdatelstvo Ministerstva Oborony SSSR, 1956.

von Zydowitz, Kurt. Die Geschichte der 58. Infanterie-Division 1939–1945. Kiel, Germany: Verlag Hans-Henning Podzun, 1952.

GERMAN DOCUMENTS

The captured German military documents cited in the study, copies of which are in my possession, were selected from the records of various German army units and commands. Most of them were documents issued by various intelligence units of the Eighteenth Army and of its corps and divisions, while some others were issued by special economic, security, or police administrations or headquarters.

The principle of classification here is arbitrary. The documents are classified by sender, and chronologically within sender units. The senders fall into two main classifications: the Eighteenth Army and Its Components (notably the XXVI, XXVIII, and L Corps and their divisions), and Other Documents (including messages from military units not in the Eighteenth Army, from the Abwehr and the Sicherheitsdienst, and from semi-military and nonmilitary sources). The documents are referred to in the Notes by the bracketed numbers that precede them here.

THE EIGHTEENTH ARMY AND ITS COMPONENTS

18th Army HQ

[1] A.O.K. 18, Abt. Ic., "Horchergebnisse," Sept. 7, 1941, A.O.K. 18, 17562/293.

[2] —. "Funksprechverkehr," Sept. 8, 1941, A.O.K. 18, 17562/293.

[3] —. "Horchergebnisse," Sept. 9, 1941, A.O.K. 18, 17562/293.

[4] —. "Vernehmung des russischen Majors K. am 14.ix.1941," A.O.K. 18, 11562/293.

[5] —. "Lage in Petersburg," Sept. 25, 1941, A.O.K. 18, 17562/294.

[6] —. "Nachrichten über Petersburg," Nos. 1, 2, 4–7, 9, Oct. 2–Dec. 4, 1941, A.O.K. 18, 17562/294–95.

[7] —. "Abschrift eines russischen Beutebefehls, 22.ix.1941," Oct. 3, 1941, XXVI A.K., 21473/13.

[8] —. "Tagebuch eines Partisanen," Oct. 17, 1941, A.O.K. 18, 17562/294.

[9] —. "Zivilbevölkerung Petersburg," Nov. 26, 1941, A.O.K. 18, 17562/295.

[10] —. "Vernehmung," Dec. 2, 1941, A.O.K. 18, 17562/295.

[11] —. "Allgemeiner Eindruck, Moskau-Petersburg," Dec. 17, 1941–Jan. 17, 1942. 1941 dates A.O.K. 18, 17562/286; 1942 dates A.O.K. 18, 19601/109–10.

[12] —. "Aufgefangene Briefe, gesandt durch die Zensur und NKWD, 2 Spezial Abt.," Dec. 18, 1941, A.O.K. 18, 19601/3.

[13] —. "Leningradskaja Prawda–Sonderausgabe, 18.xii.1941," A.O.K. 18, 19601/118.

[14] —. "Kurzer Inhalt der Briefe über die Evakuierung von Privatpersonen," Dec. 21, 1941, A.O.K. 18, 19801/3.

[15] —. "Übersetzung eines an den Rotarmisten 2/II Batl. von seiner Frau aus Leningrad gesandten Einschreibebriefes von 28.xii.1941," A.O.K. 18, 19601/118.

[16] —. "Auszug aus dem Brief eines Leningrader Bürgers," Jan. 22, 1942, A.O.K. 18, 19601/118.

[17] —. "Tagebuchaufzeichnungen eines gefallenen Rotarmisten," Jan. 30, 1942, A.O.K. 18, 19601/119.

[18] —. "Auszüge aus Feindbriefen," Feb. 13, 1942, A.O.K. 18, 19601/118.

[19] —. "Nachstehend eine V-Mann Meldung zur Kenntnisnahme," Mar. 14, 1942, A.O.K. 18, 19601/119.

[20] —. "Übersetzung eines Briefes einer russischen Soldatenfrau," Mar. 14, 1942, A.O.K. 18, 19601/119.

[21] —. "Auszug aus 17 Lagebericht," Apr. 17, 1942, A.O.K. 18, 22864/109.

[22] —. "Zusammenstellung von Aussagen von Kriegsgefangenen," May 15, 1942, A.O.K. 18, 22864/110.

[23] —. "An Oberkommando des Heeres, Abt. Fremde Heere-Ost. I Staffel," June 19, 1942, A.O.K. 18, 22864/108.

[24] —. "An die Luftflotte 1," Aug. 1, 1942, A.O.K. 18, 20381/211.

[25] —. "Aufklärungsforderung Ost, 1942," Sept. 17, 1942, A.O.K. 18, 30281/212.

[26] —. "Vernehmung des Überläufers N... A... I...," Oct. 26, 1942, A.O.K. 18, 19601/109.

[27] —. "Bericht über das Leben in Leningrad vom Anfang des Krieges bis zum 15.i.1944," A.O.K. 18, 52614/252.

XXVI Army Corps

[28] Gen. Kdo. XXVI A.K., Abt. Ic., "Feindnachrichten von 4.x.41," Oct. 4, 1941, XXVI A.K., 21473/14.

[29] —. "Funksprechverkehr Moskau-Petersburg," Oct. 19, 1941, A.O.K. 18, 17562/282.

[30] —. "Feindnachrichtenblatt von 20.xi.41," Nov. 20, 1941, A.O.K. 18, 17562/285.

[31] —. N.A.Z. 193, "Moskau-Petersburg," Dec. 21, 1941, A.O.K. 18, 17562/286.

[32] —. "Erkundigung Petersburg," Apr. 20, 1942, XXVI A.K., 21473/13.

[33] —. "Feindnachrichtenblatt," May 23, 1942, XXVI A.K., 30142/22.

[34] Kdo. 217 I.D. Abt. Ic., "Auszüge aus Feindbriefen," Feb. 12, 1942, XXVI A. K., 21473/13.

[35] —. "Vernehmung eines Überläufers," Feb. 20, 1942, A.O.K. 18, 19601/118.

XXVIII Army Corps

[36] Gen. Kdo. XXVIII A.K., Abt. Ic., "Befehl an die Truppen der Nordwest Front No. 1," Aug. 20, 1941, XXVIII A.K., 18233/13.

[37] —. "Befehl an die Truppen der 55 Armee," Sept. 9, 1941, XXVIII A.K., 18233/1.

[38] —. "Gefechtsbefehl No. 0031 des Stabes der Leningrader Front," Sept. 11, 1941, XXVIII A.K., 18233/1.

[39] —. "Beutebefehl," Sept. 25, 1941, XXVIII A.K., 18233/1.

[40] —. "Tätigkeitsbericht III, Anlage 20," Oct. 3, 1941, XXVIII A.K., 18233/1.

[41] —. "Gefangenenaussagen," Dec. 3, 1941, A.O.K. 18, 17562/298.

[42] —. "Gefangenenvernehmungen," Dec. 3, 1941, A.O.K. 18, 17562/298.
[43] —. "Gefangenenvernehmungen," Dec. 31, 1941, XXVIII A.K., 207-06/4.
[44] —. "Vernehmung des M...," Jan. 26, 1942, XXVIII A.K., 20706/7.
[45] —. "Entwurf eines Flugblattes," Feb. 2, 1942, A.O.K. 18, 19601/118.
[46] —. "Vernehmung des Leutnant D...," Mar. 2, 1942, XXVIII A.K., 20706/5.
[47] —. "Gefangenenvernehmung der Eleonore Winterholer," Mar. 12, 1942, XXVIII A.K., 20706/7.
[48] —. "Gefangenenvernehmung," May 1, 1942, XXVIII A.K., 20706/5.
[49] —. "Vernehmung des O... A... W...," May 2, 1942, XXVIII A.K. 20706/7.
[50] —. "Vernehmung eines Gefangenen Agenten," May 2, 1942, XXVIII A.K., 20706/7.
[51] —. "Vernehmung der D... A... G...," May 3, 1942, XXVIII A.K., 20706/7.
[52] —. "Vernehmung des P... I... W...," May 23, 1942, XXVIII A.K., 25175/12.
[53] —. "Vernehmung des Kundschafters M...," Sept. 26, 1942, XXVIII A.K., 25175/11.
[54] Kdo. 1 I.D., Abt. Ic., "Aussagen eines Überläufers...," Mar. 9, 1942, XXVIII A.K., 20706/7.
[55] —. "Vernehmung einer Überläuferin in Abschnitt I/I.R. 374," Mar. 29, 1942, XXVIII A.K., 20706/5.
[56] Kdo. 227 I.D., Abt. Ic., "Beobachtungsbericht über die 'Eisstrasse' auf dem Ladoga-See," Dec. 26, 1941, A.O.K. 18, 17562/286.
[57] —. "Feindnachrichtenblatt No. 6," Mar. 5, 1942, 227 I.D., 17799/5.
[58] —. "Feindnachrichtenblatt No. 7," Mar. 27, 1942, 227 I.D., 17799/5.
[59] Kdo. 269 I.D., Abt. Ic., "Lagebericht No. 17," Sept. 15, 1941, 269 I.D., 21867/28.
[60] —. "Feindnachrichtenblatt No. 10," Mar. 2, 1942, 269 I.D., 21867/28.
[61] —. "Feindnachrichtenblatt No. 11," Mar. 8, 1942, 269 I.D., 21867/28.

L Army Corps

[62] Gen. Kdo. L A.K., Abt. Ic., "Feindnachrichtenblatt Anlage 26," Sept. 12, 1941, L A.K. 14997/4.
[63] —. "Feindnachrichtenblatt," Sept. 18, 1941–Nov. 30, 1942, L A.K., 21717/11.
[64] —. "Auswertung von in Postamt Krasnogwardeisk vorgefundenen Briefen," Sept. 23, 1941, A.O.K. 18, 17562/297.
[65] —. "Anlage zu Feindnachrichtenblatt," Oct. 2, 1941, L A.K., 21717/11.
[66] —. "Auszug aus dem Brief des Artilleristen X... 48 Artl. Regt. 3 Abtlg...," Nov. 10, 1941, A.O.K. 18, 17562/298.
[67] —. "Übersetzung eines Artikels aus der Leningradskaja Prawda," November 1941, A.O.K. 18, 17562/298.
[68] —. "Bericht des gefallenen jüdischen Kommissars Weinberg vom 1 Batl. des 880 Schtz. Regts. an den Regt.-Kommissar," Nov. 26, 1941, A.O.K. 18, 17562/298.

[69] —. "Bericht über die Vernehmung der Überläufer," Dec. 18, 1941, A.O.K. 18, 19601/118.

[70] —. "13 Lagebericht," Dec. 24, 1941, L A.K., 21717/11.

[71] —. "Gefangenenvernehmungen vom 10.i.42," Jan. 12, 1942, A.O.K. 18, 19601/118.

[72] —. "Russische Feldpost," Feb. 2, 1942, A.O.K. 18, 19601/118.

[73] —. "Aus einem Lagebericht des S.D. über Leningrad," May 26, 1942, 5 Geb. Div., 25268/15.

[74] —. "Gefangenenvernehmung," Aug. 14, 1942, A.O.K. 18, 30281/210–13.

[75] Kdo. 121 I.D., Abt. Ic., "Ergebnis der Durchsicht der in Tosno aufgefundenen Briefpost," 121 I.D., 23295/15.

[76] Kdo. 122 I.D., Abt. Ic., "Aussagen eines Zivilisten," Sept. 15, 1941, XXVIII A.K., 18233/1.

[77] —. "Tagebuch eines Überläufers," Dec. 5, 1941, L A.K., 17562/285.

[78] —. "Beutepapiere," Feb. 2, 1942, A. O. K. 18, 19601/118.

Miscellaneous Lesser Units

[79] Dulag 154, Abt. Ic./A.O. "Vernehmung betr. Leningrad," Aug. 13, 1942, A.O.K. 18, 30281/212.

[80] —. "Zusammenstellungen von Fabriken und Rüstungsbetrieben in UdSSR," Aug. 28, 1943, A.O.K. 18, 44911/251.

[81] Wi. Kdo. Krasnogwardeisk, "Aufstellung über die Evakuierung von Leningrad Industriewerken," Jan. 19, 1942, A.O.K. 18, 19601/118.

OTHER GERMAN DOCUMENTS

Other Military Units above Division Level

[82] H. Gp. Nord, Ic./A.O., "S... und P... Verhältnisse und Stimmung in Leningrad," H. Gp. Nord, 75131/97.

[83] A.O.K. 11, Ic./A.O., "Die Lage in Leningrad seit Beginn der Einschliessung bis September 1942," A.O.K. 11, 35873/8.

[84] —. "Anlage 1 zum F. Nachrichtenblatt 322/42," [Nov. 18, 1942?], A.O.K. 11, 35873/8.

[85] A.O.K. 16, Abt. Ic., "Übersetzung, Leningrad Gebietsausschuss der bolschewistischen Partei," Nov. 13, 1941, A.O.K. 18, 17562/297.

[86] —. "Befehl an die Truppen der Leningrader Front No. 0098, Stadt Leningrad, 5.x.41," Nov. 14, 1941, A.O.K. 18, 17562/297.

[87] —. "Zusatzvernehmung, Oberst... 20. NKWD-Division," Nov. 17, 1941, A.O.K. 18, 17562/298.

[88] [16th Army.] Gen. Kdo. XXXVIII, Abt. Ic., "Zusammenfassung der Feindnachrichten für die Zeit vom 25.ix bis 15.x.1941," Oct. 21, 1941, A.O.K. 18, 17562/282.

[89] [16th Army.] Gen. Kdo. XXXIX A.K., Abt. Ic., "Kriegstagebuch eines russischen Reserve-Offiziers," XXXIX A.K., 23854/4.

[90] A.O.K. 20, Abt. Ic., "Auszüge aus der Armee Tageszeitung des Leningrader Militärbezirks 'Auf der Wacht für Heimat,' vom August 1941," Aug. 25, 1941, A.O.K. 20, 25353/2.

[91] Kd. Pz. Gp. 4, Abt. Ic., "Auswertung von Gefangenen Aussagen im Abschnitt der Panzergruppe 4, in der Zeit von 7.viii bis 20.viii.41," A.O.K. 18, 17562/296.

Abwehr (Army Intelligence) and S.D. (Security Service)

[92] Abw. Einsatzgruppe beim A.O.K. 18, "An die Abwehrgruppe Nord," Oct. 21, 1941, A.O.K. 18, 17562/297.
[93] —. "An die Abwehrgruppe Nord," Nov. 21, 1941, A.O.K. 18, 17562/298.
[94] —. "Aussagen," Dec. 4, 1941, A.O.K. 18, 17562/298.
[95] —. "Auszüge aus russischen original-Privatbriefen," Dec. 12, 1941, A.O.K. 18, 17562/298.
[96] Abwehrtruppe I/A.O.K. 18, "An Abteilung Ic.," June 25, 1942, A.O.K. 18, 22864/108.
[97] Abwehrkommando 104/Iwi, "Lage in Leningrad," Oct. 9, 1942, H. Gp. Nord 75843.

[98] Sipo. u. S.D., Einsatzgruppe A, "11 Lagebericht," Nov. 19, 1941, L A.K., 21717/11.
[99] —. "12 Lagebericht," Dec. 4, 1941, L A.K., 21717/11.
[100] —. "13 Lagebericht," Dec. 24, 1941, L A.K., 21717/11.
[101] —. "Auswertung einer Sowjetischen Zeitung," Jan. 1, 1942, A.O.K. 18, 19601/118.
[102] —. "15 Lagebericht," Feb. 11, 1942, A.O.K. 18, 19601/119.
[103] —. "Vernehmungsniederschrift," May 8, 1942, A.O.K. 18, 22864/108.
[104] Chef der Sipo. u. S.D., "Ereignismeldung UdSSR No. 150," Jan. 2, 1942, S.D. Reports 43.
[105] —. "Ereignismeldung UdSSR No. 170," Feb. 18, 1942, S.D. Reports 46.
[106] —. "Ereignismeldung UdSSR No. 182," Mar. 18, 1942, S.D. Reports 47.
[107] —. "Ereignismeldung UdSSR No. 191," Apr. 10, 1942, S.D. Reports 48.
[108] Sipo. u. S.D., Sonderkommando 16, Kdo. Loknja, "Vorgeführt erscheint der Russe M... und erklärt," Apr. 24, 1942, A.O.K. 18, 22864/108.
[109] SS-Polizei Division, Abt. Ic., "Lage in Leningrad, Anlage 2 zu Ic.," Mar. 29, 1943, 4. SS-Polizei Grenadier Division, 38712/5.

Miscellaneous

[110] OKM-Weisungen, "Der Führer an Obersten Befehlshaber der Wehrmacht," Weisung No. 35, Sept. 6, 1941, O.K.M. Weisungen, O.K.W. (Führer), Band 2, OKM/59.
[111] OKW/WFSt. Abt. 1 Roem Eins. Op. No. 441530/41, Sept. 13, 1941, O.K.M. Weisungen O.K.W. (Führer), Band 2, OKM/59.
[112] 28 Jäger Division, Abt. Ic., "Militärgeographisches Merkblatt," Oct. 16, 1942, 28 I.D. 30148/19.
[113] Wi. Kdo. Goerlitz, "Lagebericht 13," Nov. 3, 1941, Wi/ID 2.368.
[114] Höh. Art. Kdr. 303, Abt. Ic., "An A.O.K. 18," Nov. 12, 1941, A.O.K. 18, 17562/298.

[115] —. "Vernehmung des Kgf. K... S...," Aug. 28, 1943, A.O.K. 18, 44911/251.

[116] Glavnoe Politicheskoe Upravlenie RKKA, "Ob usilenii vospitatelnoi raboty v razvedyvatelnykh podrazdeleniiakh, No. 287," Dec. 16, 1941, A.O.K. 18, 19601/3.

[117] Lds. Schtz. Batl. 868, "Vernehmungsprotokoll," Dec. 20, 1941, A.O.K. 18, 17562/298.

[118] "UdSSR, Sowjet f.d. Evakuierung-Verordnung Nr. 16841 se," Dec. 25, 1941, A.O.K. 19601/3.

[119] Sdf. v. Breitenstein, "Auszug aus einem russischen Brief aus Leningrad vom 12. xii. 1941," Jan. 9, 1942, A.O.K. 18, 19601/118.

[120] Sonderkommando Ia, Teilkommando Ost, "Agentenvernehmung, Erkundigung Leningrad," Mar. 12, 1942, A.O.K. 18, 19601/121.

[121] Reichssicherheitshauptamt, "An den Reichsführer SS und Chef der Deutschen Polizei—Sonderzug Heinrich," July 1, 1942, E.A.P. 161-b-12/333, Footlocker 58.

INDEX

*I*NDEX

OTHER VOLUMES OF RAND RESEARCH

COLUMBIA UNIVERSITY PRESS, NEW YORK:

Bergson, Abram, and Hans Heymann, Jr., *Soviet National Income and Product, 1940–48,* 1954
Galenson, Walter, *Labor Productivity in Soviet and American Industry,* 1955
Hoeffding, Oleg, *Soviet National Income and Product in 1928,* 1954

THE FREE PRESS, GLENCOE, ILLINOIS:

Dinerstein, Herbert S., and Leon Goure, *Two Studies in Soviet Controls: Communism and the Russian Peasant; Moscow in Crisis,* 1955
Garthoff, Raymond L., *Soviet Military Doctrine,* 1953
Goldhamer, Herbert, and Andrew W. Marshall, *Psychosis and Civilization,* 1953
Leites, Nathan, *A Study of Bolshevism,* 1953
Leites, Nathan, and Elsa Bernaut, *Ritual of Liquidation: The Case of the Moscow Trials,* 1954
The RAND Corporation, *A Million Random Digits with 100,000 Normal Deviates,* 1955

HARVARD UNIVERSITY PRESS, CAMBRIDGE, MASSACHUSETTS:

Bergson, Abram, *The Real National Income of Soviet Russia Since 1928,* 1961
Fainsod, Merle, *Smolensk Under Soviet Rule,* 1958
Hitch, Charles J., and Roland McKean, *The Economics of Defense in the Nuclear Age,* 1960
Moorsteen, Richard, *Prices and Production of Machinery in the Soviet Union, 1928–1958,* 1962

THE MACMILLAN COMPANY, NEW YORK:

Dubyago, A. D., *The Determination of Orbits,* translated from the Russian by R. D. Burke, G. Gordon, L. N. Rowell, and F. T. Smith, 1961.
O'Sullivan, J. J. (ed.), *Protective Construction in a Nuclear Age,* 1961
Whiting, Allen S., *China Crosses the Yalu: The Decision to Enter the Korean War,* 1960

MCGRAW-HILL BOOK COMPANY, INC., NEW YORK:

Bellman, Richard, *Introduction to Matrix Analysis*, 1960
Dorfman, Robert, Paul A. Samuelson, and Robert M. Solow, *Linear Programming and Economic Analysis*, 1958
Gale, David, *The Theory of Linear Economic Models*, 1960
Janis, Irving L., *Air War and Emotional Stress: Psychological Studies of Bombing and Civilian Defense*, 1951
Leites, Nathan, *The Operational Code of the Politburo*, 1951
· McKinsey, J. C. C., *Introduction to the Theory of Games*, 1952
Mead, Margaret, *Soviet Attitudes Toward Authority: An Interdisciplinary Approach to Problems of Soviet Character*, 1951
Scitovsky, Tibor, Edward Shaw, and Lorie Tarshis, *Mobilizing Resources for War: The Economic Alternatives*, 1951
Selznick, Philip, *The Organizational Weapon: A Study of Bolshevik Strategy and Tactics*, 1952
Shanley, F. R., *Weight-Strength Analysis of Aircraft Structures*, 1952
Williams, J. D., *The Compleat Strategyst: Being a Primer on the Theory of Games of Strategy*, 1954

THE MICROCARD FOUNDATION, MADISON, WISCONSIN:

Baker, C. L., and F. J. Gruenberger, *The First Six Million Prime Numbers*, 1959

NORTH-HOLLAND PUBLISHING COMPANY, AMSTERDAM, HOLLAND:

Arrow, Kenneth J., and Marvin Hoffenberg, *A Time Series Analysis of Interindustry Demands*, 1959.

FREDERICK A. PRAEGER, INC., NEW YORK:

Dinerstein, H. S., *War and the Soviet Union: Nuclear Weapons and the Revolution in Soviet Military and Political Thinking*, 1959
Speier, Hans, *Divided Berlin: The Anatomy of Soviet Political Blackmail*, 1961
Tanham, G. K., *Communist Revolutionary Warfare. The Viet Minh in Indochina*, 1961.

PRENTICE-HALL, INC., ENGLEWOOD CLIFFS, NEW JERSEY:

Dresher, Melvin, *Games of Strategy: Theory and Applications*, 1961
Hsieh, Alice L., *Communist China's Strategy in the Nuclear Era*, 1962
Newell, Allen (ed.), *Information Processing Language-V Manual*, 1961

PRINCETON UNIVERSITY PRESS, PRINCETON, NEW JERSEY:

Baum, Warren C., *The French Economy and the State*, 1958
Bellman, Richard, *Adaptive Control Processes: A Guided Tour*, 1961
Bellman, Richard, *Dynamic Programming*, 1957
Bellman, Richard E., and Stuart E. Dreyfus, *Applied Dynamic Programming*, 1962
Brodie, Bernard, *Strategy in the Missile Age*, 1959

Davison, W. Phillips, *The Berlin Blockade: A Study in Cold War Politics*, 1958

Ford, L. R., Jr., and D. R. Fulkerson, *Flows in Networks*, 1962

Hastings, Cecil, Jr., *Approximations for Digital Computers*, 1955

Johnson, John J. (ed.), *The Role of the Military in Underdeveloped Countries*, 1962

Smith, Bruce Lannes, and Chitra M. Smith, *International Communication and Political Opinion: A Guide to the Literature*, 1956.

Wolf, Charles, Jr., *Foreign Aid: Theory and Practice in Southern Asia*, 1960

PUBLIC AFFAIRS PRESS, WASHINGTON, D.C.:

Krieger, F. J., *Behind the Sputniks: A Survey of Soviet Space Science*, 1958

Rush, Myron, *The Rise of Khrushchev*, 1958

RANDOM HOUSE, INC., NEW YORK:

Buchheim, Robert W., and the Staff of The RAND Corporation, *Space Handbook: Astronautics and Its Applications*, 1959

ROW, PETERSON AND COMPANY, EVANSTON, ILLINOIS:

George, Alexander L., *Propaganda Analysis: A Study of Inferences Made from Nazi Propaganda in World War II*, 1959

Melnik, Constantin, and Nathan Leites, *The House without Windows: France Selects a President*, 1958

Speier, Hans, *German Rearmament and Atomic War: The Views of German Military and Political Leaders*, 1957

Speier, Hans, and W. Phillips Davison (eds.), *West German Leadership and Foreign Policy*, 1957

STANFORD UNIVERSITY PRESS, STANFORD, CALIFORNIA:

Kecskemeti, Paul, *Strategic Surrender: The Politics of Victory and Defeat*, 1958

Kecskemeti, Paul, *The Unexpected Revolution: Social Forces in the Hungarian Uprising*, 1961

Kramish, Arnold, *Atomic Energy in the Soviet Union*, 1959

Leites, Nathan, *On the Game of Politics in France*, 1959

Trager, Frank N. (ed.), *Marxism in Southeast Asia: A Study of Four Countries*, 1959

UNIVERSITY OF CALIFORNIA PRESS, BERKELEY, CALIFORNIA:

Goure, Leon, *Civil Defense in the Soviet Union*, 1962

THE UNIVERSITY OF CHICAGO PRESS, CHICAGO, ILLINOIS:

Hirshleifer, Jack, James C. DeHaven, and Jerome W. Milliman, *Water Supply: Economics, Technology, and Policy*, 1960

JOHN WILEY & SONS, INC., NEW YORK:

McKean, Roland N., *Efficiency in Government through Systems Analysis: With Emphasis on Water Resource Development*, 1958